C000259577

LETTERS

OF

JOHN KEATS

LETTERS

OF

JOHN KEATS

TO HIS FAMILY AND FRIENDS

EDITED BY

SIDNEY COLVIN

London

MACMILLAN AND CO.

AND NEW YORK

1891

First Edition June 1891
Reprinted October 1891

CONTENTS

b

CONTENTS

PREFACE

THE object of the present volume is to supply the want, which many readers must have felt, of a separate and convenient edition of the letters of Keats to his family and friends. He is one of those poets whose genius makes itself felt in prose-writing almost as decisively as in verse, and at their best these letters are among the most beautiful in our language. Portions of them lent an especial charm to a book charming at any rate —the biography of the poet first published more than forty years ago by Lord Houghton. But the correspondence as given by Lord Houghton is neither accurate nor complete. He had in few cases the originals before him, but made use of copies, some of them quite fragmentary, especially those supplied him from America; and moreover, working while many of the poet's friends were still alive, he thought it right to exercise a degree of editorial freedom for which there would now be neither occasion nor excuse. While I was engaged in preparing the life of Keats for Mr. Morley's series some years since, the following materials for an improved edition of his letters came into my hands :—

(1) The copies made by Richard Woodhouse, a few years after Keats's death, of the poet's correspondence with his principal friends, viz. the publishers, Messrs. Taylor and Hessey; the transcriber, Woodhouse himself, who was a young barrister of literary tastes in the confidence of those gentlemen; John Hamilton Reynolds, solicitor, poet, humourist, and critic (born 1796, died

1852); Jane and Mariane Reynolds, sisters of the last-
named, the former afterwards Mrs. Tom Hood; James
Rice, the bosom friend of Reynolds, and like him a young
solicitor; Benjamin Bailey, undergraduate of Magdalen
Hall, Oxford, afterwards Archdeacon of Colombo (1794?-
1852), and one or two more.

(2) The imperfect copies of the poet's letters to his
brother and sister-in-law in America, which were made
by the sister-in-law's second husband, Mr. Jeffrey of
Louisville, and sent by him to Lord Houghton, who
published them with further omissions and alterations of
his own.

(3) Somewhat later, after the publication of my book,
the autograph originals of some of these same letters to
America were put into my hands, including almost the
entire text of Nos. lxiii. lxxiii. lxxx. and xcii. in the
present edition. The three last are the long and famous
journal-letters written in the autumn of 1818 and spring
of 1819, and between them occupy nearly a quarter of the
whole volume. I have shown elsewhere [1] how much of
their value and interest was sacrificed by Mr. Jeffrey's
omissions.

Besides these manuscript sources, I have drawn largely
on Mr. Buxton Forman's elaborate edition of Keats's works
in four volumes (1883),[2] and to a much less extent on the

---

[1] *Macmillan's Magazine*, August 1888.

[2] For the letters already printed by Lord Houghton, Mr.
Forman as a rule simply copied the text of that editor. The letters
to Fanny Brawne and Fanny Keats, on the other hand, he printed
with great accuracy from the autographs, and had autographs
also before him in revising those to Dilke, Haydon, and several
besides. The correspondence with Fanny Keats he kindly gave
me leave to use for the present volume, receiving from me in
return the right to use my MS. materials for a revised issue of
his own work. In that issue, which appeared at the end of 1889,
the new matter is, however, printed separately, in the form of
scraps and addenda detached from their context; and the present
edition (the appearance of which has been delayed for two years
by accidental circumstances) is the only one in which the true text
of the American and miscellaneous letters is given consecutively
and in proper order.

edition published by the poet's American grand-nephew, Mr. Speed (1884)[1]. Even thus, the correspondence is still probably not quite complete. In some of the voluminous journal-letters there may still be gaps, where a sheet of the autograph has gone astray ; and since the following pages have been in print, I have heard of the existence in private collections of one or two letters which I have not been able to include. But it is not a case in which absolute completeness is of much importance.

In matters of the date and sequence of the letters, I have taken pains to be more exact than previous editors, especially in tracing the daily progress and different halting-places of the poet on his Scotch tour (which it takes some knowledge of the ground to do), and in dating the successive parts, written at intervals sometimes during two or three months, of the long journal-letters to America. On these particulars Keats himself is very vague, and his manuscript sometimes runs on without a break at points where the sense shows that he has dropped and taken it up again after a pause of days or weeks.[2] Again, I have in all cases given in full the verse and other quotations contained in the correspondence, where other editors have only indicated them by their first lines. It is indeed from these that the letters derive a great part of their character. Writing to his nearest relatives or most intimate friends, he is always quoting for their pleasure poems of his own now classical, then warm from his brain, sent forth uncertain whether to live or die, or snatches of doggrel nonsense as the humour of the moment takes him. The former, familiar as we may be with them, gain a new interest and freshness from the context: the latter are nothing apart from it, and to

---

[1] The letters in which I have relied wholly or in part on Mr. Speed's text are Nos. xxv. lxxx. (only for a few passages missing in the autograph) cxvi. and cxxxi.

[2] Where the dates in my text are printed without brackets, they are those given by Keats himself ; the dates within brackets have been supplied either from the postmarks (as was done by Woodhouse in all his transcripts) or by inference from the text.

print them gravely, as has been done, among the Poetical Works, is to punish the levities of genius too hard.

As to the text, I have followed the autograph wherever it was possible, and in other cases the manuscript or printed version which I judged nearest the autograph; with this exception, that I have not thought it worth while to preserve mere slips of the pen or tricks of spelling. The curious in such matters will find them religiously reproduced by Mr. Buxton Forman wherever he has had the opportunity. The poet's punctuation, on the other hand, and his use of capitals, which is odd and full of character, I have preserved. As is well known, his handwriting is as a rule clear and beautiful, quite free from unsteadiness or sign of fatigue; and as mere specimens for the collector, few autographs can compare with these close-written quarto (or sometimes extra folio) sheets, in which the young poet has poured out to those he loved his whole self indiscriminately, generosity and fretfulness, ardour and despondency, boyish petulance side by side with manful good sense, the tattle of suburban parlours with the speculations of a spirit unsurpassed for native poetic gift and insight.

The editor of familiar correspondence has at all times a difficult task before him in the choice what to give and what to withhold. In the case of Keats the difficulty is greater than in most, from the ferment of opposing elements and impulses in his nature, and from the extreme unreserve with which he lays himself open alike in his weakness and his strength. The other great letter-writers in English are men to some degree on their guard: men, if not of the world, at least of some worldly training and experience, and of characters in some degree formed and set. The phase of unlimited youthful expansiveness, of enthusiastic or fretful outcry, they have either escaped or left behind, and never give themselves away completely. Gray is of course an extreme case in point. With a masterly breadth of mind he unites an even finicking degree of academic fastidiousness

and personal reserve, and his correspondence charms, not
by impulse or openness, but by urbanity and irony, by
ripeness of judgment and knowledge, by his playful
kindliness towards the few intimates he has, and the sober
wistfulness with which he looks out, from his Pisgah-
height of universal culture, over regions of imaginative
delight into which it was not given to him nor his
contemporaries to enter fully. To take others differing
most widely both as men and poets : Cowper, whether
affectionately "chatting and chirping" to his cousin
Lady Hesketh, or confiding his spiritual terrors to the
Rev. John Newton, that unwise monitor who would not let
them sleep,—Cowper is a letter-writer the most unaffected
and sincere, but has nevertheless the degree of reticence
natural to his breeding, as well as a touch of staidness
and formality proper to his age. Byron offers an
extreme contrast ; unrestrained he is, but far indeed
from being unaffected ; the greatest attitudinist in
literature as in life, and the most brilliant of all letter-
writers after his fashion, with his wit, his wilfulness,
his flash, his extraordinary unscrupulousness and resource, his vulgar pride of caste, his everlasting restless-
ness and egotism, his occasional true irradiations of the
divine fire. Shelley, again—but he, as has been justly
said, must have his singing robes about him to be quite
truly Shelley, and in his correspondence is little more
than any other amiable and enthusiastic gentleman and
scholar on his travels. To the case of Keats, at any
rate, none of these other distinguished letter-writers
affords any close parallel. That admirable genius was
from the social point of view an unformed lad in the
flush and rawness of youth. His passion for beauty, his
instinctive insight into the vital sources of imaginative
delight in nature, in romance, and in antiquity, went
along with perceptions painfully acute in matters of
daily life, and nerves high-strung in the extreme. He
was moreover almost incapable of artifice or disguise.
Writing to his brothers and sister or to friends as dear,

he is secret with them on one thing only, and that is his unlucky love-passion after he became a prey to it: for the rest he is open as the day, and keeps back nothing of what crosses his mind, nothing that vexes or jars on him or tries his patience. His character, as thus laid bare, contains elements of rare nobility and attraction—modesty, humour, sweetness, courage, impulsive disinterestedness, strong and tender family affection, the gift of righteous indignation, the gift of sober and strict self-knowledge. But it is only a character in the making. A strain of hereditary disease, lurking in his constitution from the first, was developed by over-exertion and aggravated by mischance, so that he never lived to be himself; and from about his twenty-fourth birthday his utterances are those of one struggling in vain against a hopeless distemper both of body and mind.

If a selection could be made from those parts only of Keats's correspondence which show him at his best, we should have an anthology full of intuitions of beauty, even of wisdom, and breathing the very spirit of generous youth; one unrivalled for zest, whim, fancy, and amiability, and written in an English which by its peculiar alert and varied movement sometimes recalls, perhaps more closely than that of any other writer (for the young Cockney has Shakspeare in his blood), the prose passages of *Hamlet* and *Much Ado about Nothing*. Had the correspondence never been printed before, were it there to be dealt with for the first time, this method of selection would no doubt be the tempting one to apply to it. But such a treatment is now hardly possible, and in any case would hardly be quite fair; since the object, or at all events the effect, of publishing a man's correspondence is not merely to give literary pleasure—it is to make the man himself known; and the revelation, though it need not be wholly without reserve, is bound to be just and proportionate as far as it goes. Even as an artist, in the work which he himself published to the world, Keats was not one of those of whom it

could be said, " his worst he kept, his best he gave."
Rather he gave promiscuously, in the just confidence
that among the failures and half-successes of his inex-
perienced youth would be found enough of the best to
establish his place among the poets after his death.
Considering all things, the nature of the man, the difficulty of separating the exquisite from the common, the
healthful from the diseased, in his mind and work,
considering also the use that has already been made of
the materials, I have decided in this edition to give the
correspondence almost unpruned ; omitting a few passages
of mere crudity, hardly more than two pages in all, but
not attempting to suppress those which betray the weak
places in the writer's nature, his flaws of taste and
training, his movements of waywardness, irritability, and
morbid suspicion. Only the biographer without tact,
the critic without balance, will insist on these. A truer
as well as more charitable judgment will recognise that
what was best in Keats was also what was most real,
and will be fortified by remembering that to those who
knew him his faults were almost unapparent, and that
no man was ever held by his friends in more devoted
or more unanimous affection while he lived and afterwards.

There is one thing, however, which I have not chosen
to do, and that is to include in this collection the poet's
love-letters to Fanny Brawne. As it is, the intimate
nature of the correspondence must sometimes give the
reader a sense of eavesdropping, of being admitted into
petty private matters with which he has no concern. If
this is to some extent inevitable, it is by no means inevitable that the public should be farther asked to look
over the shoulder of the sick and presently dying youth
while he declares the impatience and torment of his
passion to the object, careless and unresponsive as she
seems to have been, who inspired it. These letters too
have been printed. As a matter of feeling I cannot put
myself in the place of the reader who desires to possess

them; while as a matter of literature they are in a
different key from the rest,—not lacking passages of
beauty, but constrained and painful in the main, and
quite without the genial ease and play of mind which
make the letters to his family and friends so attractive.
Therefore in this, which I hope may become the standard
edition of his correspondence, they shall find no place.

As to the persons, other than those already mentioned,
to whom the letters here given are addressed :—Shelley
of course needs no words; nor should any be needed for
the painter Haydon (1786-1846), or the poet and critic
Leigh Hunt (1784-1859). Theirs were the chief inspiring
influences which determined the young medical student,
about his twentieth year, at the time when this correspondence opens, to give up his intended profession for poetry.
Both were men of remarkable gifts and strong intellectual enthusiasm, hampered in either case by foibles of
character which their young friend and follower, who
has left so far more illustrious a name, was only too
quick to detect. Charles Cowden Clarke (1787-1877),
the son of Keats's schoolmaster at Enfield, had exercised
a still earlier influence on the lad's opening mind, and
was himself afterwards long and justly distinguished as
a Shakspearean student and lecturer and essayist on
English literature. Charles Wentworth Dilke (1789-
1864), having begun life in the Civil Service, early
abandoned that calling for letters, and lived to be one
of the most influential of English critics and journalists;
he is chiefly known from his connection with the *Athen-
æum*, and through the memoir published by his grand-
son. Charles Brown, afterwards styling himself Charles
Armitage Brown (1786 - 1842), who became known
to Keats through Dilke in · the summer of 1817,
and was his most intimate companion during the two
years June 1818 to June 1820, had begun life as a
merchant in St. Petersburg, and failing, came home, and
took, he also, to literature, chiefly as a contributor to the
various periodicals edited by Leigh Hunt. He lived

mostly in Italy from 1822 to 1834, then for six years at Plymouth, and in 1841 emigrated to New Zealand, where he died the following year. Joseph Severn (1793-1879) was the son of an engraver, himself beginning to practise as a painter when Keats knew him. His devoted tendance of the poet during the last sad months in Italy was the determining event of Severn's career, earning him the permanent regard and gratitude of all lovers of genius. He established himself for good in Rome, where he continued to practise his art, and was for many years English consul, and one of the most familiar figures in the society of the city.

Lastly, of the poet's own relations, George Keats (1799-1842) after his brother's death continued to live at Louisville in America, where he made and lost a fortune in business before he died. His widow (born Georgiana Augusta Wylie), so often and affectionately addressed in these letters, by and by took a second husband, a Mr. Jeffrey, already mentioned as the correspondent of Lord Houghton. Frances Mary Keats (1803-1889), always called Fanny in the delightful series of letters which her brother addressed to her as a young girl,[1] in course of time married a Spanish gentleman, Señor Llanos, and lived in Madrid to a great old age. Several other members of the poet's circle enjoyed unusual length of days—Mr. William Dilke, for instance, dying a few years ago at ninety, and Mr. Gleig, long Chaplain-General of the Forces, at ninety-two. But with the death of his sister a year and a half ago, passed away probably the last survivor of those who could bear in memory the voice and features of Adonais.

S. C.

May 1891.

---

[1] The autographs of these letters are now in the British Museum.

LETTERS OF JOHN KEATS

TO

HIS FAMILY AND FRIENDS

I.—TO CHARLES COWDEN CLARKE.

[London, October 31, 1816.]

My DAINTIE DAVIE—I will be as punctual as the Bee
to the Clover.   Very glad am I at the thoughts of
seeing so soon this glorious Haydon and all his creation.
I pray thee let me know when you go to Ollier's and
where he resides—this I forgot to ask you—and tell me
also when you will help me waste a sullen day—God
'ield you [1]—   J. K.

II.—TO BENJAMIN ROBERT HAYDON.

[London,] November 20, 1816.

My dear Sir—Last evening wrought me up, and I
cannot forbear sending you the following—

Yours unfeignedly,   JOHN KEATS.
Removed to 76 Cheapside.

[1] The early letters of Keats are full of these Shakspearean tags
and allusions: some of the less familiar I have thought it worth
while to mark in the footnotes.

B

Great spirits now on earth are sojourning ;
   He of the cloud, the cataract, the lake,
   Who on Helvellyn's summit, wide awake,
Catches his freshness from Archangel's wing :
He of the rose, the violet, the spring,
   The social smile, the chain for Freedom's sake :
   And lo !—whose stedfastness would never take
A meaner sound than Raphael's whispering.
And other spirits there are standing apart
   Upon the forehead of the age to come ;
These, these will give the world another heart,
   And other pulses.   Hear ye not the hum
Of mighty workings in the human mart ?
Listen awhile ye nations, and be dumb.[1]

III.—TO BENJAMIN ROBERT HAYDON.

[London,] Thursday afternoon, November 20, 1816.

My dear Sir—Your letter has filled me with a proud pleasure, and shall be kept by me as a stimulus to exertion—I begin to fix my eye upon one horizon.   My feelings entirely fall in with yours in regard to the Ellipsis, and I glory in it.   The Idea of your sending it to Wordsworth put me out of breath—you know with what Reverence I would send my Well-wishes to him.

   Yours sincerely   JOHN KEATS.

IV.—TO CHARLES COWDEN CLARKE.

[London,] Tuesday [December 17, 1816].

My dear Charles—You may now look at Minerva's Ægis with impunity, seeing that my awful Visage [2] did not turn you into a John Doree.   You have accordingly a legitimate title to a Copy—I will use my interest to procure it for you.   I'll tell you what—I met Reynolds at Haydon's a few mornings since—he promised to be with me this Evening and Yesterday I had the same

---

[1] The references are of course to Wordsworth, Leigh Hunt, and Haydon. In the sonnet as printed in the *Poems* of 1817, and all later editions, the last line but one breaks off at "workings," the words "in the human mart" having been omitted by Haydon's advice.

[2] Presumably as shown in some drawing or miniature.

promise from Severn and I must put you in mind that
on last All hallowmas' day you gave me your word
that you would spend this Evening with me—so no
putting off. I have done little to Endymion lately [1]—I
hope to finish it in one more attack. I believe you I
went to Richards's—it was so whoreson a Night that I
stopped there all the next day. His Remembrances to
you. (Ext. from the common place Book of my Mind—
Mem.—Wednesday—Hampstead—call in Warner Street
—a sketch of Mr. Hunt.)—I will ever consider you my
sincere and affectionate friend—you will not doubt that
I am yours.

God bless you—   JOHN KEATS.

V.—TO JOHN HAMILTON REYNOLDS.

[London,] Sunday Evening [March 2, 1817 ?].[2]

My dear Reynolds—Your kindness affects me so
sensibly that I can merely put down a few mono-sentences.
Your Criticism only makes me extremely anxious that I
should not deceive you.

It's the finest thing by God as Hazlitt would say.
However I hope I may not deceive you. There are
some acquaintances of mine who will scratch their
Beards and although I have, I hope, some Charity, I
wish their Nails may be long. I will be ready at the
time you mention in all Happiness.

There is a report that a young Lady of 16 has
written the new Tragedy, God bless her—I will know
her by Hook or by Crook in less than a week. My
Brothers' and my Remembrances to your kind Sisters.

Yours most sincerely   JOHN KEATS.

[1] Not the long poem published under that title in 1818, but
the earlier attempt beginning, "I stood tiptoe upon a little hill,"
which was printed as a fragment in the *Poems* of 1817.

[2] This letter, which is marked by Woodhouse in his copy "no
date, sent by hand," I take to be an answer to the commendatory
sonnet addressed by Reynolds to Keats on February 27, 1817: see
Keats (Men of Letters Series), Appendix, p. 223.

VI.—TO JOHN HAMILTON REYNOLDS.

[London, March 17, 1817.]

My dear Reynolds—My Brothers are anxious that I should go by myself into the country—they have always been extremely fond of me, and now that Haydon has pointed out how necessary it is that I should be alone to improve myself, they give up the temporary pleasure of living with me continually for a great good which I hope will follow. So I shall soon be out of Town. You must soon bring all your present troubles to a close, and so must I, but we must, like the Fox, prepare for a fresh swarm of flies. Banish money—Banish sofas—Banish Wine—Banish Music; but right Jack Health, honest Jack Health, true Jack Health—Banish health and banish all the world. I must . . . if I come this evening, I shall horribly commit myself elsewhere. So I will send my excuses to them and Mrs. Dilke by my brothers.

Your sincere friend   JOHN KEATS.

VII.—TO GEORGE AND THOMAS KEATS.

[Southampton,] Tuesday Morn [April 15, 1817].

My dear Brothers—I am safe at Southampton—after having ridden three stages outside and the rest in for it began to be very cold. I did not know the Names of any of the Towns I passed through—all I can tell you is that sometimes I saw dusty Hedges—sometimes Ponds—then nothing—then a little Wood with trees look you like Launce's Sister "as white as a Lily and as small as a Wand"—then came houses which died away into a few straggling Barns—then came hedge trees aforesaid again. As the Lamplight crept along the following things were discovered—"long heath broom furze"—Hurdles here and there half a Mile—Park palings when the Windows of a House were always discovered by

reflection—One Nymph of Fountain—*N.B. Stone*—
lopped Trees—Cow ruminating—ditto Donkey—Man
and Woman going gingerly along—William seeing his
Sisters over the Heath—John waiting with a Lanthorn
for his Mistress—Barber's Pole—Doctor's Shop—However after having had my fill of these I popped my Head
out just as it began to Dawn—*N.B. this Tuesday Morn
saw the Sun rise*—of which I shall say nothing at
present. I felt rather lonely this Morning at Breakfast
so I went and unbox'd a Shakspeare—"There's my
Comfort."[1]   I went immediately after Breakfast to
Southampton Water where I enquired for the Boat to
the Isle of Wight as I intend seeing that place before
I settle—it will go at 3, so shall I after having taken a
Chop. I know nothing of this place but that it is long
—tolerably broad—has bye streets—two or three
Churches—a very respectable old Gate with two Lions
to guard it. The Men and Women do not materially
differ from those I have been in the Habit of seeing. I
forgot to say that from dawn till half-past six I went
through a most delightful Country—some open Down
but for the most part thickly wooded. What surprised
me most was an immense quantity of blooming Furze
on each side the road cutting a most rural dash. The
Southampton water when I saw it just now was no better
than a low Water Water which did no more than answer
my expectations—it will have mended its Manners by
3. From the Wharf are seen the shores on each side
stretching to the Isle of Wight. You, Haydon, Reynolds,
etc. have been pushing each other out of my Brain by
turns. I have conned over every Head in Haydon's
Picture—you must warn them not to be afraid should
my Ghost visit them on Wednesday—tell Haydon to
Kiss his Hand at Betty over the Way for me yea and to
spy at her for me. I hope one of you will be competent
to take part in a Trio while I am away—you need only

---

[1] For Stephano's "Here's my comfort," twice in *Tempest*,
II. ii.

aggravate your voices a little and mind not to speak
Cues and all—when you have said Rum-ti-ti—you must
not be rum any more or else another will take up the
ti-ti alone and then he might be taken God shield us for
little better than a Titmouse. By the by talking of
Titmouse Remember me particularly to all my Friends—
give my Love to the Miss Reynoldses and to Fanny who
I hope you will soon see.   Write to me soon about them
all—and you George particularly how you get on with
Wilkinson's plan.   What could I have done without my
Plaid?   I don't feel inclined to write any more at
present for I feel rather muzzy—you must be content
with this fac simile of the rough plan of Aunt Dinah's
Counterpane.

    Your most affectionate Brother   JOHN KEATS.
Reynolds shall hear from me soon.

VIII.—TO JOHN HAMILTON REYNOLDS.

                         Carisbrooke, April 17th [1817].

    My dear Reynolds — Ever since I wrote to my
Brothers from Southampton I have been in a taking—
and at this moment I am about to become settled—for I
have unpacked my books, put them into a snug corner,
pinned up Haydon, Mary Queen of Scots, and Milton
with his daughters in a row. In the passage I found a
head of Shakspeare which I had not before seen. It is
most likely the same that George spoke so well of, for I
like it extremely. Well—this head I have hung over my
Books, just above the three in a row, having first discarded
a French Ambassador—now this alone is a good morning's
work. Yesterday I went to Shanklin, which occasioned
a great debate in my mind whether I should live there
or at Carisbrooke. Shanklin is a most beautiful place—
Sloping wood and meadow ground reach round the Chine,
which is a cleft between the Cliffs of the depth of nearly
300 feet at least. This cleft is filled with trees and

bushes in the narrow part, and as it widens becomes
bare, if it were not for primroses on one side, which
spread to the very verge of the Sea, and some fishermen's
huts on the other, perched midway in the Balustrades of
beautiful green Hedges along their steps down to the
sands. But the sea, Jack, the sea—the little waterfall—
then the white cliff—then St. Catherine's Hill—"the
sheep in the meadows, the cows in the corn." Then, why
are you at Carisbrooke? say you. Because, in the first
place, I should be at twice the Expense, and three times
the inconvenience—next that from here I can see your
continent—from a little hill close by the whole north
Angle of the Isle of Wight, with the water between us.
In the 3rd place, I see Carisbrooke Castle from my
window, and have found several delightful wood-alleys,
and copses, and quick freshes.[1] As for primroses—the
Island ought to be called Primrose Island—that is, if the
nation of Cowslips agree thereto, of which there are
divers Clans just beginning to lift up their heads.
Another reason of my fixing is, that I am more in reach
of the places around me. I intend to walk over the
Island east—West—North—South. I have not seen
many specimens of Ruins—I don't think however I shall
ever see one to surpass Carisbrooke Castle. The trench
is overgrown with the smoothest turf, and the Walls
with ivy. The Keep within side is one Bower of ivy—
a colony of Jackdaws have been there for many years. I
dare say I have seen many a descendant of some old
cawer who peeped through the Bars at Charles the first,
when he was there in Confinement. On the road from
Cowes to Newport I saw some extensive Barracks, which
disgusted me extremely with the Government for placing
such a Nest of Debauchery in so beautiful a place. I
asked a man on the Coach about this—and he said that
the people had been spoiled. In the room where I slept

---

[1] "I'll not show him
Where the quick freshes are."
                    Caliban in *Tempest*, III. ii.

at Newport, I found this on the Window—" O Isle spoilt by the mil*a*tary ! . . ."

The wind is in a sulky fit, and I feel that it would be no bad thing to be the favourite of some Fairy, who would give one the power of seeing how our Friends got on at a Distance. I should like, of all Loves, a sketch of you and Tom and George in ink which Haydon will do if you tell him how I want them. From want of regular rest I have been rather *narvus*—and the passage in *Lear*—" Do you not hear the sea ?"—has haunted me intensely.

ON THE SEA

It keeps eternal whisperings around
  Desolate shores, and with its mighty swell
  Gluts twice ten thousand Caverns, till the spell
Of Hecate leaves them their old shadowy sound.
Often 'tis in such gentle temper found,
  That scarcely will the very smallest shell
  Be mov'd for days from where it sometime fell,
When last the winds of Heaven were unbound.
O ye ! who have your eye-balls vex'd and tir'd,
  Feast them upon the wideness of the Sea ;
    O ye ! whose Ears are dinn'd with uproar rude,
  Or fed too much with cloying melody—
    Sit ye near some old Cavern's Mouth, and brood
Until ye start as if the sea Nymphs quired—[1]

                    April 18th.

Will you have the goodness to do this ? Borrow a Botanical Dictionary—turn to the words Laurel and Prunus, show the explanations to your sisters and Mrs. Dilke and without more ado let them send me the Cups Basket and Books they trifled and put off and off while I was in town. Ask them what they can say for themselves—ask Mrs. Dilke wherefore she does so distress me —let me know how Jane has her health—the Weather is unfavourable for her. Tell George and Tom to write. I'll tell you what—on the 23d was Shakspeare born.

---

[1] This sonnet was first published in the *Champion* (edited by John Scott) for August 17, 1817.

Now if I should receive a letter from you and another from my Brothers on that day 'twould be a parlous good thing. Whenever you write say a word or two on some Passage in Shakspeare that may have come rather new to you, which must be continually happening, notwithstanding that we read the same Play forty times —for instance, the following from the Tempest never struck me so forcibly as at present,

> " Urchins
> *Shall, for the vast of night that they may work,*
> All exercise on thee—"

How can I help bringing to your mind the line—

> *In the dark backward and abysm of time—*

I find I cannot exist without Poetry—without eternal Poetry—half the day will not do—the whole of it—I began with a little, but habit has made me a Leviathan. I had become all in a Tremble from not having written anything of late—the Sonnet overleaf did me good. I slept the better last night for it—this Morning, however, I am nearly as bad again. Just now I opened Spenser, and the first Lines I saw were these—

> "The noble heart that harbours virtuous thought,
> And is with child of glorious great intent,
> Can never rest until it forth have brought
> Th' eternal brood of glory excellent—"

Let me know particularly about Haydon, ask him to write to me about Hunt, if it be only ten lines—I hope all is well—I shall forthwith begin my Endymion, which I hope I shall have got some way with by the time you come, when we will read our verses in a delightful place I have set my heart upon, near the Castle. Give my Love to your Sisters severally—to George and Tom. Remember me to Rice, Mr. and Mrs. Dilke and all we know.

Your sincere Friend   JOHN KEATS.

Direct J. Keats, Mrs. Cook's, New Village, Carisbrooke.

IX.—TO LEIGH HUNT.

Margate, May 10, 1817.

My dear Hunt—The little gentleman that sometimes lurks in a gossip's bowl, ought to have come in the very likeness of a *roasted* crab, and choaked me outright for not answering your letter ere this: however, you must not suppose that I was in town to receive it: no, it followed me to the Isle of Wight, and I got it just as I was going to pack up for Margate, for reasons which you anon shall hear.   On arriving at this treeless affair, I wrote to my brother George to request C. C. C.[1] to do the thing you wot of respecting Rimini; and George tells me he has undertaken it with great pleasure; so I hope there has been an understanding between you for many proofs: C. C. C. is well acquainted with Bensley.   Now why did you not send the key of your cupboard, which, I know, was full of papers?   We would have locked them all in a trunk, together with those you told me to destroy, which indeed I did not do, for fear of demolishing receipts, there not being a more unpleasant thing in the world (saving a thousand and one others) than to pay a bill twice.   Mind you, old Wood's a "very varmint," shrouded in covetousness :— and now I am upon a horrid subject—what a horrid one you were upon last Sunday, and well you handled it.   The last Examiner[2] was a battering-ram against Christianity, blasphemy, Tertullian, Erasmus, Sir Philip Sidney ; and then the dreadful Petzelians and their expiation by blood ; and do Christians shudder at the same thing in a newspaper which they attribute to their God in its most aggravated form ?   What is to be the end of this?   I must mention Hazlitt's Southey.[3]   O that he had left

---

[1] Charles Cowden Clarke.

[2] For Sunday, May 4, 1817.

[3] The first part, published in the same number of the *Examiner*, of a ferocious review by Hazlitt of Southey's *Letter to William Smith, Esq., M.P.*

out the grey hairs; or that they had been in any other
paper not concluding with such a thunderclap! That
sentence about making a page of the feeling of a whole
life, appears to me like a whale's back in the sea of prose.
I ought to have said a word on Shakspeare's Christianity.
There are two which I have not looked over with you,
touching the thing: the one for, the other against: that
in favour is in Measure for Measure, Act II. Scene ii.—

> *Isab.* Alas, alas!
> Why, all the souls that were, were forfeit once;
> And He that might the 'vantage best have took,
> Found out the remedy.

That against is in Twelfth Night, Act III. Scene ii.—

> *Maria.* For there is no Christian that means to be saved by
> believing rightly, can ever believe such impossible passages of
> grossness.

Before I come to the Nymphs,[1] I must get through
all disagreeables. I went to the Isle of Wight, thought
so much about poetry, so long together, that I could not
get to sleep at night; and, moreover, I know not how it
was, I could not get wholesome food. By this means, in
a week or so, I became not over capable in my upper stories,
and set off pell-mell for Margate, at least a hundred and
fifty miles, because, forsooth, I fancied that I should like
my old lodging here, and could contrive to do without trees.
Another thing, I was too much in solitude, and consequently was obliged to be in continual burning of thought,
as an only resource. However, Tom is with me at
present, and we are very comfortable. We intend,
though, to get among some trees. How have you got
on among them? How are the Nymphs? I suppose
they have led you a fine dance. Where are you now?—
in Judea, Cappadocia, or the parts of Libya about Cyrene?
Stranger from "Heaven, Hues, and Prototypes," I wager
you have given several new turns to the old saying,
"Now the maid was fair and pleasant to look on," as

---

[1] The poem so entitled on which Hunt was now at work, and
which was published in the volume called *Foliage* (1818).

well as made a little variation in "Once upon a time."
Perhaps, too, you have rather varied, "Here endeth the
first lesson." Thus I hope you have made a horseshoe
business of "unsuperfluous life," "faint bowers," and
fibrous roots. I vow that I have been down in the
mouth lately at this work. These last two days, however,
I have felt more confident—I have asked myself so often
why I should be a poet more than other men, seeing how
great a thing it is,—how great things are to be gained by
it, what a thing to be in the mouth of Fame,—that at last
the idea has grown so monstrously beyond my seeming
power of attainment, that the other day I nearly consented with myself to drop into a Phaethon. Yet 'tis a
disgrace to fail, even in a huge attempt; and at this
moment I drive the thought from me. I began my poem
about a fortnight since, and have done some every day,
except travelling ones. Perhaps I may have done a
good deal for the time, but it appears such a pin's point
to me, that I will not copy any out. When I consider
that so many of these pin-points go to form a bodkin-
point (God send I end not my life with a bare bodkin,
in its modern sense!), and that it requires a thousand
bodkins to make a spear bright enough to throw any light
to posterity, I see nothing but continual uphill journeying.
Now is there anything more unpleasant (it may come
among the thousand and one) than to be so journeying
and to miss the goal at last? But I intend to whistle
all these cogitations into the sea, where I hope they will
breed storms violent enough to block up all exit from
Russia. Does Shelley go on telling strange stories of
the deaths of kings?[1] Tell him, there are strange stories
of the deaths of poets. Some have died before they were
conceived. "How do you make that out, Master
Vellum?" Does Mrs. S. cut bread and butter as neatly

---

[1] Alluding to the well-known story of Shelley dismaying an
old lady in a stage-coach by suddenly, à propos of nothing, crying
out to Leigh Hunt in the words of Richard II., "For God's sake,
let us sit upon the ground," etc.

as ever ? Tell her to procure some fatal scissors, and cut
the thread of life of all to-be-disappointed poets. Does
Mrs. Hunt tear linen as straight as ever ? Tell her to
tear from the book of life all blank leaves. Remember
me to them all ; to Miss Kent and the little ones all.

Your sincere Friend JOHN KEATS *alias* JUNKETS.

You shall hear where we move.

X.—TO BENJAMIN ROBERT HAYDON.

Margate, Saturday Eve [May 10, 1817].

My dear Haydon,

> "Let Fame, that all pant after in their lives,
> Live register'd upon our brazen tombs,
> And so grace us in the disgrace of death :
> When spite of cormorant devouring Time
> The endeavour of this present breath may buy
> That Honour which shall bate his Scythe's keen edge
> And make us heirs of all eternity." [1]

To think that I have no right to couple myself with
you in this speech would be death to me, so I have e'en
written it, and I pray God that our "brazen tombs" be
nigh neighbours. It cannot be long first; the "endeavour of this present breath" will soon be over, and yet
it is as well to breathe freely during our sojourn—it is
as well as if you have not been teased with that Money
affair, that bill-pestilence. However, I must think that
difficulties nerve the Spirit of a Man—they make our
Prime Objects a Refuge as well as a Passion. The
Trumpet of Fame is as a tower of Strength, the ambitious
bloweth it and is safe. I suppose, by your telling me
not to give way to forebodings, George has mentioned to
you what I have lately said in my Letters to him—
truth is I have been in such a state of Mind as to read
over my Lines and hate them. I am one that "gathers
Samphire, dreadful trade "—the Cliff of Poesy towers
above me—yet when Tom who meets with some of Pope's

---

[1] Opening speech of the King in *Love's Labour's Lost.*

Homer in Plutarch's Lives reads some of those to me
they seem like Mice to mine. I read and write about
eight hours a day. There is an old saying "well begun
is half done"—'tis a bad one. I would use instead,
"Not begun at all till half done;" so according to that
I have not begun my Poem and consequently (à priori)
can say nothing about it. Thank God! I do begin
arduously where I leave off, notwithstanding occasional
depressions; and I hope for the support of a High
Power while I climb this little eminence, and especially
in my Years of more momentous Labour. I remember
your saying that you had notions of a good Genius pre-
siding over you. I have of late had the same thought,
for things which I do half at Random are afterwards
confirmed by my judgment in a dozen features of Propriety. Is it too daring to fancy Shakspeare this
Presider? When in the Isle of Wight I met with a
Shakspeare in the Passage of the House at which I
lodged—it comes nearer to my idea of him than any I
have seen—I was but there a Week, yet the old woman
made me take it with me though I went off in a hurry.
Do you not think this is ominous of good? I am glad
you say every man of great views is at times tormented
as I am.

Sunday after [May 11].

This Morning I received a letter from George by
which it appears that Money Troubles are to follow us
up for some time to come—perhaps for always—these
vexations are a great hindrance to one—they are not
like Envy and detraction stimulants to further exertion
as being immediately relative and reflected on at the same
time with the prime object—but rather like a nettle leaf
or two in your bed. So now I revoke my Promise of
finishing my Poem by the Autumn which I should have
done had I gone on as I have done—but I cannot write
while my spirit is fevered in a contrary direction and I
am now sure of having plenty of it this Summer. At
this moment I am in no enviable Situation—I feel that

I am not in a Mood to write any to-day; and it appears that the loss of it is the beginning of all sorts of irregularities. I am extremely glad that a time must come when everything will leave not a wrack behind. You tell me never to despair—I wish it was as easy for me to observe the saying—truth is I have a horrid Morbidity of Temperament which has shown itself at intervals—it is I have no doubt the greatest Enemy and stumbling-block I have to fear—I may even say that it is likely to be the cause of my disappointment. However every ill has its share of good—this very bane would at any time enable me to look with an obstinate eye on the Devil Himself—aye to be as proud of being the lowest of the human race as Alfred could be in being of the highest. I feel confident I should have been a rebel angel had the opportunity been mine. I am very sure that you do love me as your very Brother—I have seen it in your continual anxiety for me—and I assure you that your welfare and fame is and will be a chief pleasure to me all my Life. I know no one but you who can be fully sensible of the turmoil and anxiety, the sacrifice of all what is called comfort, the readiness to measure time by what is done and to die in six hours could plans be brought to conclusions—the looking upon the Sun, the Moon, the Stars, the Earth and its contents, as materials to form greater things—that is to say ethereal things—but here I am talking like a Madman,—greater things than our Creator himself made ! !

I wrote to Hunt yesterday—scarcely know what I said in it. I could not talk about Poetry in the way I should have liked for I was not in humor with either his or mine. His self-delusions are very lamentable—they have enticed him into a Situation which I should be less eager after than that of a galley Slave—what you observe thereon is very true must be in time.

Perhaps it is a self-delusion to say so—but I think I could not be deceived in the manner that Hunt is—may I die to-morrow if I am to be. There is no greater

Sin after the seven deadly than to flatter oneself into an idea of being a great Poet——or one of those beings who are privileged to wear out their Lives in the pursuit of Honor——how comfortable a feel it is to feel that such a Crime must bring its heavy Penalty? That if one be a Self-deluder accounts must be balanced? I am glad you are hard at Work——'t will now soon be done——I long to see Wordsworth's as well as to have mine in :[1] but I would rather not show my face in Town till the end of the Year——if that will be time enough——if not I shall be disappointed if you do not write for me even when you think best. I never quite despair and I read Shakspeare ——indeed I shall I think never read any other Book much. Now this might lead me into a long Confab but I desist. I am very near agreeing with Hazlitt that Shakspeare is enough for us. By the by what a tremendous Southean article his last was——I wish he had left out "grey hairs." It was very gratifying to meet your remarks on the manuscript——I was reading Anthony and Cleopatra when I got the Paper and there are several Passages applicable to the events you commentate. You say that he arrived by degrees and not by any single struggle to the height of his ambition——and that his Life had been as common in particulars as other Men's. Shakspeare makes Enobarb say——

> Where's Antony?
> *Eros.*——He's walking in the garden, and *spurns*
> *The rush that lies* before him ; cries, Fool, Lepidus !

In the same scene we find——

>   Let determined things
> To destiny hold unbewailed their way.

Dolabella says of Anthony's Messenger,

> An argument that he is pluck'd when hither
> He sends so poor a pinion of his wing.

Then again——

---

[1] *I.e.*, their likenesses, as introduced by Haydon into his picture of Christ's Entry into Jerusalem.

> *Eno.*—I see Men's Judgments are
> A parcel of their fortunes ; and things outward
> Do draw the inward quality after them,
> To suffer all alike.

The following applies well to Bertrand [1]—

> Yet he that can endure
> To follow with allegiance a fallen Lord,
> Does conquer him that did his Master conquer,
> And earns a place i' the story.

But how differently does Buonaparte bear his fate from Anthony !

'Tis good, too, that the Duke of Wellington has a good Word or so in the Examiner. A Man ought to have the Fame he deserves—and I begin to think that detracting from him as well as from Wordsworth is the same thing. I wish he had a little more taste—and did not in that respect " deal in Lieutenantry." You should have heard from me before this—but in the first place I did not like to do so before I had got a little way in the First Book, and in the next as G. told me you were going to write I delayed till I had heard from you. Give my Respects the next time you write to the North and also to John Hunt. Remember me to Reynolds and tell him to write. Ay, and when you send Westward tell your Sister that I mentioned her in this. So now in the name of Shakspeare, Raphael and all our Saints, I commend you to the care of heaven !

    Your everlasting Friend   JOHN KEATS.

XI.—TO MESSRS. TAYLOR AND HESSEY.

Margate, May 16, 1817.

My dear Sirs—I am extremely indebted to you for your liberality in the shape of manufactured rag, value £20, and shall immediately proceed to destroy some of the minor heads of that hydra the dun ; to conquer which the knight need have no Sword Shield Cuirass, Cuisses Herbadgeon Spear Casque Greaves Paldrons spurs Chev-

---

[1] General Bertrand, who followed Napoleon to St. Helena.

ron or any other scaly commodity, but he need only take the Bank-note of Faith and Cash of Salvation, and set out against the monster, invoking the aid of no Archimago or Urganda, but finger me the paper, light as the Sibyl's leaves in Virgil, whereat the fiend skulks off with his tail between his legs. Touch him with this enchanted paper, and he whips you his head away as fast as a snail's horn—but then the horrid propensity he has to put it up again has discouraged many very valiant Knights. He is such a never-ending still-beginning sort of a body—like my landlady of the Bell. I should conjecture that the very spright that "the green sour ringlets makes Whereof the ewe not bites" had manufactured it of the dew fallen on said sour ringlets. I think I could make a nice little allegorical poem, called "The Dun," where we would have the Castle of Carelessness, the drawbridge of credit, Sir Novelty Fashion's expedition against the City of Tailors, etc. etc. I went day by day at my poem for a Month—at the end of which time the other day I found my Brain so over-wrought that I had neither rhyme nor reason in it—so was obliged to give up for a few days. I hope soon to be able to resume my work—I have endeavoured to do so once or twice; but to no purpose. Instead of Poetry, I have a swimming in my head and feel all the effects of a Mental debauch, lowness of Spirits, anxiety to go on without the power to do so, which does not at all tend to my ultimate progression. However to-morrow I will begin my next month. This evening I go to Canterbury, having got tired of Margate. I was not right in my head when I came — At Canterbury I hope the remembrance of Chaucer will set me forward like a Billiard Ball. I am glad to hear of Mr. T.'s health, and of the welfare of the "In-town-stayers." And think Reynolds will like his Trip—I have some idea of seeing the Continent some time this summer. In repeating how sensible I am of your kindness, I remain

    Yr obedt servt and friend   JOHN KEATS.

I shall be happy to hear any little intelligence in the literary or friendly way when you have time to scribble.

XII.—TO MESSRS. TAYLOR AND HESSEY.

[London] Tuesday Morn [July 8, 1817].

My dear Sirs—I must endeavour to lose my maidenhead with respect to money Matters as soon as possible —And I will too—So, here goes! A couple of Duns that I thought would be silent till the beginning, at least, of next month (when I am certain to be on my legs, for certain sure), have opened upon me with a cry most "untuneable"; never did you hear such *un*-"gallant chiding." Now you must know, I am not desolate, but have, thank God, 25 good notes in my fob. But then, you know, I laid them by to write with and would stand at bay a fortnight ere they should grab me. In a month's time I must pay, but it would relieve my mind if I owed you, instead of these Pelican duns.

I am afraid you will say I have "wound about with circumstance," when I should have asked plainly—however as I said I am a little maidenish or so, and I feel my virginity come strong upon me, the while I request the loan of a £20 and a £10, which, if you would enclose to me, I would acknowledge and save myself a hot forehead. I am sure you are confident of my responsibility, and in the sense of squareness that is always in me.

Your obliged friend   JOHN KEATS.

XIII.—TO MARIAN AND JANE REYNOLDS.

Oxf[ord,[1] September 5, 1817].

My dear Friends—You are I am glad to hear comfortable at Hampton,[2] where I hope you will receive the Biscuits we ate the other night at Little Britain.[3] I hope you found them good. There you are among sands,

[1] On a visit to Benjamin Bailey at Magdalen Hall.
[2] Littlehampton.   [3] Reynolds's family lived in Little Britain.

stones, Pebbles, Beeches, Cliffs, Rocks, Deeps, Shallows,
weeds, ships, Boats (at a distance), Carrots, Turnips,
sun, moon, and stars and all those sort of things—here
am I among Colleges, halls, Stalls, Plenty of Trees,
thank God—Plenty of water, thank heaven—Plenty of
Books, thank the Muses—Plenty of Snuff, thank Sir
Walter Raleigh—Plenty of segars,—Ditto—Plenty of
flat country, thank Tellus's rolling-pin.   I'm on the sofa
—Buonaparte is on the snuff-box—But you are by the
seaside—argal, you bathe—you walk—you say "how
beautiful"—find out resemblances between waves and
camels—rocks and dancing-masters—fireshovels and tele-
scopes—Dolphins and Madonas—which word, by the
way, I must acquaint you was derived from the Syriac,
and came down in a way which neither of you I am
sorry to say are at all capable of comprehending.   But as
a time may come when by your occasional converse with
me you may arrive at "something like prophetic strain,"
I will unbar the gates of my pride and let my condescen-
sion stalk forth like a ghost at the Circus.—The word
Ma-don-a, my dear Ladies—or—the word Mad—Ona—so
I say! I am not mad—Howsumever when that aged
Tamer Kewthon sold a certain camel called Peter to the
overseer of the Babel Sky-works, he thus spake, adjusting
his cravat round the tip of his chin—"My dear Ten-
story-up-in-air! this here Beast, though I say it as
shouldn't say't, not only has the power of subsisting 40
days and 40 nights without fire and candle but he can
sing.—Here I have in my Pocket a Certificate from Signor
Nicolini of the King's Theatre; a Certificate to this
effect——" I have had dinner since I left that effect upon you, and feel too heavy in mentibus to display all the
Profundity of the Polygon—so you had better each of
you take a glass of cherry Brandy and drink to the health
of Archimedes, who was of so benign a disposition that
he never would leave Syracuse in his life—So kept
himself out of all Knight-Errantry.—This I know to be
a fact; for it is written in the 45th book of Winkine's

treatise on garden-rollers, that he trod on a fishwoman's toe in Liverpool, and never begged her pardon. Now the long and short is this—that is by comparison—for a long day may be a short year—A long Pole may be a very stupid fellow as a man. But let us refresh ourself from this depth of thinking, and turn to some innocent jocularity—the Bow cannot always be bent—nor the gun always loaded, if you ever let it off—and the life of man is like a great Mountain—his breath is like a Shrewsbury cake—he comes into the world like a shoeblack, and goes out of it like a cobbler—he eats like a chimney-sweeper, drinks like a gingerbread baker—and breathes like Achilles—so it being that we are such sublunary creatures, let us endeavour to correct all our bad spelling—all our most delightful abominations, and let us wish health to Marian and Jane, whoever they be and wherever.

Yours truly   JOHN KEATS.

XIV —TO FANNY KEATS.

Oxford, September 10 [1817].

My dear Fanny—Let us now begin a regular question and answer—a little pro and con ; letting it interfere as a pleasant method of my coming at your favorite little wants and enjoyments, that I may meet them in a way befitting a brother.

We have been so little together since you have been able to reflect on things that I know not whether you prefer the History of King Pepin to Bunyan's Pilgrim's Progress—or Cinderella and her glass slipper to Moore's Almanack. However in a few Letters I hope I shall be able to come at that and adapt my scribblings to your Pleasure. You must tell me about all you read if it be only six Pages in a Week and this transmitted to me every now and then will procure you full sheets of Writing from me pretty frequently.—This I feel as a necessity for we ought to become intimately acquainted, in order that I may not only, as you grow up love you as my only Sister, but confide in you as my dearest friend. When I saw you last I told you of my intention of going to Oxford and 'tis now a Week since I disembark'd from his Whipship's Coach the Defiance in this place. I am living in Magdalen Hall on a visit to a young Man with whom I have not been long acquainted, but whom I like very much—we lead very industrious lives—he in general Studies and I in proceeding at a pretty good rate with a Poem which I hope you will see early in the next year. —Perhaps you might like to know what I am writing about. I will tell you. Many Years ago there was a young handsome Shepherd who fed his flocks on a Mountain's Side called Latmus—he was a very contemplative sort of a Person and lived solitary among the trees and Plains little thinking that such a beautiful Creature as the Moon was growing mad in Love with him.—However so it was ; and when he was asleep on the Grass she used to come down from heaven and admire him excessively for a long time; and at last could not refrain from carrying him away in her arms to the top of that high Mountain Latmus while he was a dreaming —but I daresay you have read this and all the other beautiful Tales which have come down from the ancient times of that beautiful Greece. If you have not let me know and I will tell you more at large of others quite as delightful. This Oxford I have no doubt is the finest City in the world—it is full of old Gothic buildings— Spires—towers—Quadrangles—Cloisters—Groves, etc., and is surrounded with more clear streams than ever I saw together. I take a Walk by the Side of one of them every Evening and, thank God, we have not had a drop of rain these many days. I had a long and interesting Letter from George, cross lines by a short one from Tom yesterday dated Paris. They both send their loves to you. Like most Englishmen they feel a mighty preference for everything English—the French Meadows, the trees, the People, the Towns, the Churches, the Books, the everything—although they may be in themselves good : yet when put in comparison with our green Island they all vanish like Swallows in October. They have seen Cathedrals, Manuscripts, Fountains, Pictures, Tragedy, Comedy,—with other things you may by chance meet with in this Country such as Washerwomen, Lamplighters, Turnpikemen, Fishkettles, Dancing Masters, Kettle drums, Sentry Boxes, Rocking Horses, etc.—and, now they have taken them over a set of boxing-gloves.

I have written to George and requested him, as you wish I should, to write to you. I have been writing very hard lately, even till an utter incapacity came on, and I feel it now about my head : so you must not mind a little out-of-the-way sayings—though by the bye were my brain as clear as a bell I think I should have a little propensity thereto. I shall stop here till I have finished the 3d Book of my Story ; which I hope will be accomplish'd in at most three Weeks from to-day—about which time you shall see me. How do you like Miss Taylor's essays in Rhyme—I just look'd into the Book and it appeared to me suitable to you—especially since I remember your liking for those pleasant little things the Original Poems—the essays are the more mature production of the same hand. While I was speaking about France it occurred to me to speak a few Words on their Language—it is perhaps the poorest one ever spoken since the jabbering in the Tower of Babel, and when you come to know that the real use and greatness of a Tongue is to be referred to its Literature—you will be astonished to find how very inferior it is to our native Speech.—I wish the Italian would supersede French in every school throughout the Country, for that is full of real Poetry and Romance of a kind more fitted for the Pleasure of Ladies than perhaps our own.—It seems that the only end to be gained in acquiring French is the immense accomplishment of speaking it—it is none at all—a most lamentable mistake indeed. Italian indeed would sound most musically from Lips which had began to pronounce it as early as French is crammed down our Mouths, as if we were young Jack-

daws at the mercy of an overfeeding Schoolboy. Now
Fanny you must write soon—and write all you think
about, never mind what—only let me have a good deal
of your writing—You need not do it all at once—be two
or three or four days about it, and let it be a diary of
your little Life. You will preserve all my Letters and I
will secure yours—and thus in the course of time we
shall each of us have a good Bundle—which, hereafter,
when things may have strangely altered and God knows
what happened, we may read over together and look with
pleasure on times past—that now are to come. Give my
Respects to the Ladies—and so my dear Fanny I am
ever

Your most affectionate Brother   JOHN.

If you direct—Post Office, Oxford—your Letter will
be brought to me.

XV.—TO JANE REYNOLDS.

Oxford, Sunday Evg. [September 14, 1817].

My dear Jane—You are such a literal translator, that
I shall some day amuse myself with looking over some
foreign sentences, and imagining how you would render
them into English. This is an age for typical Curiosities;
and I would advise you, as a good speculation, to study
Hebrew, and astonish the world with a figurative version
in our native tongue. The Mountains skipping like rams,
and the little hills like lambs, you will leave as far behind
as the hare did the tortoise. It must be so or you would
never have thought that I really meant you would like
to pro and con about those Honeycombs—no, I had no
such idea, or, if I had, 'twould be only to tease you a
little for love. So now let me put down in black and
white briefly my sentiments thereon. —Imprimis—I
sincerely believe that Imogen is the finest creature, and
that I should have been disappointed at hearing you
prefer Juliet—Item—Yet I feel such a yearning towards

Juliet that I would rather follow her into Pandemonium than Imogen into Paradise—heartily wishing myself a Romeo to be worthy of her, and to hear the Devils quote the old proverb, "Birds of a feather flock together"—Amen.—

Now let us turn to the Seashore. Believe me, my dear Jane, it is a great happiness to see that you are in this finest part of the year winning a little enjoyment from the hard world. In truth, the great Elements we know of, are no mean comforters : the open sky sits upon our senses like a sapphire crown—the Air is our robe of state—the Earth is our throne, and the Sea a mighty minstrel playing before it—able, like David's harp, to make such a one as you forget almost the tempest cares of life. I have found in the ocean's music,—varying (tho self-same) more than the passion of Timotheus, an enjoyment not to be put into words ; and, "though inland far I be," I now hear the voice most audibly while pleasing myself in the idea of your sensations. ·

——— is getting well apace, and if you have a few trees, and a little harvesting about you, I'll snap my fingers in Lucifer's eye. I hope you bathe too—if you do not, I earnestly recommend it. Bathe thrice a week, and let us have no more sitting up next winter. Which is the best of Shakspeare's plays ? I mean in what mood and with what accompaniment do you like the sea best ? It is very fine in the morning, when the sun,

> " Opening on Neptune with fair blessed beams,
> Turns into yellow gold his salt sea streams,"

and superb when

> " The sun from meridian height
> Illumines the depth of the sea,
> And the fishes, beginning to sweat,
> Cry d—— it ! how hot we shall be,"

and gorgeous, when the fair planet hastens

> " To his home
> Within the Western foam."

But don't you think there is something extremely fine
after sunset, when there are a few white clouds about
and a few stars blinking—when the waters are ebbing,
and the horizon a mystery? This state of things has
been so fulfilling to me that I am anxious to hear
whether it is a favourite with you. So when you and
Marianne club your letter to me put in a word or two
about it. Tell Dilke that it would be perhaps as well if
he left a Pheasant or Partridge alive here and there to
keep up a supply of game for next season—tell him to
rein in if Possible all the Nimrod of his disposition, he
being a mighty hunter before the Lord—of the Manor.
Tell him to shoot fair, and not to have at the Poor devils
in a furrow—when they are flying, he may fire, and
nobody will be the wiser.

Give my sincerest respects to Mrs. Dilke, saying that
I have not forgiven myself for not having got her the
little box of medicine I promised, and that, had I remained at Hampstead I would have made precious havoc
with her house and furniture—drawn a great harrow over
her garden—poisoned Boxer—eaten her clothes-pegs—
fried her cabbages—fricaseed (how is it spelt?) her
radishes—ragout'd her Onions—belaboured her *beat*-root
—outstripped her scarlet-runners—parlez-vous'd with her
french-beans—devoured her mignon or mignionette—
metamorphosed her bell-handles—splintered her looking-
glasses—bullocked at her cups and saucers—agonised her
decanters—put old Phillips to pickle in the brine-tub—
dis*organ*ised her piano—dislocated her candlesticks—
emptied her wine-bins in a fit of despair—turned out her
maid to grass—and astonished Brown; whose letter to
her on these events I would rather see than the original
Copy of the Book of Genesis. Should you see Mr. W.
D.[1] remember me to him, and to little Robinson Crusoe,
and to Mr. Snook. Poor Bailey, scarcely ever well,

---

[1] William Dilke, a younger brother of Charles Dilke, who had
served in the Commissariat department in the Peninsula, America,
and Paris. He died in 1885 at the age of 90.

has gone to bed, pleased that I am writing to you. To your brother John (whom henceforth I shall consider as mine) and to you, my dear friends, Marianne and Jane, I shall ever feel grateful for having made known to me so real a fellow as Bailey. He delights me in the selfish and (please God) the disinterested part of my disposition. If the old Poets have any pleasure in looking down at the enjoyers of their works, their eyes must bend with a double satisfaction upon him. I sit as at a feast when he is over them, and pray that if, after my death, any of my labours should be worth saving, they may have so "honest a chronicler" as Bailey. Out of this, his enthusiasm in his own pursuit and for all good things is of an exalted kind—worthy a more healthful frame and an untorn spirit. He must have happy years to come—"he shall not die by God."

A letter from John the other day was a chief happiness to me. I made a little mistake when, just now, I talked of being far inland. How can that be when Endymion and I are at the bottom of the sea? whence I hope to bring him in safety before you leave the seaside; and, if I can so contrive it, you shall be greeted by him upon the sea-sands, and he shall tell you all his adventures, which having finished, he shall thus proceed—"My dear Ladies, favourites of my gentle mistress, however my friend Keats may have teased and vexed you, believe me he loves you not the less—for instance, I am deep in his favour, and yet he has been hauling me through the earth and sea with unrelenting perseverance. I know for all this that he is mighty fond of me, by his contriving me all sorts of pleasures. Nor is this the least, fair ladies, this one of meeting you on the desert shore, and greeting you in his name. He sends you moreover this little scroll—" My dear Girls, I send you, per favour of Endymion, the assurance of my esteem for you, and my utmost wishes for your health and pleasure, being ever,

Your affectionate Brother   JOHN KEATS.

XVI.—TO JOHN HAMILTON REYNOLDS.

Oxford, Sunday Morn [September 21, 1817].

My dear Reynolds—So you are determined to be my
mortal foe—draw a Sword at me, and I will forgive—Put
a Bullet in my Brain, and I will shake it out as a dew-
drop from the Lion's Mane—put me on a Gridiron, and I
will fry with great complacency—but—oh, horror! to
come upon me in the shape of a Dun! Send me bills!
as I say to my Tailor, send me Bills and I'll never employ
you more. However, needs must, when the devil drives:
and for fear of "before and behind Mr. Honeycomb" I'll
proceed. I have not time to elucidate the forms and
shapes of the grass and trees; for, rot it! I forgot to
bring my mathematical case with me, which unfortunately
contained my triangular Prism so that the hues of the
grass cannot be dissected for you—

For these last five or six days, we have had regularly
a Boat on the Isis, and explored all the streams about,
which are more in number than your eye-lashes. We
sometimes skim into a Bed of rushes, and there become
naturalised river-folks,—there is one particularly nice
nest, which we have christened "Reynolds's Cove," in
which we have read Wordsworth and talked as may be.
I think I see you and Hunt meeting in the Pit.—What
a very pleasant fellow he is, if he would give up the
sovereignty of a Room pro bono. What Evenings we
might pass with him, could we have him from Mrs. H.
Failings I am always rather rejoiced to find in a man
than sorry for; they bring us to a Level. He has them,
but then his makes-up are very good. He agrees with
the Northern Poet in this, "He is not one of those who
much delight to season their fireside with personal talk"
—I must confess however having a little itch that way,
and at this present moment I have a few neighbourly
remarks to make. The world, and especially our England,
has, within the last thirty years, been vexed and teased

by a set of Devils, whom I detest so much that I almost
hunger after an Acherontic promotion to a Torturer,
purposely for their accommodation.   These devils are a
set of women, who having taken a snack or Luncheon of
Literary scraps, set themselves up for towers of Babel in
languages, Sapphos in Poetry, Euclids in Geometry, and
everything in nothing.   Among such the name of Mon-
tague has been pre-eminent.   The thing has made a very
uncomfortable impression on me.   I had longed for some
real feminine Modesty in these things, and was therefore
gladdened in the extreme on opening the other day,
one of Bailey's Books—a book of poetry written by one
beautiful Mrs. Philips, a friend of Jeremy Taylor's, and
called "The Matchless Orinda—"   You must have heard
of her, and most likely read her Poetry—I wish you have
not, that I may have the pleasure of treating you with a
few stanzas—I do it at a venture—You will not regret
reading them once more.   The following, to her friend
Mrs. M. A. at parting, you will judge of.

1

I have examin'd and do find,
  Of all that favour me
There's none I grieve to leave behind
  But only, only thee.
To part with thee I needs must die,
Could parting sep'rate thee and I.

2

But neither Chance nor Complement
  Lid element our Love ;
'Twas sacred sympathy was lent
  Us from the Quire above.
That Friendship Fortune did create,
Still fears a wound from Time or Fate.

3

Our chang'd and mingled Souls are grown
  To such acquaintance now,
That if each would resume their own,
  Alas ! we know not how.
We have each other so engrost,
That each is in the Union lost.

4

And thus we can no Absence know,
   Nor shall we be confin'd ;
Our active Souls will daily go
   To learn each others mind.
Nay, should we never meet to Sense,
Our Souls would hold Intelligence.

5

Inspired with a Flame Divine
   I scorn to court a stay ;
For from that noble Soul of thine
   I ne're can be away.
But I shall weep when thou dost grieve ;
Nor can I die whil'st thou dost live.

6

By my own temper I shall guess
   At thy felicity,
And only like my happiness
   Because it pleaseth thee.
Our hearts at any time will tell
If thou, or I, be sick, or well.

7

All Honour sure I must pretend,
   All that is good or great ;
She that would be *Rosania's* Friend,
   Must be at least compleat.*
If I have any bravery,
'Tis cause I have so much of thee.

   * A complete friend.   This line sounded very oddly
to me at first.

8

Thy Leiger Soul in me shall lie,
   And all thy thoughts reveal ;
Then back again with mine shall flie,
   And thence to me shall steal.
Thus still to one another tend ;
Such is the sacred name of *Friend.*

9

Thus our twin-Souls in one shall grow,
   And teach the World new Love,
Redeem the Age and Sex, and show
   A Flame Fate dares not move :
And courting Death to be our friend,
Our Lives together too shall end.

10

A Dew shall dwell upon our Tomb
　Of such a quality,
That fighting Armies, thither come,
　Shall reconciled be.
We'll ask no Epitaph, but say
Orinda and Rosania.

In other of her poems there is a most delicate fancy of the Fletcher kind—which we will con over together. So Haydon is in Town. I had a letter from him yesterday. We will contrive as the winter comes on—but that is neither here nor there. Have you heard from Rice? Has Martin met with the Cumberland Beggar, or been wondering at the old Leech-gatherer? Has he a turn for fossils? that is, is he capable of sinking up to his Middle in a Morass? How is Hazlitt? We were reading his Table [1] last night. I know he thinks himself not estimated by ten people in the world—I wish he knew he is. I am getting on famous with my third Book—have written 800 lines thereof, and hope to finish it next Week. Bailey likes what I have done very much. Believe me, my dear Reynolds, one of my chief layings-up is the pleasure I shall have in showing it to you, I may now say, in a few days. I have heard twice from my Brothers, they are going on very well, and send their Remembrances to you. We expected to have had notices from little-Hampton this morning—we must wait till Tuesday. I am glad of their Days with the Dilkes. You are, I know, very much teased in that precious London, and want all the rest possible ; so I shall be contented with as brief a scrawl—a Word or two, till there comes a pat hour.

Send us a few of your stanzas to read in " Reynolds's Cove." Give my Love and respects to your Mother, and remember me kindly to all at home.

Yours faithfully　　　　JOHN KEATS.

I have left the doublings for Bailey, who is going to say that he will write to you to-morrow.

---

[1] The *Round Table* : republished from the *Examiner* of the two preceding years.

XVII.—TO BENJAMIN ROBERT HAYDON.

Oxford, September 28 [1817].

My dear Haydon—I read your letter to the young Man, whose Name is Cripps. He seemed more than ever anxious to avail himself of your offer. I think I told you we asked him to ascertain his Means. He does not possess the Philosopher's stone—nor Fortunatus's purse, nor Gyges's ring—but at Bailey's suggestion, whom I assure you is a very capital fellow, we have stummed up a kind of contrivance whereby he will be enabled to do himself the benefits you will lay in his Path. I have a great Idea that he will be a tolerable neat brush. 'Tis perhaps the finest thing that will befal him this many a year : for he is just of an age to get grounded in bad habits from which you will pluck him. He brought a copy of Mary Queen of Scots : it appears to me that he has copied the bad style of the painting, as well as coloured the eyeballs yellow like the original. He has also the fault that you pointed out to me in Hazlitt on the constringing and diffusing of substance. However I really believe that he will take fire at the sight of your Picture—and set about things. If he can get ready in time to return to town with me, which will be in a few days—I will bring him to you. You will be glad to hear that within these last three weeks I have written 1000 lines—which are the third Book of my Poem. My Ideas with respect to it I assure you are very low—and I would write the subject thoroughly again—but I am tired of it and think the time would be better spent in writing a new Romance which I have in my eye for next summer—Rome was not built in a Day—and all the good I expect from my employment this summer is the fruit of Experience which I hope to gather in my next Poem. Bailey's kindest wishes, and my vow of being

    Yours eternally   JOHN KEATS.

XVIII.—TO BENJAMIN BAILEY.

Hampstead, Wednesday [October 8, 1817].

My dear Bailey—After a tolerable journey, I went
from Coach to Coach as far as Hampstead where I found
my Brothers—the next Morning finding myself tolerably
well I went to Lamb's Conduit Street and delivered
your parcel.   Jane and Marianne were greatly improved.
Marianne especially, she has no unhealthy plumpness in
the face, but she comes me healthy and angular to the
chin—I did not see John—I was extremely sorry to
hear that poor Rice, after having had capital health
during his tour, was very ill.   I daresay you have
heard from him.   From No. 19 I went to Hunt's and
Haydon's who live now neighbours.—Shelley was there—
I know nothing about anything in this part of the world
—every Body seems at Loggerheads.   There's Hunt in-
fatuated—there's Haydon's picture in statu quo—There's
Hunt walks up and down his painting room criticising
every head most unmercifully.   There's Horace Smith
tired of Hunt.   "The web of our life is of mingled
yarn."[1]   Haydon having removed entirely from Marl-
borough Street, Cripps must direct his letter to Lisson
Grove, North Paddington.   Yesterday Morning while I
was at Brown's, in came Reynolds, he was pretty bobbish,
we had a pleasant day—he would walk home at night
that cursed cold distance.   Mrs. Bentley's children are
making a horrid row[2]—whereby I regret I cannot be
transported to your Room to write to you.   I am quite
disgusted with literary men and will never know another
except Wordsworth—no not even Byron.   Here is an
instance of the friendship of such.   Haydon and Hunt

[1] First Lord in *All's Well that Ends Well*, IV. iii.
[2] Bentley, the Hampstead postman, was Keats's landlord at the
house in Well Walk where he and his brothers had taken up their
quarters the previous June.

have known each other many years—now they live,
pour ainsi dire, jealous neighbours—Haydon says to me,
Keats, don't show your lines to Hunt on any Account, or
he will have done half for you—so it appears Hunt
wishes it to be thought.   When he met Reynolds in the
Theatre, John told him that I was getting on to the
completion of 4000 lines—Ah! says Hunt, had it not
been for me they would have been 7000!   If he will
say this to Reynolds, what would he to other people?
Haydon received a Letter a little while back on this
subject from some Lady—which contains a caution to me,
through him, on the subject—now is not all this a most
paltry thing to think about?   You may see the whole of
the case by the following Extract from a Letter I wrote
to George in the Spring—"As to what you say about
my being a Poet, I can return no Answer but by saying
that the high Idea I have of poetical fame makes me
think I see it towering too high above me.   At any rate,
I have no right to talk until Endymion is finished—it will
be a test, a trial of my Powers of Imagination, and
chiefly of my invention, which is a rare thing indeed—
by which I must make 4000 lines of one bare circumstance, and fill them with poetry : and when I consider
that this is a great task, and that when done it will take
me but a dozen paces towards the temple of fame—it makes
me say—God forbid that I should be without such a task!
I have heard Hunt say, and I may be asked—*why endeavour after a long Poem?*   To which I should answer, Do
not the Lovers of Poetry. like to have a little Region to
wander in, where they may pick and choose, and in which
the images are so numerous that many are forgotten and
found new in a second Reading : which may be food
for a Week's stroll in the Summer?   Do not they like
this better than what they can read through before Mrs.
Williams comes down stairs? a Morning work at most.

"Besides, a long poem is a test of invention, which I
take to be the Polar star of Poetry, as Fancy is the Sails
—and Imagination the rudder.   Did our great Poets

ever write short Pieces ? I mean in the shape of Tales—
this same invention seems indeed of late years to have
been forgotten as a Poetical excellence—But enough of
this, I put on no Laurels till I shall have finished
Endymion, and I hope Apollo is not angered at my
having made a Mockery at him at Hunt's "——

You see, Bailey, how independent my Writing has
been. Hunt's dissuasion was of no avail—I refused to
visit Shelley that I might have my own unfettered scope;—
and after all, I shall have the Reputation of Hunt's
élève. His corrections and amputations will by the
knowing ones be traced in the Poem. This is, to be
sure, the vexation of a day, nor would I say so many
words about it to any but those whom I know to have
my welfare and reputation at heart. Haydon promised
to give directions for those Casts, and you may expect
to see them soon, with as many Letters—You will soon
hear the dinning of Bells—never mind ! you and Gleig [1]
will defy the foul fiend—But do not sacrifice your health
to Books : do take it kindly and not so voraciously. I
am certain if you are your own Physician, your Stomach
will resume its proper strength and then what great
benefits will follow.—My sister wrote a Letter to me,
which I think must be at the post-office—Ax Will to see.
My Brother's kindest remembrances to you—we are
going to dine at Brown's where I have some hopes of
meeting Reynolds. The little Mercury I have taken has
corrected the poison and improved my health—though I
feel from my employment that I shall never be again
secure in Robustness. Would that you were as well as

Your Sincere friend and brother   JOHN KEATS.

---

[1] G. R. Gleig, son of the Bishop of Stirling : born 1796, died
1888 : served in the Peninsula War and afterwards took orders :
Chaplain-General to the Forces from 1846 to 1875 : author of the
Subaltern and many military tales and histories.

XIX—TO BENJAMIN BAILEY.

[Hampstead : about November 1, 1817.]

My dear Bailey—So you have got a Curacy—good, but I suppose you will be obliged to stop among your Oxford favourites during Term time. Never mind. When do you preach your first sermon ?—tell me, for I shall propose to the two R.'s[1] to hear it,—so don't look into any of the old corner oaken pews, for fear of being put out by us. Poor Johnny Moultrie can't be there. He is ill, I expect—but that's neither here nor there. All I can say, I wish him as well through it as I am like to be. For this fortnight I have been confined at Hampstead. Saturday evening was my first day in town, when I went to Rice's—as we intend to do every Saturday till we know not when. We hit upon an old gent we had known some few years ago, and had a *veiry pleasante daye*. In this world there is no quiet,—nothing but teasing and snubbing and vexation. My brother Tom looked very unwell yesterday, and I am for shipping him off to Lisbon. Perhaps I ship there with him. I have not seen Mrs. Reynolds since I left you, wherefore my conscience smites me. I think of seeing her to-morrow ; have you any message ? I hope Gleig came soon after I left. I don't suppose I've written as many lines as you have read volumes, or at least chapters, since I saw you. However, I am in a fair way now to come to a conclusion in at least three weeks, when I assure you I shall be glad to dismount for a month or two ; although I'll keep as tight a rein as possible till then, nor suffer myself to sleep. I will copy for you the opening of the Fourth Book, in which you will see from the manner I had not an opportunity of mentioning any poets, for fear of spoiling the effect of the passage by particularising them.

Thus far had I written when I received your last, which made me at the sight of the direction caper for

[1] Reynolds and Rice.

despair; but for one thing I am glad that I have been
neglectful, and that is, therefrom I have received a proof
of your utmost kindness, which at this present I feel very
much, and I wish I had a heart always open to such
sensations; but there is no altering a man's nature, and
mine must be radically wrong, for it will lie dormant a
whole month. This leads me to suppose that there are
no men thoroughly wicked, so as never to be self-spiritual-
ised into a kind of sublime misery; but, alas! 'tis but
for an hour. He is the only Man "who has kept watch
on man's mortality," who has philanthropy enough to
overcome the disposition to an indolent enjoyment of
intellect, who is brave enough to volunteer for uncomfortable hours. You remember in Hazlitt's essay on
commonplace people he says, "they read the Edinburgh
and Quarterly, and think as they do." Now, with
respect to Wordsworth's "Gipsy," I think he is right, and
yet I think Hazlitt is right, and yet I think Wordsworth
is rightest. If Wordsworth had not been idle, he had
not been without his task; nor had the "Gipsies"—they
in the visible world had been as picturesque an object as
he in the invisible. The smoke of their fire, their
attitudes, their voices, were all in harmony with the
evenings. It is a bold thing to say—and I would not
say it in print—but it seems to me that if Wordsworth
had thought a little deeper at that moment, he would
not have written the poem at all. I should judge it to
have been written in one of the most comfortable moods
of his life—it is a kind of sketchy intellectual landscape,
not a search after truth, nor is it fair to attack him on
such a subject; for it is with the critic as with the poet;
had Hazlitt thought a little deeper, and been in a good
temper, he would never have spied out imaginary faults
there. The Sunday before last I asked Haydon to dine
with me, when I thought of settling all matters with
him in regard to Cripps, and let you know about it.
Now, although I engaged him a fortnight before, he sent
illness as an excuse. He never will come. I have not

been well enough to stand the chance of a wet night, and so have not seen him, nor been able to expurgatorise more masks for you; but I will not speak—your speakers are never doers. Then Reynolds,—every time I see him and mention you, he puts his hand to his head and looks like a son of Niobe's; but he'll write soon.

Rome, you know, was not built in a day. I shall be able, by a little perseverance, to read your letters off-hand. I am afraid your health will suffer from over study before your examination. I think you might regulate the thing according to your own pleasure,—and I would too. They were talking of your being up at Christmas. Will it be before you have passed? There is nothing, my dear Bailey, I should rejoice at more than to see you comfortable with a little Peona wife; an affectionate wife, I have a sort of confidence, would do you a great happiness. May that be one of the many blessings I wish you. Let me be but the one-tenth of one to you, and I shall think it great. My brother George's kindest wishes to you. My dear Bailey, I am,

Your affectionate friend   JOHN KEATS.

I should not like to be pages in your way; when in a tolerable hungry mood you have no mercy. Your teeth are the Rock Tarpeian down which you capsize epic poems like mad. I would not for forty shillings be Coleridge's Lays in your way. I hope you will soon get through this abominable writing in the schools, and be able to keep the terms with more comfort in the hope of retiring to a comfortable and quiet home out of the way of all Hopkinses and black beetles. When you are settled, I will come and take a peep at your church, your house; try whether I shall have grown too lusty for my chair by the fireside, and take a peep at my earliest bower. A question is the best beacon towards a little speculation. Then ask me after my health and spirits. This question ratifies in my mind what I have said above. Health and spirits can only belong unalloyed to the selfish man

—the man who thinks much of his fellows can never be
in spirits. You must forgive, although I have only
written three hundred lines; they would have been five,
but I have been obliged to go to town. Yesterday I
called at Lamb's. St. Jane looked very flush when I
first looked in, but was much better before I left.

XX.—TO BENJAMIN BAILEY.

*[Fragment from an outside sheet:
postmark London, November 5, 1817.]*

. . . I will speak of something else, or my spleen will
get higher and higher—and I am a bearer of the two-
edged sword.—I hope you will receive an answer from
Haydon soon—if not, Pride! Pride! Pride! I have
received no more subscription—but shall soon have a
full health, Liberty and leisure to give a good part of my
time to him. I will certainly be in time for him. We
have promised him one year: let that have elapsed, then
do as we think proper. If I did not know how impossible it is, I should say—"do not at this time of
disappointments, disturb yourself about others."

There has been a flaming attack upon Hunt in the
Endinburgh Magazine. I never read anything so
virulent—accusing him of the greatest Crimes, depreci-
ating his Wife, his Poetry, his Habits, his Company, his
Conversation. These Philippics are to come out in
numbers—called "the Cockney School of Poetry."
There has been but one number published—that on
Hunt—to which they have prefixed a motto from one
Cornelius Webb Poetaster—who unfortunately was of
our party occasionally at Hampstead and took it into
his head to write the following,—something about "we'll
talk on Wordsworth, Byron, a theme we never tire on;"
and so forth till he comes to Hunt and Keats. In the
Motto they have put Hunt and Keats in large letters—
I have no doubt that the second number was intended
for me: but have hopes of its non-appearance, from the

following Advertisement in last Sunday's Examiner :—
"To Ƶ.—The Writer of the Article signed Z., in Blackwood's Edinburgh Magazine for October 1817 is invited
to send his address to the printer of the Examiner, in
order that Justice may be Executed on the proper person."
I don't mind the thing much—but if he should go to
such lengths with me as he has done with Hunt, I must
infallibly call him to an Account if he be a human being,
and appears in Squares and Theatres, where we might
possibly meet—I don't relish his abuse. . . .

XXI.—TO CHARLES WENTWORTH DILKE.

[Hampstead, November 1817.]

My dear Dilke—Mrs. Dilke or Mr. Wm. Dilke, whoever of you shall receive this present, have the kindness
to send pr. bearer Sibylline Leaves, and your petitioner
shall ever pray as in duty bound.

Given under my hand this Wednesday morning of
Novr. 1817.   JOHN KEATS.

Vivant Rex et Regina—amen.

XXII.—TO BENJAMIN BAILEY. *

[Burford Bridge, November 22, 1817.]

My dear Bailey—I will get over the first part of this
(*un*said [1]) Letter as soon as possible, for it relates to the
affairs of poor Cripps.—To a Man of your nature such a
Letter as Haydon's must have been extremely cutting—
What occasions the greater part of the World's Quarrels?
—simply this—two Minds meet, and do not understand
each other time enough to prevent any shock or surprise
at the conduct of either party—As soon as I had known
Haydon three days, I had got enough of his Character not
to have been surprised at such a Letter as he has hurt you

---

[1] *Sic:* for "unpaid"?

with. Nor, when I knew it, was it a principle with me to drop his acquaintance; although with you it would have been an imperious feeling. I wish you knew all that I think about Genius and the Heart—and yet I think that you are thoroughly acquainted with my innermost breast in that respect, or you could not have known me even thus long, and still hold me worthy to be your dear Friend. In passing, however, I must say one thing that has pressed upon me lately, and increased my Humility and capability of submission—and that is this truth— Men of Genius are great as certain ethereal Chemicals operating on the Mass of neutral intellect—but they have not any individuality, any determined Character—I would call the top and head of those who have a proper self Men of Power.

But I am running my head into a subject which I am certain I could not do justice to under five Years' study, and 3 vols. octavo—and, moreover, I long to be talking about the Imagination—so my dear Bailey, do not think of this unpleasant affair, if possible do not—I defy any harm to come of it—I defy. I shall write to Cripps this week, and request him to tell me all his goings-on from time to time by Letter wherever I may be. It will go on well—so don't because you have suddenly discovered a Coldness in Haydon suffer yourself to be teased—Do not my dear fellow—O! I wish I was as certain of the end of all your troubles as that of your momentary start about the authenticity of the Imagination. I am certain of nothing but of the holiness of the Heart's affections, and the truth of Imagination. What the Imagination seizes as Beauty must be truth—whether it existed before or not,—for I have the same idea of all our passions as of Love: they are all, in their sublime, creative of essential Beauty. In a Word, you may know my favourite speculation by my first Book, and the little Song I sent in my last, which is a representation from the fancy of the probable mode of operating in these Matters. The Imagination may be compared to Adam's dream,—he

awoke and found it truth :[1]—I am more zealous in this
affair, because I have never yet been able to perceive how
anything can be known for truth by consecutive reasoning
—and yet it must be.   Can it be that even the greatest
Philosopher ever arrived at his Goal without putting aside
numerous objections?   However it may be, O for a life
of Sensations rather than of Thoughts!   It is "a Vision
in the form of Youth," a shadow of reality to come—And
this consideration has further convinced me,—for it has
come as auxiliary to another favourite speculation of
mine,—that we shall enjoy ourselves hereafter by having
what we called happiness on Earth repeated in a finer
tone—And yet such a fate can only befall those who
delight in Sensation, rather than hunger as you do after
Truth.   Adam's dream will do here, and seems to be a
Conviction that Imagination and its empyreal reflection, is
the same as human life and its spiritual repetition. But,
as I was saying, the Simple imaginative Mind may have
its rewards in the repetition of its own silent Working
coming continually on the Spirit with a fine Suddenness—
to compare great things with small, have you never by
being surprised with an old Melody, in a delicious place
by a delicious voice, *felt* over again your very speculations
and surmises at the time it first operated on your soul?
—do you not remember forming to yourself the Singer's
face—more beautiful than it was possible, and yet with
the elevation of the Moment you did not think so?
Even then you were mounted on the Wings of Imagination, so high that the prototype must be hereafter—that
delicious face you will see.   What a time!   I am continually running away from the subject.   Sure this cannot

---

[1] "She disappear'd, and left me dark : I waked
     To find her, or for ever to deplore
     Her loss, and other pleasures all abjure :
     When, out of hope, behold her not far off, ·
     Such as I saw her in my dream, adorn'd
     With what all Earth or Heaven could bestow
     To make her amiable."
                    Paradise Lost, Book VIII.

be exactly the Case with a complex mind—one that is
imaginative, and at the same time careful of its fruits,—
who would exist partly on Sensation, partly on thought—
to whom it is necessary that years should bring the philosophic Mind? Such a one I consider yours, and therefore
it is necessary to your eternal happiness that you not
only drink this old Wine of Heaven, which I shall call the
redigestion of our most ethereal Musings upon Earth, but
also increase in knowledge and know all things. I am
glad to hear that you are in a fair way for Easter. You
will soon get through your unpleasant reading, and
then!—but the world is full of troubles, and I have
not much reason to think myself pestered with many.

I think Jane or Marianne has a better opinion of me
than I deserve : for, really and truly, I do not think my
Brother's illness connected with mine—you know more
of the real Cause than they do ; nor have I any chance
of being rack'd as you have been. You perhaps at one
time thought there was such a thing as worldly happiness to be arrived at, at certain periods of time marked
out,—you have of necessity from your disposition been
thus led away—I scarcely remember counting upon any
Happiness—I look not for it if it be not in the present
hour,—nothing startles me beyond the moment. The
Setting Sun will always set me to rights, or if a Sparrow
come before my Window, I take part in its existence and
pick about the gravel. The first thing that strikes me
on hearing a Misfortune having befallen another is this—
"Well, it cannot be helped : he will have the pleasure of
trying the resources of his Spirit"—and I beg now, my
dear Bailey, that hereafter should you observe anything
cold in me not to put it to the account of heartlessness,
but abstraction—for I assure you I sometimes feel not
the influence of a passion or affection during a whole
Week—and so long this sometimes continues, I begin to
suspect myself, and the genuineness of my feelings at
other times—thinking them a few barren Tragedy Tears.

My brother Tom is much improved—he is going to

Devonshire—whither I shall follow him.   At present, I am just arrived at Dorking—to change the Scene—change the Air, and give me a spur to wind up my Poem, of which there are wanting 500 lines.   I should have been here a day sooner, but the Reynoldses persuaded me to stop in Town to meet your friend Christie.   There were Rice and Martin—we talked about Ghosts.   I will have some Talk with Taylor and let you know,—when please God I come down at Christmas.   I will find that Examiner if possible.   My best regards to Gleig, my Brothers' to you and Mrs. Bentley.

Your affectionate Friend   JOHN KEATS.

I want to say much more to you—a few hints will set me going.   Direct Burford Bridge near Dorking.

XXIII.—TO JOHN HAMILTON REYNOLDS.

[Burford Bridge,] November 22, 1817.

My dear Reynolds—There are two things which tease me here—one of them Cripps, and the other that I cannot go with Tom into Devonshire.   However, I hope to do my duty to myself in a week or so; and then I'll try what I can do for my neighbour—now, is not this virtuous? On returning to Town I'll damm all Idleness—indeed, in superabundance of employment, I must not be content to run here and there on little two-penny errands, but turn Rakehell, *i.e.* go a masking, or Bailey will think me just as great a Promise Keeper as *he* thinks you; for myself I do not, and do not remember above one complaint against you for matter o' that.   Bailey writes so abominable a hand, to give his Letter a fair reading requires a little time: so I had not seen, when I saw you last, his invitation to Oxford at Christmas.   I'll go with you. You know how poorly Rice was.   I do not think it was all corporeal,—bodily pain was not used to keep him silent.   I'll tell you what; he was hurt at what your Sisters said about his joking with your Mother, he was,

soothly to sain. It will all blow over. God knows, my
dear Reynolds, I should not talk any sorrow to you—you
must have enough vexations—so I won't any more. If I
ever start a rueful subject in a letter to you—blow me!
Why don't you?—now I am going to ask you a very
silly Question neither you nor anybody else could answer,
under a folio, or at least a Pamphlet—you shall judge—
why don't you, as I do, look unconcerned at what may
be called more particularly Heart-vexations? They never
surprise me—lord! a man should have the fine point of
his soul taken off to become fit for this world.

I like this place very much. There is Hill and Dale
and a little River. I went up Box hill this Evening after
the Moon—"you a' seen the Moon"—came down, and
wrote some lines. Whenever I am separated from you,
and not engaged in a continued Poem, every letter shall
bring you a lyric—but I am too anxious for you to enjoy
the whole to send you a particle. One of the three books
I have with me is Shakspeare's Poems : I never found
so many beauties in the sonnets—they seem to be full of
fine things said unintentionally—in the intensity of working out conceits. Is this to be borne? Hark ye!

> When lofty trees I see barren of leaves,
>   Which erst from heat did canopy the head,
> And Summer's green all girded up in sheaves,
>   Borne on the bier with white and bristly head.

He has left nothing to say about nothing or anything :
for look at snails—you know what he says about Snails—
you know when he talks about "cockled Snails"—well,
in one of these sonnets, he says—the chap slips into—
no! I lie! this is in the Venus and Adonis : the simile
brought it to my Mind.

> As the snail, whose tender horns being hit,
>   Shrinks back into his shelly cave with pain,
> And there all smothered up in shade doth sit,
>   Long after fearing to put forth again ;
> So at his bloody view her eyes are fled,
> Into the deep dark Cabins of her head.

He overwhelms a genuine Lover of poesy with all manner .
of abuse, talking about—

> "a poet's rage
> And stretched metre of an antique song."

Which, by the bye, will be a capital motto for my poem,
won't it? He speaks too of "Time's antique pen"—and
"April's first-born flowers"—and "Death's eternal cold."
—By the Whim-King! I'll give you a stanza, because
it is not material in connection, and when I wrote it I
wanted you—to give your vote, pro or con.—

> Crystalline Brother of the belt of Heaven,
> Aquarius! to whom King Jove hath given
> Two liquid pulse-streams, 'stead of feather'd wings—
> Two fan-like fountains—thine illuminings
> For Dian play :
> Dissolve the frozen purity of air ;
> Let thy white shoulders, silvery and bare,
> Show cold through wat'ry pinions : make more bright
> The Star-Queen's Crescent on her marriage night :
> Haste, haste away !

. . . I see there is an advertisement in the *Chronicle*
to Poets—he is so over-loaded with poems on the "late
Princess." I suppose you do not lack—send me a few—
lend me thy hand to laugh a little—send me a little
pullet-sperm, a few finch-eggs—and remember me to each
of our card-playing Club. When you die you will all be
turned into Dice, and be put in pawn with the devil: for
cards, they crumple up like anything. . . .
I rest Your affectionate friend   JOHN KEATS.

Give my love to both houses—hinc atque illinc.

XXIV.—TO GEORGE AND THOMAS KEATS.

Hampstead, December 22, 1817.

My dear Brothers—I must crave your pardon for not
having written ere this. . . . I saw Kean return to
the public in Richard III., and finely he did it, and, at
the request of Reynolds, I went to criticise his *Duke* in

Rich^d.—the critique is in to-day's Champion, which I
send you with the Examiner, in which you will find
very proper lamentation on the obsoletion of Christmas
Gambols and pastimes: but it was mixed up with so
much egotism of that drivelling nature that pleasure is
entirely lost.   Hone the publisher's trial, you must find
very amusing, and as Englishmen very encouraging: his
Not Guilty is a thing, which not to have been, would
have dulled still more Liberty's Emblazoning—Lord
Ellenborough has been paid in his own coin—Wooler
and Hone have done us an essential service.   I have had
two very pleasant evenings with Dilke yesterday and
to-day, and am at this moment just come from him, and
feel in the humour to go on with this, begun in the
morning, and from which he came to fetch me.   I spent
Friday evening with Wells[1] and went next morning
to see *Death on the Pale horse*.   It is a wonderful
picture, when West's age is considered; but there is
nothing to be intense upon, no women one feels mad to
kiss, no face swelling into reality.   The excellence of
every art is its intensity, capable of making all disagreeables evaporate from their being in close relationship with
Beauty and Truth—Examine King Lear, and you will
find this exemplified throughout; but in this picture we
have unpleasantness without any momentous depth of
speculation excited, in which to bury its repulsiveness—
The picture is larger than Christ rejected.

   I dined with Haydon the Sunday after you left, and
had a very pleasant day, I dined too (for I have been
out too much lately) with Horace Smith and met his
two Brothers with Hill and Kingston and one Du Bois,
they only served to convince me how superior humour
is to wit, in respect to enjoyment—These men say things
which make one start, without making one feel, they are

---

[1] Charles Wells, a schoolmate of Tom Keats; afterwards
author of *Stories after Nature* and *Joseph and his Brethren*.   For
Keats's subsequent cause of quarrel with him see below, Letter
XCII.

all alike; their manners are alike; they all know fashionables; they have all a mannerism in their very eating and
drinking, in their mere handling a Decanter. They talked
of Kean and his low company—would I were with that
company instead of yours said I to myself! I know
such like acquaintance will never do for me and yet I am
going to Reynolds, on Wednesday. Brown and Dilke
walked with me and back from the Christmas pantomime.
I had not a dispute, but a disquisition, with Dilke upon
various subjects; several things dove-tailed in my mind,
and at once it struck me what quality went to form a
Man of Achievement, especially in Literature, and which
Shakspeare possessed so enormously—I mean *Negative
Capability*, that is, when a man is capable of being in
uncertainties, mysteries, doubts, without any irritable
reaching after fact and reason. Coleridge, for instance,
would let go by a fine isolated verisimilitude caught from
the Penetralium of mystery,[1] from being incapable of
remaining content with half-knowledge. This pursued
through volumes would perhaps take us no further than
this, that with a great poet the sense of Beauty over-
comes every other consideration, or rather obliterates all
consideration.

Shelley's poem[2] is out and there are words about its
being objected to, as much as Queen Mab was. Poor
Shelley I think he has his Quota of good qualities, in
sooth la! Write soon to your most sincere friend and
affectionate Brother   JOHN.

XXV.—TO GEORGE AND THOMAS KEATS.

Featherstone Buildings,[3] Monday [January 5, 1818].

My dear Brothers—I ought to have written before,
and you should have had a long letter last week, but I

---

[1] An admirable phrase!—if only *penetralium* were Latin.
[2] *Laon and Cythna*, presently changed to *The Revolt of Islam*.
[3] The family of Charles Wells lived at this address.

undertook the Champion for Reynolds, who is at
Exeter. I wrote two articles, one on the Drury Lane
Pantomime, the other on the Covent Garden new
Tragedy, which they have not put in;[1] the one they have
inserted is so badly punctuated that you perceive I am
determined never to write more, without some care in
that particular. Wells tells me that you are licking your
chops, Tom, in expectation of my book coming out. I
am sorry to say I have not begun my corrections yet:
to-morrow I set out. I called on Sawrey[2] this morning.
He did not seem to be at all put out at anything I said and
the inquiries I made with regard to your spitting of blood,
and moreover desired me to ask you to send him a correct
account of all your sensations and symptoms concerning
the palpitation and the spitting and the cough—if you
have any. Your last letter gave me a great pleasure,
for I think the invalid is in a better spirit there along the
Edge; and as for George, I must immediately, now I
think of it, correct a little misconception of a part of my
last letter. The Misses Reynolds have never said one
word against me about you, or by any means endeavoured to
lessen you in my estimation. That is not what I referred
to; but the manner and thoughts which I knew they
internally had towards you, time will show. Wells and
Severn dined with me yesterday. We had a very
pleasant day. I pitched upon another bottle of claret,
we enjoyed ourselves very much; were all very witty
and full of Rhymes. We played a concert from 4 o'clock
till 10—drank your healths, the Hunts', and (*N.B.*)
seven Peter Pindars. I said on that day the only
good thing I was ever guilty of. We were talking about
Stephens and the 1st Gallery. I said I wondered that
careful folks would go there, for although it was but a
shilling, still you had to pay through the Nose. I saw
the Peachey family in a box at Drury one night. I have

---

[1] Both in fact appeared in the number for Sunday, January 4:
see postscript below.
[2] The Hampstead doctor who attended the Keats brothers.

got such a curious[1] . . . or rather I had such, now I am
in my own hand.

I have had a great deal of pleasant time with Rice
lately, and am getting initiated into a little band. They
call drinking deep dyin' scarlet. They call good wine a
pretty tipple, and call getting a child knocking out an
apple; stopping at a tavern they call hanging out.
Where do you sup? is where do you hang out?

Thursday I promised to dine with Wordsworth, and
the weather is so bad that I am undecided, for he lives
at Mortimer Street. I had an invitation to meet him at
Kingston's,[2] but not liking that place I sent my excuse.
What I think of doing to-day is to dine in Mortimer
Street (Words[th]), and sup here in the Feath[r] buildings,
as Mr. Wells has invited me. On Saturday, I called on
Wordsworth before he went to Kingston's, and was surprised to find him with a stiff collar. I saw his spouse,
and I think his daughter. I forget whether I had
written my last before my Sunday evening at Haydon's
—no, I did not, or I should have told you, Tom, of a
young man you met at Paris, at Scott's, . . . Ritchie. I
think he is going to Fezan, in Africa; then to proceed
if possible like Mungo Park. He was very polite to me,
and inquired very particularly after you. Then there
was Wordsworth, Lamb, Monkhouse, Landseer, Kingston,
and your humble servant. Lamb got tipsy and blew up
Kingston—proceeding so far as to take the candle across
the room, hold it to his face, and show us what a soft
fellow he was.[3] I astonished Kingston at supper with a

[1] The text of this letter is described by its American editor
(who seems to have mistaken the order of one or two passages)
as written in an evident hurry and almost illegible.

[2] Mr. Kingston was a Commissioner of Stamps, an acquaintance
and tiresome hanger-on of Wordsworth.

[3] For a more glowing account of this supper party of December
28, 1817, compare Haydon, *Autobiography*, i. p. 384. The Mr.
Ritchie referred to started on a Government mission to Fezzan in
September 1818, and died at Morzouk the following November.
An account of the expedition was published by his travelling com-
panion, Captain G. F. Lyon, R.N.

pertinacity in favour of drinking, keeping my two glasses
at work in a knowing way.

I have seen Fanny twice lately—she inquired particularly after you and wants a co-partnership letter from you.
She has been unwell, but is improving.   I think she will
be quick.   Mrs. Abbey was saying that the Keatses were
ever indolent, that they would ever be so, and that it is
born in them.   Well, whispered Fanny to me, if it is
born with us, how can we help it?   She seems very
anxious for a letter.   As I asked her what I should get
for her, she said a "Medal of the Princess."   I called on
Haslam—we dined very snugly together.   He sent me
a Hare last week, which I sent to Mrs. Dilke.   Brown
is not come back.   I and Dilke are getting capital friends.
He is going to take the Champion.   He has sent his
farce to Covent Garden.   I met Bob Harris[1] on the
steps at Covent Garden ; we had a good deal of curious
chat.   He came out with his old humble opinion.   The
Covent Garden pantomime is a very nice one, but they
have a middling Harlequin, a bad Pantaloon, a worse
Clown, and a shocking Columbine, who is one of the Miss
Dennets.   I suppose you will see my critique on the new
tragedy in the next week's Champion.   It is a shocking bad
one.   I have not seen Hunt ; he was out when I called.
Mrs. Hunt looks as well as ever I saw her after her confinement.   There is an article in the se'nnight Examiner
on Godwin's Mandeville, signed E. K.—I think it Miss
Kent's—I will send it.   There are fine subscriptions
going on for Hone.

You ask me what degrees there are between Scott's
novels and those of Smollett.   They appear to me to be
quite distinct in every particular, more especially in their
aims.   Scott endeavours to throw so interesting and
romantic a colouring into common and low characters as
to give them a touch of the sublime.   Smollett on the
contrary pulls down and levels what with other men

---

[1] The manager : of whom Macready in his *Reminiscences* has
so much that is pleasant to say.

would continue romance. The grand parts of Scott are within the reach of more minds than the finest humours in Humphrey Clinker. I forget whether that fine thing of the Serjeant is Fielding or Smollett, but it gives me more pleasure than the whole novel of the Antiquary. You must remember what I mean. Some one says to the Serjeant : "That's a non-sequitur! "—"If you come to that," replies the Serjeant, "you're another ! "—

I see by Wells's letter Mr. Abbey[1] does not overstock you with money. You must write. I have not seen . . . yet, but expect it on Wednesday. I am afraid it is gone. Severn tells me he has an order for some drawings for the Emperor of Russia.

You must get well Tom, and then I shall feel whole and genial as the winter air. Give me as many letters as you like, and write to Sawrey soon. I received a short letter from Bailey about Cripps, and one from Haydon, ditto. Haydon thinks he improved very much. Mrs. Wells desires particularly . . . to Tom and her respects to George, and I desire no better than to be ever your most affectionate Brother   JOHN.

P.S.—I had not opened the Champion before I found both my articles in it.

I was at a dance at Redhall's, and passed a pleasant time enough—drank deep, and won 10·6 at cutting for half guineas. . . . Bailey was there and seemed to enjoy the evening. Rice said he cared less about the hour than any one, and the proof is his dancing—he cares not for time, dancing as if he was deaf. Old Redhall not being used to give parties, had no idea of the quantity of wine that would be drank, and he actually put in readiness on the kitchen stairs eight dozen.

Every one inquires after you, and desires their remembrances to you.

Your Brother   JOHN.

[1] Tea-merchant, of Pancras Lane and Walthamstow : guardian to the Keats brothers and their sister.

XXVI.—TO BENJAMIN ROBERT HAYDON.

[Hampstead,] Saturday Morn [January 10, 1818].

My dear Haydon—I should have seen you ere this, but on account of my sister being in Town : so that when I have sometimes made ten paces towards you, Fanny has called me into the City ; and the Christmas Holydays are your only time to see Sisters, that is if they are so situated as mine. I will be with you early next week— to-night it should be, but we have a sort of a Club every Saturday evening—to-morrow, but I have on that day an insuperable engagement. Cripps has been down to me, and appears sensible that a binding to you would be of the greatest advantage to him—if such a thing be done it cannot be before £150 or £200 are secured in subscriptions to him. I will write to Bailey about it, give a Copy of the Subscribers' names to every one I know who is likely to get a £5 for him. I will leave a Copy at Taylor and Hessey's, Rodwell and Martin, and will ask Kingston and Co. to cash up.

Your friendship for me is now getting into its teens— and I feel the past. Also every day older I get—the greater is my idea of your achievements in Art : and I am convinced that there are three things to rejoice at in this Age—The Excursion, Your Pictures, and Hazlitt's depth of Taste.

Yours affectionately   JOHN KEATS.

XXVII.—TO JOHN TAYLOR.

[Hampstead,] Saturday Morning [January 10, 1818].

My dear Taylor—Several things have kept me from you lately :—first you had got into a little hell, which I was not anxious to reconnoitre—secondly, I have made a vow not to call again without my first book : so you may expect to see me in four days. Thirdly, I have been racketing too much, and do not feel over well. I have seen Wordsworth frequently—Dined with him last Monday—Reynolds, I suppose you have seen.   Just scribble me thus many lines, to let me know you are in the land of the living, and well.   Remember me to the Fleet Street Household—and should you see any from Percy Street, give my kindest regards to them.

    Your sincere friend   JOHN KEATS.

XXVIII.—TO GEORGE AND THOMAS KEATS.

[Hampstead,] Tuesday [January 13, 1818].

My dear Brothers—I am certain I think of having a letter to-morrow morning for I expected one so much this morning, having been in town two days, at the end of which my expectations began to get up a little.   I found two on the table, one from Bailey and one from Haydon, I am quite perplexed in a world of doubts and fancies—there is nothing stable in the world; uproar's your only music—I don't mean to include Bailey in this and so dismiss him from this with all the opprobrium he deserves—that is in so many words, he is one of the noblest men alive at the present day.   In a note to Haydon about a week ago (which I wrote with a full sense of what he had done, and how he had never manifested any little mean drawback in his value of me) I said if there were three things superior in the modern world, they were "the Excursion," "Haydon's pictures," and "Hazlitt's depth of Taste"—so I do believe—Not thus speaking with any poor vanity that works of genius were the first things in this world.   No! for that sort of probity and disinterestedness which such men as Bailey possess, does hold and grasp the tiptop of any spiritual honours that can be paid to anything in this world—And moreover having this feeling at this present come over me in its full force, I sat down to write to you with a grateful heart, in that I had not a Brother who did not feel and credit me for a deeper feeling and devotion for his uprightness, than for any marks of genius however splendid.   I was speaking about doubts and fancies—I mean there has been a quarrel of a severe nature between Haydon and Reynolds and another ("the Devil rides upon a fiddlestick") between Hunt and Haydon—the first grew from the Sunday on which Haydon invited some friends to meet Wordsworth.   Reynolds never went, and never sent any Notice about it, this offended Haydon more than it ought to have done—he wrote a very sharp and high note to Reynolds and then another in palliation—but which Reynolds feels as an aggravation of the first—Considering all things, Haydon's frequent neglect of his Appointments, etc. his notes were bad enough to put Reynolds on the right side of the question —but then Reynolds has no power of sufferance; no idea of having the thing against him; so he answered Haydon in one of the most cutting letters I ever read; exposing to himself all his own weaknesses and going on to an excess, which whether it is just or no, is what I would fain have unsaid, the fact is, they are both in the right and both in the wrong.

The quarrel with Hunt I understand thus far.   Mrs. H. was in the habit of borrowing silver of Haydon—the last time she did so, Haydon asked her to return it at a certain time—she did not—Haydon sent for it—Hunt went to expostulate on the indelicacy, etc.—they got to words and parted for ever.   All I hope is at some time to bring them together again.—Lawk! Molly there's been such doings—Yesterday evening I made an appointment with Wells to go to a private theatre, and it being in the neighbourhood of Drury Lane, and thinking we might be fatigued with sitting the whole evening in one dirty hole, I got the Drury Lane ticket, and therewith we divided the evening with a spice of Richard III——

[Later, January 19 or 20.]

Good Lord! I began this letter nearly a week ago, what have I been doing since—I have been—I mean

not been—sending last Sunday's paper to you.   I believe
because it was not near me—for I cannot find it, and my
conscience presses heavy on me for not sending it.   You
would have had one last Thursday, but I was called
away, and have been about somewhere ever since.
Where?   What!   Well I rejoice almost that I have not
heard from you because no news is good news.   I cannot
for the world recollect why I was called away, all I
know is that there has been a dance at Dilke's, and
another at the London Coffee House; to both of which I
went.   But I must tell you in another letter the circumstances thereof—for though a week should have passed
since I wrote on the other side it quite appals me.   I
can only write in scraps and patches.   Brown is returned
from Hampstead.   Haydon has returned an answer in
the same style—they are all dreadfully irritated against
each other.   On Sunday I saw Hunt and dined with Haydon, met Hazlitt and Bewick there, and took Haslam with
me—forgot to speak about Cripps though I broke my engagement to Haslam's on purpose.   Mem.—Haslam came
to meet me, found me at Breakfast, had the goodness
to go with me my way—I have just finished the revision
of my first book, and shall take it to Taylor's to-morrow
—intend to persevere—Do not let me see many days
pass without hearing from you.

Your most affectionate Brother   JOHN.

XXIX.—TO JOHN TAYLOR.

[Hampstead,] Friday 23d [January 1818].

My dear Taylor—I have spoken to Haydon about the
drawing.   He would do it with all his Art and Heart
too, if so I will it; however, he has written thus to me;
but I must tell you, first, he intends painting a finished
Picture from the Poem.   Thus he writes—"When I do
anything for your Poem it must be effectual—an honour
to both of us: to hurry up a sketch for the season won't
do.   I think an engraving from your head, from a Chalk

drawing of mine, done with all my might, to which I would put my name, would answer Taylor's idea better than the other. Indeed, I am sure of it. This I will do, and this will be effectual, and as I have not done it for any other human being, it will have an effect."

What think you of this? Let me hear. I shall have my second Book in readiness forthwith.

Yours most sincerely   JOHN KEATS.

If Reynolds calls tell him three lines will be acceptable, for I am squat at Hampstead.

XXX.—TO GEORGE AND THOMAS KEATS.

[Hampstead,] Friday 23d January [1818].

My dear Brothers—I was thinking what hindered me from writing so long, for I have so many things to say to you, and know not where to begin. It shall be upon a thing most interesting to you, my Poem. Well! I have given the first Book to Taylor; he seemed more than satisfied with it, and to my surprise proposed publishing it in Quarto if Haydon would make a drawing of some event therein, for a Frontispiece. I called on Haydon, he said he would do anything I liked, but said he would rather paint a finished picture, from it, which he seems eager to do; this in a year or two will be a glorious thing for us; and it will be, for Haydon is struck with the 1st Book. I left Haydon and the next day received a letter from him, proposing to make, as he says, with all his might, a finished chalk sketch of my head, to be engraved in the first style and put at the head of my Poem, saying at the same time he had never done the thing for any human being, and that it must have considerable effect as he will put his name to it—I begin to-day to copy my 2nd Book— "thus far into the bowels of the land"—You shall hear whether it will be Quarto or non Quarto, picture or non picture. Leigh Hunt I showed my 1st Book to—he

allows it not much merit as a whole ; says it is unnatural
and made ten objections to it in the mere skimming over.
He says the conversation is unnatural and too high-flown
for Brother and Sister—says it should be simple forgetting do ye mind that they are both overshadowed by a
supernatural Power, and of force could not speak like
Francesca in the Rimini.   He must first prove that
Caliban's poetry is unnatural—This with me completely overturns his objections—the fact is he and
Shelley are hurt, and perhaps justly, at my not having
showed them the affair officiously and from several hints
I have had they appear much disposed to dissect and
anatomise any trip or slip I may have made.—But who's
afraid ? Ay! Tom! Demme if I am.   I went last
Tuesday, an hour too late, to Hazlitt's Lecture on poetry,
got there just as they were coming out, when all these
pounced upon me.   Hazlitt, John Hunt and Son, Wells,
Bewick, all the Landseers, Bob Harris, aye and more—
the Landseers enquired after you particularly—I know
not whether Wordsworth has left town—But Sunday I
dined with Hazlitt and Haydon, also that I took Haslam
with me—I dined with Brown lately.   Dilke having
taken the Champion Theatricals was obliged to be in
town—Fanny has returned to Walthamstow.—Mr.
Abbey appeared very glum, the last time I went to see
her, and said in an indirect way, that I had no business
there—Rice has been ill, but has been mending much
lately—

I think a little change has taken place in my intellect
lately—I cannot bear to be uninterested or unemployed,
I, who for so long a time have been addicted to passive-
ness.   Nothing is finer for the purposes of great produc-
tions than a very gradual ripening of the intellectual
powers.   As an instance of this—observe—I sat down
yesterday to read King Lear once again : the thing
appeared to demand the prologue of a sonnet, I wrote
it, and began to read—(I know you would like to see
it.)

ON SITTING DOWN TO KING LEAR ONCE AGAIN.

O golden-tongued Romance with serene Lute !
Fair-plumed Syren, Queen of far-away !
Leave melodising on this wintry day,
Shut up thine olden volume and be mute.
Adieu ! for once again the fierce dispute
Betwixt Hell torment and impassion'd Clay
Must I burn through ; once more assay
The bitter sweet of this Shakspearian fruit.
Chief Poet ! and ye clouds of Albion,
Begetters of our deep eternal theme,
When I am through the old oak forest gone
Let me not wander in a barren dream,
But, when I am consumed with the Fire,
Give me new Phœnix-wings to fly at my desire.

So you see I am getting at it, with a sort of determination and strength, though verily I do not feel it at this
moment—this is my fourth letter this morning, and I
feel rather tired, and my head rather swimming—so I
will leave it open till to-morrow's post.—

I am in the habit of taking my papers to Dilke's and
copying there ; so I chat and proceed at the same time.
I have been there at my work this evening, and the walk
over the Heath takes off all sleep, so I will even proceed
with you. I left off short in my last just as I began an
account of a private theatrical—Well it was of the
lowest order, all greasy and oily, insomuch that if they
had lived in olden times, when signs were hung over the
doors, the only appropriate one for that oily place would
have been—a guttered Candle. They played John Bull,
The Review, and it was to conclude with Bombastes
Furioso—I saw from a Box the first Act of John Bull,
then went to Drury and did not return till it was over—
when by Wells's interest we got behind the scenes—there
was not a yard wide all the way round for actors, scene-
shifters, and interlopers to move in—for ' Nota Bene '
the Green Room was under the stage, and there was I
threatened over and over again to be turned out by the
oily scene-shifters, there did I hear a little painted

Trollop own, very candidly, that she had failed in Mary, with a "damn'd if she'd play a serious part again, as long as she lived," and at the same time she was habited as the Quaker in the Review.—There was a quarrel, and a fat good-natured looking girl in soldiers' clothes wished she had only been a man for Tom's sake. One fellow began a song, but an unlucky finger-point from the Gallery sent him off like a shot. One chap was dressed to kill for the King in Bombastes, and he stood at the edge of the scene in the very sweat of anxiety to show himself, but Alas the thing was not played. The sweetest morsel of the night moreover was, that the musicians began pegging and fagging away—at an overture—never did you see faces more in earnest, three times did they play it over, dropping all kinds of corrections and still did not the curtain go up. Well then they went into a country dance, then into a region they well knew, into the old boonsome Pothouse, and then to see how pompous o' the sudden they turned; how they looked about and chatted; how they did not care a damn; was a great treat——

I hope I have not tired you by this filling up of the dash in my last. Constable the bookseller has offered Reynolds ten guineas a sheet to write for his Magazine— it is an Edinburgh one, which Blackwood's started up in opposition to. Hunt said he was nearly sure that the 'Cockney School' was written by Scott [1] so you are right Tom !—There are no more little bits of news I can remember at present.

I remain, My dear Brothers, Your very affectionate Brother   JOHN.

[1] Of course a mere delusion; but Hunt and those of his circle retained for years afterwards an impression that Scott had in some way inspired or encouraged the *Cockney School* articles.

XXXI.—TO BENJAMIN BAILEY.

[Hampstead,] Friday Jan*· 23 [1818].

My dear Bailey—Twelve days have pass'd since your last reached me.—What has gone through the myriads of human minds since the 12th? We talk of the immense Number of Books, the Volumes ranged thousands by thousands—but perhaps more goes through the human intelligence in Twelve days than ever was written.—*How has that unfortunate family lived through the twelve?* One saying of yours I shall never forget—you may not recollect it—it being perhaps said when you were looking on the Surface and seeming of Humanity alone, without a thought of the past or the future—or the deeps of good and evil—you were at that moment estranged from speculation, and I think you have arguments ready for the Man who would utter it to you—this is a formidable preface for a simple thing—merely you said, " *Why should woman suffer?* " Aye, why should she? " By heavens I'd coin my very Soul, and drop my Blood for Drachmas ! " These things are, and he, who feels how incompetent the most skyey Knight-errantry is to heal this bruised fairness, is like a sensitive leaf on the hot hand of thought.—Your tearing, my dear friend, a spiritless and gloomy letter up, to re-write to me, is what I shall never forget—it was to me a real thing—Things have happened lately of great perplexity—you must have heard of them—Reynolds and Haydon retorting and recriminating—and parting for ever—the same thing has happened between Haydon and Hunt. It is unfortunate—Men should bear with each other: there lives not the Man who may not be cut up, aye Lashed to pieces on his weakest side. The best of Men have but a portion of good in them—a kind of spiritual yeast in their frames, which creates the ferment of existence—by which a Man is propelled to act, and strive, and buffet with Circumstance. The sure way, Bailey, is first to know a Man's faults, and then be passive—if after that he insensibly draws you towards him then you have no power to break the link.   Before I felt interested in either Reynolds or Haydon, I was well read in their faults; yet, knowing them, I have been cementing gradually with both.   I have an affection for them both, for reasons almost opposite—and to both must I of necessity cling, supported always by the hope that, when a little time, a few years, shall have tried me more fully in their esteem, I may be able to bring them together.   The time must come, because they have both hearts : and they will recollect the best parts of each other, when this gust is overblown.—I had a message from you through a letter to Jane—I think, about Cripps—there can be no idea of binding until a sufficient sum is sure for him—and even then the thing should be maturely considered by all his helpers—I shall try my luck upon as many fat purses as I can meet with.—Cripps is improving very fast : I have the greater hopes of him because he is so slow in development.   A Man of great executing powers at 20, with a look and a speech almost stupid, is sure to do something.

I have just looked through the Second Side of your Letter—I feel a great content at it.—I was at Hunt's the other day, and he surprised me with a real authenticated lock of *Milton's Hair*.   I know you would like what I wrote thereon, so here it is—*as they say of a Sheep in a Nursery Book* :—

ON SEEING A LOCK OF MILTON'S HAIR.

Chief of Organic Numbers !
  Old Scholar of the Spheres !
Thy spirit never slumbers,
  But rolls about our ears
For ever, and for ever !
O what a mad endeavour
      Worketh he,
Who to thy sacred and ennobled hearse
Would offer a burnt sacrifice of verse
      And melody.

How heavenward thou soundest,
  Live Temple of sweet noise,
And Discord unconfoundest,
  Giving Delight new joys,
And Pleasure nobler pinions !
O, where are thy dominions ?
    Lend thine ear
To a young Delian oath,—aye, by thy soul,
By all that from thy mortal lips did roll,
And by the kernel of thine earthly love,
Beauty, in things on earth, and things above,
    I swear !
  When every childish fashion
    Has vanish'd from my rhyme,
  Will I, gray-gone in passion,
    Leave to an after-time,
    Hymning and harmony
Of thee, and of thy works, and of thy life ;
But vain is now the burning and the strife,
Pangs are in vain, until I grow high-rife
    With old Philosophy,
And mad with glimpses of futurity !

For many years my offering must be hush'd ;
  When I do speak, I'll think upon this hour,
Because I feel my forehead hot and flush'd,
  Even at the simplest vassal of thy power,—
    A lock of thy bright hair, ✗
    Sudden it came,
And I was startled, when I caught thy name
    Coupled so unaware ;
Yet, at the moment, temperate was my blood.
I thought I had beheld it from the flood.

This I did at Hunt's at his request—perhaps I
should have done something better alone and at home.—
I have sent my first Book to the press, and this afternoon shall begin preparing the Second—my visit to you
will be a great spur to quicken the proceeding.—I have
not had your Sermon returned—I long to make it the
Subject of a Letter to you—What do they say at Oxford ?
  I trust you and Gleig pass much fine time together.
Remember me to him and Whitehead. My Brother Tom
is getting stronger, but his spitting of Blood continues.
I sat down to read King Lear yesterday, and felt the

✗ A bracelet of bright hair

greatness of the thing up to the Writing of a Sonnet pre-
paratory thereto—in my next you shall have it.—There
were some miserable reports of Rice's health—I went,
and lo! Master Jemmy had been to the play the night
before, and was out at the time—he always comes on
his legs like a Cat. I have seen a good deal of Wordsworth. Hazlitt is lecturing on Poetry at the Surrey
Institution—I shall be there next Tuesday.

Your most affectionate friend   JOHN KEATS.

XXXII.—TO JOHN TAYLOR.

[Hampstead, January 30, 1818.]

My dear Taylor—These lines as they now stand
about "happiness," have rung in my ears like "a chime
a mending"—See here,

> " Behold
> Wherein lies happiness, Peona ? fold, etc."

It appears to me the very contrary of blessed. I hope
this will appear to you more eligible.

> " Wherein lies Happiness ? In that which becks
> Our ready minds to fellowship divine,
> A fellowship with Essence till we shine
> Full alchemised, and free of space—Behold
> The clear religion of Heaven—fold, etc."

You must indulge me by putting this in, for setting
aside the badness of the other, such a preface is necessary
to the subject. The whole thing must, I think, have
appeared to you, who are a consecutive man, as a thing
almost of mere words, but I assure you that, when I
wrote it, it was a regular stepping of the Imagination
towards a truth. My having written that argument will
perhaps be of the greatest service to me of anything I
ever did. It set before me the gradations of happiness,
even like a kind of pleasure thermometer, and is my first
step towards the chief attempt in the drama. The playing
of different natures with joy and Sorrow—

Do me this favour, and believe me
Your sincere friend　　　　　　**J. KEATS.**

I hope your next work will be of a more general
Interest. I suppose you cogitate a little about it, now
and then.

XXXIII.—TO JOHN HAMILTON REYNOLDS.

Hampstead, Saturday [January 31, 1818].

My dear Reynolds—I have parcelled out this day for
Letter Writing—more resolved thereon because your
Letter will come as a refreshment and will have (sic
parvis etc.) the same effect as a Kiss in certain situations
where people become over-generous. I have read this
first sentence over, and think it savours rather; however
an inward innocence is like a nested dove, as the old
song says. . . .

Now I purposed to write to you a serious poetical letter,
but I find that a maxim I met with the other day is a
just one : " On cause mieux quand on ne dit pas *causons.*"
I was hindered, however, from my first intention by a
mere muslin Handkerchief very neatly pinned—but
" Hence, vain deluding," etc. Yet I cannot write in
prose ; it is a sunshiny day and I cannot, so here goes,—

> Hence Burgundy, Claret, and Port,
> 　Away with old Hock and Madeira,
> Too earthly ye are for my sport ;
> 　There's a beverage brighter and clearer.
> Instead of a pitiful rummer,
> My wine overbrims a whole summer ;
> 　My bowl is the sky,
> 　And I drink at my eye,
> 　Till I feel in the brain
> 　A Delphian pain—
> Then follow, my Caius ! then follow :
> 　On the green of the hill
> 　We will drink our fill
> 　Of golden sunshine,
> 　Till our brains intertwine
> With the glory and grace of Apollo !

F

God of the Meridian,
  And of the East and West,
To thee my soul is flown,
  And my body is earthward press'd. —
It is an awful mission,
A terrible division ;
And leaves a gulph austere
To be fill'd with worldly fear.
Aye, when the soul is fled
Too high above our head,
Affrighted do we gaze
After its airy maze,
As doth a mother wild,
When her young infant child
Is in an eagle's claws—
And is not this the cause
Of madness ?—God of Song,
Thou bearest me along
Through sights I scarce can bear :
O let me, let me share
With the hot lyre and thee,
The staid Philosophy.
Temper my lonely hours,
And let me see thy bowers
More unalarm'd !

My dear Reynolds, you must forgive all this ranting
—but the fact is, I cannot write sense this Morning—
however you shall have some—I will copy out my last
Sonnet.

When I have fears that I may cease to be
  Before my pen has glean'd my teeming brain,
Before high piled Books in charactery,
  Hold like rich garners the full ripen'd grain—
When I behold, upon the night's starr'd face,
  Huge cloudy symbols of a high romance,
And think that I may never live to trace
  Their shadows, with the magic hand of chance ;
And when I feel, fair creature of an hour,
  That I shall never look upon thee more,
Never have relish in the faery power
  Of unreflecting Love ;—then on the shore
    Of the wide world I stand alone, and think
    Till Love and Fame to nothingness do sink.

I must take a turn, and then write to Teignmouth.
Remember me to all, not excepting yourself.

Your sincere friend   JOHN KEATS.

XXXIV.—TO JOHN HAMILTON REYNOLDS.

Hampstead, Tuesday [February 3, 1818].

My dear Reynolds—I thank you for your dish of
Filberts—would I could get a basket of them by way of
dessert every day for the sum of twopence.[1] Would we
were a sort of ethereal Pigs, and turned loose to feed
upon spiritual Mast and Acorns—which would be merely
being a squirrel and feeding upon filberts, for what is a
squirrel but an airy pig, or a filbert but a sort of arch-
angelical acorn? About the nuts being worth cracking,
all I can say is, that where there are a throng of delightful
Images ready drawn, simplicity is the only thing. The
first is the best on account of the first line, and the
"arrow, foil'd of its antler'd food," and moreover (and
this is the only word or two I find fault with, the more
because I have had so much reason to shun it as a quick-
sand) the last has " tender and true." We must cut
this, and not be rattlesnaked into any more of the like.
It may be said that we ought to read our contemporaries,
that Wordsworth, etc., should have their due from us.
But, for the sake of a few fine imaginative or domestic
passages, are we to be bullied into a certain Philosophy
engendered in the whims of an Egotist? Every man has
his speculations, but every man does not brood and
peacock over them till he makes a false coinage and
deceives himself. Many a man can travel to the very
bourne of Heaven, and yet want confidence to put down
his half-seeing. Sancho will invent a Journey heaven-

---

[1] Alluding to two sonnets of Reynolds *On Robin Hood*,
copies of which Keats had just received from him by post.
They were printed in the *Yellow Dwarf* (edited by John Hunt)
for February 21, 1818, and again in the collection of poems published by Reynolds in 1821 under the title *A Garden of Florence*.

ward as well as anybody. We hate poetry that has a
palpable design upon us, and, if we do not agree, seems
to put its hand into its breeches pocket.   Poetry should
be great and unobtrusive, a thing which enters into one's
soul, and does not startle it or amaze it with itself—but
with its subject.   How beautiful are the retired flowers !
—how would they lose their beauty were they to throng
into the highway, crying out, "Admire me, I am a violet!
Dote upon me, I am a primrose!"   Modern poets differ
from the Elizabethans in this : each of the moderns like
an Elector of Hanover governs his petty state and
knows how many straws are swept daily from the Cause-
ways in all his dominions, and has a continual itching
that all the Housewives should have their coppers well
scoured : The ancients were Emperors of vast Provinces,
they had only heard of the remote ones and scarcely
cared to visit them.   I will cut all this—I will have
no more of Wordsworth or Hunt in particular—Why
should we be of the tribe of Manasseh, when we can
wander with Esau?   Why should we kick against the
Pricks, when we can walk on Roses ?   Why should we be
owls, when we can be eagles?   Why be teased with
"nice-eyed wagtails," when we have in sight "the
Cherub Contemplation"?   Why with Wordsworth's
"Matthew with a bough of wilding in his hand," when
we can have Jacques "under an oak," etc. ?   The secret
of the Bough of Wilding will run through your head
faster than I can write it.   Old Matthew spoke to him
some years ago on some nothing, and because he happens
in an Evening Walk to imagine the figure of the old Man,
he must stamp it down. in black and white, and it is
henceforth sacred.   I don't mean to deny Wordsworth's
grandeur and Hunt's merit, but I mean to say we need not
be teased with grandeur and merit when we can have them
uncontaminated and unobtrusive.   Let us have the old
Poets and Robin Hood.   Your letter and its sonnets gave
me more pleasure than will the Fourth Book of Childe
Harold and the whole of anybody's life and opinions.

In return for your Dish of Filberts, I have gathered a
few Catkins, I hope they'll look pretty.

TO J. H. R. IN ANSWER TO HIS ROBIN HOOD SONNETS.

No ! those days are gone away,
And their hours are old and gray,
And their minutes buried all
Under the down-trodden pall
Of the leaves of many years.
Many times have Winter's shears,
Frozen North and chilling East,
Sounded tempests to the feast
Of the forest's whispering fleeces,
Since men paid no rent on Leases.

No ! the Bugle sounds no more,
And the twanging bow no more ;
Silent is the ivory shrill
Past the heath and up the Hill ;
There is no mid-forest laugh,
Where lone Echo gives the half
To some wight amaz'd to hear
Jesting, deep in forest drear.

On the fairest time of June
You may go with Sun or Moon,
Or the seven stars to light you,
Or the polar ray to right you ;
But you never may behold
Little John or Robin bold ;
Never any of all the clan,
Thrumming on an empty can
Some old hunting ditty, while
He doth his green way beguile
To fair Hostess Merriment
Down beside the pasture Trent,
For he left the merry tale,
Messenger for spicy ale.

Gone the merry morris din,
Gone the song of Gamelyn,
Gone the tough-belted outlaw
Idling in the " grenè shawe ":
All are gone away and past !
And if Robin *should* be cast
Sudden from his turfed grave,
And if Marian *should* have
Once again her forest days,
She would weep, and he would craze :

He would swear, for all his oaks,
Fall'n beneath the Dock-yard strokes,
Have rotted on the briny seas ;
She would weep that her wild bees
Sang not to her—"strange that honey
Can't be got without hard money"

So it is ! yet let us sing,
Honour to the old bow-string,
Honour to the bugle-horn,
Honour to the woods unshorn,
Honour to the Lincoln green,
Honour to the archer keen,
Honour to tight little John,
And the horse he rode upon :
Honour to bold Robin Hood,
Sleeping in the underwood !
Honour to maid Marian,
And to all the Sherwood clan—
Though their days have hurried by
Let us two a burden try.

I hope you will like them—they are at least written in the Spirit of Outlawry.   Here are the Mermaid lines,

Souls of Poets dead and gone,
What Elysium have ye known,
Happy field, or mossy cavern,
Fairer than the Mermaid Tavern !
Have ye tippled drink more fine
Than mine Host's Canary wine ?
Or are fruits of paradise
Sweeter than those dainty pies
Of Venison ?   O generous food
Drest as though bold Robin Hood
Would with his Maid Marian,
Sup and bowse from horn and can.
I have heard that, on a day,
Mine host's sign-board flew away,
No body knew whither, till
An astrologer's old Quill
To a sheepskin gave the story,
Said he saw you in your glory,
Underneath a new old-sign
Sipping beverage divine,
And pledging with contented smack,
The Mermaid in the Zodiac.

> Souls of Poets dead and gone,
> Are the winds a sweeter home?
> Richer is uncellar'd cavern,
> Than the merry mermaid Tavern?[1]

I will call on you at 4 to-morrow, and we will trudge to-gether, for it is not the thing to be a stranger in the Land of Harpsicols. I hope also to bring you my 2nd Book. In the hope that these Scribblings will be some amuse-ment for you this Evening, I remain, copying on the Hill,

Your sincere friend and Co-scribbler

JOHN KEATS.

XXXV.—TO JOHN TAYLOR.

Fleet Street, Thursday Morn [February 5, 1818].

My dear Taylor—I have finished copying my Second Book—but I want it for one day to overlook it. And moreover this day I have very particular employ in the affair of Cripps—so I trespass on your indulgence, and take advantage of your good nature. You shall hear from me or see me soon. I will tell Reynolds of your engagement to-morrow.

Yours unfeignedly   JOHN KEATS.

XXXVI.—TO GEORGE AND THOMAS KEATS.

Hampstead, Saturday Night [February 14, 1818].

My dear Brothers—When once a man delays a letter beyond the proper time, he delays it longer, for one or two reasons—first, because he must begin in a very common-place style, that is to say, with an excuse; and secondly things and circumstances become so jumbled in his mind, that he knows not what, or what not, he has said in his last—I shall visit you as soon as I have copied my poem all out, I am now much beforehand with the printer, they have done none yet, and I am

---

[1] Both the *Robin Hood* and the *Mermaid* lines as afterwards printed vary in several places from these first drafts.

half afraid they will let half the season by before the
printing. I am determined they shall not trouble me
when I have copied it all.—Horace Smith has lent me
his manuscript called "Nehemiah Muggs, an exposure of
the Methodists"—perhaps I may send you a few extracts
—Hazlitt's last Lecture was on Thomson, Cowper, and
Crabbe, he praised Thomson and Cowper but he gave
Crabbe an unmerciful licking—I think Hunt's article
of Fazio—no it was not, but I saw Fazio the first
night, it hung rather heavily on me—I am in the high
way of being introduced to a squad of people, Peter
Pindar, Mrs. Opie, Mrs. Scott—Mr. Robinson a great
friend of Coleridge's called on me.[1] Richards tells me
that my poems are known in the west country, and that
he saw a very clever copy of verses, headed with a Motto
from my Sonnet to George—Honours rush so thickly upon
me that I shall not be able to bear up against them.
What think you—am I to be crowned in the Capitol,
am I to be made a Mandarin—No! I am to be invited,
Mrs. Hunt tells me, to a party at Ollier's, to keep Shakspeare's birthday—Shakspeare would stare to see me
there.[2] The Wednesday before last Shelley, Hunt and
I wrote each a Sonnet on the River Nile, some day you
shall read them all. I saw a sheet of Endymion, and
have all reason to suppose they will soon get it done,
there shall be nothing wanting on my part. I have been
writing at intervals many songs and Sonnets, and I long
to be at Teignmouth, to read them over to you : however
I think I had better wait till this Book is off my mind;
it will not be long first.

Reynolds has been writing two very capital articles, in
the Yellow Dwarf, on popular Preachers—All the talk
here is about Dr. Croft the Duke of Devon etc.

Your most affectionate Brother   JOHN.

[1] Henry Crabb Robinson, author of the *Diaries*.
[2] The Olliers (Shelley's publishers) had brought out Keats's
Poems the previous spring, and the ill success of the volume had
led to a sharp quarrel between them and the Keats brothers.

XXXVII.—TO JOHN HAMILTON REYNOLDS.

[Hampstead, February 19; 1818.]

My dear Reynolds—I had an idea that a Man might
pass a very pleasant life in this manner—Let him on a
certain day read a certain page of full Poesy or distilled
Prose, and let him wander with it, and muse upon it,
and reflect from it, and bring home to it, and prophesy
upon it, and dream upon it: until it becomes stale—But
when will it do so? Never—When Man has arrived at
a certain ripeness in intellect any one grand and spiritual
passage serves him as a starting-post towards all "the
two-and-thirty Palaces." How happy is such a voyage
of conception, what delicious diligent indolence! A doze
upon a sofa does not hinder it, and a nap upon Clover
engenders ethereal finger-pointings—the prattle of a child
gives it wings, and the converse of middle-age a strength
to beat them—a strain of music conducts to "an odd
angle of the Isle," and when the leaves whisper it puts a
girdle round the earth.—Nor will this sparing touch of
noble Books be any irreverence to their Writers—for
perhaps the honors paid by Man to Man are trifles in
comparison to the benefit done by great works to the
"spirit and pulse of good" by their mere passive existence.
Memory should not be called Knowledge—Many have
original minds who do not think it—they are led away
by Custom. Now it appears to me that almost any Man
may like the spider spin from his own inwards his own
airy Citadel—the points of leaves and twigs on which the
spider begins her work are few, and she fills the air with a
beautiful circuiting. Man should be content with as few
points to tip with the fine Web of his Soul, and weave
a tapestry empyrean—full of symbols for his spiritual
eye, of softness for his spiritual touch, of space for his
wandering, of distinctness for his luxury. But the minds
of mortals are so different and bent on such diverse
journeys that it may at first appear impossible for any

common taste and fellowship to exist between two or
three under these suppositions. It is however quite the
contrary. Minds would leave each other in contrary
directions, traverse each other in numberless points, and
at last greet each other at the journey's end. An old
man and a child would talk together and the old man
be led on his path and the child left thinking. Man
should not dispute or assert, but whisper results to his
Neighbour, and thus by every germ of spirit sucking the
sap from mould ethereal every human might become
great, and humanity instead of being a wide heath
of furze and briars, with here and there a remote Oak
or Pine, would become a grand democracy of forest
trees. It has been an old comparison for our urging on
—the beehive—however it seems to me that we should
rather be the flower than the Bee—for it is a false notion
that more is gained by receiving than giving—no, the
receiver and the giver are equal in their benefits. The
flower, I doubt not, receives a fair guerdon from the Bee
—its leaves blush deeper in the next spring—and who
shall say between Man and Woman which is the most
delighted? Now it is more noble to sit like Jove than
to fly like Mercury :—let us not therefore go hurrying
about and collecting honey, bee-like, buzzing here and
there impatiently from a knowledge of what is to be
arrived at. But let us open our leaves like a flower, and be
passive and receptive ; budding patiently under the eye
of Apollo and taking hints from every noble insect that
favours us with a visit—Sap will be given us for meat,
and dew for drink. I was led into these thoughts, my
dear Reynolds, by the beauty of the morning operating
on a sense of Idleness. I have not read any Books—the
Morning said I was right—I had no idea but of the
Morning, and the Thrush said I was right—seeming to
say,

" O thou whose face hath felt the Winter's wind,
Whose eye has seen the snow-clouds hung in Mist,
And the black Elmtops 'mong the freezing stars :

To thee the Spring will be a harvest-time—
O thou, whose only book has been the light
Of supreme darkness which thou feddest on
Night after night, when Phœbus was away,
To thee the Spring shall be a triple morn—
O fret not after knowledge—I have none,
And yet my song comes native with the warmth.
O fret not after knowledge—I have none,
And yet the Evening listens.   He who saddens
At thought of idleness cannot be idle,
And he's awake who thinks himself asleep."

Now I am sensible all this is a mere sophistication (however it may neighbour to any truths), to excuse my own indolence—So I will not deceive myself that Man should be equal with Jove—but think himself very well off as a sort of scullion-Mercury or even a humble-bee. It is no matter whether I am right or wrong either one way or another, if there is sufficient to lift a little time from your shoulders—

Your affectionate friend   JOHN KEATS.

XXXVIII.—TO GEORGE AND THOMAS KEATS.

Hampstead, Saturday [February 21, 1818].

My dear Brothers—I am extremely sorry to have given you so much uneasiness by not writing; however, you know good news is no news or vice versâ. I do not like to write a short letter to you, or you would have had one long before. The weather although boisterous to-day has been very much milder; and I think Devonshire is not the last place to receive a temperate Change. I have been abominably idle since you left, but have just turned over a new leaf, and used as a marker a letter of excuse to an invitation from Horace Smith. The occasion of my writing to-day is the enclosed letter—by Postmark from Miss W——[1] Does she expect you in town George? I received a letter the other day from Haydon, in which he says, his Essays on the Elgin Marbles are being translated into Italian, the which he superintends. I did not

[1] Georgiana Wylie, to whom George Keats was engaged.

mention that I had seen the British Gallery, there are some nice things by Stark, and Bathsheba by Wilkie, which is condemned.   I could not bear Alston's Uriel.

Reynolds has been very ill for some time, confined to the house, and had leeches applied to his chest; when I saw him on Wednesday he was much the same, and he is in the worst place for amendment, among the strife of women's tongues, in a hot and parch'd room : I wish he would move to Butler's for a short time.   The Thrushes and Blackbirds have been singing me into an idea that it was Spring, and almost that leaves were on the trees. So that black clouds and boisterous winds seem to have mustered and collected in full Divan, for the purpose of convincing me to the contrary.   Taylor says my poem shall be out in a month, I think he will be out before it. . . .

The thrushes are singing now as if they would speak to the winds, because their big brother Jack, the Spring, was not far off.   I am reading Voltaire and Gibbon, although I wrote to Reynolds the other day to prove reading of no use; I have not seen Hunt since, I am a good deal with Dilke and Brown, we are very thick ; they are very kind to me, they are well.   I don't think I could stop in Hampstead but for their neighbourhood.   I hear Hazlitt's lectures regularly, his last was on Gray, Collins, Young, etc., and he gave a very fine piece of discriminating Criticism on Swift, Voltaire, and Rabelais.   I was very disappointed at his treatment of Chatterton.   I generally meet with many I know there.   Lord Byron's 4th Canto is expected out, and I heard somewhere, that Walter Scott has a new Poem in readiness.   I am sorry that Wordsworth has left a bad impression wherever he visited in town by his egotism, Vanity, and bigotry.   Yet he is a great poet if not a philosopher.   I have not yet read Shelley's Poem, I do not suppose you have it yet, at the Teignmouth libraries.   These double letters must come rather heavy, I hope you have a moderate portion of cash, but don't fret at all, if you have not—Lord ! I intend to play at

cut and run as well as Falstaff, that is to say, before he
got so lusty.

I remain praying for your health my dear Brothers
Your affectionate Brother   JOHN.

XXXIX.—TO JOHN TAYLOR.

Hampstead, February 27 [1818].

My dear Taylor—Your alteration strikes me as being
a great Improvement—And now I will attend to the
punctuations you speak of—The comma should be at
soberly, and in the other passage, the Comma should follow
quiet. I am extremely indebted to you for this alteration,
and also for your after admonitions. It is a sorry thing
for me that any one should have to overcome prejudices
in reading my verses—that affects me more than any
hypercriticism on any particular passage—In Endymion,
I have most likely but moved into the go-cart from the
leading-strings—In poetry I have a few axioms, and you
will see how far I am from their centre.

1st. I think poetry should surprise by a fine excess,
and not by singularity; It should strike the reader as a
wording of his own highest thoughts, and appear almost
a remembrance.

2d. Its touches of beauty should never be half-way,
thereby making the reader breathless, instead of content.
The rise, the progress, the setting of Imagery should,
like the sun, come natural to him, shine over him, and
set soberly, although in magnificence, leaving him in the
luxury of twilight. But it is easier to think what poetry
should be, than to write it—And this leads me to

Another axiom—That if poetry comes not as naturally
as the leaves to a tree, it had better not come at all.—
However it may be with me, I cannot help looking into
new countries with "O for a Muse of Fire to ascend!"
If Endymion serves me as a pioneer, perhaps I ought
to be content—I have great reason to be content, for
thank God I can read, and perhaps understand Shak-

speare to his depths; and I have I am sure many friends,
who, if I fail, will attribute any change in my life and
temper to humbleness rather than pride—to a cowering
under the wings of great poets, rather than to a bitterness that I am not appreciated.   I am anxious to get
Endymion printed that I may forget it and proceed.   I
have copied the 3rd Book and begun the 4th.   On running
my eye over the proofs, I saw one mistake—I will notice
it presently, and also any others, if there be any.   There
should be no comma in " the raft branch down sweeping
from a tall ash-top." I have besides made one or two
alterations, and also altered the thirteenth line p. 32 to
make sense of it, as you will see.   I will take care the
printer shall not trip up my heels.   There should be no
dash after Dryope, in the line " Dryope's lone lulling of
her child."

Remember me to Percy Street.

Your sincere and obliged friend   JOHN KEATS.

P.S.—You shall have a short preface in good time.

XL.—TO MESSRS. TAYLOR AND HESSEY.

[Hampstead, March 1818?]

My dear Sirs—I am this morning making a general
clearance of all lent Books—all—I am afraid I do not
return all—I must fog your memories about them—however with many thanks here are the remainder—which I
am afraid are not worth so much now as they were six
months ago—I mean the fashions may have changed—

Yours truly   JOHN KEATS.

XLI.—TO BENJAMIN BAILEY.

Teignmouth, Friday [March 13, 1818].[1]

My dear Bailey—When a poor devil is drowning, it
is said he comes thrice to the surface ere he makes his

[1] This letter has been hitherto erroneously printed under date
September 1818.

final sink—if however even at the third rise he can
manage to catch hold of a piece of weed or rock he
stands a fair chance, as I hope I do now, of being saved.
I have sunk twice in our correspondence, have risen
twice, and have been too idle, or something worse, to
extricate myself. I have sunk the third time, and just
now risen again at this two of the Clock P.M., and saved
myself from utter perdition by beginning this, all drenched
as I am, and fresh from the water. And I would rather
endure the present inconvenience of a wet jacket than
you should keep a laced one in store for me. Why did
I not stop at Oxford in my way? How can you ask
such a Question? Why, did I not promise to do so?
Did I not in a letter to you make a promise to do so?
Then how can you be so unreasonable as to ask me why
I did not? This is the thing—(for I have been rubbing
up my Invention—trying several sleights—I first polished
a cold, felt it in my fingers, tried it on the table, but
could not pocket it:—I tried Chillblains, Rheumatism,
Gout, tight boots,—nothing of that sort would do,—so
this is, as I was going to say, the thing)—I had a letter
from Tom, saying how much better he had got, and
thinking he had better stop—I went down to prevent
his coming up. Will not this do? turn it which way
you like—it is selvaged all round. I have used it, these
three last days, to keep out the abominable Devonshire
weather—by the by, you may say what you will of
Devonshire: the truth is, it is a splashy, rainy, misty,
snowy, foggy, haily, floody, muddy, slipshod county.
The hills are very beautiful, when you get a sight of 'em
—the primroses are out, but then you are in—the Cliffs
are of a fine deep colour, but then the Clouds are continually vieing with them—the Women like your London
people in a sort of negative way—because the native
men are the poorest creatures in England—because
Government never have thought it worth while to send a
recruiting party among them. When I think of Wordsworth's sonnet "Vanguard of Liberty! ye men of Kent!"

the degenerated race about me are Pulvis ipecac. simplex
—a strong dose. Were I a corsair, I'd make a descent
on the south coast of Devon ; if I did not run the chance
of having Cowardice imputed to me.   As for the men,
they'd run away into the Methodist meeting-houses, and
the women would be glad of it.   Had England been a
large Devonshire, we should not have won the Battle of
Waterloo.   There are knotted oaks—there are lusty rivu-
lets? there are meadows such as are not—there are
valleys of feminine[1] climate—but there are no thews and
sinews—Moore's Almanack is here a Curiosity—Arms,
neck, and shoulders may at least be seen there, and the
ladies read it as some out-of-the-way Romance.   Such a
quelling Power have these thoughts over me that I fancy
the very air of a deteriorating quality.   I fancy the flowers,
all precocious, have an Acrasian spell about them—I feel
able to beat off the Devonshire waves like soapfroth.   I
think it well for the honour of Britain that Julius Cæsar
did not first land in this County.   A Devonshirer standing
on his native hills is not a distinct object—he does not
show against the light—a wolf or two would dispossess him.
I like, I love England.   I like its living men—give me
a long brown plain "for my morning,"[1] so I may meet with
some of Edmund Ironside's descendants.   Give me a
barren mould, so I may meet with some shadowing of
Alfred in the shape of a Gipsy, a huntsman or a shepherd.   Scenery is fine—but human nature is finer—the
sward is richer for the tread of a real nervous English
foot—the Eagle's nest is finer, for the Mountaineer has
looked into it,   Are these facts or prejudices?   Whatever
they be, for them I shall never be able to relish entirely
any Devonshire scenery—Homer is fine, Achilles is fine,
Diomed is fine, Shakspeare is fine, Hamlet is fine, Lear
is fine, but dwindled Englishmen are not fine.   Where
too the women are so passable, and have such English
names, such as Ophelia, Cordelia etc. that they should
have such Paramours or rather Imparamours—As for

[1] Reading doubtful.

them, I cannot in thought help wishing, as did the cruel Emperor, that they had but one head, and I might cut it off to deliver them from any horrible Courtesy they may do their undeserving country-men.　I wonder I meet with no born monsters—O Devonshire, last night I thought the moon had dwindled in heaven——

I have never had your Sermon from Wordsworth, but Mr. Dilke lent it me.　You know my ideas about Reli-gion.　I do not think myself more in the right than other people, and that nothing in this world is proveable. I wish I could enter into all your feelings on the subject, merely for one short 10 minutes, and give you a page or two to your liking.　I am sometimes so very sceptical as to think Poetry itself a mere Jack o' Lantern to amuse whoever may chance to be struck with its brilliance.　As tradesmen say everything is worth what it will fetch, so probably every mental pursuit takes its reality and worth from the ardour of the pursuer—being in itself a Nothing. Ethereal things may at least be thus real, divided under three heads—Things real—things semireal—and nothings. Things real, such as existences of Sun moon and Stars— and passages of Shakspeare.—Things semireal, such as love, the Clouds etc., which require a greeting of the Spirit to make them wholly exist—and Nothings, which are made great and dignified by an ardent pursuit— which, by the by, stamp the Burgundy mark on the bottles of our minds, insomuch as they are able to "*consecrate whate'er they look upon.*"　I have written a sonnet here of a somewhat collateral nature—so don't imagine it an "apropos des bottes "—

Four Seasons fill the measure of the year ;
　There are four seasons in the mind of Man :
He hath his lusty Spring, when Fancy clear
　Takes in all beauty with an easy span :
He has his Summer, when luxuriously
　He chews the honied cud of fair Spring thoughts,
Till in his Soul, dissolv'd, they come to be
　Part of himself : He hath his Autumn Ports

G

And havens of repose, when his tired wings
Are folded up, and he content to look [1]
On Mists in idleness—to let fair things
Pass by unheeded as a threshold brook.
He has his winter too of Pale misfeature,
Or else he would forego his mortal nature.

Aye, this may be carried—but what am I talking of?
—it is an old maxim of mine, and of course must be well
known, that every point of thought is the Centre of an
intellectual world.   The two uppermost thoughts in a
Man's mind are the two poles of his world—he revolves
on them, and everything is Southward or Northward to
him through their means.—We take but three steps from
feathers to iron.—Now, my dear fellow, I must once for
all tell you I have not one idea of the truth of any of my
speculations—I shall never be a reasoner, because I care
not to be in the right, when retired from bickering and
in a proper philosophical temper.   So you must not stare
if in any future letter, I endeavour to prove that Apollo,
as he had catgut strings to his lyre, used a cat's paw
as a pecten—and further from said Pecten's reiterated
and continual teasing came the term *hen-pecked*.   My
Brother Tom desires to be remembered to you; he has
just this moment had a spitting of blood, poor fellow—
Remember me to Gleig and Whitehead.

Your affectionate friend   JOHN KEATS.

XLII.—TO JOHN HAMILTON REYNOLDS.

Teignmouth, Saturday [March 14, 1818].

Dear Reynolds—I escaped being blown over and
blown under and trees and house being toppled on me.—I
have since hearing of Brown's accident had an aversion
to a dose of parapet, and being also a lover of antiquities

---

[1] The five lines ending here Keats afterwards re-cast, doubtless
in order to get rid of the cockney rhyme "ports" and "thoughts."

I would sooner have a harmless piece of Herculaneum sent me quietly as a present than ever so modern a chimney-pot tumbled on to my head—Being agog to see some Devonshire, I would have taken a walk the first day, but the rain would not let me; and the second, but the rain would not let me; and the third, but the rain forbade it. Ditto 4—ditto 5—ditto—so I made up my Mind to stop indoors, and catch a sight flying between the showers: and, behold I saw a pretty valley—pretty cliffs, pretty Brooks, pretty Meadows, pretty trees, both standing as they were created, and blown down as they are uncreated—The green is beautiful, as they say, and pity it is that it is amphibious—*mais !* but alas ! the flowers here wait as naturally for the rain twice a day as the Mussels do for the Tide; so we look upon a brook in these parts as you look upon a splash in your Country. There must be something to support this—aye, fog, hail, snow, rain, Mist blanketing up three parts of the year. This Devonshire is like Lydia Languish, very entertaining when it smiles, but cursedly subject to sympathetic moisture. You have the sensation of walking under one great Lamplighter: and you can't go on the other side of the ladder to keep your frock clean, and cosset your superstition. Buy a girdle—put a pebble in your mouth—loosen your braces—for I am going among scenery whence I intend to tip you the Damosel Radcliffe—I'll cavern you, and grotto you, and waterfall you, and wood you, and water you, and immense-rock you, and tremendous-sound you, and solitude you. I'll make a lodgment on your glacis by a row of Pines, and storm your covered way with bramble Bushes. I'll have at you with hip and haw small-shot, and cannonade you with Shingles—I'll be witty upon salt-fish, and impede your cavalry with clotted cream. But ah Coward! to talk at this rate to a sick man, or, I hope, to one that was sick—for I hope by this you stand on your right foot. If you are not—that's all, —I intend to cut all sick people if they do not make up their minds to cut Sickness—a fellow to whom I have a

complete aversion, and who strange to say is harboured
and countenanced in several houses where I visit—he is
sitting now quite impudent between me and Tom—He
insults me at poor Jem Rice's—and you have seated him
before now between us at the Theatre, when I thought
he looked with a longing eye at poor Kean.   I shall say,
once for all, to my friends generally and severally, cut
that fellow, or I cut you—

I went to the Theatre here the other night, which I
forgot to tell George, and got insulted, which I ought to
remember to forget to tell any Body; for I did not fight,
and as yet have had no redress—"Lie thou there, sweetheart!"[1]   I wrote to Bailey yesterday, obliged to speak
in a high way, and a damme who's afraid—for I had
owed him so long; however, he shall see I will be better
in future.   Is he in town yet?   I have directed to Oxford
as the better chance.   I have copied my fourth Book,
and shall write the Preface soon.   I wish it was all done;
for I want to forget it and make my mind free for something new—Atkins the Coachman, Bartlett the Surgeon,
Simmons the Barber, and the Girls over at the Bonnet-
shop, say we shall now have a month of seasonable
weather—warm, witty, and full of invention—Write to
me and tell me that you are well or thereabouts, or by
the holy Beaucœur, which I suppose is the Virgin Mary,
or the repented Magdalen (beautiful name, that Magdalen),
I'll take to my Wings and fly away to anywhere but old
or Nova Scotia—I wish I had a little innocent bit of
Metaphysic in my head, to criss-cross the letter: but
you know a favourite tune is hardest to be remembered
when one wants it most and you, I know, have long
ere this taken it for granted that I never have any
speculations without associating you in them, where
they are of a pleasant nature, and you know enough
of me to tell the places where I haunt most, so that
if you think for five minutes after having read this, you

---

[1] "And, sweetheart, lie thou there":—Pistol (to his sword) in
Henry IV., Part 2, II. iv.

will find it a long letter, and see written in the Air above you,

Your most affectionate friend   JOHN KEATS.

Remember me to all.   Tom's remembrances to you.

XLIII.—TO BENJAMIN ROBERT HAYDON.

Teignmouth, Saturday Morn [March 21, 1818].

My dear Haydon—In sooth, I hope you are not too sanguine about that seal—in sooth I hope it is not Brumidgeum—in double sooth I hope it is his—and in triple sooth I hope I shall have an impression.[1]   Such a piece of intelligence came doubly welcome to me while in your own County and in your own hand—not but I have blown up the said County for its urinal qualifications— the six first days I was here it did nothing but rain ; and at that time having to write to a friend I gave Devonshire a good blowing up—it has been fine for almost three days, and I was coming round a bit ; but to-day it rains again—with me the County is yet upon its good behaviour.   I have enjoyed the most delightful Walks these three fine days beautiful enough to make me content.

> Here all the summer could I stay,
>   For there's Bishop's teign
>   And King's teign
> And Coomb at the clear teign head—
>   Where close by the stream
>   You may have your cream
> All spread upon barley bread.
>
>   There's arch Brook
>   And there's larch Brook
> Both turning many a mill ;
>   And cooling the drouth
>   Of the salmon's mouth,
> And fattening his silver gill.

[1] Replying to an ecstatic note of Haydon's about a seal with a true lover's knot and the initials W. S., lately found in a field at Stratford-on-Avon.

There is Wild wood,
A Mild hood
To the sheep on the lea o' the down,
Where the golden furze,
With its green, thin spurs,
Doth catch at the maiden's gown.

There is Newton marsh
With its spear grass harsh—
A pleasant summer level
Where the maidens sweet
Of the Market Street,
Do meet in the dusk to revel.

There's the Barton rich
With dyke and ditch
And hedge for the thrush to live in
And the hollow tree
For the buzzing bee
And a bank for the wasp to hive in.

And O, and O
The daisies blow
And the primroses are waken'd,
And the violets white
Sit in silver plight,
And the green bud's as long as the spike end.

Then who would go
Into dark Soho,
And chatter with dack'd hair'd critics,
When he can stay
For the new-mown hay,
And startle the dappled Prickets ?

I know not if this rhyming fit has done anything—
it will be safe with you if worthy to put among my
Lyrics. Here's some doggrel for you—Perhaps you would
like a bit of b——hrell—

Where be ye going, you Devon Maid ?
And what have you there in the Basket ?
Ye tight little fairy just fresh from the dairy,
Will ye give me some cream if I ask it ?

I love your Meads, and I love your flowers,
  And I love your junkets mainly,
But 'hind the door I love kissing more,
  O look not so disdainly.

I love your hills, and I love your dales,
  And I love your flocks a-bleating—
But O, on the heather to lie together,
  With both our hearts a-beating !

I'll put your Basket all safe in a nook,
  Your shawl I hang up on the willow,
And we will sigh in the daisy's eye
  And kiss on a grass green pillow.

How does the work go on ? I should like to bring out
my "Dentatus"[1] at the time your Epic makes its appearance. I expect to have my Mind soon clear for something
new. Tom has been much worse : but is now getting
better—his remembrances to you. I think of seeing the
Dart and Plymouth—but I don't know. It has as yet
been a Mystery to me how and where Wordsworth went.
I can't help thinking he has returned to his Shell—with
his beautiful Wife and his enchanting Sister. It is a
great Pity that People should by associating themselves
with the finest things, spoil them. Hunt has damned
Hampstead and masks and sonnets and Italian tales.
Wordsworth has damned the lakes—Milman has damned
the old drama—West has damned—— wholesale. Peacock
has damned satire—Ollier has damn'd Music—Hazlitt
has damned the bigoted and the blue-stockinged ; how
durst the Man ?! he is your only good damner, and if
ever I am damn'd—damn me if I shouldn't like him to
damn me. It will not be long ere I see you, but I
thought I would just give you a line out of Devon.
  Yours affectionately   JOHN KEATS.

Remember me to all we know.

  [1] *Dentatus* was the subject of Haydon's new picture.

XLIV.—TO MESSRS. TAYLOR AND HESSEY.

Teignmouth, Saturday Morn [March 21, 1818].

My dear Sirs—I had no idea of your getting on so
fast—I thought of bringing my 4th Book to Town all in
good time for you—especially after the late unfortunate
chance.

I did not however for my own sake delay finishing
the copy which was done a few days after my arrival
here.   I send it off to-day, and will tell you in a Postscript at what time to send for it from the Bull and
Mouth or other Inn.   You will find the Preface and
dedication and the title Page as I should wish it to
stand—for a Romance is a fine thing notwithstanding the
circulating Libraries.   My respects to Mrs. Hessey and
to Percy Street.

Yours very sincerely   JOHN KEATS.

P.S.—I have been advised to send it to you—you
may expect it on Monday—for I sent it by the Postman
to Exeter at the same time with this Letter.   Adieu!

XLV.—TO JAMES RICE.

Teignmouth, Tuesday [March 24, 1818].

My dear Rice—Being in the midst of your favourite
Devon, I should not, by rights, pen one word but it
should contain a vast portion of Wit, Wisdom and learning—for I have heard that Milton ere he wrote his answer
to Salmasius came into these parts, and for one whole
month, rolled himself for three whole hours (per day?), in
a certain meadow hard by us—where the mark of his
nose at equidistances is still shown.   The exhibitor of the
said meadow further saith, that, after these rollings, not
a nettle sprang up in all the seven acres for seven years,
and that from the said time, a new sort of plant was
made from the whitethorn, of a thornless nature, very

much used by the bucks of the present day to rap their
boots withal.   This account made me very naturally
suppose that the nettles and thorns etherealised by the
scholar's rotatory motion, and garnered in his head,
thence flew after a process of fermentation against the
luckless Salmasius and occasioned his well-known and
unhappy end.   What a happy thing it would be if we
could settle our thoughts and make our minds up on any
matter in five minutes, and remain content—that is, build
a sort of mental cottage of feelings, quiet and pleasant—
to have a sort of Philosophical back-garden, and cheerful
holiday-keeping front one—but alas ! this never can be :
for as the material cottager knows there are such places
as France and Italy, and the Andes and burning mountains, so the spiritual Cottager has knowledge of the terra
semi-incognita of things unearthly, and cannot for his
life keep in the check-rein—or I should stop here quiet
and comfortable in my theory of nettles.— You will see,
however, I am obliged to run wild being attracted by
the load-stone concatenation.   No sooner had I settled
the knotty point of Salmasius, than the Devil put this
whim into my head in the likeness of one of Pythagoras's
questionings—Did Milton do more good or harm in the
world ?   He wrote, let me inform you (for I have it
from a friend, who had it of ——,) he wrote Lycidas,
Comus, Paradise Lost and other Poems, with much
delectable prose—He was moreover an active friend to
man all his life, and has been since his death.—Very
good—but, my dear Fellow, I must let you know that,
as there is ever the same quantity of matter constituting
this habitable globe—as the ocean notwithstanding the
enormous changes and revolutions taking place in some
or other of its demesnes—notwithstanding Waterspouts
whirlpools and mighty rivers emptying themselves into
it—still is made up of the same bulk, nor ever varies the
number of its atoms—and as a certain bulk of water
was instituted at the creation—so very likely a certain
portion of intellect was spun forth into the thin air, for

the brains of man to prey upon it. You will see my
drift without any unnecessary parenthesis. That which
is contained in the Pacific could not lie in the hollow of
the Caspian—that which was in Milton's head could not
find room in Charles the Second's—He like a Moon
attracted intellect to its flow—it has not ebbed yet, but
has left the shore-pebbles all bare—I mean all Bucks,
Authors of Hengist, and Castlereaghs of the present day;
who without Milton's gormandising might have been all
wise men—Now forasmuch as I was very predisposed
to a country I had heard you speak so highly of, I took
particular notice of everything during my journey, and
have bought some folio asses' skins for memorandums.
I have seen everything but the wind—and that, they
say, becomes visible by taking a dose of acorns, or sleeping one night in a hog-trough, with your tail to the Sow-
Sow-West.   Some of the little Bar-maids look'd at me as
if I knew Jem Rice. . . . Well, I can't tell! I hope
you are showing poor Reynolds the way to get well.
Send me a good account of him, and if I can, I'll send
you one of Tom—Oh! for a day and all well!
   I went yesterday to Dawlish fair.

> Over the Hill and over the Dale,
>   And over the Bourne to Dawlish,
> Where ginger-bread wives have a scanty sale,
>   And ginger-bread nuts are smallish, etc. etc.

Tom's remembrances and mine to you all.
Your sincere friend   JOHN KEATS.

XLVI.—TO JOHN HAMILTON REYNOLDS.

[Teignmouth, March 25, 1818.]

   My dear Reynolds—In hopes of cheering you through
a Minute or two, I was determined will he nill he to
send you some lines, so you will excuse the unconnected
subject and careless verse. You know, I am sure,

Claude's Enchanted Castle,[1] and I wish you may be pleased with my remembrance of it.   The Rain is come on again—I think with me Devonshire stands a very poor chance.   I shall damn it up hill and down dale, if it keep up to the average of six fine days in three weeks. Let me have better news of you.

Tom's remembrances to you.   Remember us to all. Your affectionate friend,   JOHN KEATS.

Dear Reynolds ! as last night I lay in bed,
There came before my eyes that wonted thread
Of shapes, and shadows, and remembrances,
That every other minute vex and please :
Things all disjointed come from north and south,—
Two Witch's eyes above a Cherub's mouth,
Voltaire with casque and shield and habergeon,
And Alexander with his nightcap on ;
Old Socrates a-tying his cravat,
And Hazlitt playing with Miss Edgeworth's cat ;
And Junius Brutus, pretty well so so,
Making the best of's way towards Soho.

Few are there who escape these visitings,—
Perhaps one or two whose lives have patent wings,
And thro' whose curtains peeps no hellish nose,
No wild-boar tushes, and no Mermaid's toes ;
But flowers bursting out with lusty pride,
And young Æolian harps personify'd ;
Some Titian colours touch'd into real life,—
The sacrifice goes on ; the pontiff knife
Gleams in the Sun, the milk-white heifer lows,
The pipes go shrilly, the libation flows :
A white sail shows above the green-head cliff,

---

[1] The famous picture now belonging to Lady Wantage, and exhibited at Burlington House in 1888.   Whether Keats ever saw the original is doubtful (it was not shown at the British Institution in his time), but he must have been familiar with the subject as engraved by Vivarès and Woollett, and its suggestive power worked in his mind until it yielded at last the distilled poetic essence of the "magic casement" passage in the *Ode to a Nightingale*.   It is interesting to note the theme of the Grecian Urn ode coming in also amidst the "unconnected subject and careless verse" of this rhymed epistle.

Moves round the point, and throws her anchor stiff ;
The mariners join hymn with those on land.

You know the Enchanted Castle,—it doth stand
Upon a rock, on the border of a Lake,
Nested in trees, which all do seem to shake
From some old magic-like Urganda's Sword.
O Phœbus ! that I had thy sacred word
To show this Castle, in fair dreaming wise,
Unto my friend, while sick and ill he lies !

You know it well enough, where it doth seem
A mossy place, a Merlin's Hall, a dream ;
You know the clear Lake, and the little Isles,
The mountains blue, and cold near neighbour rills,
All which elsewhere are but half animate ;
There do they look alive to love and hate,
To smiles and frowns ; they seem a lifted mound
Above some giant, pulsing underground.

Part of the Building was a chosen See,
Built by a banish'd Santon of Chaldee ;
The other part, two thousand years from him,
Was built by Cuthbert de Saint Aldebrim ;
Then there's a little wing, far from the Sun,
Built by a Lapland Witch turn'd maudlin Nun ;
And many other juts of aged stone
Founded with many a mason-devil's groan.

The doors all look as if they op'd themselves
The windows as if latch'd by Fays and Elves,
And from them comes a silver flash of light,
As from the westward of a Summer's night ;
Or like a beauteous woman's large blue eyes
Gone mad thro' olden songs and poesies.

See ! what is coming from the distance dim !
A golden Galley all in silken trim !
Three rows of oars are lightening, moment whiles
Into the verd'rous bosoms of those isles ;
Towards the shade, under the Castle wall,
It comes in silence,—now 'tis hidden all.
The Clarion sounds, and from a Postern-gate
An echo of sweet music doth create
A fear in the poor Herdsman, who doth bring
His beasts to trouble the enchanted spring,—
He tells of the sweet music, and the spot,
To all his friends, and they believe him not.

O that our dreamings all, of sleep or wake,
Would all their colours from the sunset take :
From something of material sublime,
Rather than shadow our own soul's day-time
In the dark void of night.   For in the world
We jostle,—but my flag is not unfurl'd
On the Admiral-staff,—and so philosophise
I dare not yet !   Oh, never will the prize,
High reason, and the love of good and ill,
Be my award !   Things cannot to the will
Be settled, but they tease us out of thought ;
Or is it that imagination brought
Beyond its proper bound, yet still confin'd,
Lost in a sort of Purgatory blind,
Cannot refer to any standard law
Of either earth or heaven !   It is a flaw
In happiness, to see beyond our bourn,—
It forces us in summer skies to mourn,
It spoils the singing of the Nightingale.

Dear Reynolds !   I have a mysterious tale,
And cannot speak it : the first page I read
Upon a Lampit rock of green sea-weed
Among the breakers ; 'twas a quiet eve,
The rocks were silent, the wide sea did weave
An untumultuous fringe of silver foam
Along the flat brown sand ; I was at home
And should have been most happy,—but I saw
Too far into the sea, where every maw
The greater on the less feeds evermore.—
But I saw too distinct into the core
Of an eternal fierce destruction,
And so from happiness I far was gone.
Still am I sick of it, and tho' to-day,
I've gather'd young spring-leaves, and flowers gay
Of periwinkle and wild strawberry,
Still do I that most fierce destruction see,—
The Shark at savage prey,—the Hawk at pounce,—
The gentle Robin, like a Pard or Ounce,
Ravening a worm,—Away, ye horrid moods !
Moods of one's mind !   You know I hate them well.
You know I'd sooner be a clapping Bell
To some Kamtschatkan Missionary Church,
Than with these horrid moods be left i' the lurch.

XLVII.—TO BENJAMIN ROBERT HAYDON.

Wednesday, [Teignmouth, April 8, 1818].

My dear Haydon—I am glad you were pleased with my nonsense, and if it so happen that the humour takes me when I have set down to prose to you I will not gainsay it. I should be (God forgive me) ready to swear because I cannot make use of your assistance in going through Devon if I was not in my own Mind determined to visit it thoroughly at some more favourable time of the year. But now Tom (who is getting greatly better) is anxious to be in Town—therefore I put off my threading the County. I purpose within a month to put my knapsack at my back and make a pedestrian tour through the North of England, and part of Scotland—to make a sort of Prologue to the Life I intend to pursue—that is to write, to study and to see all Europe at the lowest expence. I will clamber through the Clouds and exist. I will get such an accumulation of stupendous recollections that as I walk through the suburbs of London I may not see them—I will stand upon Mount Blanc and remember this coming Summer when I intend to straddle Ben Lomond—with my soul !—galligaskins are out of the Question. I am nearer myself to hear your " Christ " is being tinted into immortality. Believe me Haydon your picture is part of myself—I have ever been too sensible of the labyrinthian path to eminence in Art (judging from Poetry) ever to think I understood the emphasis of painting. The innumerable compositions and decompositions which take place between the intellect and its thousand materials before it arrives at that trembling delicate and snail-horn perception of beauty. I know not your many havens of intenseness—nor ever can know them : but for this I hope not you achieve is lost upon me [1]: for when a Schoolboy the abstract Idea I had

---

[1] *Sic:* probably, as suggested by Mr. Forman, for " I hope what you achieve is not lost upon me."

of an heroic painting—was what I cannot describe. I
saw it somewhat sideways, large, prominent, round, and
colour'd with magnificence—somewhat like the feel I
have of Anthony and Cleopatra.   Or of Alcibiades leaning
on his Crimson Couch in his Galley, his broad shoulders
imperceptibly heaving with the Sea.   That passage in
Shakspeare is finer than this—

> See how the surly Warwick mans the Wall.

I like your consignment of Corneille—that's the humour
of it—they shall be called your Posthumous Works.[1]
I don't understand your bit of Italian.   I hope she will
awake from her dream and flourish fair—my respects to
her.   The Hedges by this time are beginning to leaf—
Cats are becoming more vociferous—young Ladies who
wear Watches are always looking at them.   Women
about forty-five think the Season very backward—
Ladies' Mares have but half an allowance of food.   It
rains here again, has been doing so for three days—however as I told you I'll take a trial in June, July, or
August next year.

I am afraid Wordsworth went rather huff'd out of
Town—I am sorry for it—he cannot expect his fireside
Divan to be infallible—he cannot expect but that every
man of worth is as proud as himself.   O that he had not
fit with a Warrener[2]—that is dined at Kingston's.   I shall
be in town in about a fortnight and then we will have a
day or so now and then before I set out on my northern
expedition—we will have no more abominable Rows—
for they leave one in a fearful silence—having settled the

---

[1] The English rebels against tradition in poetry and art at this
time took much the same view of the French dramatists of the
grand siècle as was taken by the *romantiques* of their own nation
a few years later ; and Haydon had written to Keats in his last
letter, "When I die I'll have Shakspeare placed on my heart,
with Homer in my right hand and Ariosto in the other, Dante at
my head, Tasso at my feet, and Corneille under my ——"

[2] "He hath fought with a Warrener" :—Simple in *Merry
Wives*, I. iv.

Methodists let us be rational—not upon compulsion—no
—if it will out let it—but I will not play the Bassoon
any more deliberately.   Remember me to Hazlitt, and
Bewick—

Your affectionate friend,   JOHN KEATS.

XLVIII.—TO JOHN HAMILTON REYNOLDS.

Thy. morng., [Teignmouth, April 9, 1818].

My dear Reynolds—Since you all agree that the thing [1]
is bad, it must be so—though I am not aware there is
anything like Hunt in it (and if there is, it is my natural
way, and I have something in common with Hunt).   Look
it over again, and examine into the motives, the seeds,
from which any one sentence sprung—I have not the
slightest feel of humility towards the public—or to anything in existence,—but the eternal Being, the Principle
of Beauty, and the Memory of great Men.   When I am
writing for myself for the mere sake of the moment's
enjoyment, perhaps nature has its course with me—
but a Preface is written to the Public; a thing I
cannot help looking upon as an Enemy, and which I
cannot address without feelings of Hostility.   If I write
a Preface in a supple or subdued style, it will not be in
character with me as a public speaker—I would be subdued before my friends, and thank them for subduing
me—but among Multitudes of Men—I have no feel of
stooping, I hate the idea of humility to them.

I never wrote one single Line of Poetry with the least
Shadow of public thought.

Forgive me for vexing you and making a Trojan horse
of such a Trifle, both with respect to the matter in Question,
and myself—but it eases me to tell you—I could not live
without the love of my friends—I would jump down Ætna
for any great Public good—but I hate a Mawkish Popu-

---

[1] The first draught of the proposed preface to *Endymion.*

larity. I cannot be subdued before them—My glory would be to daunt and dazzle the thousand jabberers about Pictures and Books—I see swarms of Porcupines with their Quills erect "like lime-twigs set to catch my Wingèd Book," and I would fright them away with a torch. You will say my Preface is not much of a Torch. It would have been too insulting "to begin from Jove," and I could not set a golden head upon a thing of clay. If there is any fault in the Preface it is not affectation, but an undersong of disrespect to the Public—if I write another Preface it must be done without a thought of those people—I will think about it. If it should not reach you in four or five days, tell Taylor to publish it without a Preface, and let the Dedication simply stand— "inscribed to the Memory of Thomas Chatterton."

I had resolved last night to write to you this morning —I wish it had been about something else—something to greet you towards the close of your long illness. I have had one or two intimations of your going to Hampstead for a space; and I regret to see your confounded Rheumatism keeps you in Little Britain where I am sure the air is too confined. Devonshire continues rainy. As the drops beat against the window, they give me the same sensation as a quart of cold water offered to revive a half-drowned devil—no feel of the clouds dropping fatness; but as if the roots of the earth were rotten, cold, and drenched. I have not been able to go to Kent's cave at Babbicombe—however on one very beautiful day I had a fine Clamber over the rocks all along as far as that place. I shall be in Town in about Ten days—We go by way of Bath on purpose to call on Bailey. I hope soon to be writing to you about the things of the north, purposing to wayfare all over those parts. I have settled my accoutrements in my own mind, and will go to gorge wonders. However, we'll have some days together before I set out—

I have many reasons for going wonder-ways : to make my winter chair free from spleen—to enlarge my vision—

H

to escape disquisitions on Poetry and Kingston Criticism;
to promote digestion and economise shoe-leather.   I'll
have leather buttons and belt; and, if Brown holds his
mind, over the Hills we go.   If my Books will help me
to it, then will I take all Europe in turn, and see the
Kingdoms of the Earth and the glory of them.   Tom is
getting better, he hopes you may meet him at the top o'
the hill.   My Love to your nurses.   I am ever
Your affectionate Friend   JOHN KEATS.

XLIX.—TO JOHN HAMILTON REYNOLDS.

[Teignmouth,] Friday [April 10, 1818].

My dear Reynolds—I am anxious you should find this
Preface tolerable.   If there is an affectation in it 'tis
natural to me.   Do let the Printer's Devil cook it, and
let me be as "the casing air."

You are too good in this Matter—were I in your state,
I am certain I should have no thought but of discontent
and illness—I might though be taught patience: I
had an idea of giving no Preface; however, don't you
think this had better go?   O, let it—one should not be
too timid—of committing faults.

The climate here weighs us down completely; Tom
is quite low-spirited.   It is impossible to live in a country
which is continually under hatches.   Who would live in
a region of Mists, Game Laws, indemnity Bills, etc., when
there is such a place as Italy?   It is said this England
from its Clime produces a Spleen, able to engender the
finest Sentiments, and cover the whole face of the isle
with Green—so it ought, I'm sure.—I should still like
the Dedication simply, as I said in my last.

I wanted to send you a few songs written in your
favorite Devon—it cannot be—Rain! Rain! Rain!   I
am going this morning to take a facsimile of a Letter of
Nelson's, very much to his honour—you will be greatly
pleased when you see it—in about a week.   What a spite

it is one cannot get out—the little way I went yesterday, I found a lane banked on each side with store of Primroses, while the earlier bushes are beginning to leaf.

I shall hear a good account of you soon.

Your affectionate Friend   JOHN KEATS.

My Love to all and remember me to Taylor.

L.—TO JOHN TAYLOR.

Teignmouth, Friday [April 24, 1818].

My dear Taylor—I think I did wrong to leave to you all the trouble of Endymion—But I could not help it then—another time I shall be more bent to all sorts of troubles and disagreeables. Young men for some time have an idea that such a thing as happiness is to be had, and therefore are extremely impatient under any unpleasant restraining. In time however, of such stuff is the world about them, they know better, and instead of striving from uneasiness, greet it as an habitual sensation, a pannier which is to weigh upon them through life—And in proportion to my disgust at the task is my sense of your kindness and anxiety. The book pleased me much. It is very free from faults: and, although there are one or two words I should wish replaced, I see in many places an improvement greatly to the purpose.

I think those speeches which are related—those parts where the speaker repeats a speech, such as Glaucus's repetition of Circe's words, should have inverted commas to every line. In this there is a little confusion.—If we divide the speeches into *identical* and *related;* and to the former put merely one inverted Comma at the beginning and another at the end ; and to the latter inverted Commas before every line, the book will be better understood at the 1st glance. Look at pages 126, 127, you will find in the 3d line the beginning of a related speech marked thus "Ah! art awake—" while, at the same time, in the next page the continuation of the *identical* speech is

marked in the same manner, "Young man of Latmos—"
You will find on the other side all the parts which should
have inverted commas to every line.

I was proposing to travel over the North this summer.
There is but one thing to prevent me.—I know nothing
—I have read nothing—and I mean to follow Solomon's
directions, "Get learning—get understanding." I find
earlier days are gone by—I find that I can have no
enjoyment in the world but continual drinking of knowledge. I find there is no worthy pursuit but the idea of
doing some good for the world—Some do it with their
Society—some with their wit—some with their benevol-
ence—some with a sort of power of conferring pleasure
and good-humour on all they meet—and in a thousand
ways, all dutiful to the command of great Nature—there
is but one way for me. The road lies through application,
study, and thought.—I will pursue it; and for that end,
purpose retiring for some years. I have been hovering
for some time between an exquisite sense of the luxurious,
and a love for philosophy,—were I calculated for the
former, I should be glad. But as I am not, I shall turn
all my soul to the latter.—My brother Tom is getting
better, and I hope I shall see both him and Reynolds
better before I retire from the world. - I shall see you
soon, and have some talk about what Books I shall take
with me.

Your very sincere friend   JOHN KEATS.

Pray remember me to Hessey Woodhouse and Percy
Street.

LI.—TO JOHN HAMILTON REYNOLDS.

Teignmouth, April 27, 1818.

My dear Reynolds—It is an awful while since you
have heard from me—I hope I may not be punished,
when I see you well, and so anxious as you always are
for me, with the remembrance of my so seldom writing
when you were so horribly confined. The most unhappy

hours in our lives are those in which we recollect times
past to our own blushing—If we are immortal that
must be the Hell. If I must be immortal, I hope it
will be after having taken a little of "that watery labyrinth" in order to forget some of my school-boy days
and others since those.

I have heard from George at different times how
slowly you were recovering—It is a tedious thing—but
all Medical Men will tell you how. far a very gradual
amendment is preferable ; you will be strong after this,
never fear. We are here still enveloped in clouds—I
lay awake last night listening to the Rain with a sense
of being drowned and rotted like a grain of wheat. There
is a continual courtesy between the Heavens and the Earth.
The heavens rain down their unwelcomeness, and the
Earth sends it up again to be returned to-morrow. Tom
has taken a fancy to a physician here, Dr. Turton, and
I think is getting better—therefore I shall perhaps remain
here some Months. I have written to George for some
Books—shall learn Greek, and very likely Italian—and
in other ways prepare myself to ask Hazlitt in about a
year's time the best metaphysical road I can take. For
although I take poetry to be Chief, yet there is something
else wanting to one who passes his life among Books and
thoughts on Books—I long to feast upon old Homer as
we have upon Shakspeare, and as I have lately upon
Milton. If you understood Greek, and would read me
passages, now and then, explaining their meaning, 'twould
be, from its mistiness, perhaps, a greater luxury than
reading the thing one's self. I shall be happy when I
can do the same for you. I have written for my folio
Shakspeare, in which there are the first few stanzas of
my "Pot of Basil." I have the rest here finished, and will
copy the whole out fair shortly, and George will bring it
you—The compliment is paid by us to Boccace, whether
we publish or no: so there is content in this world—
mine is short—you must be deliberate about yours : you
must not think of it till many months after you are

quite well :—then put your passion to it, and I shall be bound up with you in the shadows of Mind, as we are in our matters of human life. Perhaps a Stanza or two will not be too foreign to your Sickness.

Were they unhappy then ?—It cannot be—
   Too many tears for lovers have been shed,
Too many sighs give we to them in fee,
   Too much of pity after they are dead,
Too many doleful stories do we see,
   Whose matter in bright gold were best be read ;
Except in such a page where Theseus' spouse
Over the pathless waves towards him bows.

But, for the general award of love,
   The little sweet doth kill much bitterness ;
Though Dido silent is in under-grove,
   And Isabella's was a great distress,
Though young Lorenzo in warm Indian clove
   Was not embalm'd, this truth is not the less—
Even bees, the little almsmen of spring-bowers,
Know there is richest juice in poison-flowers.

She wept alone for pleasures not to be ;
   Sorely she wept until the night came on,
And then, instead of love, O misery !
   She brooded o'er the luxury alone :
What might have been too plainly did she see,[1]
   And to the silence made a gentle moan,
Spreading her perfect arms upon the air,
And on her couch low murmuring "Where ? O where ?"

I heard from Rice this morning—very witty—and have just written to Bailey. Don't you think I am brushing up in the letter way ? and being in for it, you shall hear again from me very shortly :—if you will promise not to put hand to paper for me until you can do it with a tolerable ease of health—except it be a line or two. Give my Love to your Mother and Sisters. Remember me to the Butlers—not forgetting Sarah.

   Your affectionate Friend   JOHN KEATS.

[1] Changed in the printed version to—"His image in the dusk she seemed to see."

LII.—TO JOHN HAMILTON REYNOLDS.

Teignmouth, May 3d [1818].

My dear Reynolds—What I complain of is that I
have been in so uneasy a state of Mind as not to be fit
to write to an invalid. I cannot write to any length
under a disguised feeling. I should have loaded you
with an addition of gloom, which I am sure you do not
want. I am now thank God in a humour to give you
a good groat's worth—for Tom, after a Night without a
Wink of sleep, and over-burthened with fever, has got up
after a refreshing day-sleep and is better than he has
been for a long time; and you I trust have been again
round the common without any effect but refreshment.
As to the Matter I hope I can say with Sir Andrew
"I have matter enough in my head" in your favour—
And now, in the second place, for I reckon that I have
finished my Imprimis, I am glad you blow up the weather—
all through your letter there is a leaning towards a
climate-curse, and you know what a delicate satisfaction
there is in having a vexation anathematised : one would
think there has been growing up for these last four
thousand years, a grand-child Scion of the old forbidden
tree, and that some modern Eve had just violated it ;
and that there was come with double charge

> "Notus and Afer, black with thundrous clouds
> From Serraliona—"

I shall breathe worsted stockings[1] sooner than I thought
for—Tom wants to be in Town—we will have some
such days upon the heath like that of last summer—and
why not with the same book? or what say you to a
black Letter Chaucer, printed in 1596 : aye I've got
one huzza ! I shall have it bound en gothique—a nice
sombre binding—it will go a little way to unmodernise.
And also I see no reason, because I have been away
this last month, why I should not have a peep at your

[1] Meaning the atmosphere of the little Bentleys in Well Walk.

Spenserian—notwithstanding you speak of your office, in
my thought a little too early, for I do not see why a
Mind like yours is not capable of harbouring and digesting
the whole Mystery of Law as easily as Parson Hugh does
pippins, which did not hinder him from his poetic canary.[1]
Were I to study physic or rather Medicine again, I feel
it would not make the least difference in my Poetry ;
when the mind is in its infancy a Bias is in reality a Bias,
but when we have acquired more strength, a Bias becomes
no Bias. Every department of Knowledge we see excellent and calculated towards a great whole—I am so
convinced of this that I am glad at not having given
away my medical Books, which I shall again look over
to keep alive the little I know thitherwards ; and moreover intend through you and Rice to become a sort of
pip-civilian.   An extensive knowledge is needful to
thinking people—it takes away the heat and fever ; and
helps, by widening speculation, to ease the Burden of
the Mystery, a thing which I begin to understand a
little, and which weighed upon you in the most gloomy
and true sentence in your Letter.   The difference of high
Sensations with and without knowledge appears to me
this : in the latter case we are falling continually ten
thousand fathoms deep and being blown up again, without wings, and with all horror of a bare-shouldered
Creature—in the former case, our shoulders are fledged,
and we go through the same air and space without fear.
This is running one's rigs on the score of abstracted
benefit—when we come to human Life and the affections,
it is impossible to know how a parallel of breast and
head can be drawn (you will forgive me for thus privately
treading out of my depth, and take it for treading as
school-boys tread the water) ; it is impossible to know
how far knowledge will console us for the death of a
friend, and the ill " that flesh is heir to." With respect
to the affections and Poetry you must know by a sym-

---

[1] "I will make an end of my dinner ; there's pippins and cheese
to come ":—Sir Hugh Evans in *Merry Wives of Windsor*, I. ii.

pathy my thoughts that way, and I daresay these few
lines will be but a ratification : I wrote them on May-
day—and intend to finish the ode all in good time—

> Mother of Hermes ! and still youthful Maia !
> 　　May I sing to thee
> As thou wast hymned on the shores of Baiæ ?
> 　　Or may I woo thee
> In earlier Sicilian ? or thy smiles
> Seek as they once were sought, in Grecian isles,
> By Bards who died content on pleasant sward,
> Leaving great verse unto a little clan ?
> O, give me their old vigour, and unheard
> Save of the quiet Primrose, and the span
> 　　Of heaven and few ears,
> Rounded by thee, my song should die away
> 　　Content as theirs,
> Rich in the simple worship of a day.—

You may perhaps be anxious to know for fact to what
sentence in your Letter I allude. You say, "I fear there
is little chance of anything else in this life"—you seem
by that to have been going through with a more painful
and acute zest the same labyrinth that I have—I have
come to the same conclusion thus far. My Branchings
out therefrom have been numerous : one of them is the
consideration of Wordsworth's genius and as a help, in
the manner of gold being the meridian Line of worldly
wealth, how he differs from Milton. And here I have
nothing but surmises, from an uncertainty whether Milton's
apparently less anxiety for Humanity proceeds from his
seeing further or not than Wordsworth : And whether
Wordsworth has in truth epic passion, and martyrs
himself to the human heart, the main region of his song.
In regard to his genius alone—we find what he says true
as far as we have experienced, and we can judge no further
but by larger experience—for axioms in philosophy are
not axioms until they are proved upon our pulses.
We read fine things, but never feel them to the full
until we have gone the same steps as the author.—I know
this is not plain ; you will know exactly my meaning

when I say that now I shall relish Hamlet more than
I ever have done—Or, better—you are sensible no man
can set down Venery as a bestial or joyless thing until
he is sick of it, and therefore all philosophising on it
would be mere wording.   Until we are sick, we understand not; in fine, as Byron says, "Knowledge is
sorrow"; and I go on to say that "Sorrow is wisdom"—
and further for aught we can know for certainty
"Wisdom is folly"—So you see how I have run away
from Wordsworth and Milton, and shall still run away
from what was in my head, to observe, that some kind of
letters are good squares, others handsome ovals, and other
some orbicular, others spheroid—and why should not there
be another species with two rough edges like a Rat-trap?
I hope you will find all my long letters of that species,
and all will be well; for by merely touching the spring
delicately and ethereally, the rough-edged will fly immediately into a proper compactness; and thus you may make
a good wholesome loaf, with your own leaven in it, of
my fragments—If you cannot find this said Rat-trap
sufficiently tractable, alas for me, it being an impos-
sibility in grain for my ink to stain otherwise: If I
scribble long letters I must play my vagaries—I must
be too heavy, or too light, for whole pages—I must be
quaint and free of Tropes and figures—I must play my
draughts as I please, and for my advantage and your
erudition, crown a white with a black, or a black with a
white, and move into black or white, far and near as I
please—I must go from Hazlitt to Patmore, and make
Wordsworth and Coleman play at leap-frog, or keep one
of them down a whole half-holiday at fly-the-garter—
"From Gray to Gay, from Little to Shakspeare."   Also
as a long cause requires two or more sittings of the
Court, so a long letter will require two or more
sittings of the Breech, wherefore I shall resume after
dinner—

Have you not seen a Gull, an orc, a Sea-Mew, or anything to bring this Line to a proper length, and also fill

up this clear part; that like the Gull I may *dip*[1]—I
hope, not out of sight—and also, like a Gull, I hope to
be lucky in a good-sized fish—This crossing a letter
is not without its association—for chequer-work leads
us naturally to a Milkmaid, a Milkmaid to Hogarth,
Hogarth to Shakspeare — Shakspeare to Hazlitt —
Hazlitt to Shakspeare—and thus by merely pulling an
apron-string we set a pretty peal of Chimes at work—
Let them chime on while, with your patience, I will
return to Wordsworth — whether or no he has an ex-
tended vision or a circumscribed grandeur—whether
he is an eagle in his nest or on the wing—And to be
more explicit and to show you how tall I stand by
the giant, I will put down a simile of human life as far
as I now perceive it; that is, to the point to which I
say we both have arrived at—Well—I compare human
life to a large Mansion of Many apartments, two of which
I can only describe, the doors of the rest being as yet
shut upon me—The first we step into we call the infant
or thoughtless Chamber, in which we remain as long as
we do not think—We remain there a long while, and
notwithstanding the doors of the second Chamber remain
wide open, showing a bright appearance, we care not to
hasten to it; but are at length imperceptibly impelled by
the awakening of the thinking principle within us—we
no sooner get into the second Chamber, which I shall call
the Chamber of Maiden-Thought, than we become intoxi-
cated with the light and the atmosphere, we see nothing
but pleasant wonders, and think of delaying there for
ever in delight: However among the effects this breathing is father of is that tremendous one of sharpening one's
vision into the heart and nature of Man—of convincing
one's nerves that the world is full of Misery and Heart-
break, Pain, Sickness, and oppression—whereby this
Chamber of Maiden Thought becomes gradually darkened,
and at the same time, on all sides of it, many doors are

---

[1] The crossing of the letter, begun at the words "Have you
not," here *dips* into the original writing.

set open—but all dark—all leading to dark passages—
We see not the balance of good and evil—we are in a
mist—*we* are now in that state—We feel the "burden of
the Mystery." To this point was Wordsworth come, as
far as I can conceive, when he wrote 'Tintern Abbey,'
and it seems to me that his Genius is explorative of those
dark Passages. Now if we live, and go on thinking, we
too shall explore them—He is a genius and superior to
us, in so far as he can, more than we, make discoveries
and shed a light in them—Here I must think Wordsworth is deeper than Milton, though I think it has
depended more upon the general and gregarious advance
of intellect, than individual greatness of Mind—From
the Paradise Lost and the other Works of Milton, I
hope it is not too presuming, even between ourselves, to
say, that his Philosophy, human and divine, may be
tolerably understood by one not much advanced in years.
In his time, Englishmen were just emancipated from a
great superstition, and Men had got hold of certain points
and resting-places in reasoning which were too newly
born to be doubted, and too much opposed by the Mass
of Europe not to be thought ethereal and authentically
divine—Who could gainsay his ideas on virtue, vice,
and Chastity in Comus, just at the time of the dis-
missal of a hundred disgraces? who would not rest
satisfied with his hintings at good and evil in the
Paradise Lost, when just free from the Inquisition
and burning in Smithfield? The Reformation produced
such immediate and great benefits, that Protestantism
was considered under the immediate eye of heaven, and
its own remaining Dogmas and superstitions then, as it
were, regenerated, constituted those resting-places and
seeming sure points of Reasoning—from that I have
mentioned, Milton, whatever he may have thought in
the sequel, appears to have been content with these by
his writings—He did not think into the human heart as
Wordsworth has done—Yet Milton as a Philosopher
had sure as great powers as Wordsworth—What is

then to be inferred? O many things—It proves there
is really a grand march of intellect,—It proves that a
mighty providence subdues the mightiest Minds to the
service of the time being, whether it be in human Knowledge or Religion. I have often pitied a tutor who has
to hear "Nom. Musa" so often dinn'd into his ears—I
hope you may not have the same pain in this scribbling
—I may have read these things before, but I never had
even a thus dim perception of them; and moreover I like
to say my lesson to one who will endure my tediousness
for my own sake—After all there is certainly something
real in the world—Moore's present to Hazlitt is real—I
like that Moore, and am glad I saw him at the Theatre
just before I left Town. Tom has spit a *leetle* blood this
afternoon, and that is rather a damper—but I know—the
truth is there is something real in the World. Your third
Chamber of Life shall be a lucky and a gentle one—
stored with the wine of love—and the Bread of Friendship
—When you see George if he should not have received
a letter from me tell him he will find one at home most
likely—tell Bailey I hope soon to see him—Remember
me to all. The leaves have been out here for mony a
day—I have written to George for the first stanzas of
my Isabel—I shall have them soon, and will copy the
whole out for you.

Your affectionate Friend   JOHN KEATS.

LIII.—TO BENJAMIN BAILEY.

Hampstead, Thursday [May 28, 1818].

My dear Bailey—I should have answered your Letter
on the Moment, if I could have said yes to your invitation. What hinders me is insuperable: I will tell it at
a little length. You know my Brother George has been
out of employ for some time: it has weighed very much
upon him, and driven him to scheme and turn over things
in his Mind. The result has been his resolution to
emigrate to the back Settlements of America, become

Farmer and work with his own hands, after purchasing 14 hundred acres of the American Government. This for many reasons has met with my entire Consent —and the chief one is this ; he is of too independent and liberal a Mind to get on in Trade in this Country, in which a generous Man with a scanty resource must be ruïned. I would sooner he should till the ground than bow to a customer. There is no choice with him : he could not bring himself to the latter. I would not consent to his going alone ;—no—but that objection is done away with : he will marry before he sets sail a young lady he has known for several years, of a nature liberal and high-spirited enough to follow him to the Banks of the Mississippi. He will set off in a month or six weeks, and you will see how I should wish to pass that time with him.— And then I must set out on a journey of my own. Brown and I are going a pedestrian tour through the north of England and Scotland as far as John o' Grot's. I have this morning such a lethargy that I cannot write. The reason of my delaying is oftentimes from this feeling,—I wait for a proper temper. Now you ask for an immediate answer, I do not like to wait even till to-morrow. However, I am now so depressed that I have not an idea to put to paper—my hand feels like lead—and yet it is an unpleasant numbness ; it does not take away the pain of Existence. I don't know what to write.

                                    Monday [June 1].

You see how I have delayed ; and even now I have but a confused idea of what I should be about. My intellect must be in a degenerating state—it must be—for when I should be writing about—God knows what—I am troubling you with moods of my own mind, or rather body, for mind there is none. I am in that temper that if I were under water I would scarcely kick to come up to the top—I know very well 'tis all nonsense—In a short time I hope I shall be in a temper to feel sensibly your mention of my book. In vain have

I waited till Monday to have any Interest in that or anything else.   I feel no spur at my Brother's going to
America, and am almost stony-hearted about his wedding.
All this will blow over—All I am sorry for is having to
write to you in such a time—but I cannot force my
letters in a hotbed.   I could not feel comfortable in
making sentences for you.   I am your debtor—I must
ever remain so—nor do I wish to be clear of any Rational
debt: there is a comfort in throwing oneself on the
charity of one's friends —'tis like the albatross sleeping
on its wings.   I will be to you wine in the cellar, and
the more modestly, or rather, indolently, I retire into the
backward bin, the more Falerne will I be at the drinking.
There is one thing I must mention—my Brother talks of
sailing in a fortnight—if so I will most probably be with
you a week before I set out for Scotland.   The middle
of your first page should be sufficient to rouse me.   What
I said is true, and I have dreamt of your mention of it,
and my not answering it has weighed on me since.   If I
come, I will bring your letter, and hear more fully your
sentiments on one or two points.   I will call about the
Lectures at Taylor's, and at Little Britain, to-morrow.
Yesterday I dined with Hazlitt, Barnes, and Wilkie, at
Haydon's.   The topic was the Duke of Wellington—very
amusingly pro-and-con'd.   Reynolds has been getting
much better; and Rice may begin to crow, for he got a
little so-so at a party of his, and was none the worse for
it the next morning.   I hope I shall soon see you, for we
must have many new thoughts and feelings to analyse,
and to discover whether a little more knowledge has not
made us more ignorant.
   Yours affectionately   JOHN KEATS.

               LIV.—TO BENJAMIN BAILEY.

                              London [June 10, 1818].

   My dear Bailey—I have been very much gratified
and very much hurt by your letters in the Oxford

Paper :[1] because independent of that unlawful and mortal feeling of pleasure at praise, there is a glory in enthusiasm; and because the world is malignant enough to chuckle at the most honourable Simplicity. Yes, on my soul, my dear Bailey, you are too simple for the world—and that Idea makes me sick of it. How is it that by extreme opposites we have, as it were, got discontented nerves? You have all your life (I think so) believed everybody. I have suspected everybody. And, although you have been so deceived, you make a simple appeal—the world has something else to do, and I am glad of it—Were it in my choice, I would reject a Petrarchal coronation—on account of my dying day, and because women have cancers. I should not by rights speak in this tone to you for it is an incendiary spirit that would do so. Yet I am not old enough or magnanimous enough to annihilate self— and it would perhaps be paying you an ill compliment. I was in hopes some little time back to be able to relieve your dulness by my spirits—to point out things in the world worth your enjoyment—and now I am never alone without rejoicing that there is such a thing as death— without placing my ultimate in the glory of dying for a great human purpose. Perhaps if my affairs were in a different state, I should not have written the above—you shall judge : I have two brothers; one is driven, by the "burden of Society," to America; the other with an exquisite love of life, is in a lingering state—My love for my Brothers, from the early loss of our Parents, and even from earlier misfortunes,[2] has grown into an affection "passing the love of women." I have been ill-tempered with them—I have vexed them—but the thought of them has always stifled the impression that any woman might otherwise have made upon me. I have a sister too, and may not follow them either to America or to the grave. Life must be undergone, and I certainly derive some

[1] The *Oxford Herald* for June 6, 1818.
[2] Referring probably to the unfortunate second marriage made by their mother.

consolation from the thought of writing one or two more poems before it ceases.

I have heard some hints of your retiring to Scotland—I should like to know your feeling on it—it seems rather remote. Perhaps Gleig will have a duty near you. I am not certain whether I shall be able to go any journey, on account of my Brother Tom, and a little indisposition of my own. If I do not you shall see me soon, if *no* on my return or I'll quarter myself on you next winter. I had known my sister-in-law some time before she was my sister, and was very fond of her. I like her better and better. She is the most disinterested woman I ever knew—that is to say, she goes beyond degree in it. To see an entirely disinterested girl quite happy is the most pleasant and extraordinary thing in the world—It depends upon a thousand circumstances—On my word it is extraordinary. Women must want Imagination, and they may thank God for it; and so may we, that a delicate being can feel happy without any sense of crime. It puzzles me, and I have no sort of logic to comfort me—I shall think it over. I am not at home, and your letter being there I cannot look it over to answer any particular—only I must say I feel that passage of Dante. If I take any book with me it shall be those minute volumes of Carey, for they will go into the aptest corner.

Reynolds is getting, I may say, robust, his illness has been of service to him—like every one just recovered, he is high-spirited—I hear also good accounts of Rice. With respect to domestic literature, the Edinburgh Magazine, in another blow-up against Hunt, calls me "the amiable Mister Keats"—and I have more than a laurel from the Quarterly Reviewers for they have smothered me in "Foliage." I want to read you my "Pot of Basil"—if you go to Scotland, I should much like to read it there to you, among the snows of next winter. My Brothers' remembrances to you.

Your affectionate friend   JOHN KEATS.

LV.—TO JOHN TAYLOR.

[Hampstead,] Sunday Evening [June 21, 1818].

My dear Taylor—I am sorry I have not had time to call and wish you health till my return—Really I have been hard run these last three days—However, au revoir, God keep us all well! I start to-morrow Morning. My brother Tom will I am afraid be lonely. I can scarce ask a loan of books for him, since I still keep those you lent me a year ago. If I am overweening, you will I know be indulgent. Therefore when you shall write, do send him some you think will be most amusing—he will be careful in returning them. Let him have one of my books bound. I am ashamed to catalogue these messages. There is but one more, which ought to go for nothing as there is a lady concerned. I promised Mrs. Reynolds one of my books bound. As I cannot write in it let the opposite [1] be pasted in 'prythee. Remember me to Percy St.—Tell Hilton that one gratification on my return will be to find him engaged on a history piece to his own content—And tell Dewint I shall become a disputant on the landscape—Bow for me very genteelly to Mrs. D. or she will not admit your diploma. Remember me to Hessey, saying I hope he'll *Cary* his point. I would not forget Woodhouse. Adieu!

Your sincere friend   JOHN O' GROTS.

LVI.—TO THOMAS KEATS.

Keswick, June 29th [1818].

My dear Tom—I cannot make my Journal as distinct and actual as I could wish, from having been engaged in writing to George, and therefore I must tell you without circumstance that we proceeded from Ambleside to Rydal, saw the Waterfalls there, and called on Words-

---

[1] A leaf with the name and "from the Author," notes Wood-house.

worth, who was not at home, nor was any one of his
family. I wrote a note and left it on the mantel-piece.
Thence on we came to the foot of Helvellyn, where we
slept, but could not ascend it for the mist. I must
mention that from Rydal we passed Thirlswater, and a
fine pass in the Mountains—from Helvellyn we came to
Keswick on Derwent Water. The approach to Derwent
Water surpassed Windermere—it is richly wooded, and
shut in with rich-toned Mountains. From Helvellyn to
Keswick was eight miles to Breakfast, after which we
took a complete circuit of the Lake, going about ten miles,
and seeing on our way the Fall of Lowdore. I had an easy
climb among the streams, about the fragments of Rocks
and should have got I think to the summit, but unfortunately I was damped by slipping one leg into a
squashy hole. There is no great body of water, but the
accompaniment is delightful; for it oozes out from a cleft
in perpendicular Rocks, all fledged with Ash and other
beautiful trees.[1] It is a strange thing how they got
there. At the south end of the Lake, the Mountains of
Borrowdale are perhaps as fine as anything we have seen.
On our return from this circuit, we ordered dinner, and
set forth about a mile and a half on the Penrith road, to
see the Druid temple. We had a fag up hill, rather too
near dinner-time, which was rendered void by the gratification of seeing those aged stones on a gentle rise in the
midst of the Mountains, which at that time darkened all
around, except at the fresh opening of the Vale of St.
John. We went to bed rather fatigued, but not so much
so as to hinder us getting up this morning to mount
Skiddaw. It promised all along to be fair, and we had
fagged and tugged nearly to the top, when, at half-past
six, there came a Mist upon us and shut out the view.
We did not, however, lose anything by it: we were high
enough without mist to see the coast of Scotland—the

[1] Compare the *Ode to Psyche* :—

"Far, far around shall those dark-crested trees
Fledge the wild-ridged mountains steep by steep."

Irish Sea—the hills beyond Lancaster—and nearly all the large ones of Cumberland and Westmoreland, particularly Helvellyn and Scawfell. It grew colder and colder as we ascended, and we were glad, at about three parts of the way, to taste a little rum which the Guide brought with him, mixed, mind ye, with Mountain water. I took two glasses going and one returning. It is about six miles from where I am writing to the top—So we have walked ten miles before Breakfast to-day. We went up with two others, very good sort of fellows—All felt, on arising into the cold air, that same elevation which a cold bath gives one—I felt as if I were going to a Tournament.

Wordsworth's house is situated just on the rise of the foot of Mount Rydal; his parlour-window looks directly down Winandermere; I do not think I told you how fine the Vale of Grasmere is, and how I discovered "the ancient woman seated on Helm Crag"[1]—We shall proceed immediately to Carlisle, intending to enter Scotland on the 1st of July viâ—

[Carlisle,] July 1st.

We are this morning at Carlisle. After Skiddaw, we walked to Treby the oldest market town in Cumberland—where we were greatly amused by a country dancing-school holden at the Tun, it was indeed "no new cotillon fresh from France." No, they kickit and jumpit with mettle extraordinary, and whiskit, and friskit, and toed it, and go'd it, and twirl'd it, and whirl'd it, and stamped it, and sweated it, tattooing the floor like mad. The difference between our country dances and these Scottish figures is about the same as leisurely stirring a cup o' Tea and beating up a batter-pudding. I was extremely gratified to think that, if I had pleasures they knew nothing of, they had also some into which I could not possibly enter. I hope I shall not return without having got the Highland fling.

[1] Wordsworth's lines "To Joanna" seem to have been special favourites with Keats.

There was as fine a row of boys and girls as you ever saw; some beautiful faces, and one exquisite mouth. I never felt so near the glory of Patriotism, the glory of making by any means a country happier. This is what I like better than scenery. I fear our continued moving from place to place will prevent our becoming learned in village affairs: we are mere creatures of Rivers, Lakes, and Mountains. Our yesterday's journey was from Treby to Wigton, and from Wigton to Carlisle. The Cathedral does not appear very fine—the Castle is very ancient, and of brick. The City is very various—old white-washed narrow streets—broad red-brick ones more modern—I will tell you anon whether the inside of the Cathedral is worth looking at. It is built of sandy red stone or Brick. We have now walked 114 miles, and are merely a little tired in the thighs, and a little blistered. We shall ride 38 miles to Dumfries, when we shall linger awhile about Nithsdale and Galloway. I have written two letters to Liverpool. I found a letter from sister George; very delightful indeed: I shall preserve it in the bottom of my knapsack for you.

[Dumfries, evening of same day, July 1.]

ON VISITING THE TOMB OF BURNS.

The Town, the churchyard, and the setting sun,
The Clouds, the trees, the rounded hills all seem,
Though beautiful, Cold—strange—as in a dream,
I dreamed long ago, now new begun.
The short-liv'd, paly Summer is but won
From Winter's ague, for one hour's gleam;
Though sapphire-warm, their stars do never beam:
All is cold Beauty; pain is never done:
For who has mind to relish, Minos-wise,
The Real of Beauty, free from that dead hue
Sickly imagination and sick pride
Cast wan upon it! Burns! with honour due
I oft have honour'd thee. Great shadow, hide
Thy face; I sin against thy native skies.

You will see by this sonnet that I am at Dumfries. We have dined in Scotland. Burns's tomb is in the

Churchyard corner, not very much to my taste, though on a scale large enough to show they wanted to honour him. Mrs. Burns lives in this place; most likely we shall see her to-morrow—This Sonnet I have written in a strange mood, half-asleep. I know not how it is, the Clouds, the Sky, the Houses, all seem anti-Grecian and anti-Charlemagnish. I will endeavour to get rid of my prejudices and tell you fairly about the Scotch.

[Dumfries,] July 2nd.

In Devonshire they say, "Well, where be ye going?" Here it is, "How is it wi' yoursel?" A man on the Coach said the horses took a Hellish heap o' drivin'; the same fellow pointed out Burns's Tomb with a deal of life—"There de ye see it, amang the trees—white, wi' a roond tap?" The first well-dressed Scotchman we had any conversation with, to our surprise confessed himself a Deist. The careful manner of delivering his opinions, not before he had received several encouraging hints from us, was very amusing. Yesterday was an immense Horse-fair at Dumfries, so that we met numbers of men and women on the road, the women nearly all barefoot, with their shoes and clean stockings in hand, ready to put on and look smart in the Towns. There are plenty of wretched cottages whose smoke has no outlet but by the door. We have now begun upon Whisky, called here Whuskey,—very smart stuff it is. Mixed like our liquors, with sugar and water, 'tis called toddy; very pretty drink, and much praised by Burns.

LVII.—TO FANNY KEATS.

Dumfries, July 2nd [1818].

My dear Fanny—I intended to have written to you from Kirkcudbright, the town I shall be in to-morrow—but I will write now because my Knapsack has worn my coat in the Seams, my coat has gone to the Tailor's and I have but one Coat to my back in these parts

I must tell you how I went to Liverpool with George and our new Sister and the Gentleman my fellow traveller through the Summer and autumn—We had a tolerable journey to Liverpool—which I left the next morning before George was up for Lancaster—Then we set off from Lancaster on foot with our Knapsacks on, and have walked a Little zig-zag through the mountains and Lakes of Cumberland and Westmoreland—We came from Carlisle yesterday to this place—We are employed in going up Mountains, looking at strange towns, prying into old ruins and eating very hearty breakfasts. Here we are full in the Midst of broad Scotch "How is it a' wi' yoursel"—the Girls are walking about bare-footed and in the worst cottages the smoke finds its way out of the door. I shall come home full of news for you and for fear I should choak you by too great a dose at once I must make you used to it by a letter or two. We have been taken for travelling Jewellers, Razor sellers and Spectacle vendors because friend Brown wears a pair. The first place we stopped at with our Knapsacks contained one Richard Bradshaw, a notorious tippler. He stood in the shape of a 5 and ballanced himself as well as he could saying with his nose right in Mr. Brown's face "Do—yo—u sell spect—ta—cles?" Mr. Abbey says we are Don Quixotes—tell him we are more generally taken for Pedlars. All I hope is that we may not be taken for excisemen in this whisky country. We are generally up about 5 walking before breakfast and we complete our 20 miles before dinner.—Yesterday we visited Burns's Tomb and this morning the fine Ruins of Lincluden.

[Auchencairn, same day, July 2.]

I had done thus far when my coat came back fortified at all points—so as we lose no time we set forth again through Galloway—all very pleasant and pretty with no fatigue when one is used to it—We are in the midst of Meg Merrilies's country of whom I suppose you have heard.

Old Meg she was a Gipsy,
  And liv'd upon the Moors :
Her bed it was the brown heath turf,
  And her house was out of doors.

Her apples were swart blackberries,
  Her currants pods o' broom ;
Her wine was dew of the wild white rose,
  Her book a churchyard tomb.

Her Brothers were the craggy hills,
  Her Sisters larchen trees—
Alone with her great family
  She liv'd as she did please.

No breakfast had she many a morn,
  No dinner many a noon,
And 'stead of supper she would stare
  Full hard against the Moon.

But every morn of woodbine fresh
  She made her garlanding,
And every night the dark glen Yew
  She wove, and she would sing.

And with her fingers old and brown
  She plaited Mats o' Rushes,
And gave them to the Cottagers
  She met among the Bushes.

Old Meg was brave as Margaret Queen
  And tall as Amazon :
An old red blanket cloak she wore ;
  A chip hat had she on.
God rest her aged bones somewhere—
  She died full long agone !

If you like these sort of Ballads I will now and then
scribble one for you—if I send any to Tom I'll tell him
to send them to you.

[Kirkcudbright, evening of same day, July 2.]

I have so many interruptions that I cannot manage
to fill a Letter in one day—since I scribbled the song
we have walked through a beautiful Country to Kirkcudbright—at which place I will write you a song about
myself—

There was a naughty Boy,
A naughty boy was he,
He would not stop at home,
He could not quiet be—
  He took
  In his Knapsack
  A Book
  Full of vowels
  And a shirt
  With some towels—
  A slight cap
  For night cap—
  A hair brush,
  Comb ditto,
  New Stockings
  For old ones
  Would split O!
  This Knapsack
  Tight at's back
  He rivetted close
And followéd his Nose
  To the North,
  To the North,
And follow'd his nose
  To the North.

There was a naughty boy
  And a naughty boy was he,
For nothing would he do
  But scribble poetry—
  He took
  An inkstand
  In his hand
  And a Pen
  Big as ten
  In the other,
  And away
  In a Pother
  He ran
  To the mountains
  And fountains
  And ghostes
  And Postes
  And witches
  And ditches
  And wrote
  In his coat

When the weather
  Was cool,
  Fear of gout,
  And without
When the weather
  Was warm—
  Och the charm
  When we choose
To follow one's nose
  To the north,
  To the north,
To follow one's nose
  To the north!

There was a naughty boy
  And a naughty boy was he,
He kept little fishes
  In washing tubs three
  In spite
  Of the might
  Of the Maid
  Nor afraid
  Of his Granny-good—
  He often would
  Hurly burly
  Get up early
  And go
  By hook or crook
  To the brook
  And bring home
  Miller's thumb,
  Tittlebat
  Not over fat,
  Minnows small
  As the stall
  Of a glove,
  Not above
  The size
  Of a nice
  Little Baby's
  Little fingers—
  O he made
  'Twas his trade
Of Fish a pretty Kettle
  A Kettle—
  A Kettle
Of Fish a pretty Kettle
  A Kettle!

There was a naughty Boy,
  And a naughty Boy was
    he,
He ran away to Scotland
  The people for to see—
    Then he found
    That the ground
    Was as hard,
    That a yard
    Was as long,
    That a song
    Was as merry,
    That a cherry
    Was as red—
    That lead
    Was as weighty,
    That fourscore
    Was as eighty,
    That a door
    Was as wooden
    As in England—
So he stood in his shoes
  And he wonder'd,
    He wonder'd,
He stood in his shoes
  And he wonder'd.

[Newton Stewart, July 4.]

My dear Fanny, I am ashamed of writing you such stuff, nor would I if it were not for being tired after my day's walking, and ready to tumble into bed so fatigued that when I am asleep you might sew my nose to my great toe and trundle me round the town, like a Hoop, without waking me. Then I get so hungry a Ham goes but a very little way and fowls are like Larks to me—A Batch of Bread I make no more ado with than a sheet of parliament; and I can eat a Bull's head as easily as I used to do Bull's eyes. I take a whole string of Pork Sausages down as easily as a Pen'orth of Lady's fingers. Ah dear I must soon be contented with an acre or two of oaten cake a hogshead of Milk and a Clothes-basket of Eggs morning noon and night when I get among the Highlanders. Before we see them we shall pass into Ireland and have a chat with the Paddies, and look at the Giant's Causeway which you must have heard of—I have not time to tell you particularly for I have to send a Journal to Tom of whom you shall hear all particulars or from me when I return. Since I began this we have walked sixty miles to Newton Stewart at which place I put in this Letter—to-night we sleep at Glenluce—to-morrow at Portpatrick and the next day we shall cross in the passage boat to Ireland. I hope Miss Abbey has quite recovered.   Present my Respects to her and to Mr. and Mrs. Abbey.   God bless you.

Your affectionate Brother,   JOHN.

Do write me a Letter directed to *Inverness*, Scotland.

LVIII.—TO THOMAS KEATS.

Auchtercairn [for Auchencairn,] 3rd [for 2d] July 1818.

My dear Tom—We are now in Meg Merrilies's country, and have this morning passed through some parts exactly suited to her.   Kirkcudbright County is very beautiful, very wild, with craggy hills, somewhat in the Westmoreland fashion.   We have come down from Dumfries to the sea-coast part of it.   The following song you will have from Dilke, but perhaps you would like it here.[1] . . .

[Newton Stewart,] July 5th [for 4th].

Yesterday was passed in Kirkcudbright, the country is very rich, very fine, and with a little of Devon.   I am now writing at Newton Stewart, six miles into Wigtown. Our landlady of yesterday said very few southerners passed hereaways.   The children jabber away, as if in a foreign language ; the bare-footed girls look very much in keeping, I mean with the scenery about them. Brown praises their cleanliness and appearance of comfort, the neatness of their cottages, etc.—it may be—they are very squat among trees and fern and heath and broom, on levels slopes and heights—but I wish they were as snug as those up the Devonshire valleys.   We are lodged and entertained in great varieties.   We dined yesterday on dirty Bacon, dirtier eggs, and dirtiest potatoes, with a slice of salmon—we breakfast this morning in a nice carpeted room, with sofa, hair-bottomed Chairs, and green-baized Mahogany.   A spring by the road-side is always welcome : we drink water for dinner, diluted with a Gill of whisky.

[1] Keats here repeats for his brother the Meg Merrilies piece contained in the preceding letter to Fanny.

[Donaghadee] July 6.

Yesterday morning we set out from Glenluce, going some distance round to see some rivers: they were scarcely worth the while. We went on to Stranraer, in a burning sun, and had gone about six miles when the Mail overtook us: we got up, were at Port Patrick in a jiffey, and I am writing now in little Ireland. The dialects on the neighbouring shores of Scotland and Ireland are much the same, yet I can perceive a great difference in the nations, from the chamber-maid at this *nate toone* kept by Mr. Kelly. She is fair, kind, and ready to laugh, because she is out of the horrible dominion of the Scotch Kirk. A Scotch girl stands in terrible awe of the Elders—poor little Susannahs, they will scarcely laugh, and their Kirk is greatly to be damned. These Kirk-men have done Scotland good (Query?). They have made men, women; old men, young men; old women, young women; boys, girls; and all infants careful—so that they are formed into regular Phalanges of savers and gainers. Such a thrifty army cannot fail to enrich their Country, and give it a greater appearance of Comfort, than that of their poor rash neighbourhood—these Kirk-men have done Scotland harm; they have banished puns, and laughing, and kissing, etc. (except in cases where the very danger and crime must make it very gustful). I shall make a full stop at kissing, for after that there should be a better parenthesis, and go on to remind you of the fate of Burns—poor unfortunate fellow, his disposition was Southern—how sad it is when a luxurious imagination is obliged, in self-defence, to deaden its delicacy in vulgarity, and rot[1] in things attainable, that it may not have leisure to go mad after things which are not. No man, in such matters, will be content with the experience of others—It is true that out of suffering there is no dignity, no greatness, that in the most abstracted pleasure there is no lasting happiness—Yet who would not like

---

[1] Reading doubtful.

to discover over again that Cleopatra was a Gipsy, Helen a rogue, and Ruth a deep one? I have not sufficient reasoning faculty to settle the doctrine of thrift, as it is consistent with the dignity of human Society—with the happiness of Cottagers. All I can do is by plump contrasts; were the fingers made to squeeze a guinea or a white hand?—were the lips made to hold a pen or a kiss? and yet in Cities man is shut out from his fellows if he is poor—the cottager must be very dirty, and very wretched, if she be not thrifty—the present state of society demands this, and this convinces me that the world is very young, and in a very ignorant state— We live in a barbarous age—I would sooner be a wild deer, than a girl under the dominion of the Kirk; and I would sooner be a wild hog, than be the occasion of a poor Creature's penance before those execrable elders.

It is not so far to the Giant's Causeway as we supposed—We thought it 70, and hear it is only 48 miles—So we shall leave one of our knapsacks here at Donaghadee, take our immediate wants, and be back in a week, when we shall proceed to the County of Ayr. In the Packet yesterday we heard some ballads from two old men—One was a Romance which seemed very poor—then there was "The Battle of the Boyne," then "Robin Huid," as they call him—"Before the King you shall go, go, go; before the King you shall go."

[Stranraer,] July 9th.

We stopped very little in Ireland, and that you may not have leisure to marvel at our speedy return to Port Patrick, I will tell you that it is as dear living in Ireland as at the Hummums—thrice the expense of Scotland—it would have cost us £15 before our return; moreover we found those 48 miles to be Irish ones, which reach to 70 English—so having walked to Belfast one day, and back to Donaghadee the next, we left Ireland with a fair breeze. We slept last night at Port Patrick, when I was gratified by a letter from you. On

our walk in Ireland, we had too much opportunity to see
the worse than nakedness, the rags, the dirt and misery,
of the poor common Irish—A Scotch cottage, though
in that sometimes the smoke has no exit but at the
door, is a palace to an Irish one. We could observe that
impetuosity in Man and Woman—We had the pleasure
of finding our way through a Peat-bog, three miles
long at least—dreary, flat, dank, black, and spongy—
here and there were poor dirty Creatures, and a few
strong men cutting or carting Peat—We heard on
passing into Belfast through a most wretched suburb,
that most disgusting of all noises, worse than the Bag-
pipes—the laugh of a Monkey—the chatter of women—the
scream of a Macaw—I mean the sound of the Shuttle.
What a tremendous difficulty is the improvement of such
people.   I cannot conceive how a mind *"with child"* of
philanthrophy could grasp at its possibility—with me it
is absolute despair—

At a miserable house of entertainment, half-way
between Donaghadee and Belfast, were two men sitting
at Whisky—one a labourer, and the other I took to be
a drunken weaver—the labourer took me to be a
Frenchman, and the other hinted at bounty-money;
saying he was ready to take it—On calling for the
letters at Port Patrick, the man snapped out "what
Regiment?"   On our return from Belfast we met a sedan
—the Duchess of Dunghill.   It is no laughing matter
though.   Imagine the worst dog-kennel you ever saw,
placed upon two poles from a mouldy fencing—In such
a wretched thing sat a squalid old woman, squat like an
ape half-starved, from a scarcity of biscuit in its passage
from Madagascar to the Cape, with a pipe in her mouth,
and looking out with a round-eyed skinny-lidded inanity;
with a sort of horizontal idiotic movement of her head—
Squat and lean she sat, and puffed out the smoke, while
two ragged tattered girls carried her along.   What a
thing would be a history of her life and sensations; I
shall endeavour when I have thought a little more, to

give you my idea of the difference between the Scotch
and Irish—The two Irishmen I mentioned were speaking
of their treatment in England, when the weaver said—
" Ah you were a civil man, but I was a drinker."

Till further notice you must direct to Inverness.

Your most affectionate Brother   JOHN.

LIX.—TO THOMAS KEATS.

Belantree [for Ballantrae,] July 10.

Ah ! ken ye what I met the day
  Out oure the Mountains
A coming down by craggies gray
  An mossie fountains—
Ah goud-hair'd Marie yeve I pray
  Ane minute's guessing—
For that I met upon the way
  Is past expressing.
As I stood where a rocky brig
  A torrent crosses
I spied upon a misty rig
  A troup o' Horses—
And as they trotted down the glen
  I sped to meet them
To see if I might know the Men
  To stop and greet them.
First Willie on his sleek mare came
  At canting gallop
His long hair rustled like a flame
  On board a shallop,
Then came his brother Rab and then
  Young Peggy's Mither
And Peggy too—adown the glen
  They went togither—
I saw her wrappit in her hood
  Frae wind and raining—
Her cheek was flush wi' timid blood
  Twixt growth and waning—
She turn'd her dazed head full oft
  For there her Brithers
Came riding with her Bridegroom soft
  And mony ithers
Young Tam came up and eyed me quick
  With reddened cheek—

Braw Tam was daffed like a chick—
    He could na speak—
Ah Marie they are all gane hame
    Through blustering weather
An' every heart is full on flame
    An' light as feather.
Ah ! Marie they are all gone hame
    Frae happy wadding,
Whilst I—Ah is it not a shame ?
    Sad tears am shedding.

My dear Tom—The reason for my writing these lines
was that Brown wanted to impose a Galloway song upon
Dilke—but it won't do.   The subject I got from meeting
a wedding just as we came down into this place—where
I am afraid we shall be imprisoned a while by the
weather.   Yesterday we came 27 Miles from Stranraer
—entered Ayrshire a little beyond Cairn, and had our
path through a delightful Country.   I shall endeavour
that you may follow our steps in this walk—it would be
uninteresting in a Book of Travels—it can not be interesting but by my having gone through it.   When we left
Cairn our Road lay half way up the sides of a green
mountainous shore, full of clefts of verdure and eternally
varying—sometimes up sometimes down, and over little
Bridges going across green chasms of moss, rock and
trees—winding about everywhere.   After two or three
Miles of this we turned suddenly into a magnificent glen
finely wooded in Parts—seven Miles long—with a Mountain stream winding down the Midst—full of cottages in
the most happy situations—the sides of the Hills covered
with sheep—the effect of cattle lowing I never had so
finely.   At the end we had a gradual ascent and got
among the tops of the Mountains whence in a little time
I descried in the Sea Ailsa Rock 940 feet high—it was
15 Miles distant and seemed close upon us.   The effect
of Ailsa with the peculiar perspective of the Sea in connection with the ground we stood on, and the misty rain
then falling gave me a complete Idea of a deluge.   Ailsa
struck me very suddenly—really I was a little alarmed.

[Girvan, same day, July 10.]

Thus far had I written before we set out this morning. Now we are at Girvan 13 Miles north of Belantree. Our Walk has been along a more grand shore to-day than yesterday—Ailsa beside us all the way.—From the heights we could see quite at home Cantire and the large Mountains of Arran, one of the Hebrides. We are in comfortable Quarters. The Rain we feared held up bravely and it has been "fu fine this day."——To-morrow we shall be at Ayr.

[Kirkoswald, July 11.]

'Tis now the 11th of July and we have come 8 Miles to Breakfast to Kirkoswald. I hope the next Kirk will be Kirk Alloway. I have nothing of consequence to say now concerning our journey—so I will speak as far as I can judge on the Irish and Scotch—I know nothing of the higher Classes—yet I have a persuasion that there the Irish are victorious. As to the profanum vulgus I must incline to the Scotch. They never laugh—but they are always comparatively neat and clean. Their constitutions are not so remote and puzzling as the Irish. The Scotchman will never give a decision on any point—he will never commit himself in a sentence which may be referred to as a meridian in his notion of things—so that you do not know him—and yet you may come in nigher neighbourhood to him than to the Irishman who commits himself in so many places that it dazes your head. A Scotchman's motive is more easily discovered than an Irishman's. A Scotchman will go wisely about to deceive you, an Irishman cunningly. An Irishman would bluster out of any discovery to his disadvantage. A Scotchman would retire perhaps without much desire for revenge. An Irishman likes to be thought a gallous fellow. A Scotchman is contented with himself. It seems to me they are both sensible of the Character they hold in England and act accordingly to Englishmen. Thus

K

the Scotchman will become over grave and over decent
and the Irishman over-impetuous. I like a Scotchman
best because he is less of a bore—I like the Irishman
best because he ought to be more comfortable.—The
Scotchman has made up his Mind within himself in a
sort of snail shell wisdom. The Irishman is full of
strongheaded instinct. The Scotchman is farther in
Humanity than the Irishman—there he will stick perhaps when the Irishman will be refined beyond him—for
the former thinks he cannot be improved—the latter
would grasp at it for ever, place but the good plain
before him.

Maybole, [same day, July 11].

Since breakfast we have come only four Miles to
dinner, not merely, for we have examined in the way
two Ruins, one of them very fine, called Crossraguel
Abbey—there is a winding Staircase to the top of a little
Watch Tower.

Kingswells, July 13.

I have been writing to Reynolds—therefore any particulars since Kirkoswald have escaped me—from said
Kirk we went to Maybole to dinner—then we set forward
to Burness' town Ayr—the approach to it is extremely
fine—quite outwent my expectations—richly meadowed,
wooded, heathed and rivuleted—with a grand Sea view
terminated by the black Mountains of the isle of Arran.
As soon as I saw them so nearly I said to myself " How
is it they did not beckon Burns to some grand attempt
at Epic ?"
The bonny Doon is the sweetest river I ever saw—
overhung with fine trees as far as we could see—We
stood some time on the Brig across it, over which Tam
o' Shanter fled—we took a pinch of snuff on the Key
stone—then we proceeded to the " auld Kirk Alloway."
As we were looking at it a Farmer pointed the spots
where Mungo's Mither hang'd hersel' and "drunken
Charlie brake's neck's bane." Then we proceeded to the
Cottage he was born in—there was a board to that effect

by the door side—it had the same effect as the same sort of memorial at Stratford on Avon. We drank some Toddy to Burns's Memory with an old Man who knew Burns—damn him and damn his anecdotes—he was a great bore—it was impossible for a Southron to understand above 5 words in a hundred.—There was something good in his description of Burns's melancholy the last time he saw him. I was determined to write a sonnet in the Cottage—I did—but it was so bad I cannot venture it here.

Next we walked into Ayr Town and before we went to Tea saw the new Brig and the Auld Brig and Wallace tower. Yesterday we dined with a Traveller. We were talking about Kean. He said he had seen him at Glasgow "in Othello in the Jew, I mean er, er, er, the Jew in Shylock." He got bother'd completely in vague ideas of the Jew in Othello, Shylock in the Jew, Shylock in Othello, Othello in Shylock, the Jew in Othello, etc. etc. etc.—he left himself in a mess at last.—Still satisfied with himself he went to the Window and gave an abortive whistle of some tune or other—it might have been Handel. There is no end to these Mistakes—he'll go and tell people how he has seen "Malvolio in the Countess"—"Twelfth night in Midsummer night's dream"—Bottom in much ado about Nothing—Viola in Barrymore—Antony in Cleopatra—Falstaff in the mouse Trap.—

[Glasgow,] July 14.

We enter'd Glasgow last Evening under the most oppressive Stare a body could feel. When we had crossed the Bridge Brown look'd back and said its whole population had turned out to wonder at us—we came on till a drunken Man came up to me—I put him off with my Arm—he returned all up in Arms saying aloud that, "he had seen all foreigners bu-u-ut he never saw the like o' me." I was obliged to mention the word Officer and Police before he would desist.—The City of Glasgow I take to be a very fine

one—I was astonished to hear it was twice the size of
Edinburgh.   It is built of Stone and has a much more
solid appearance than London.   We shall see the Cathedral this morning—they have devilled it into "High
Kirk."   I want very much to know the name of the
ship George is gone in—also what port he will land in
—I know nothing about it.   I hope you are leading a
quiet Life and gradually improving.   Make a long lounge
of the whole Summer—by the time the Leaves fall I
shall be near you with plenty of confab—there are a
thousand things I cannot write.   Take care of yourself
—I mean in not being vexed or bothered at anything.

   God bless you !   JOHN ——.

LX.—TO JOHN HAMILTON REYNOLDS.

Maybole, July 11 [1818].

   My dear Reynolds—I'll not run over the Ground we
have passed ; that would be merely as bad as telling a
dream—unless perhaps I do it in the manner of the
Laputan printing press—that is I put down Mountains,
Rivers Lakes, dells, glens, Rocks, and Clouds, with
beautiful enchanting, Gothic picturesque fine, delightful,
enchanting, Grand, sublime—a few blisters, etc.—and
now you have our journey thus far : where I begin a letter
to you because I am approaching Burns's Cottage very fast.
We have made continual inquiries from the time we saw
his Tomb at Dumfries—his name of course is known all
about—his great reputation among the plodding people
is, "that he wrote a good *mony* sensible things."   One
of the pleasantest means of annulling self is approaching
such a shrine as the Cottage of Burns—we need not think
of his misery—that is all gone, bad luck to it—I shall
look upon it hereafter with unmixed pleasure, as I do
upon my Stratford-on-Avon day with Bailey.   I shall fill
this sheet for you in the Bardie's country, going no further
than this till I get into the town of Ayr which will be a
9 miles' walk to Tea.

[Kingswells, July 13.]

We were talking on different and indifferent things, when on a sudden we turned a corner upon the immediate Country of Ayr—the Sight was as rich as possible. I had no Conception that the native place of Burns was so beautiful—the idea I had was more desolate, his 'rigs of Barley' seemed always to me but a few strips of Green on a cold hill—O prejudice! it was as rich as Devon—I endeavoured to drink in the Prospect, that I might spin it out to you as the Silkworm makes silk from Mulberry leaves—I cannot recollect it—Besides all the Beauty, there were the Mountains of Arran Isle, black and huge over the Sea. We came down upon everything suddenly—there were in our way the 'bonny Doon,' with the Brig that Tam o' Shanter crossed, Kirk Alloway, Burns's Cottage, and then the Brigs of Ayr. First we stood upon the Bridge across the Doon; surrounded by every Phantasy of green in Tree, Meadow, and Hill,—the stream of the Doon, as a Farmer told us, is covered with trees from head to foot — you know those beautiful heaths so fresh against the weather of a summer's evening—there was one stretching along behind the trees. I wish I knew always the humour my friends would be in at opening a letter of mine, to suit it to them as nearly as possible. I could always find an egg shell for Melancholy, and as for Merriment a Witty humour will turn anything to Account—My head is sometimes in such a whirl in considering the million likings and antipathies of our Moments—that I can get into no settled strain in my Letters. My Wig! Burns and sentimentality coming across you and Frank Fladgate in the office— O scenery that thou shouldst be crushed between two Puns—As for them I venture the rascalliest in the Scotch Region—I hope Brown does not put them punctually in his journal—If he does I must sit on the cutty-stool all next winter. We went to Kirk Alloway—"a Prophet is no Prophet in his own Country"—We went to the Cottage

and took some Whisky. I wrote a sonnet for the mere
sake of writing some lines under the roof—they are so
bad I cannot transcribe them—The Man at the Cottage
was a great Bore with his Anecdotes—I hate the rascal
—his Life consists in fuz, fuzzy, fuzziest—He drinks
glasses five for the Quarter and twelve for the hour—he
is a mahogany-faced old Jackass who knew Burns—He
ought to have been kicked for having spoken to him.
He calls himself " a curious old Bitch "—but he is a flat
old dog—I should like to employ Caliph Vathek to kick
him.   O the flummery of a birthplace !   Cant ! Cant !
Cant ! It is enough to give a spirit the guts-ache—Many
a true word, they say, is spoken in jest—this may be
because his gab hindered my sublimity : the flat dog
made me write a flat sonnet.   My dear Reynolds—I
cannot write about scenery and visitings — Fancy is
indeed less than a present palpable reality, but it is
greater than remembrance — you would lift your eyes
from Homer only to see close before you the real Isle of
Tenedos—you would rather read Homer afterwards than
remember yourself—One song of Burns's is of more worth
to you than all I could think for a whole year in his
native country.   His Misery is a dead weight upon the
nimbleness of one's quill—I tried to forget it—to drink
Toddy without any Care—to write a merry sonnet—it
won't do—he talked with Bitches—he drank with Black-
guards, he was miserable—We can see horribly clear,
in the works of such a Man his whole life, as if we were
God's spies.—What were his addresses to Jean in the
latter part of his life ?   I should not speak so to you—
yet why not—you are not in the same case—you are
in the right path, and you shall not be deceived.   I have
spoken to you against Marriage, but it was general—the
Prospect in those matters has been to me so blank, that
I have not been unwilling to die—I would not now, for
I have inducements to Life—I must see my little Nephews
in America, and I must see you marry your lovely Wife.
My sensations are sometimes deadened for weeks together

— but believe me I have more than once yearned for the time of your happiness to come, as much as I could for myself after the lips of Juliet.—From the tenor of my occasional rodomontade in chit-chat, you might have been deceived concerning me in these points—upon my soul, I have been getting more and more close to you, every day, ever since I knew you, and now one of the first pleasures I look to is your happy Marriage—the more, since I have felt the pleasure of loving a sister in Law.   I did not think it possible to become so much attached in so short a time—Things like these, and they are real, have made me resolve to have a care of my health—you must be as careful.

The rain has stopped us to-day at the end of a dozen Miles, yet we hope to see Loch Lomond the day after to-morrow ;—I will piddle out my information, as Rice says, next Winter, at any time when a substitute is wanted for Vingt-un.   We bear the fatigue very well—20 Miles a day in general—A Cloud came over us in getting up Skiddaw—I hope to be more lucky in Ben Lomond—and more lucky still in Ben Nevis.   What I think you would enjoy is poking about Ruins—sometimes Abbey, sometimes Castle.   The short stay we made in Ireland has left few remembrances—but an old woman in a dog-kennel Sedan with a pipe in her Mouth, is what I can never forget— I wish I may be able to give you an idea of her—Remember me to your Mother and Sisters, and tell your Mother how I hope she will pardon me for having a scrap of paper pasted in the Book sent to her.   I was driven on all sides and had not time to call on Taylor— So Bailey is coming to Cumberland—well, if you'll let me know where at Inverness, I will call on my return and pass a little time with him—I am glad 'tis not Scotland —Tell my friends I do all I can for them, that is, drink their healths in Toddy.   Perhaps I may have some lines by and by to send you fresh, on your own Letter—Tom has a few to show you.

Your affectionate friend   JOHN KEATS.

LXI.—TO THOMAS KEATS.

Cairn-something [for Cairndow,] July 17, [1818].

My dear Tom—Here's Brown going on so that I cannot bring to mind how the two last days have vanished—for example he says The Lady of the Lake went to Rock herself to sleep on Arthur's seat and the Lord of the Isles coming to Press a Piece. . . . I told you last how we were stared at in Glasgow—we are not out of the Crowd yet. Steam Boats on Loch Lomond and Barouches on its sides take a little from the Pleasure of such romantic chaps as Brown and I. The Banks of the Clyde are extremely beautiful—the north end of Loch Lomond grand in excess—the entrance at the lower end to the narrow part from a little distance is precious good—the Evening was beautiful nothing could surpass our fortune in the weather—yet was I worldly enough to wish for a fleet of chivalry Barges with Trumpets and Banners just to die away before me into that blue place among the mountains—I must give you an outline as well as I can.[1]

No^t B — the Water was a fine Blue silvered and the Mountains a dark purple, the Sun setting aslant behind them—meantime the head of ben Lomond was covered with a rich Pink Cloud. We did not ascend Ben Lomond—the price being very high and a half a day of rest being quite acceptable. We were up at 4 this morning and have walked to breakfast 15 Miles through two Tremendous Glens—at the end of the first there is a place called rest and be thankful which we took for an Inn—it was nothing but a Stone and so we were cheated into 5 more Miles to Breakfast—I have just been bathing in Loch Fyne a salt water Lake opposite the Windows,---quite pat and fresh but for the cursed Gad flies—damn 'em they have been at me ever since I left the Swan and two necks.[2]

[1] Here follows a sketch.

[2] The Swan and Two Necks, Lad Lane, London, seems to have been the coach office for Liverpool and the North-West; compare Lamb's *Letters* (ed. Ainger), vol. i. p. 241.

All gentle folks who owe a grudge
  To any living thing
Open your ears and stay your trudge
  Whilst I in dudgeon sing.

The Gadfly he hath stung me sore—
  O may he ne'er sting you !
But we have many a horrid bore
  He may sting black and blue.

Has any here an old gray Mare
  With three legs all her store,
O put it to her Buttocks bare
  And straight she'll run on four.

Has any here a Lawyer suit
  Of 1743,
Take Lawyer's nose and put it to't
  And you the end will see.

Is there a Man in Parliament
  Dumbfounder'd in his speech,
O let his neighbour make a rent
  And put one in his breech.

O Lowther how much better thou
  Hadst figur'd t'other day
When to the folks thou mad'st a bow
  And hadst no more to say

If lucky Gadfly had but ta'en
  His seat upon thine A—e
And put thee to a little pain
  To save thee from a worse.

Better than Southey it had been,
  Better than Mr. D——,
Better than Wordsworth too, I ween,
  Better than Mr. V——.

Forgive me pray good people all
  For deviating so—
In spirit sure I had a call—
  And now I on will go.

Has any here a daughter fair
  Too fond of reading novels,
Too apt to fall in love with care
  And charming Mister Lovels,

O put a Gadfly to that thing
   She keeps so white and pert—
I mean the finger for the ring,
   And it will breed a wort.

Has any here a pious spouse
   Who seven times a day
Scolds as King David pray'd, to chouse
   And have her holy way—

O let a Gadfly's little sting
   Persuade her sacred tongue
That noises are a common thing,
   But that her bell has rung.

And as this is the summum bo-
   num of all conquering,
I leave "withouten wordes mo"
   The Gadfly's little sting.

                        [Inverary, July 18.]

Last Evening we came round the End of Loch Fyne to Inverary—the Duke of Argyle's Castle is very modern magnificent and more so from the place it is in—the woods seem old enough to remember two or three changes in the Crags about them—the Lake was beautiful and there was a Band at a distance by the Castle. I must say I enjoyed two or three common tunes—but nothing could stifle the horrors of a solo on the Bag-pipe—I thought the Beast would never have done.—Yet was I doomed to hear another.—On entering Inverary we saw a Play Bill. Brown was knocked up from new shoes—so I went to the Barn alone where I saw the Stranger accompanied by a Bag-pipe. There they went on about interesting creaters and human nater till the Curtain fell and then came the Bag-pipe. When Mrs. Haller fainted down went the Curtain and out came the Bag-pipe—at the heartrending, shoemending reconciliation the Piper blew amain. I never read or saw this play before; not the Bag-pipe nor the wretched players themselves were

little in comparison with it—thank heaven it has been
scoffed at lately almost to a fashion—

> Of late two dainties were before me placed
>   Sweet, holy, pure, sacred and innocent,
>   From the ninth sphere to me benignly sent
> That Gods might know my own particular taste :
> First the soft Bag-pipe mourn'd with zealous haste,
>   The Stranger next with head on bosom bent
>   Sigh'd ; rueful again the piteous Bag-pipe went,
> Again the Stranger sighings fresh did waste.
> O Bag-pipe thou didst steal my heart away—
>   O Stranger thou my nerves from Pipe didst charm—
> O Bag-pipe thou didst re-assert thy sway—
>   Again thou Stranger gav'st me fresh alarm—
> Alas ! I could not choose.   Ah ! my poor heart
> Mumchance art thou with both oblig'd to part.

I think we are the luckiest fellows in Christendom—
Brown could not proceed this morning on account of his
feet and lo there is thunder and rain.

[Kilmelfort,] July 20th.

For these two days past we have been so badly
accommodated more particularly in coarse food that I
have not been at all in cue to write.   Last night poor
Brown with his feet blistered and scarcely able to
walk, after a trudge of 20 Miles down the Side of
Loch Awe had no supper but Eggs and Oat Cake—we
have lost the sight of white bread entirely—Now we
had eaten nothing but Eggs all day—about 10 a piece
and they had become sickening—To-day we have fared
rather better—but no oat Cake wanting—we had a small
Chicken and even a good bottle of Port but all together
the fare is too coarse—I feel it a little.—Another week
will break us in.   I forgot to tell you that when we came
through Glenside it was early in the morning and we
were pleased with the noise of Shepherds, Sheep and
dogs in the misty heights close above us—we saw none
of them for some time, till two came in sight creeping
among the Crags like Emmets, yet their voices came

quite plainly to us—The approach to Loch Awe was very
solemn towards nightfall—the first glance was a streak
of water deep in the Bases of large black Mountains.—
We had come along a complete mountain road, where if
one listened there was not a sound but that of Mountain
Streams. We walked 20 Miles by the side of Loch Awe
—every ten steps creating a new and beautiful picture—
sometimes through little wood—there are two islands on
the Lake each with a beautiful ruin—one of them rich
in ivy.—We are detained this morning by the rain.   I
will tell you exactly where we are. We are between
Loch Craignish and the sea just opposite Long Island.[1]
Yesterday our walk was of this description—the near
Hills were not very lofty but many of them steep,
beautifully wooded—the distant Mountains in the Hebrides very grand, the Saltwater Lakes coming up between
Crags and Islands full tide and scarcely ruffled—sometimes appearing as one large Lake, sometimes as three
distinct ones in different directions. At one point we
saw afar off a rocky opening into the main sea.—We
have also seen an Eagle or two. They move about without the least motion of Wings when in an indolent fit.—
I am for the first time in a country where a foreign Language is spoken—they gabble away Gaelic at a vast rate
—numbers of them speak English. There are not many
Kilts in Argyleshire—at Fort William they say a Man is
not admitted into Society without one—the Ladies there
have a horror at the indecency of Breeches. I cannot
give you a better idea of Highland Life than by describ-
ing the place we are in. The Inn or public is by far the
best house in the immediate neighbourhood. It has a
white front with tolerable windows—the table I am

---

[1] By Long Island Keats means, not of course the great chain
of the Outer Hebrides so styled, but the little island of Luing,
east of Scarba Sound. His account of the place from which he
is writing, and its distance from Oban as specified in the para-
graph added there next day, seem to identify it certainly as Kil-
melfort.

writing on surprises me as being a nice flapped Mahogany one. . . . You may if you peep see through the floor chinks into the ground rooms. The old Grandmother of the house seems intelligent though not over clean. *N.B.* No snuff being to be had in the village she made us some. The Guid Man is a rough-looking hardy stout Man who I think does not speak so much English as the Guid wife who is very obliging and sensible and moreover though stockingless has a pair of old Shoes —Last night some Whisky Men sat up clattering Gaelic till I am sure one o'Clock to our great annoyance. There is a Gaelic testament on the Drawers in the next room. White and blue China ware has crept all about here— Yesterday there passed a Donkey laden with tin-pots— opposite the Window there are hills in a Mist—a few Ash trees and a mountain stream at a little distance.— They possess a few head of Cattle.—If you had gone round to the back of the House just now—you would have seen more hills in a Mist—some dozen wretched black Cottages scented of peat smoke which finds its way by the door or a hole in the roof—a girl here and there barefoot. There was one little thing driving Cows down a slope like a mad thing. There was another standing at the cowhouse door rather pretty fac'd all up to the ankles in dirt.

[Oban, July 21.]

We have walk'd 15 Miles in a soaking rain to Oban opposite the Isle of Mull which is so near Staffa we had thought to pass to it — but the expense is 7 Guineas and those rather extorted.—Staffa you see is a fashionable place and therefore every one concerned with it either in this town or the Island are what you call up. 'Tis like paying sixpence for an apple at the playhouse—this irritated me and Brown was not best pleased—we have therefore resolved to set northward for fort William to-morrow morning. I fed upon a bit of white Bread to-day like a Sparrow—it was very fine—I

cannot manage the cursed Oat Cake.   Remember me to
all and let me hear a good account of you at Inverness—
I am sorry Georgy had not those lines.   Good-bye.

    Your affectionate Brother   JOHN ——.

LXII.—TO BENJAMIN BAILEY.

Inverary, July 18 [1818].

    My dear Bailey—The only day I have had a chance
of seeing you when you were last in London I took
every advantage of—some devil led you out of the way
—Now I have written to Reynolds to tell me where you
will be in Cumberland—so that I cannot miss you.   And
when I see you, the first thing I shall do will be to read
that about Milton and Ceres, and Proserpine—for though
I am not going after you to John o' Grot's, it will be but
poetical to say so.   And here, Bailey, I will say a few
words written in a sane and sober mind, a very scarce
thing with me, for they may, hereafter, save you a great
deal of trouble about me, which you do not deserve, and
for which I ought to be bastinadoed.   I carry all matters
to an extreme—so that when I have any little vexation,
it grows in five minutes into a theme for Sophocles.
Then, and in that temper, if I write to any friend, I have
so little self-possession that I give him matter for grieving at the very time perhaps when I am laughing at a
Pun.   Your last letter made me blush for the pain I had
given you—I know my own disposition so well that I
am certain of writing many times hereafter in the same
strain to you—now, you know how far to believe in
them.   You must allow for Imagination.   I know I
shall not be able to help it.

    I am sorry you are grieved at my not continuing my
visits to Little Britain—Yet I think I have as far as a
Man can do who has Books to read and subjects to think
upon—for that reason I have been nowhere else except
to Wentworth Place so nigh at hand—moreover I have

been too often in a state of health that made it prudent
not to hazard the night air.   Yet, further, I will confess
to you that I cannot enjoy Society small or numerous—
I am certain that our fair friends are glad I should come
for the mere sake of my coming; but I am certain I
bring with me a vexation they are better without—If I
can possibly at any time feel my temper coming upon
me I refrain even from a promised visit.   I am certain
I have not a right feeling towards women—at this moment, I am striving to be just to them, but I cannot—
Is it because they fall so far beneath my boyish Imagination?   When I was a schoolboy I thought a fair woman
a pure Goddess ; my mind was a soft nest in which some
one of them slept, though she knew it not.   I have no
right to expect more than their reality—I thought them
ethereal above men—I find them perhaps equal—great
by comparison is very small.   Insult may be inflicted in
more ways than by word or action—One who is tender
of being insulted does not like to think an insult against
another.   I do not like to think insults in a lady's company—I commit a crime with her which absence would
not have known.   Is it not extraordinary ?—when among
men, I have no evil thoughts, no malice, no spleen—I
feel free to speak or to be silent—I can listen, and from
every one I can learn—my hands are in my pockets, I
am free from all suspicion and comfortable.   When I am
among women, I have evil thoughts, malice, spleen—I
cannot speak, or be silent—I am full of suspicions and
therefore listen to nothing—I am in a hurry to be gone.
You must be charitable and put all this perversity to my
being disappointed since my boyhood.   Yet with such
feelings I am happier alone among crowds of men, by
myself, or with a friend or two.   With all this, trust me,
I have not the least idea that men of different feelings
and inclinations are more short-sighted than myself.   I
never rejoiced more than at my Brother's marriage, and
shall do so at that of any of my friends.   I must abso-
lutely get over this—but how ? the only way is to find

the root of the evil, and so cure it "with backward mutters of dissevering power "—that is a difficult thing ; for an obstinate Prejudice can seldom be produced but from a gordian complication of feelings, which must take time to unravel, and care to keep unravelled. I could say a good deal about this, but I will leave it, in hopes of better and more worthy dispositions—and also content that I am wronging no one, for after all I do think better of womankind than to suppose they care whether Mister John Keats five feet high likes them or not. You appeared to wish to know my moods on this subject— don't think it a bore my dear fellow, it shall be my Amen. I should not have consented to myself these four months tramping in the highlands, but that I thought it would give me more experience, rub off more prejudice, use to more hardship, identify finer scenes, load me with grander mountains, and strengthen more my reach in Poetry, than would stopping at home among books, even though I should reach Homer. By this time I am comparatively a Mountaineer. I have been among wilds and mountains too much to break out much about their grandeur. I have fed upon oat-cake—not long enough to be very much attached to it.—The first mountains I saw, though not so large as some I have since seen, weighed very solemnly upon me. The effect is wearing away—yet I like them mainly.

[Island of Mull, July 22.]

We have come this Evening with a guide—for without was impossible—into the middle of the Isle of Mull, pursuing our cheap journey to Iona, and perhaps Staffa. We would not follow the common and fashionable mode, from the great Imposition of Expense. We have come over heath and rock, and river and bog, to what in England would be called a horrid place. Yet it belongs to a Shepherd pretty well off perhaps. The family speak not a word but Gaelic, and we have not yet seen their faces for the smoke, which, after visiting every cranny (not excepting my eyes very much incommoded for writing), finds its way out at the door. I am more comfortable than I could have imagined in such a place, and so is Brown. The people are all very kind—We lost our way a little yesterday; and inquiring at a Cottage, a young woman without a word threw on her cloak and walked a mile in a mizzling rain and splashy way to put us right again.

I could not have had a greater pleasure in these parts than your mention of my sister. She is very much prisoned from me. I am afraid it will be some time before I can take her to many places I wish. I trust we shall see you ere long in Cumberland—At least I hope I shall, before my visit to America, more than once. I intend to pass a whole year there, if I live to the completion of the three next. My sister's welfare, and the hopes of such a stay in America, will make me observe your advice. I shall be prudent and more careful of my health than I have been. I hope you will be about paying your first visit to Town after settling when we come into Cumberland— Cumberland however will be no distance to me after my present journey. I shall spin to you in a Minute. I begin to get rather a contempt of distances. I hope you will have a nice convenient room for a library. Now you are so well in health, do keep it up by never missing your dinner, by not reading hard, and by taking proper exercise. You'll have a horse, I suppose, so you must make a point of sweating him. You say I must study Dante —well, the only Books I have with me are those 3 little volumes.[1] I read that fine passage you mention a few days ago. Your letter followed me from Hampstead to Port-Patrick, and thence to Glasgow. You must think me by this time a very pretty fellow. One of the pleasantest bouts we have had was our walk to Burns's Cottage, over the Doon, and past Kirk Alloway. I had determined to write a Sonnet in the Cottage. I did— but lawk ! it was so wretched I destroyed it—however in a few days afterwards I wrote some lines cousin-german

[1] Cary's translation.

to the circumstance, which I will transcribe, or rather cross-scribe in the front of this.

Reynolds's illness has made him a new man—he will be stronger than ever—before I left London he was really getting a fat face. Brown keeps on writing volumes of adventures to Dilke. When we get in of an evening and I have perhaps taken my rest on a couple of chairs, he affronts my indolence and Luxury by pulling out of his knapsack 1st his paper—2ndly his pens and last his ink. Now I would not care if he would change a little. I say now why not Bailey, take out his pens first sometimes—But I might as well tell a hen to hold up her head before she drinks instead of afterwards.

Your affectionate Friend,   JOHN KEATS.

LINES WRITTEN IN THE HIGHLANDS AFTER A VISIT TO BURNS'S COUNTRY

There is a charm in footing slow across a silent plain,
Where patriot Battle has been fought, where glory had the gain ;
There is a pleasure on the heath where Druids old have been,
Where Mantles gray have rustled by and swept the nettles green ;
There is a Joy in every spot made known by times of old,
New to the feet, although each tale a hundred times be told ;
There is a deeper Joy than all, more solemn in the heart,
More parching to the tongue than all, of more divine a smart,
When weary steps forget themselves, upon a pleasant turf,
Upon hot sand, or flinty road, or sea-shore iron scurf,
Toward the Castle, or the Cot, where long ago was born
One who was great through mortal days, and died of fame unshorn.
Light heather-bells may tremble then, but they are far away ;
Wood-lark may sing from sandy fern,—the sun may hear his Lay ;
Runnels may kiss the grass on shelves and shallows clear,
But their low voices are not heard, though come on travels drear ;
Blood-red the sun may set behind black mountain peaks ;
Blue tides may sluice and drench their time in Caves and weedy
      creeks ;
Eagles may seem to sleep wing-wide upon the Air ;
Ring-doves may fly convuls'd across to some high-cedar'd lair ;
But the forgotten eye is still fast lidded to the ground,
As Palmer's, that, with weariness, mid-desert shrine hath found.
   At such a time the Soul's a child, in childhood is the brain ;
Forgotten is the worldly heart—alone, it beats in vain.—

Aye, if a Madman could have leave to pass a healthful day
To tell his forehead's swoon and faint when first began decay,
He might make tremble many a one whose spirit had gone forth
To find a Bard's low cradle-place about the silent North.
· Scanty the hour and few the steps beyond the bourn of Care,
Beyond the sweet and bitter world,—beyond it unaware !
Scanty the hour and few the steps, because a longer stay
Would bar return, and make a man forget his mortal way :
O horrible ! to lose the sight of well remember'd face,
Of Brother's eyes, of Sister's brow—constant to every place ;
Filling the Air, as on we move, with Portraiture intense ;
More warm than those heroic tints that pain a Painter's sense,
When shapes of old come striding by, and visages of old,
Locks shining black, hair scanty gray, and passions manifold.
No No, that horror cannot be, for at the cable's length
Man feels the gentle anchor pull and gladdens in its strength :—
One hour, half-idiot, he stands by mossy waterfall,
But in the very next he reads his soul's Memorial :—
He reads it on the mountain's height, where chance he may sit
        down
Upon rough marble diadem—that hill's eternal Crown.
Yet be his Anchor e'er so fast, room is there for a prayer
That man may never lose his Mind on Mountains black and bare ;
That he may stray league after league some Great birthplace to
        find
And keep his vision clear from speck, his inward sight unblind.

LXIII.—TO THOMAS KEATS.

Dun an cullen,[1] Island of Mull [July 23, 1818].

My dear Tom—Just after my last had gone to the
Post, in came one of the Men with whom we endeavoured
to agree about going to Staffa—he said what a pity it was
we should turn aside and not see the curiosities.   So we
had a little talk, and finally agreed that he should be our
guide across the Isle of Mull.   We set out, crossed two
ferries—one to the Isle of Kerrara, of little distance ; the
other from Kerrara to Mull 9 Miles across—we did it

---

[1] No place so named appears on any map : but at the foot of
the Cruach-Doire-nan-Cuilean, off the road, is a house named
Derrynaculan, and a few miles farther on, at the head of Loch
Seridain, an ancient fortified site or *Dun*, with an inn on the road
near by.

in forty minutes with a fine Breeze.   The road through
the Island, or rather the track, is the most dreary you can
think of—between dreary Mountains, over bog and rock
and river with our Breeches tucked up and our Stockings
in hand.   About 8 o'Clock we arrived at a shepherd's
Hut, into which we could scarcely get for the Smoke
through a door lower than my Shoulders.   We found our
way into a little compartment with the rafters and turf-
thatch blackened with smoke, the earth floor full of Hills
and Dales.   We had some white Bread with us, made a
good supper, and slept in our Clothes in some Blankets ;
our Guide snored on another little bed about an Arm's
length off.   This morning we came about sax Miles to
Breakfast, by rather a better path, and we are now in by
comparison a Mansion.   Our Guide is I think a very
obliging fellow—in the way this morning he sang us
two Gaelic songs—one made by a Mrs. Brown on her
husband's being drowned, the other a jacobin one on
Charles Stuart.   For some days Brown has been enquiring
out his Genealogy here—he thinks his Grandfather came
from long Island.   He got a parcel of people about him
at a Cottage door last Evening, chatted with ane who had
been a Miss Brown, and who I think from a likeness,
must have been a Relation—he jawed with the old Woman
—flattered a young one—kissed a child who was afraid of
his Spectacles and finally drank a pint of Milk.   They
handle his Spectacles as we do a sensitive leaf.

[Oban,] July 26th.

Well—we had a most wretched walk of 37 Miles
across the Island of Mull and then we crossed to Iona
or Icolmkill—from Icolmkill we took a boat at a
bargain to take us to Staffa and land us at the head
of Loch Nakgal,[1] whence we should only have to walk
half the distance to Oban again and on a better road.
All this is well passed and done, with this singular
piece of Luck, that there was an interruption in the bad

[1] For Loch na Keal.

Weather just as we saw Staffa at which it is impossible
to land but in a tolerable Calm sea. But I will first
mention Icolmkill—I know not whether you have heard
much about this Island; I never did before I came nigh
it. It is rich in the most interesting Antiquities. Who
would expect to find the ruins of a fine Cathedral Church,
of Cloisters Colleges Monasteries and Nunneries in so
remote an Island? The Beginning of these things was
in the sixth Century, under the superstition of a would-
be-Bishop-saint, who landed from Ireland, and chose the
spot from its Beauty—for at that time the now treeless
place was covered with magnificent Woods. Columba
in the Gaelic is Colm, signifying Dove—Kill signifies
church, and I is as good as Island—so I-colm-kill means
the Island of Saint Columba's Church. Now this Saint
Columba became the Dominic of the barbarian Christians of the north and was famed also far south—but
more especially was reverenced by the Scots the Picts
the Norwegians the Irish. In a course of years perhaps the Island was considered the most holy ground of
the north, and the old Kings of the aforementioned
nations chose it for their burial-place. We were shown
a spot in the Churchyard where they say 61 Kings
are buried 48 Scotch from Fergus II. to Macbeth
8 Irish 4 Norwegians and 1 French—they lie in rows
compact. Then we were shown other matters of later
date, but still very ancient—many tombs of Highland
Chieftains—their effigies in complete armour, face up-
wards, black and moss-covered—Abbots and Bishops of
the island always of one of the chief Clans. There were
plenty Macleans and Macdonnels; among these latter,
the famous Macdonel Lord of the Isles. There have
been 300 Crosses in the Island but the Presbyterians
destroyed all but two, one of which is a very fine one,
and completely covered with a shaggy coarse Moss. The
old Schoolmaster, an ignorant little man but reckoned
very clever, showed us these things. He is a Maclean,
and as much above 4 foot as he is under 4 foot three

inches.   He stops at one glass of whisky unless you
press another and at the second unless you press a
third—

I· am puzzled how to give you an Idea of Staffa.   It
can only be represented by a first-rate drawing.   One
may compare the surface of the Island to a roof—this
roof is supported by grand pillars of basalt standing
together as thick as honeycombs.   The finest thing is
Fingal's Cave—it is entirely a hollowing out of Basalt
Pillars.   Suppose now the Giants who rebelled against
Jove had taken a whole Mass of black Columns and
bound them together like bunches of matches—and then
with immense axes had made a cavern in the body of
these columns—Of course the roof and floor must be
composed of the broken ends of the Columns—such is
Fingal's Cave, except that the Sea has done the work of
excavations, and is continually dashing there—so that
we walk along the sides of the cave on the pillars which
are left as if for convenient stairs.   The roof is arched
somewhat gothic-wise, and the length of some of the
entire side-pillars is fifty feet.   About the island you
might seat an army of Men each on a pillar.   The length
of the Cave is 120 feet, and from its extremity the view
into the sea, through the large Arch at the entrance—the
colour of the columns is a sort of black with a lurking
gloom of purple therein.   For solemnity and grandeur it
far surpasses the finest Cathedral.   At the extremity of
the Cave there is a small perforation into another cave,
at which the waters meeting and buffeting each other
there is sometimes produced a report as of a cannon
heard as far as Iona, which must be 12 Miles.   As we
approached in the boat, there was such a fine swell of
the sea that the pillars appeared rising immediately out
of the crystal.   But it is impossible to describe it—

> Not Aladdin magian
> Ever such a work began.
> Not the Wizard of the Dee
> Ever such a dream could see,

Not St. John in Patmos Isle
In the passion of his toil
When he saw the churches seven
Golden-aisled built up in heaven
Gaz'd at such a rugged wonder.
As I stood its roofing under
Lo! I saw one sleeping there
On the marble cold and bare.
While the surges wash'd his feet
And his garments white did beat
Drench'd about the sombre rocks,
On his neck his well-grown locks
Lifted dry above the Main
Were upon the curl again—
"What is this? and what art thou?"
Whisper'd I, and touch'd his brow;
"What art thou? and what is this?"
Whisper'd I, and strove to kiss
The Spirit's hand, to wake his eyes;
Up he started in a trice:
"I am Lycidas, "said he,
"Fam'd in funeral Minstrelsy—
This was architected thus
By the great Oceanus.
Here his mighty waters play
Hollow Organs all the day,
Here, by turns, his dolphins all,
Finny palmers great and small,
Come to pay devotion due—
Each a mouth of pearls must strew!
Many a Mortal of these days
Dares to pass our sacred ways,
Dares to touch, audaciously
This Cathedral of the sea—
I have been the Pontiff-priest,
Where the Waters never rest,
Where a fledgy sea-bird choir
Soars for ever—holy fire
I have hid from Mortal Man.
Proteus is my Sacristan.
But the stupid eye of Mortal
Hath pass'd beyond the Rocky portal,
So for ever will I leave
Such a taint and soon unweave
All the magic of the place—
'Tis now free to stupid face—
To cutters and to fashion boats,

> To cravats and to Petticoats.
> The great Sea shall war it down,
> For its fame shall not be blown
> At every farthing quadrille dance."[1]
> So saying with a Spirit's glance
> He dived——

I am sorry I am so indolent as to write such stuff as this. It can't be helped. The western coast of Scotland is a most strange place—it is composed of rocks, Mountains, mountainous and rocky Islands intersected by lochs—you can go but a short distance anywhere from salt water in the highlands.

I have a slight sore throat and think it best to stay a day or two at Oban—then we shall proceed to Fort William and Inverness, where I am anxious to be on account of a Letter from you. Brown in his Letters puts down every little circumstance. I should like to do the same, but I confess myself too indolent, and besides next winter everything will come up in prime order as we verge on such and such things.

Have you heard in any way of George? I should think by this time he must have landed. I in my carelessness never thought of knowing where a letter would find him on the other side—I think Baltimore, but I am afraid of directing it to the wrong place. I shall begin some chequer work for him directly, and it will be ripe for the post by the time I hear from you next after this. I assure you I often long for a seat and a Cup o' tea at Well Walk, especially now that mountains, castles, and Lakes are becoming common to me. Yet I would rather summer it out, for on the whole I am happier than when I have time to be glum—perhaps it may cure me. Immediately on my return I shall begin studying hard, with a peep at the theatre now and then—and depend upon it I shall be very luxurious. With respect to Women I think I shall be able to conquer my passions

---

[1] The six lines from "place" to "dance" were judiciously omitted by Keats in copying these verses later.

hereafter better than I have yet done. You will help me to talk of George next winter, and we will go now and then to see Fanny. Let me hear a good account of your health and comfort, telling me truly how you do alone. Remember me to all including Mr. and Mrs. Bentley.

Your most affectionate Brother   JOHN.

LXIV.—TO THOMAS KEATS.

Letter Findlay, August 3 [1818].

Ah mio Ben.

My dear Tom—We have made but poor progress lately, chiefly from bad weather, for my throat is in a fair way of getting quite well, so I have had nothing of consequence to tell you till yesterday when we went up Ben Nevis, the highest Mountain in Great Britain. On that account I will never ascend another in this empire—Skiddaw is nothing to it either in height or in difficulty. It is above 4300 feet from the Sea level, and Fortwilliam stands at the head of a Salt water Lake, consequently we took it completely from that level. I am heartily glad it is done—it is almost like a fly crawling up a wainscoat. Imagine the task of mounting ten Saint Pauls without the convenience of Staircases. We set out about five in the morning with a Guide in the Tartan and Cap, and soon arrived at the foot of the first ascent which we immediately began upon. After much fag and tug and a rest and a glass of whisky apiece we gained the top of the first rise and saw then a tremendous chap above us, which the guide said was still far from the top. After the first Rise our way lay along a heath valley in which there was a Loch—after about a Mile in this Valley we began upon the next ascent, more formidable by far than the last, and kept mounting with short intervals of rest until we got above all vegetation, among nothing but loose Stones which lasted us to the very top. The Guide said we had three Miles of a stony ascent—we gained the first tolerable level after the valley to the height of what in the Valley we had thought the top and saw still above us another huge crag which still the Guide said was not the top—to that we made with an obstinate fag, and having gained it there came on a Mist, so that from that part to the very top we walked in a Mist. The whole immense head of the Mountain is composed of large loose stones—thousands of acres. Before we had got halfway up we passed large patches of snow and near the top there is a chasm some hundred feet deep completely glutted with it.—Talking of chasms they are the finest wonder of the whole—they appear great rents in the very heart of the mountain though they are not, being at the side of it, but other huge crags arising round it give the appearance to Nevis of a shattered heart or Core in itself. These Chasms are 1500 feet in depth and are the most tremendous places I have ever seen— they turn one giddy if you choose to give way to it. We tumbled in large stones and set the echoes at work in fine style. Sometimes these chasms are tolerably clear, sometimes there is a misty cloud which seems to steam up and sometimes they are entirely smothered with clouds.

After a little time the Mist cleared away but still there were large Clouds about attracted by old Ben to a certain distance so as to form as it appeared large dome curtains which kept sailing about, opening and shutting at intervals here and there and everywhere: so that although we did not see one vast wide extent of prospect all round we saw something perhaps finer—these cloud-veils opening with a dissolving motion and showing us the mountainous region beneath as through a loophole— these cloudy loopholes ever varying and discovering fresh prospect east, west, north and south. Then it was misty again, and again it was fair—then puff came a cold breeze of wind and bared a craggy chap we had not yet seen though in close neighbourhood. Every now and then we had overhead blue Sky clear and the sun pretty warm. I do not know whether I can give you an Idea of the prospect from a large Mountain top.   You are on a stony plain which of course makes you forget you are on any but low ground—the horizon or rather edges of this plain being above 4000 feet above the Sea hide all the Country immediately beneath you, so that the next object you see all round next to the edges of the flat top are the Summits of Mountains of some distance off.   As you move about on all sides you see more or less of the near neighbour country according as the Mountain you stand upon is in different parts steep or rounded—but the most new thing of all is the sudden leap of the eye from the extremity of what appears a plain into so vast a distance. On one part of the top there is a handsome pile of Stones done pointedly by some soldiers of artillery; I clim[b]ed on to them and so got a little higher than old Ben himself. It was not so cold as I expected—yet cold enough for a glass of Whisky now and then.   There is not a more fickle thing than the top of a Mountain—what would a Lady give to change her head-dress as often and with as little trouble!—There are a good many red deer upon Ben Nevis—we did not see one—the dog we had with us kept a very sharp look out and really languished for a bit of a worry.   I have said nothing yet of our getting on among the loose stones large and small sometimes on two, sometimes on three, sometimes four legs—sometimes two and stick, sometimes three and stick, then four again, then two, then a jump, so that we kept on ringing changes on foot, hand, stick, jump, boggle, stumble, foot, hand, foot (very gingerly), stick again, and then again a game at all fours.   After all there was one Mrs. Cameron of 50 years of age and the fattest woman in all Inverness-shire who got up this Mountain some few years ago—true she had her servants—but then she had her self.   She ought to have hired Sisyphus,—"Up the high hill he heaves a huge round—Mrs. Cameron."   'Tis said a little conversation took place between the mountain and the Lady.   After taking a glass of Whisky as she was tolerably seated at ease she thus began—

Mrs. C.

Upon my Life Sir Nevis I am pique'd
That I have so far panted tugg'd and reek'd
To do an honor to your old bald pate
And now am sitting on you just to bait,
Without your paying me one compliment.
Alas 'tis so with all, when our intent
Is plain, and in the eye of all Mankind
We fair ones show a preference, too blind !
You Gentle man immediately turn tail—
O let me then my hapless fate bewail !
Ungrateful Baldpate have I not disdain'd
The pleasant Valleys—have I not madbrain'd
Deserted all my Pickles and preserves
My China closet too—with wretched Nerves
To boot—say wretched ingrate have I not
Left my soft cushion chair and caudle pot.
'Tis true I had no corns—no ! thank the fates
My Shoemaker was always Mr. Bates.
And if not Mr. Bates why I'm not old !
Still dumb ungrateful Nevis—still so cold !

Here the Lady took some more whisky and was putting
even more to her lips when she dashed it to the Ground
for the Mountain began to grumble—which continued
for a few minutes before he thus began—

Ben Nevis.

What whining bit of tongue and Mouth thus dares
Disturb my slumber of a thousand years ?
Even so long my sleep has been secure—
And to be so awaked I'll not endure.
Oh pain—for since the Eagle's earliest scream
I've had a damn'd confounded ugly dream,
A Nightmare sure.   What Madam was it you ?
It cannot be !   My old eyes are not true !
Red-Crag, my Spectacles !   Now let me see !
Good Heavens Lady how the gemini
Did you get here ?   O I shall split my sides !
I shall earthquake——

Mrs. C.

Sweet Nevis do not quake, for though I love
Your honest Countenance all things above

Truly I should not like to be convey'd
So far into your Bosom—gentle Maid
Loves not too rough a treatment gentle Sir—
Pray thee be calm and do not quake nor stir
No not a Stone or I shall go in fits—

Ben Nevis.

I must—I shall—I meet not such tit bits—
I meet not such sweet creatures every day—
By my old night cap night cap night and day
I must have one sweet Buss—I must and shall !
Red Crag !—What Madam can you then repent
Of all the toil and vigour you have spent
To see Ben Nevis and to touch his nose ?
Red Crag I say !   O I must have them close !
Red Crag, there lies beneath my farthest toe
A vein of Sulphur—go dear Red Crag, go—
And rub your flinty back against it—budge !
Dear Madam I must kiss you, faith I must !
I must Embrace you with my dearest gust !
Block-head, d'ye hear—Block-head I'll make her feel
There lies beneath my east leg's northern heel
A cave of young earth dragons—well my boy
Go thither quick and so complete my joy
Take you a bundle of the largest pines
And when the sun on fiercest Phosphor shines
Fire them and ram them in the Dragon's nest
Then will the dragons fry and fizz their best
Until ten thousand now no bigger than
Poor Alligators—poor things of one span—
Will each one swell to twice ten times the size
Of northern whale—then for the tender prize—
The moment then—for then will Red Crag rub
His flinty back—and I shall kiss and snub
And press my dainty morsel to my breast.
Block-head make haste !
                    O Muses weep the rest—
The Lady fainted and he thought her dead
So pulled the clouds again about his head
And went to sleep again—soon she was rous'd
By her affrighted servants—next day hous'd
Safe on the lowly ground she bless'd her fate
That fainting fit was not delayed too late.

But what surprises me above all is how this Lady got
down again. I felt it horribly. 'Twas the most vile

descent—shook me all to pieces.   Over leaf you will find a Sonnet I wrote on the top of Ben Nevis.   We have just entered Inverness.   I have three Letters from you and one from Fanny—and one from Dilke.   I would set about crossing this all over for you but I will first write to Fanny and Mrs. Wylie.   Then I will begin another to you and not before because I think it better you should have this as soon as possible.   My Sore throat is not quite well and I intend stopping here a few days.

> Read me a lesson, Muse, and speak it loud
>   Upon the top of Nevis, blind in mist !
> I look into the chasms, and a shroud
>   Vapourous doth hide them,—just so much I wist
> Mankind do know of hell ; I look o'erhead,
>   And there is sullen mist,—even so much
> Mankind can tell of heaven ; mist is spread
>   Before the earth, beneath me,—even such,
> Even so vague is man's sight of himself !
>   Here are the craggy stones beneath my feet,—
>   Thus much I know that, a poor witless elf,
>   I tread on them,—that all my eye doth meet
> Is mist and crag, not only on this height,
> But in the world of thought and mental might !

Good-bye till to morrow.
Your most affectionate Brother   JOHN ——.

LXV.—TO MRS. WYLIE.

Inverness, August 6 [1818].

My dear Madam—It was a great regret to me that I should leave all my friends, just at the moment when I might have helped to soften away the time for them.   I wanted not to leave my brother Tom, but more especially, believe me, I should like to have remained near you, were it but for an atom of consolation after parting with so dear a daughter.   My brother George has ever been more than a brother to me ; he has been my greatest friend, and I can never forget the sacrifice you have made for his happiness.   As I walk along the Mountains here I am

full of these things, and lay in wait, as it were, for the
pleasure of seeing you immediately on my return to town.
I wish, above all things, to say a word of Comfort to you,
but I know not how. It is impossible to prove that
black is white; it is impossible to make out that sorrow
is joy, or joy is sorrow.

Tom tells me that you called on Mr. Haslam, with a
newspaper giving an account of a gentleman in a Fur cap
falling over a precipice in Kirkcudbrightshire. If it was
me, I did it in a dream, or in some magic interval between
the first and second cup of tea; which is nothing extraordinary when we hear that Mahomet, in getting out of
Bed, upset a jug of water, and, whilst it was falling, took
a fortnight's trip, as it seemed, to Heaven; yet was back
in time to save one drop of water being spilt. As for Fur
caps, I do not remember one beside my own, except at
Carlisle : this was a very good Fur cap I met in High
Street, and I daresay was the unfortunate one. I daresay that the fates, seeing but two Fur caps in the north,
thought it too extraordinary, and so threw the dies which
of them should be drowned. The lot fell upon Jones : I
daresay his name was Jones. All I hope is that the
gaunt Ladies said not a word about hanging; if they did I
shall repent that I was not half-drowned in Kirkcudbright.
Stop! let me see !—being half-drowned by falling from a
precipice, is a . very romantic affair : why should I not
take it to myself? How glorious to be introduced in a
drawing-room to a Lady who reads Novels, with "Mr.
So-and-so—Miss So-and-so; Miss So-and-so, this is Mr.
So-and-so, who fell off a precipice and was half-drowned."
Now I refer to you, whether I should lose so fine an
opportunity of making my fortune. No romance lady
could resist me—none. Being run under a Waggon—side-
lamed in a playhouse, Apoplectic through Brandy—and a
thousand other tolerably decent things for badness, would
be nothing, but being tumbled over a precipice into the
sea—oh! it would make my fortune—especially if you
could contrive to hint, from this bulletin's authority, that

I was not upset on my own account, but that I dashed into the waves after Jessy of Dumblane, and pulled her out by the hair.   But that, alas! she was dead, or she would have made me happy with her hand—however in this you may use your own discretion.   But I must leave joking, and seriously aver, that I have been very romantic indeed among these Mountains and Lakes.   I have got wet through, day after day—eaten oat-cake, and drank Whisky—walked up to my knees in Bog—got a sore throat—gone to see Icolmkill and Staffa; met with wholesome food just here and there as it happened—went up Ben Nevis, and—*N.B.*, came down again.   Sometimes when I am rather tired I lean rather languishingly on a rock, and long for some famous Beauty to get down from her Palfrey in passing, approach me, with—her saddle-bags, and give me—a dozen or two capital roast-beef Sandwiches.

When I come into a large town, you know there is no putting one's Knapsack into one's fob, so the people stare. We have been taken for Spectacle-vendors, Razor-sellers, Jewellers, travelling linendrapers, Spies, Excisemen, and many things I have no idea of.   When I asked for letters at Port Patrick, the man asked what regiment?   I have had a peep also at little Ireland.   Tell Henry I have not camped quite on the bare Earth yet, but nearly as bad, in walking through Mull, for the Shepherds' huts you can scarcely breathe in, for the Smoke which they seem to endeavour to preserve for smoking on a large scale.   Besides riding about 400, we have walked above 600 Miles, and may therefore reckon ourselves as set out.

I assure you, my dear Madam, that one of the greatest pleasures I shall have on my return, will be seeing you, and that I shall ever be

Yours, with the greatest respect and sincerity,

JOHN KEATS.

LXVI.—TO FANNY KEATS.

Hampstead, August 18 [1818].

My dear Fanny—I am afraid you will think me
very negligent in not having answered your Letter—I
see it is dated June 12. I did not arrive at Inverness
till the 8th of this Month so I am very much concerned
at your being disappointed so long a time. I did not
intend to have returned to London so soon but have a
bad sore throat from a cold I caught in the island of
Mull : therefore I thought it best to get home as soon as
possible, and went on board the Smack from Cromarty.
We had a nine days' passage and were landed at London
Bridge yesterday. I shall have a good deal to tell you
about Scotland—I would begin here but I have a confounded toothache. Tom has not been getting better
since I left London and for the last fortnight has been
worse than ever—he has been getting a little better for
these two or three days. I shall ask Mr. Abbey to let
me bring you to Hampstead. If Mr. A. should see this
Letter tell him that he still must if he pleases forward
the Post Bill to Perth as I have empowered my fellow
traveller to receive it. I have a few Scotch pebbles for
you from the Island of Icolmkill—I am afraid they are
rather shabby—I did not go near the Mountain of Cairn
Gorm. I do not know the Name of George's ship—the
Name of the Port he has gone to is Philadelphia whence
he will travel to the Settlement across the Country—I
will tell you all about this when I see you. The Title of
my last Book is Endymion—you shall have one soon.—
I would not advise you to play on the Flageolet—however
I will get you one if you please. I will speak to Mr.
Abbey on what you say concerning school. I am sorry
for your poor Canary. You shall have another volume
of my first Book. My toothache keeps on so that I
cannot write with any pleasure—all I can say now is
that your Letter is a very nice one without fault and

M

that you will hear from or see in a few days if his throat
will let him,

Your affectionate Brother   JOHN.

LXVII.—TO FANNY KEATS.

Hampstead, Tuesday [August 25, 1818].

My dear Fanny—I have just written to Mr. Abbey to
ask him to let you come and see poor Tom who has lately
been much worse.   He is better at present—sends his
Love to you and wishes much to see you—I hope he will
shortly—I have not been able to come to Walthamstow
on his account as well as a little Indisposition of my own.
I have asked Mr. A. to write me—if he does not mention
anything of it to you, I will tell you what reasons he
has though I do not think he will make any objection.
Write me what you want with a Flageolet and I will get
one ready for you by the time you come.

Your affectionate Brother   JOHN ———.

LXVIII.—TO JANE REYNOLDS.

Well Walk, September 1st [1818].

My dear Jane—Certainly your kind note would rather
refresh than trouble me, and so much the more would
your coming if as you say, it could be done without agitat-
ing my Brother too much.   Receive on your Hearth our
deepest thanks for your Solicitude concerning us.

I am glad John is not hurt, but gone safe into Devonshire—I shall be in great expectation of his Letter—but
the promise of it in so anxious and friendly a way I prize
more than a hundred.   I shall be in town to-day on some
business with my guardian "as was" with scarce a hope
of being able to call on you.   For these two last days
Tom has been more cheerful : you shall hear again soon
how he will be.

Remember us particularly to your Mother.

Your sincere friend   JOHN KEATS.

LXIX.—TO CHARLES WENTWORTH DILKE.

[Hampstead, September 21 1818.]

My dear Dilke—According to the Wentworth place Bulletin you have left Brighton much improved: therefore now a few lines will be more of a pleasure than a bore. I have things to say to you, and would fain begin upon them in this fourth line: but I have a Mind too well regulated to proceed upon anything without due preliminary remarks.—You may perhaps have observed that in the simple process of eating radishes I never begin at the root but constantly dip the little green head in the salt—that in the Game of Whist if I have an ace I constantly play it first. So how can I with any face begin without a dissertation on letter-writing? Yet when I consider that a sheet of paper contains room only for three pages and a half, how can I do justice to such a pregnant subject? However, as you have seen the history of the world stamped as it were by a diminishing glass in the form of a chronological Map, so will I "with retractile claws" draw this into the form of a table—whereby it will occupy merely the remainder of this first page—

> Folio—Parsons, Lawyers, Statesmen, Physicians out of place—ut—Eustace—Thornton—out of practice or on their travels.
>
> Foolscap—1. Superfine—Rich or noble poets—ut Byron. 2. common ut egomet.
>
> Quarto—Projectors, Patentees, Presidents, Potato growers.
>
> Bath—Boarding schools, and suburbans in general.
>
> Gilt edge—Dandies in general, male, female, and literary.
>
> Octavo or tears—All who make use of a lascivious seal.
>
> Duodec.—May be found for the most part on Milliners' and Dressmakers' Parlour tables.

Strip—At the Playhouse-doors, or anywhere.
Slip—Being but a variation.
Snip—So called from its size being disguised by a
    twist.

I suppose you will have heard that Hazlitt has on foot
a prosecution against Blackwood. I dined with him a
few days since at Hessey's—there was not a word said
about it, though I understand he is excessively vexed.
Reynolds, by what I hear, is almost over-happy, and
Rice is in town. I have not seen him, nor shall I for
some time, as my throat has become worse after getting
well, and I am determined to stop at home till I am
quite well. I was going to Town to-morrow with Mrs. D.
but I thought it best to ask her excuse this morning. I
wish I could say Tom was any better. His identity
presses upon me so all day that I am obliged to go out
—and although I intended to have given some time to
study alone, I am obliged to write and plunge into abstract
images to ease myself of his countenance, his voice, and
feebleness—so that I live now in a continual fever. It
must be poisonous to life, although I feel well. Imagine
"the hateful siege of contraries"—if I think of fame, of
poetry, it seems a crime to me, and yet I must do so or
suffer. I am sorry to give you pain—I am almost
resolved to burn this—but I really have not self-possession
and magnanimity enough to manage the thing otherwise
—after all it may be a nervousness proceeding from the
Mercury.
    Bailey I hear is gaining his spirits, and he will yet
be what I once thought impossible, a cheerful Man—I
think he is not quite so much spoken of in Little Britain.
I forgot to ask Mrs. Dilke if she had anything she wanted
to say immediately to you. This morning look'd so un-
promising that I did not think she would have gone—
but I find she has, on sending for some volumes of
Gibbon. I was in a little funk yesterday, for I sent in
an unseal'd note of sham abuse, until I recollected, from

what I heard Charles say, that the servant could neither read nor write—not even to her Mother as Charles observed.   I have just had a Letter from Reynolds—he is going on gloriously.   The following is a translation of a line of Ronsard—

> Love pour'd her beauty into my warm veins.

You have passed your Romance, and I never gave in to it, or else I think this line a feast for one of your Lovers. How goes it with Brown ?

    Your sincere friend   JOHN KEATS.

LXX.—TO JOHN HAMILTON REYNOLDS.

[Hampstead, about September 22, 1818.]

My dear Reynolds—Believe me I have rather rejoiced at your happiness than fretted at your silence.   Indeed I am grieved on your account that I am not at the same time happy—But I conjure you to think at Present of nothing but pleasure—"Gather the rose, etc."—gorge the honey of life.   I pity you as much that it cannot last for ever, as I do myself now drinking bitters.   Give yourself up to it—you cannot help it—and I have a Consolation in thinking so.   I never was in love—Yet the voice and shape of a Woman has haunted me these two days [1]—at such a time, when the relief, the feverous relief of Poetry seems a much less crime—This morning Poetry has conquered—I have relapsed into those abstractions which are my only life—I feel escaped from a new strange and threatening sorrow—And I am thankful for it—There is an awful warmth about my heart like a load of Immortality.

    Poor Tom—that woman—and Poetry were ringing changes in my senses—Now I am in comparison happy— I am sensible this will distress you—you must forgive me.   Had I known you would have set out so soon I

---

[1] Miss Charlotte Cox, an East-Indian cousin of the Reynoldses— the " Charmian " described more fully in Letter LXXIII.

could have sent you the 'Pot of Basil' for I had copied
it out ready.—Here is a free translation of a Sonnet of
Ronsard, which I think will please you—I have the loan
of his works—they have great Beauties.

> Nature withheld Cassandra in the skies,
>   For more adornment, a full thousand. years;
> She took their cream of Beauty's fairest dyes,
>   And shap'd and tinted her above all Peers:
> Meanwhile Love kept her dearly with his wings,
>   And underneath their shadow fill'd her eyes
> With such a richness that the cloudy Kings
>   Of high Olympus utter'd slavish sighs.
> When from the Heavens I saw her first descend,
>   My heart took fire, and only burning pains,
> They were my pleasures—they my Life's sad end;
>   Love pour'd her beauty into my warm veins
>
>   .   .   .   .   .   .
>   .   .   .   .   .   .

I had not the original by me when I wrote it, and
did not recollect the purport of the last lines.

I should have seen Rice ere this—but I am confined
by Sawrey's mandate in the house now, and have as
yet only gone out in fear of the damp night.—You know
what an undangerous matter it is.   I shall soon be quite
recovered—Your offer I shall remember as though it had
even now taken place in fact—I think it cannot be.
Tom is not up yet—I cannot say he is better.   I have
not heard from George.

Your affectionate friend   JOHN KEATS.

LXXI.—TO FANNY KEATS.

[Hampstead, October 9, 1818.]

My dear Fanny—Poor Tom is about. the same as
when you saw him last; perhaps weaker—were it not
for that I should have been over to pay you a. visit these
fine days.   I got to the stage half an hour before it set
out and counted the buns and tarts in a Pastry-cook's
window and was just beginning with the Jellies.   There

was no one in the Coach who had a Mind to eat me like
Mr. Sham-deaf.   I shall be punctual in enquiring about
next Thursday—
    Your affectionate Brother   JOHN.

LXXII.—TO JAMES AUGUSTUS HESSEY.

[Hampstead, October 9, 1818.]

My dear Hessey—You are very good in sending me
the letters from the Chronicle—and I am very bad in not
acknowledging such a kindness sooner—pray forgive me.
It has so chanced that I have had that paper every day—
I have seen to-day's. /I cannot but feel indebted to those
Gentlemen who have taken my part—As for the rest, I
begin to get a little acquainted with my own strength
and weakness.—Praise or blame has but a momentary
effect on the man whose love of beauty in the abstract
makes him a severe critic on his own Works.   My own
domestic criticism has given me pain without comparison beyond what Blackwood or the Quarterly could
possibly inflict—and also when I feel I am right, no
external praise can give me such a glow as my own
solitary reperception and ratification of what is fine. J. S.
is perfectly right in regard to the slip-shod Endymion.[1]
That it is so is no fault of mine.   No !—though it may
sound a little paradoxical.   It is as good as I had power
to make it—by myself—Had I been nervous about its
being a perfect piece, and with that view asked advice,
and trembled over every page, it would not have been
written ; for it is not in my nature to fumble—I will
write independently.—I have written independently *without Judgment.*   I may write independently, and *with
Judgment,* hereafter.   The Genius of Poetry must work

---

[1] Referring to these words in John Scott's letter in his defence,
Morning Chronicle, October 3, 1818 :—" That there are also many,
very many passages indicating both haste and carelessness I will
not deny ; nay, I will go further, and assert that a real friend of
the author would have dissuaded him from immediate publication."

out its own salvation in a man : It cannot be matured
by law and precept, but by sensation and watchfulness
in itself—That which is creative must create itself—In
Endymion, I leaped headlong into the sea, and thereby
have become better acquainted with the Soundings, the
quicksands, and the rocks, than if I had stayed upon the
green shore, and piped a silly pipe, and took tea and
comfortable advice.   I was never afraid of failure ; for I
would sooner fail than not be among the greatest—But
I am nigh getting into a rant.   So, with remembrances
to Taylor and Woodhouse etc. I am

Yours very sincerely   JOHN KEATS.

LXXIII.—TO GEORGE AND GEORGIANA KEATS.

[Hampstead, October 13 or 14, 1818.]

My dear George—There was a part in your Letter
which gave me a great deal of pain, that where you
lament not receiving Letters from England.   I intended
to have written immediately on my return from Scotland
(which was two Months earlier than I had intended on
account of my own as well as Tom's health) but then I
was told by Mrs. W. that you had said you would not
wish any one to write till we had heard from you.   This
I thought odd and now I see that it could not have been
so ; yet at the time I suffered my unreflecting head to be
satisfied, and went on in that sort of abstract careless
and restless Life with which you are well acquainted.
This sentence should it give you any uneasiness do not
let it last for before I finish it will be explained away to
your satisfaction—

I am grieved to say I am not sorry you had not Letters
at Philadelphia; you could have had no good news of Tom
and I have been withheld on his account from beginning
these many days ; I could not bring myself to say the
truth, that he is no better but much worse—However it
must be told ; and you must my dear Brother and Sister
take example from me and bear up against any Calamity for

my sake as I do for yours.   Our's are ties which independent of their own Sentiment are sent us by providence to
prevent the deleterious effects of one great solitary grief.
I have Fanny and I have you—three people whose Happiness to me is sacred—and it does annul that selfish
sorrow which I should otherwise fall into, living as I do
with poor Tom who looks upon me as his only comfort—
the tears will come into your Eyes—let them—and
embrace each other—thank heaven for what happiness
you have, and after thinking a moment or two that you
suffer in common with all Mankind hold it not a sin to
regain your cheerfulness—

I will relieve you of one uneasiness of overleaf: I
returned I said on account of my health—I am now well
from a bad sore throat which came of bog trotting in the
Island of Mull—of which you shall hear by the copies I
shall make from my Scotch Letters—

Your content in each other is a delight to me which
I cannot express—the Moon is now shining full and
brilliant—she is the same to me in Matter, what you
are to me in Spirit.   If you were here my dear Sister I
could not pronounce the words which I can write to you
from a distance : I have a tenderness for you, and an
admiration which I feel to be as great and more chaste
than I can have for any woman in the world.   You will
mention Fanny—her character is not formed, her identity
does not press upon me as yours does.   I hope from the
bottom of my heart that I may one day feel as much for
her as I do for you—I know not how it is, but I have
never made any acquaintance of my own—nearly all
through your medium my dear Brother—through you I
know not only a Sister but a glorious human being.   And
now I am talking of those to whom you have made me
known I cannot forbear mentioning Haslam as a most
kind and obliging and constant friend.   His behaviour
to Tom during my absence and since my return has
endeared him to me for ever—besides his anxiety about
you.   To-morrow I shall call on your Mother and

exchange information with her. On Tom's account I
have not been able to pass so much time with her as I
would otherwise have done—I have seen her but twice
—once I dined with her and Charles—She was well, in
good spirits, and I kept her laughing at my bad jokes.
We went to tea at Mrs. Millar's, and in going were particularly struck with the light and shade through the
Gate way at the Horse Guards. I intend to write you
such Volumes that it will be impossible for me to keep
any order or method in what I write : that will come
first which is uppermost in my Mind, not that which is
uppermost in my heart—besides I should wish to give
you a picture of our Lives here whenever by a touch I
can do it; even as you must see by the last sentence our
walk past Whitehall all in good health and spirits—this
I am certain of, because I felt so much pleasure from
the simple idea of your playing a game at Cricket. At
Mrs. Millar's I saw Henry quite well—there was Miss
Keasle—and the good-natured Miss Waldegrave—Mrs.
Millar began a long story and you know it is her
Daughter's way to help her on as though her tongue were
ill of the gout. Mrs. M. certainly tells a story as though
she had been taught her Alphabet in Crutched Friars.
Dilke has been very unwell; I found him very ailing
on my return—he was under Medical care for some time,
and then went to the Sea Side whence he has returned
well. Poor little Mrs. D. has had another gall-stone
attack; she was well ere I returned—she is now at
Brighton. Dilke was greatly pleased to hear from you,
and will write a letter for me to enclose—He seems
greatly desirous of hearing from you of the settlement
itself—

[October 14 or 15.]

I came by ship from Inverness, and was nine days
at Sea without being sick—a little Qualm now and then
put me in mind of you—however as soon as you touch
the shore all the horrors of Sickness are soon forgotten,
as was the case with a Lady on board who could not

hold her head up all the way.   We had not been in the
Thames an hour before her tongue began to some tune ;
paying off as it was fit she should all old scores.   I was
the only Englishman on board.   There was a downright
Scotchman who hearing that there had been a bad crop
of Potatoes in England had brought some triumphant
specimens from Scotland—these he exhibited with national
pride to all the Lightermen and Watermen from the Nore
to the Bridge.   I fed upon beef all the way ; not being
able to eat the thick Porridge which the Ladies managed
to manage with large awkward horn spoons into the
bargain.   Severn has had a narrow escape of his Life
from a Typhus fever : he is now gaining strength—Reynolds has returned from a six weeks' enjoyment in Devonshire—he is well, and persuades me to publish my pot
of Basil as an answer to the attacks made on me in
Blackwood's Magazine and the Quarterly Review.   There
have been two Letters in my defence in the Chronicle
and one in the Examiner, copied from the Alfred Exeter
Paper, and written by Reynolds.   I do not know who
wrote those in the Chronicle.   This is a mere matter of
the moment—I think I shall be among the English
Poets after my death.   Even as a Matter of present
interest the attempt to crush me in the Quarterly has
only brought me more into notice, and it is a common
expression among book men "I wonder the Quarterly
should cut its own throat."

     It does me not the least harm in Society to make
me appear little and ridiculous : I know when a man
is superior to me and give him all due respect—he will
be the last to laugh at me and as for the rest I feel that
I make an impression upon them which insures me
personal respect while I am in sight whatever they
may say when my back is turned.   Poor Haydon's
eyes will not suffer him to proceed with his picture
—he has been in the Country—I have seen him but
once since my return.   I hurry matters together here
because I do not know when the Mail sails—I shall

enquire to-morrow, and then shall know whether to be
particular or general in my letter—You shall have at least
two sheets a day till it does sail whether it be three days
or a fortnight—and then I will begin a fresh one for the
next Month.   The Miss Reynoldses are very kind to me,
but they have lately displeased me much, and in this
way—Now I am coming the Richardson.   On my return
the first day I called they were in a sort of taking or
bustle about a Cousin of theirs who having fallen out
with her Grandpapa in a serious manner was invited by
Mrs. R. to take Asylum in her house.   She is an east
indian and ought to be her Grandfather's Heir.[1]   At the
time I called Mrs. R. was in conference with her up stairs,
and the young Ladies were warm in her praises down
stairs, calling her genteel, interesting and a thousand
other pretty things to which I gave no heed, not being
partial to 9 days' wonders—Now all is completely
changed—they hate her, and from what I hear she is not
without faults—of a real kind : but she has others which
are more apt to make women of inferior charms hate her.
She is not a Cleopatra, but she is at least a Charmian.
She has a rich Eastern look ; she has fine eyes and fine
manners.   When she comes into a room she makes an
impression the same as the Beauty of a Leopardess   She
is too fine and too conscious of herself to repulse any Man
who may address her—from habit she thinks that nothing
particular.   I always find myself more at ease with such
a woman ; the picture before me always gives me a life
and animation which I cannot possibly feel with anything inferior.   I am at such times too much occupied in
admiring to be awkward or in a tremble.   I forget myself
entirely because I live in her.   You will by this time
think I am in love with her ; so before I go any further
I will tell you I am not—she kept me awake one Night
as a tune of Mozart's might do   I speak of the thing as
a pastime and an amusement, than which I can feel
none deeper than a conversation with an imperial woman,

---

[1] Miss Charlotte Cox ; see above, Letter LXX.

the very "yes" and "no" of whose Lips is to me a
Banquet. I don't cry to take the moon home with
me in my Pocket nor do I fret to leave her behind me.
I like her and her like because one has no *sensations*—
what we both are is taken for granted. You will suppose
I have by this had much talk with her—no such thing—
there are the Miss Reynoldses on the look out—They
think I don't admire her because I did not stare at her.

They call her a flirt to me—What a want of knowledge! She walks across a room in such a manner that
a Man is drawn towards her with a magnetic Power.
This they call flirting! they do not know things.
They do not know what a Woman is. I believe though
she has faults—the same as Charmian and Cleopatra
might have had. Yet she is a fine thing speaking in a
worldly way: for there are two distinct tempers of mind
in which we judge of things—the worldly, theatrical and
pantomimical; and the unearthly, spiritual and ethereal
—in the former Buonaparte, Lord Byron and this Charmian hold the first place in our Minds; in the latter,
John Howard, Bishop Hooker rocking his child's cradle
and you my dear Sister are the conquering feelings. As
a Man in the world I love the rich talk of a Charmian;
as an eternal Being I love the thought of you. I should
like her to ruin me, and I should like you to save me.
Do not think, my dear Brother, from this that my
Passions are headlong, or likely to be ever of any pain
to you—

> "I am free from Men of Pleasure's cares,
>   By dint of feelings far more deep than theirs."

This is Lord Byron, and is one of the finest things he has
said. I have no town talk for you, as I have not been
much among people—as for Politics they are in my opinion
only sleepy because they will soon be too wide awake. Perhaps not—for the long and continued Peace of England
itself has given us notions of personal safety which are likely
to prevent the re-establishment of our national Honesty.

There is, of a truth, nothing manly or sterling in any part of the Government. There are many Madmen in the Country I have no doubt, who would like to be beheaded on tower Hill merely for the sake of éclat, there are many Men like Hunt who from a principle of taste would like to see things go on better, there are many like Sir F. Burdett who like to sit at the head of political dinners, —but there are none prepared to suffer in obscurity for their Country—The motives of our worst men are Interest and of our best Vanity. We have no Milton, no Algernon Sidney—Governors in these days lose the title of Man in exchange for that of Diplomat and Minister. We breathe in a sort of Officinal Atmosphere—All the departments of Government have strayed far from Simplicity which is the greatest of Strength there is as much difference in this respect between the present Government and Oliver Cromwell's as there is between the 12 Tables of Rome and the volumes of Civil Law which were digested by Justinian. A Man now entitled Chancellor has the same honour paid to him whether he be a Hog or a Lord Bacon. No sensation is created by Greatness but by the number of Orders a Man has at his Button holes. Notwithstanding the part which the Liberals take in the Cause of Napoleon, I cannot but think he has done more harm to the life of Liberty than any one else could have done : not that the divine right Gentlemen have done or intend to do any good—no they have taken a Lesson of him, and will do all the further harm he would have done without any of the good. The worst thing he has done is, that he has taught them how to organise their monstrous armies. The Emperor Alexander it is said intends to divide his Empire as did Diocletian —creating two Czars besides himself, and continuing the supreme Monarch of the whole. Should he do this and they for a series of Years keep peaceable among themselves Russia may spread her conquest even to China—I think it a very likely thing that China itself may fall, Turkey certainly will. Meanwhile European north Russia will

hold its horns against the rest of Europe, intriguing constantly with France.   Dilke, whom you know to be a
Godwin perfectibility Man, pleases himself with the idea
that America will be the country to take up the human
intellect where England leaves off—I differ there with
him greatly—A country like the United States, whose
greatest Men are Franklins and Washingtons will never
do that.   They are great Men doubtless, but how are
they to be compared to those our countrymen Milton and
the two Sidneys ?   The one is a philosophical Quaker full
of mean and thrifty maxims, the other sold the very
Charger who had taken him through all his Battles.
Those Americans are great, but they are not sublime
Man—the humanity of the United States can never reach
the sublime.   Birkbeck's mind is too much in the American
style—you must endeavour to infuse a little Spirit of another sort into the settlement, always with great caution,
for thereby you may do your descendants more good
than you may imagine.   If I had a prayer to make for
any great good, next to Tom's recovery, it should be that
one of your Children should be the first American Poet.
I have a great mind to make a prophecy, and they say
prophecies work out their own fulfilment—

> 'Tis the witching time of night,
> Orbed is the moon and bright,
> And the Stars they glisten, glisten,.
> Seeming with bright eyes to listen.
> For what listen they ?
> For a song and for a charm,
> See they glisten in alarm
> And the Moon is waxing warm
> To hear what I shall say.
> Moon keep wide thy golden ears
> Hearken Stars and hearken Spheres
> Hearken thou eternal Sky
> I sing an infant's Lullaby,
> O pretty Lullaby !
> Listen, Listen, listen, listen
> Glisten, glisten, glisten, glisten
> And hear my Lullaby !
> Though the Rushes that will make

Its cradle still are in the lake,
Though the linen that will be
Its swathe, is on the cotton tree,
Though the woollen that will keep
It warm, is on the silly sheep ;
Listen Starlight, listen, listen
Glisten, Glisten, glisten, glisten
And hear my Lullaby !
Child ! I see thee !   Child, I've found thee
Midst of the quiet all around thee !
Child, I see thee !   Child, I spy thee
And thy mother sweet is nigh thee !—
Child, I know thee !   Child no more
But a Poet *evermore*
See, See the Lyre, The Lyre
In a flame of fire
Upon the little cradle's top
Flaring, flaring, flaring
Past the eyesight's bearing—
Awake it from its sleep,
And see if it can keep
Its eyes upon the blaze—
Amaze, Amaze !
It stares, it stares, it stares
It dares what no one dares
It lifts its little hand into the flame
Unharm'd, and on the strings
Paddles a little tune and sings
With dumb endeavour sweetly !
Bard art thou completely !
Little Child
O' the western wild,
Bard art thou completely !—
Sweetly, with dumb endeavour—
A Poet now or never !
Little Child
O' the western wild
A Poet now or never !

                                        [October 16.]

This is Friday, I know not what day of the Month—
I will enquire to-morrow, for it is fit you should know
the time I am writing.   I went to Town yesterday, and
calling at Mrs. Millar's was told that your Mother would
not be found at home—I met Henry as I turned the
corner—I had no leisure to return, so I left the letters

with him. He was looking very well. Poor Tom is no
better to-night—I am afraid to ask him what Message I
shall send from him. And here I could go on complaining
of my Misery, but I will keep myself cheerful for your
Sakes. With a great deal of trouble I have succeeded in
getting Fanny to Hampstead. She has been several times.
Mr. Lewis has been very kind to Tom all the summer,
there has scarce a day passed but he has visited him, and
not one day without bringing or sending some fruit of
the nicest kind. He has been very assiduous in his
enquiries after you—It would give the old Gentleman a
great deal of pleasure if you would send him a Sheet
enclosed in the next parcel to me, after you receive this—
how long it will be first—Why did I not write to Philadelphia? Really I am sorry for that neglect. I wish to
go on writing ad infinitum to you—I wish for interesting
matter and a pen as swift as the wind—But the fact is
I go so little into the Crowd now that I have nothing
fresh and fresh every day to speculate upon except my
own Whims and Theories. I have been but once to
Haydon's, once to Hunt's, once to Rice's, once to Hessey's.
I have not seen Taylor, I have not been to the Theatre.
Now if I had been many times to all these and was still
in the habit of going I could on my return at night have
each day something new to tell you of without any stop
—But now I have such a dearth that when I get to the
end of this sentence and to the bottom of this page I
must wait till I can find something interesting to you
before I begin another. After all it is not much matter
what it may be about, for the very words from such a
distance penned by this hand will be grateful to you—
even though I were to copy out the tale of Mother
Hubbard or Little Red Riding Hood.

[Later.]

I have been over to Dilke's this evening—there with
Brown we have been talking of different and indifferent
Matters—of Euclid, of Metaphysics, of the Bible, of Shak-

N

speare, of the horrid System and consequences of the fagging at great schools. I know not yet how large a parcel I can send—I mean by way of Letters—I hope there can be no objection to my dowling up a quire made into a small compass. That is the manner in which I shall write. I shall send you more than Letters—I mean a tale—which I must begin on account of the activity of my Mind; of its inability to remain at rest. It must be prose and not very exciting. I must do this because in the way I am at present situated I have too many interruptions to a train of feeling to be able to write Poetry. So I shall write this Tale, and if I think it worth while get a duplicate made before I send it off to you.

[October 21.]

This is a fresh beginning the 21st October. Charles and Henry were with us on Sunday, and they brought me your Letter to your Mother—we agreed to get a Packet off to you as soon as possible. I shall dine with your Mother to-morrow, when they have promised to have their Letters ready. I shall send as soon as possible without thinking of the little you may have from me in the first parcel, as I intend, as I said before, to begin another Letter of more regular information. Here I want to communicate so largely in a little time that I am puzzled where to direct my attention. Haslam has promised to let me know from Capper and Hazlewood. For want of something better I shall proceed to give you some extracts from my Scotch Letters—Yet now I think on it why not send you the letters themselves—I have three of them at present—I believe Haydon has two which I will get in time. I dined with your Mother and Henry at Mrs. Millar's on Thursday, when they gave me their Letters. Charles's I have not yet—he has promised to send it. The thought of sending my Scotch Letters has determined me to enclose a few more which I have received and which will give you the best cue to how I am going on, better than you could otherwise know. Your Mother

was well, and I was sorry I could not stop later.   I called
on Hunt yesterday—it has been always my fate to meet
Ollier there—On Thursday I walked with Hazlitt as far
as Covent Garden : he was going to play Racquets.   I
think Tom has been rather better these few last days—
he has been less nervous.   I expect Reynolds to-morrow.

[Later, about October 25.]

Since I wrote thus far I have met with that same Lady
again, whom I saw at Hastings and whom I met when
we were going to the English Opera.   It was in a street
which goes from Bedford Row to Lamb's Conduit Street.
—I passed her and turned back : she seemed glad of it—
glad to see me, and not offended at my passing her before.
We walked on towards Islington, where we called on a
friend of hers who keeps a Boarding School.   She has
always been an enigma to me—she has been in a Room
with you and Reynolds, and wishes we should be
acquainted without any of our common acquaintance
knowing it.   As we went along, sometimes through
shabby, sometimes through decent Streets, I had my
guessing at work, not knowing what it would be, and
prepared to meet any surprise.   First it ended at this
House at Islington : on parting from which I pressed to
attend her home.   She consented, and then again my
thoughts were at work what it might lead to, though
now they had received a sort of genteel hint from the
Boarding School.   Our Walk ended in 34 Gloucester
Street, Queen Square—not exactly so, for we went upstairs into her sitting-room, a very tasty sort of place
with Books, Pictures, a bronze Statue of Buonaparte,
Music, æolian Harp, a Parrot, a Linnet, a Case of choice
Liqueurs, etc. etc.   She behaved in the kindest manner—
made me take home a Grouse for Tom's dinner.   Asked for
my address for the purpose of sending more game. . . . I
expect to pass some pleasant hours with her now and then :
in which I feel I shall be of service to her in matters of
knowledge and taste : if I can I will. . . . She and your

George are the only women à peu près de mon age whom I would be content to know for their mind and friendship alone.—I shall in a short time write you as far as I know how I intend to pass my Life—I cannot think of those things now Tom is so unwell and weak. Notwithstanding your Happiness and your recommendation I hope I shall never marry. Though the most beautiful Creature were waiting for me at the end of a Journey or a Walk; though the Carpet were of Silk, the Curtains of the morning Clouds; the chairs and Sofa stuffed with Cygnet's down; the food Manna, the Wine beyond Claret, the Window opening on Winander mere, I should not feel—or rather my Happiness would not be so fine, as my Solitude is sublime. Then instead of what I have described, there is a sublimity to welcome me home—The roaring of the wind is my wife and the Stars through the window pane are my Children. The mighty abstract Idea I have of Beauty in all things stifles the more divided and minute domestic happiness—an amiable wife and sweet Children I contemplate as a part of that Beauty, but I must have a thousand of those beautiful particles to fill up my heart. I feel more and more every day, as my imagination strengthens, that I do not live in this world alone but in a thousand worlds—No sooner am I alone than shapes of epic greatness are stationed around me, and serve my Spirit the office which is equivalent to a King's bodyguard —then "Tragedy with sceptred pall comes sweeping by." According to my state of mind I am with Achilles shouting in the Trenches, or with Theocritus in the Vales of Sicily. Or I throw my whole being into Troilus, and repeating those lines, "I wander like a lost Soul upon the stygian Banks staying for waftage," I melt into the air with a voluptuousness so delicate that I am content to be alone. These things, combined with the opinion I have of the generality of women—who appear to me as children to whom I would rather give a sugar Plum than my time, form a barrier against Matrimony which I rejoice in.

I have written this that you might see I have my share of the highest pleasures, and that though I may choose to pass my days alone I shall be no Solitary.   You see there is nothing spleenical in all this.   The only thing that can ever affect me personally for more than one short passing day, is any doubt about my powers for poetry—I seldom have any, and I look with hope to the nighing time when I shall have none.   I am as happy as a Man can be— that is, in myself I should be happy if Tom was well, and I knew you were passing pleasant days.   Then I should be most enviable—with the yearning Passion I have for the beautiful, connected and made one with the ambition of my intellect.   Think of my Pleasure in Solitude in comparison of my commerce with the world—there I am a child—there they do not know me, not even my most intimate acquaintance—I give into their feelings as though I were refraining from irritating a little child.   Some think me middling, others silly, others foolish—every one thinks he sees my weak side against my will, when in truth it is with my will—I am content to be thought all this because I have in my own breast so great a resource. This is one great reason why they like me so ; because they can all show to advantage in a room and eclipse from a certain tact one who is reckoned to be a good Poet.   I hope I am not here playing tricks 'to make the angels weep' : I think not : for I have not the least contempt for my species, and though it may sound para- doxical, my greatest elevations of soul leave me every time more humbled—Enough of this—though in your Love for me you will not think it enough.

[Later, October 29 or 31.]

Haslam has been here this morning and has taken all the Letters except this sheet, which I shall send him by the Twopenny, as he will put the Parcel in the Boston post Bag by the advice of Capper and Hazlewood, who assure him of the safety and expedition that way—the Parcel will be forwarded to Warder and thence to you all the same.

There will not be a Philadelphia ship for these six weeks
—by that time I shall have another Letter to you. Mind
you I mark this Letter A. By the time you will receive
this you will have I trust passed through the greatest of
your fatigues. As it was with your Sea Sickness I shall
not hear of them till they are past. Do not set to your
occupation with too great an anxiety—take it calmly—
and let your health be the prime consideration. I hope
you will have a Son, and it is one of my first wishes to
have him in my Arms—which I will do please God
before he cuts one double tooth. Tom is rather more
easy than he has been : but is still so nervous that I
cannot speak to him of these Matters—indeed it is the
care I have had to keep his Mind aloof from feelings too
acute that has made this Letter so short a one—I did
not like to write before him a Letter he knew was to
reach your hands—I cannot even now ask him for any
Message—his heart speaks to you. Be as happy as you
can. Think of me, and for my sake be cheerful.

Believe me, my dear Brother and sister, Your anxious
and affectionate Brother   JOHN.

This day is my Birth day.

All our friends have been anxious in their enquiries,
and all send their remembrances.

LXXIV.—TO FANNY KEATS.

Hampstead, Friday Morn [October 16, 1818].

My dear Fanny—You must not condemn me for not
being punctual to Thursday, for I really did not know
whether it would not affect poor Tom too much to see
you. You know how it hurt him to part with you the
last time. At all events you shall hear from me ; and
if Tom keeps pretty well to-morrow, I will see Mr. Abbey
the next day, and endeavour to settle that you shall be
with us on Tuesday or Wednesday. I have good news
from George—He has landed safely with our Sister—
they are both in good health—their prospects are good—

and they are by this time nighing to their journey's end —you shall hear the particulars soon.

Your affectionate Brother   JOHN.
Tom's love to you.

LXXV.—TO FANNY KEATS.

[Hampstead, October 26, 1818.]

My dear Fanny—I called on Mr. Abbey in the beginning of last Week: when he seemed averse to letting you come again from having heard that you had been to other places besides Well Walk. I do not mean to say you did wrongly in speaking of it, for there should rightly be no objection to such things : but you know with what People we are obliged in the course of Childhood to associate, whose conduct forces us into duplicity and falsehood to them. To the worst of People we should be openhearted : but it is as well as things are to be prudent in making any communication to any one, that may throw an impediment in the way of any of the little pleasures you may have. I do not recommend duplicity but prudence with such people. Perhaps I am talking too deeply for you : if you do not now, you will understand what I mean in the course of a few years. I think poor Tom is a little Better : he sends his love to you. I shall call on Mr. Abbey to-morrow : when I hope to settle when to see you again. Mrs. Dilke has been for some time at Brighton—she is expected home in a day or two. She will be pleased I am sure with your present. I will try for permission for you to remain here all Night should Mrs. D. return in time.

Your affectionate Brother   JOHN ——.

LXXVI.—TO RICHARD WOODHOUSE.

[Hampstead, October 27, 1818.]

My dear Woodhouse—Your letter gave me great satisfaction, more on account of its friendliness than any relish of that matter in it which is accounted so accept-

able to the "genus irritabile."   The best answer I can
give you is in a clerklike manner to make some observations on two principal points which seem to point like
indices into the midst of the whole pro and con about
genius, and views, and achievements, and ambition, et
cætera.—1st. As to the poetical Character itself (I mean
that sort, of which, if I am anything, I am a member;
that sort distinguished from the Wordsworthian, or
egotistical Sublime; which is a thing per se, and stands
alone,) it is not itself—it has no self—It is everything
and nothing—It has no character—it enjoys light and
shade; it lives in gusto, be it foul or fair, high or low,
rich or poor, mean or elevated—It has as much delight
in conceiving an Iago as an Imogen.   What shocks the
virtuous philosopher delights the chameleon poet.   It does
no harm from its relish of the dark side of things, any
more than from its taste for the bright one, because they
both end in speculation.   A poet is the most unpoetical
of anything in existence, because he has no Identity—
he is continually in for and filling some other body.
The Sun,—the Moon,—the Sea, and men and women, who
are creatures of impulse, are poetical, and have about
them an unchangeable attribute; the poet has none, no
identity—he is certainly the most unpoetical of all God's
creatures.—If then he has no self, and if I am a poet,
where is the wonder that I should say I would write no
more?   Might I not at that very instant have been
cogitating on the Characters of Saturn and Ops?[1]   It is a
wretched thing to confess; but it is a very fact, that not
one word I ever utter can be taken for granted as an
opinion growing out of my identical Nature—how can
it, when I have no Nature?   When I am in a room
with people, if I ever am free from speculating on
creations of my own brain, then, not myself goes home

---

[1] This, notes Woodhouse, is in reply to a letter of protest he
had written Keats concerning "what had fallen from him, about
six weeks back, when we dined together at Mr. Hessey's, respecting his continuing to write; which he seemed very doubtful of."

to myself, but the identity of every one in the room
begins to press upon me, so that I am in a very little
time annihilated—not only among men; it would be
the same in a nursery of Children. I know not whether I
make myself wholly understood : I hope enough so to let
you see that no dependence is to be placed on what I
said that day.

In the 2d place, I will speak of my views, and of
the life I purpose to myself. I am ambitious of doing
the world some good : if I should be spared, that may
be the work of maturer years—in the interval I will assay
to reach to as high a summit in poetry as the nerve
bestowed upon me will suffer. The faint conceptions I
have of poems to come bring the blood frequently into
my forehead—All I hope is, that I may not lose all
interest in human affairs—that the solitary Indifference
I feel for applause, even from the finest spirits, will not
blunt any acuteness of vision I may have. I do not
think it will. I feel assured I should write from the
mere yearning and fondness I have for the beautiful, even
if my night's labours should be burnt every Morning, and
no eye ever shine upon them. But even now I am perhaps not speaking from myself, but from some Character
in whose soul I now live.

I am sure however that this next sentence is from
myself—I feel your anxiety, good opinion, and friendship,
in the highest degree, and am

Yours most sincerely   JOHN KEATS.

LXXVII.—TO FANNY KEATS.

[Hampstead, November 5, 1818.]

My dear Fanny—I have seen Mr. Abbey three times
about you, and have not been able to get his consent.
He says that once more between this and the Holidays
will be sufficient. What can I do? I should have been
at Walthamstow several times, but I am not able to
leave Tom for so long a time as that would take me.

Poor Tom has been rather better these 4 last days in consequence of obtaining a little rest a nights. Write to me as often as you can, and believe that I would do anything to give you any pleasure—we must as yet wait patiently.

Your affectionate Brother   JOHN ——.

LXXVIII.—TO JAMES RICE.

Well Walk [Hampstead,] Novr. 24, [1818].

My dear Rice—Your amende Honorable I must call "un surcroît d'Amitié," for I am not at all sensible of anything but that you were unfortunately engaged and I was unfortunately in a hurry. I completely understand your feeling in this mistake, and find in it that balance of comfort which remains after regretting your uneasiness. I have long made up my mind to take for granted the genuine-heartedness of my friends, notwithstanding any temporary ambiguousness in their behaviour or their tongues, nothing of which however I had the least scent of this morning. I say completely understand; for I am everlastingly getting my mind into such-like painful trammels—and am even at this moment suffering under them in the case of a friend of ours.—I will tell you two most unfortunate and parallel slips—it seems down-right pre-intention—A friend says to me, "Keats, I shall go and see Severn this week."—"Ah ! (says I) you want him to take your Portrait."—And again, "Keats," says a friend, "when will you come to town again?"—"I will," says I, "let you have the MS. next week." In both these cases I appeared to attribute an interested motive to each of my friends' questions—the first made him flush, the second made him look angry :— and yet I am innocent in both cases ; my mind leapt over every interval, to what I saw was per se a pleasant subject with him. You see I have no allowances to make —you see how far I am from supposing you could show me any neglect. I very much regret the long time I

have been obliged to exile from you : for I have one or
two rather pleasant occasions to confer upon with you.
What I have heard from George is favourable—I expect
a letter from the Settlement itself.

Your sincere friend   JOHN KEATS.

I cannot give any good news of Tom.

LXXIX.—TO FANNY KEATS.

[Hampstead,] Tuesday Morn [December 1, 1818].

My dear Fanny—Poor Tom has been so bad that I
have delayed your visit hither—as it would be so painful
to you both.   I cannot say he is any better this morning
—he is in a very dangerous state—I have scarce any
hopes of him.   Keep up your spirits for me my dear
Fanny—repose entirely in

Your affectionate Brother   JOHN.

LXXX.—TO GEORGE AND GEORGIANA KEATS.

[Hampstead,[1] about Decr. 18, 1818.]

My dear Brother and Sister—You will have been
prepared before this reaches you for the worst news you
could have, nay, if Haslam's letter arrives in proper time,
I have a consolation in thinking that the first shock will
be past before you receive this.   The last days of poor
Tom were of the most distressing nature; but his last
moments were not so painful, and his very last was
without a pang.   I will not enter into any parsonic
comments on death—yet the common observations of the

---

[1] On the death of his brother Tom (which took place December
1, a few hours after the last letter was written) Brown urged Keats
to leave the lodgings where the brothers had lived together, and
come and live with him at Wentworth Place—a block of two semi-
detached houses in a large garden at the bottom of John Street,
of which Dilke occupied the larger and Brown the smaller : see
Keats (Men of Letters Series), p. 128.   Keats complied ; and
henceforth his letters dated Hampstead must be understood as
written not from Well Walk, but from Wentworth Place.

commonest people on death are as true as their proverbs. I have scarce a doubt of immortality of some nature or other—neither had Tom. My friends have been exceedingly kind to me every one of them—Brown detained me at his House. I suppose no one could have had their time made smoother than mine has been. During poor Tom's illness I was not able to write and since his death the task of beginning has been a hindrance to me. Within this last Week I have been everywhere—and I will tell you as nearly as possible how all go on. With Dilke and Brown I am quite thick—with Brown indeed I am going to domesticate—that is, we shall keep house together. I shall have the front parlour and he the back one, by which I shall avoid the noise of Bentley's Children—and be the better able to go on with my Studies—which have been greatly interrupted lately, so that I have not the shadow of an idea of a book in my head, and my pen seems to have grown too gouty for sense. How are you going on now? The goings on of the world makes me dizzy—There you are with Birkbeck—here I am with Brown—sometimes I fancy an immense separation, and sometimes as at present, a direct communication of Spirit with you. That will be one of the grandeurs of immortality—There will be no space, and consequently the only commerce between spirits will be by their intelligence of each other—when they will completely understand each other, while we in this world merely comprehend each other in different degrees—the higher the degree of good so higher is our Love and friendship. I have been so little used to writing lately that I am afraid you will not smoke my meaning so I will give an example—Suppose Brown or Haslam or any one whom I understand in the next degree to what I do you, were in America, they would be so much the farther from me in proportion as their identity was less impressed upon me. Now the reason why I do not feel at the present moment so far from you is that I remember your Ways and Manners and actions; I know your manner of thinking, your

manner of feeling: I know what shape your joy or
your sorrow would take; I know the manner of your walking, standing, sauntering, sitting down, laughing, punning,
and every action so truly that you seem near to me.
You will remember me in the same manner—and the
more when I tell you that I shall read a passage of
Shakspeare every Sunday at ten o'Clock—you read one
at the same time, and we shall be as near each other as
blind bodies can be in the same room.

I saw your Mother the day before yesterday, and
intend now frequently to pass half a day with her—she
seem'd tolerably well. I called in Henrietta Street and
so was speaking with your Mother about Miss Millar—
we had a chat about Heiresses—she told me I think of
7 or eight dying Swains. Charles was not at home.
I think I have heard a little more talk about Miss
Keasle—all I know of her is she had a new sort of shoe
on of bright leather like our Knapsacks. Miss Millar
gave me one of her confounded pinches. *N.B.* did not
like it. Mrs. Dilke went with me to see Fanny last
week, and Haslam went with me last Sunday. She was
well—she gets a little plumper and had a little Colour.
On Sunday I brought from her a present of facescreens
and a work-bag for Mrs. D.—they were really very
pretty. From Walthamstow we walked to Bethnal
green—where I felt so tired from my long walk that I
was obliged to go to Bed at ten. Mr. and Mrs. Keasle
were there. Haslam has been excessively kind, and his
anxiety about you is great; I never meet him but we
have some chat thereon. He is always doing me some
good turn—he gave me this thin paper [1] for the purpose
of writing to you. I have been passing an hour this
morning with Mr. Lewis—he wants news of you very
much. Haydon was here yesterday—he amused us
much by speaking of young Hoppner who went with
Captain Ross on a voyage of discovery to the Poles.

[1] A paper of the largest folio size, used by Keats in this letter
only, and containing some eight hundred words a page of his writing.

The Ship was sometimes entirely surrounded with vast
mountains and crags of ice, and in a few Minutes not a
particle was to be seen all round the Horizon.   Once
they met with so vast a Mass that they gave themselves
over for lost ; their last resource was in meeting it with
the Bowsprit, which they did, and split it asunder and
glided through it as it parted, for a great distance—one
Mile and more.   Their eyes were so fatigued with the
eternal dazzle and whiteness that they lay down on their
backs upon deck to relieve their sight on the blue sky.
Hoppner describes his dreadful weariness at the continual
day—the sun ever moving in a circle round above their
heads—so pressing upon him that he could not rid himself of the sensation even in the dark Hold of the Ship.
The Esquimaux are described as the most wretched of
Beings—they float from their summer to their winter
residences and back again like white Bears on the ice
floats.   They seem never to have washed, and so when
their features move the red skin shows beneath the
cracking peel of dirt.   They had no notion of any
inhabitants in the World but themselves.   The sailors
who had not seen a Star for some time, when they came
again southwards on the hailing of the first revision of
one, all ran upon deck with feelings of the most joyful
nature.   Haydon's eyes will not suffer him to proceed
with his Picture—his Physician tells him he must remain
two months more, inactive.   Hunt keeps on in his old
way—I am completely tired of it all.   He has lately
publish'd a Pocket Book called the literary Pocket-Book
—full of the most sickening stuff you can imagine.
Reynolds is well ; he has become an Edinburgh Reviewer.
I have not heard from Bailey.   Rice I have seen very little
of lately—and I am very sorry for it. . The Miss R's. are
all as usual.   Archer above all people called on me one
day—he wanted some information by my means, from
Hunt and Haydon, concerning some Man they knew.   I
got him what he wanted, but know none of the whys
and wherefores.   Poor Kirkman left Wentworth Place

one evening about half-past eight and was stopped,
beaten and robbed of his Watch in Pond Street. I saw
him a few days since; he had not recovered from his
bruises. I called on Hazlitt the day I went to Romney
Street—I gave John Hunt extracts from your letters—
he has taken no notice. I have seen Lamb lately—
Brown and I were taken by Hunt to Novello's—there
we were devastated and excruciated with bad and repeated puns—Brown don't want to go again. We went
the other evening to see Brutus a new Tragedy by
Howard Payne, an American—Kean was excellent—the
play was very bad. It is the first time I have been
since I went with you to the Lyceum.

Mrs. Brawne who took Brown's house for the Summer,
still resides in Hampstead. She is a very nice woman, and
her daughter senior is I think beautiful and elegant, graceful, silly, fashionable and strange. We have a little tiff
now and then—and she behaves a little better, or I must
have sheered off.[1] I find by a sidelong report from your
Mother that I am to be invited to Miss Millar's birthday
dance. Shall I dance with Miss Waldegrave? Eh! I
shall be obliged to shirk a good many there. I shall be
the only Dandy there—and indeed I merely comply with
the invitation that the party may not be entirely destitute
of a specimen of that race. I shall appear in a complete
dress of purple, Hat and all—with a list of the beauties
I have conquered embroidered round my Calves.

Thursday [December 24].

This morning is so very fine, I should have
walked over to Walthamstow if I had thought of it
yesterday. What are you doing this morning? Have
you a clear hard frost as we have? How do you come

---

[1] This is Keats's first mention of Fanny Brawne. His sense on
first acquaintance of her power to charm and tease him must be
understood, in spite of his reticence on the subject, as having
grown quickly into the absorbing passion which tormented the
remainder of his days.

on with the gun? Have you shot a Buffalo? Have you
met with any Pheasants? My Thoughts are very frequently in a foreign Country—I live more out of
England than in it. The Mountains of Tartary are a
favourite lounge, if I happen to miss the Alleghany ridge,
or have no whim for Savoy. There must be great
pleasure in pursuing game—pointing your gun—no, it
won't do—now, no—rabbit it—now bang—smoke and
feathers—where is it? Shall you be able to get a good
pointer or so? Have you seen Mr. Trimmer? He is an
acquaintance of Peachey's. Now I am not addressing
myself to G. minor, and yet I am—for you are one.
Have you some warm furs? By your next Letters I
shall expect to hear exactly how you go on—smother
nothing—let us have all; fair and foul, all plain. Will
the little bairn have made his entrance before you have
this? Kiss it for me, and when it can first know a
cheese from a Caterpillar show it my picture twice a
Week. You will be glad to hear that Gifford's attack
upon me has done me service—it has got my Book
among several *sets*—Nor must I forget to mention once
more what I suppose Haslam has told you, the present
of a £25 note I had anonymously sent me. I have
many things to tell you—the best way will be to make
copies of my correspondence; and I must not forget the
Sonnet I received with the Note. Last Week I received
the following from Woodhouse whom you must recollect:—

"My dear Keats—I send enclosed a Letter, which when read
take the trouble to return to me. The History of its reaching me
is this. My Cousin, Miss Frogley of Hounslow, borrowed my
copy of *Endymion* for a specified time. Before she had time to
look into it, she and my friend Mr. Hy. Neville of Esher, who
was house Surgeon to the late Princess Charlotte, insisted upon
having it to read for a day or two, and undertook to make my
Cousin's peace with me on account of the extra delay. Neville
told me that one of the Misses Porter (of romance Celebrity) had
seen it on his table, dipped into it, and expressed a wish to read it.
I desired he should keep it as long and lend it to as many as he
pleased, provided it was not allowed to slumber on any one's shelf.
I learned subsequently from Miss Frogley that these Ladies had

requested of Mr. Neville, if he was acquainted with the Author,
the Pleasure of an introduction.   About a week back the enclosed
was transmitted by Mr. Neville to my Cousin, as a species of
Apology for keeping her so long without the Book, and she sent it
to me, knowing that it would give me Pleasure—I forward it to
you for somewhat the same reason, but principally because it gives
me the opportunity of naming to you (which it would have been
fruitless to do before) the opening there is for an introduction to a
class of society from which you may possibly derive advantage, as
well as qualification, if you think proper to avail yourself of it.
In such a case I should be very happy to further your Wishes.
But do just as you please.   The whole is entirely *entre nous.—*
Yours, etc.,   R. W."

Well—now this is Miss Porter's Letter to Neville—

"Dear Sir—As my Mother is sending a Messenger to Esher, I
cannot but make the same the bearer of my regrets for not having
had the pleasure of seeing you the morning you called at the
gate.   I had given orders to be denied, I was so very unwell with
my still adhesive cold ; but had I known it was you I should have
taken off the interdict for a few minutes, to say how very much I
am delighted with *Endymion.*   I had just finished the Poem and
have done as you permitted, lent it to Miss Fitzgerald.   I regret
you are not personally acquainted with the Author, for I should
have been happy to have acknowledged to him, through the
advantage of your communication, the very rare delight my sister
and myself have enjoyed from the first fruits of Genius.   I hope
the ill-natured Review will not have damaged" (or damped) "such
true Parnassian fire—it ought not, for when Life is granted, etc."

—and so she goes on.   Now I feel more obliged than
flattered by this—so obliged that I will not at present
give you an extravaganza of a Lady Romancer.   I will
be introduced to them if it be merely for the pleasure of
writing to you about it—I shall certainly see a new race
of People.   I shall more certainly have no time for them.

Hunt has asked me to meet Tom Moore some day—so
you shall hear of him.   The Night we went to Novello's
there was a complete set to of Mozart and punning.   I
was so completely tired of it that if I were to follow my
own inclinations I should never meet any one of that set
again, not even Hunt, who is certainly a pleasant fellow
in the main when you are with him—but in reality he
is vain, egotistical, and disgusting in matters of taste and

in morals.   He understands many a beautiful thing;
but then, instead of giving other minds credit for the
same degree of perception as he himself professes—he
begins an explanation in such a curious manner that our
taste and self-love is offended continually.   Hunt does
one harm by making fine things petty, and beautiful
things hateful.   Through him I am indifferent to Mozart,
I care not for white Busts—and many a glorious thing
when associated with him becomes a nothing.   This
distorts one's mind—makes one's thoughts bizarre—per-
plexes one in the standard of Beauty.   Martin is very
much irritated against Blackwood for printing some
Letters in his Magazine which were Martin's property—
he always found excuses for Blackwood till he himself
was injured, and now he is enraged.   I have been several
times thinking whether or not I should send you the
Examiners, as Birkbeck no doubt has all the good periodical Publications—I will save them at all events.   I
must not forget to mention how attentive and useful
Mrs. Bentley has been—I am very sorry to leave her—
but I must, and I hope she will not be much a loser by
it.   Bentley is very well—he has just brought me a
clothes'-basket of Books.   Brown has gone to town to-
day to take his Nephews who are on a visit here to see
the Lions.   I am passing a Quiet day—which I have not
done for a long while—and if I do continue so, I feel I
must again begin with my poetry—for if I am not in
action mind or Body I am in pain—and from that I
suffer greatly by going into parties where from the rules
of society and a natural pride I am obliged to smother
my Spirit and look like an Idiot—because I feel my
impulses given way to would too much amaze them.   I
live under an everlasting restraint—never relieved except
when I am composing—so I will write away.

Friday [December 25].

I think you knew before you left England that
my next subject would be "the fall of Hyperion."

I went on a little with it last night, but it will take
some time to get into the vein again. I will not give
you any extracts because I wish the whole to make an.
impression. I have however a few Poems which you
will like, and I will copy out on the next sheet. I shall
dine with Haydon on Sunday, and go over to Walthamstow on Monday if the frost hold. I think also of going
into Hampshire this Christmas to Mr. Snook's[1]—they say
I shall be very much amused—But I don't know—I
think I am in too huge a Mind for study—I must do it
—I must wait at home and let those who wish come to
see me. I cannot always be (how do you spell it?)
trapsing. Here I must tell you that I have not been
able to keep the journal or write the Tale I promised—
now I shall be able to do so. I will write to Haslam
this morning to know when the Packet sails, and till it
does I will write something every day—After that my
journal shall go on like clockwork, and you must not
complain of its dulness—for what I wish is to write a
quantity to you—knowing well that dulness itself will
from me be interesting to you—You may conceive how
this not having been done has weighed upon me. I shall
be able to judge from your next what sort of information
will be of most service or amusement to you. Perhaps
as you were fond of giving me sketches of character you
may like a little picnic of scandal even across the Atlantic.
But now I must speak particularly to you, my dear Sister
—for I know you love a little quizzing better than a
great bit of apple dumpling. Do you know Uncle
Redhall? He is a little Man with an innocent powdered
upright head, he lisps with a protruded under lip—he
has two Nieces, each one would weigh three of him—one
for height and the other for breadth—he knew Bartolozzi. He gave a supper, and ranged his bottles of wine
all up the Kitchen and cellar stairs—quite ignorant of
what might be drunk—It might have been a good joke

---

[1] Of Bedhampton Castle: a connection of the Dilkes and
special friend of Brown.

to pour on the sly bottle after bottle into a washing tub,
and roar for more—If you were to trip him up it would
discompose a Pigtail and bring his under lip nearer to
his nose.   He never had the good luck to lose a silk
Handkerchief in a Crowd, and therefore has only one topic
of conversation—Bartolozzi.   Shall I give you Miss
Brawne?   She is about my height—with a fine style of
countenance of the lengthened sort—she wants sentiment
in every feature—she manages to make her hair look
well—her nostrils are fine—though a little painful—her
mouth is bad and good—her Profile is better than her
full-face which indeed is not full but pale and thin
without showing any bone.   Her shape is very graceful
and so are her movements—her Arms are good her hands
baddish—her feet tolerable.   She is not seventeen—but
she is ignorant—monstrous in her behaviour, flying out
in all directions—calling people such names that I was
forced lately to make use of the term *Minx*—this is I
think not from any innate vice, but from a penchant she
has for acting stylishly—I am however tired of such
style and shall decline any more of it.   She had a friend
to visit her lately—you have known plenty such—her
face is raw as if she was standing out in a frost; her
lips raw and seem always ready for a Pullet—she plays
the Music without one sensation but the feel of the
ivory at her fingers.   She is a downright Miss without
one set off—We hated her and smoked her and baited her
and I think drove her away.   Miss B. thinks her a
Paragon of fashion, and says she is the only woman she
would change persons with.   What a stupe—She is
superior as a Rose to a Dandelion. · When we went to
bed Brown observed as he put out the Taper what a
very ugly old woman that Miss Robinson would make—
at which I must have groaned aloud for I'm sure ten
minutes.   I have not seen the thing Kingston again—
George will describe him to you—I shall insinuate some
of these Creatures into a Comedy some day—and perhaps
have Hunt among them—

Scene, a little Parlour. *Enter* Hunt—Gattie—
Hazlitt—Mrs. Novello—Ollier. *Gattie.* Ha ! Hunt, got
into your new house ? Ha ! Mrs. Novello : seen Altam
and his Wife ?—*Mrs. N.* Yes (with a grin), it's Mr.
Hunt's, isn't it ?—*Gattie.* Hunt's ? no, ha ! Mr. Ollier,
I congratulate you upon the highest compliment I ever
heard paid to the Book. Mr. Hazlitt, I hope you are
well.—*Hazlitt.* Yes Sir, no Sir.—*Mr. Hunt* (at the
Music), "La Biondina," etc. Hazlitt, did you ever hear
this ?—"La Biondina," etc.—*Hazlitt.* O no Sir—I never.
—*Ollier.* Do, Hunt, give it us over again—divine.—
Gattie. Divino—Hunt, when does your Pocket-Book come
out ?—*Hunt.* "What is this absorbs me quite ?" O we
are spinning on a little, we shall floridise soon I hope.
Such a thing was very much wanting—people think of
nothing but money getting—now for me I am rather
inclined to the liberal side of things. I am reckoned lax
in my Christian principles, etc. etc. etc.

[December 29.]

It is some days since I wrote the last page—and what
I have been about since I have no Idea. I dined at
Haslam's on Sunday—with Haydon yesterday, and saw
Fanny in the morning ; she was well. Just now I took
out my poem to go on with it, but the thought of my
writing so little to you came upon me and I could not
get on—so I have began at random and I have not a
word to say—and yet my thoughts are so full of you that
I can do nothing else. I shall be confined at Hampstead
a few days on account of a sore throat—the first thing I
do will be to visit your Mother again. The last time I
saw Henry he show'd me his first engraving, which I
thought capital. Mr. Lewis called this morning and
brought some American Papers—I have not look'd into
them—I think we ought to have heard of you before
this—I am in daily expectation of Letters—Nil desper-
andum. Mrs. Abbey wishes to take Fanny from School
—I shall strive all I can against that. There has
happened a great Misfortune in the Drewe Family—old

Drewe has been dead some time; and lately George
Drewe expired in a fit—on which account Reynolds has
gone into Devonshire.   He dined a few days since at
Horace Twisse's with Liston and Charles Kemble.   I
see very little of him now, as I seldom go to Little
Britain because the *Ennui* always seizes me there, and
John Reynolds is very dull at home.   Nor have I seen
Rice.   How you are now going on is a Mystery to me—
I hope a few days will clear it up.

[December 30.]

I never know the day of the Month.   It is very fine
here to-day, though I expect a Thundercloud, or rather
a snow cloud, in less than an hour.   I am at present alone
at Wentworth Place—Brown being at Chichester and Mr.
and Mrs. Dilke making a little stay in Town. I know not
what I should do without a sunshiny morning now and then
—it clears up one's spirits.   Dilke and I frequently have
some chat about you.   I have now and then some doubt,
but he seems to have a great confidence.   I think there
will soon be perceptible a change in the fashionable slang
literature of the day—it seems to me that Reviews have
had their day—that the public have been surfeited—
there will soon be some new folly to keep the Parlours in
talk — What it is I care not.   We have seen three
literary Kings in our Time—Scott, Byron, and then the
Scotch novels.   All now appears to be dead—or I may
mistake, literary Bodies may still keep up the Bustle
which I do not hear.   Haydon show'd me a letter he
had received from Tripoli—Ritchie was well and in good
Spirits, among Camels, Turbans, Palm Trees, and Sands.
You may remember I promised to send him an Endymion
which I did not—however he has one—you have one.
One is in the Wilds of America—the other is on a
Camel's back in the plains of Egypt.   I am looking into
a Book of Dubois's—he has written directions to the
Players—one of them is very good.   " In singing never
mind the music—observe what time you please.   It

would be a pretty degradation indeed if you were obliged
to confine your genius to the dull regularity of a fiddler
—horse hair and cat's guts—no, let him keep *your* time
and play *your* tune—*dodge him.*" I will now copy out
the Letter and Sonnet I have spoken of. The outside
cover was thus directed, "Messrs. Taylor and Hessey,
(Booksellers), No. 93 Fleet Street, London," and it contained this:

'Messrs. Taylor and Hessey are requested to forward the enclosed letter by some *safe* mode of conveyance to the Author of
Endymion, who is not known at Teignmouth : or if they have not
his address, they will return the letter by post, directed as below,
within a *fortnight*, "Mr. P. Fenbank, P. O., Teignmouth." 9th
Novr. 1818.'

In this sheet was enclosed the following, with a super-
scription—'Mr. John Keats, Teignmouth.' Then came
Sonnet to John Keats—which I would not copy for any
in the world but you—who know that I scout "mild
light and loveliness" or any such nonsense in myself.

Star of high promise !—not to this dark age
  Do thy mild light and loveliness belong ;
  For it is blind, intolerant, and wrong ;
Dead to empyreal soarings, and the rage
Of scoffing spirits bitter war doth wage
  With all that bold integrity of song.
  Yet thy clear beam shall shine through ages strong
To ripest times a light and heritage.
And there breathe now who dote upon thy fame,
  Whom thy wild numbers wrap beyond their being,
Who love the freedom of thy lays—their aim
  Above the scope of a dull tribe unseeing—
And there is one whose hand will never scant
From his poor store of fruits all *thou* canst want.

November 1818.   turn over.

I turn'd over and found a £25 note. Now this appears
to me all very proper—if I had refused it I should have
behaved in a very bragadochio dunderheaded manner—
and yet the present galls me a little, and I do not know
whether I shall not return it if I ever meet with the
donor after, whom to no purpose I have written. I have

your Miniature on the Table George the great—it's very
like—though not quite about the upper lip.   I wish we
had a better of your little George.   I must not forget to
tell you that a few days since I went with Dilke a shooting on the heath and shot a Tomtit.   There were as many
guns abroad as Birds.   I intended to have been at
Chichester this Wednesday—but on account of this sore
throat I wrote him (Brown) my excuse yesterday.

Thursday [December 31].

(I will date when I finish.)—I received a Note from
Haslam yesterday—asking if my letter is ready—now
this is only the second sheet—notwithstanding all my
promises.   But you must reflect what hindrances I
have had.   However on sealing this I shall have
nothing to prevent my proceeding in a gradual journal,
which will increase in a Month to a considerable size.   I
will insert any little pieces I may write—though I will
not give any extracts from my large poem which is scarce
began.   I want to hear very much whether Poetry and
literature in general has gained or lost interest with you—
and what sort of writing is of the highest gust with you
now.   With what sensation do you read Fielding?—and
do not Hogarth's pictures seem an old thing to you?
Yet you are very little more removed from general association than I am—recollect that no Man can live but in
one society at a time—his enjoyment in the different
states of human society must depend upon the Powers of
his Mind—that is you can imagine a Roman triumph
or an Olympic game as well as I can.   We with our
bodily eyes see but the fashion and Manners of one
country for one age—and then we die.   Now to me
manners and customs long since passed whether among
the Babylonians or the Bactrians are as real, or even
more real than those among which I now live—My
thoughts have turned lately this way—The more we
know the more inadequacy we find in the world to satisfy
us—this is an old observation; but I have made up my

Mind never to take anything for granted—but even to examine the truth of the commonest proverbs — This however is true. Mrs. Tighe and Beattie once delighted me—now I see through them and can find nothing in them but weakness, and yet how many they still delight! Perhaps a superior being may look upon Shakspeare in the same light—is it possible? No—This same inadequacy is discovered (forgive me, little George, you know I don't mean to put you in the mess) in Women with few exceptions—the Dress Maker, the blue Stocking, and the most charming sentimentalist differ but in a slight degree and are equally smokeable. But I'll go no further—I may be speaking sacrilegiously—and on my word I have thought so little that I have not one opinion upon anything except in matters of taste—I never can feel certain of any truth but from a clear perception of its Beauty— and I find myself very young minded even in that perceptive power—which I hope will increase. A year ago I could not understand in the slightest degree Raphael's cartoons—now I begin to read them a little—And how did I learn to do so? By seeing something done in quite an opposite spirit—I mean a picture of Guido's in which all the Saints, instead of that heroic simplicity and unaffected grandeur which they inherit from Raphael, had each of them both in countenance and gesture all the canting, solemn, melodramatic mawkishness of Mackenzie's father Nicholas. When I was last at Haydon's I looked over a Book of Prints taken from the fresco of the Church at Milan, the name of which I forget—in it are comprised Specimens of the first and second age of art in Italy. I do not think I ever had a greater treat out of Shakspeare. Full of Romance and the most tender feeling—magnificence of draperies beyond any I ever saw, not excepting Raphael's. But Grotesque to a curious pitch—yet still making up a fine whole—even finer to me than more accomplish'd works—as there was left so much room for Imagination. I have not heard one of this last course of Hazlitt's lectures. They were upon 'Wit and Humour,' 'the English comic writers.'

Saturday, Jany. 2nd [1819].

Yesterday Mr. and Mrs. D. and myself dined at Mrs. Brawne's — nothing particular passed. I never intend hereafter to spend any time with Ladies unless they are handsome—you lose time to no purpose. For that reason I shall beg leave to decline going again to Redall's or Butler's or any Squad where a fine feature cannot be mustered among them all—and where all the evening's amusement consists in saying 'your good health, *your* good health, and YOUR good health—and (O I beg your pardon) yours, Miss ——,' and such thing not even dull enough to keep one awake—With respect to amiable speaking I can read—let my eyes be fed or I'll never go out to dinner anywhere. Perhaps you may have heard of the dinner given to Thos. Moore in Dublin, because I have the account here by me in the Philadelphia democratic paper. The most pleasant thing that occurred was the speech Mr. Tom made on his Father's health being drank. I am afraid a great part of my Letters are filled up with promises and what I will do rather than any great deal written—but here I say once for all—that circumstances prevented me from keeping my promise in my last, but now I affirm that as there will be nothing to hinder me I will keep a journal for you. That I have not yet done so you would forgive if you knew how many hours I have been repenting of my neglect. For I have no thought pervading me so constantly and frequently as that of you—my Poem cannot frequently drive it away— you will retard it much more than you could by taking up my time if you were in England. I never forget you except after seeing now and then some beautiful woman— but that is a fever—the thought of you both is a passion with me, but for the most part a calm one. I asked Dilke for a few lines for you—he has promised them—I shall send what I have written to Haslam on Monday Morning—what I can get into another sheet to-morrow I

will—There are one or two little poems you might like.
I have given up snuff very nearly quite—Dilke has
promised to sit with me this evening, I wish he would
come this minute for I want a pinch of snuff very much
just now—I have none though in my own snuff box.
My sore throat is much better to-day—I think I might
venture on a pinch.   Here are the Poems—they will
explain themselves—as all poems should do without any
comment—

> Ever let the Fancy roam,
> Pleasure never is at home.
> At a touch sweet pleasure melteth
> Like to bubbles when rain pelteth :
> Then let winged fancy wander
> Towards heaven still spread beyond her—
> Open wide the mind's cage door,
> She'll dart forth and cloudward soar.
> O sweet Fancy, let her loose !
> Summer's joys are spoilt by use,
> And the enjoying of the spring
> Fades as doth its blossoming :
> Autumn's red-lipped fruitage too
> Blushing through the mist and dew,
> Cloys with kissing.   What do then ?
> Sit thee in an ingle when
> The sear faggot blazes bright,
> Spirit of a winter night :
> When the soundless earth is muffled,
> And the caked snow is shuffled
> From the Ploughboy's heavy shoon :
> When the night doth meet the moon
> In a dark conspiracy
> To banish vesper from the sky.
> Sit thee then and send abroad
> With a Mind self-overaw'd
> Fancy high-commission'd ; send her,—
> She'll have vassals to attend her—
> She will bring thee, spite of frost,
> Beauties that the Earth has lost ;
> She will bring thee all together
> All delights of summer weather ;
> All the faery buds of May,
> On spring turf or scented spray ;
> All the heaped Autumn's wealth
> With a still mysterious stealth ;

She will mix these pleasures up
Like three fit wines in a cup
And thou shalt quaff it—Thou shalt hear
Distant harvest carols clear,
Rustle of the reaped corn
Sweet Birds antheming the Morn ;
And in the same moment hark
To the early April lark,
And the rooks with busy caw
Foraging for sticks and straw.
Thou shalt at one glance behold
The daisy and the marigold ;
White plumed lilies and the first
Hedgerow primrose that hath burst ;
Shaded Hyacinth alway
Sapphire Queen of the Mid-may ;
And every leaf and every flower
Pearled with the same soft shower.
Thou shalt see the fieldmouse creep
Meagre from its celled sleep,
And the snake all winter shrank
Cast its skin on sunny bank ;
Freckled nest eggs shalt thou see
Hatching in the hawthorn tree ;
When the hen-bird's wing doth rest
Quiet on its mossy nest ;
Then the hurry and alarm
When the Beehive casts its swarm—
Acorns ripe down scattering
While the autumn breezes sing,
For the same sleek throated mouse
To store up in its winter house.
    O, sweet Fancy, let her loose !
Every joy is spoilt by use :
Every pleasure, every joy—
Not a Mistress but doth cloy.
Where's the cheek that doth not fade,
Too much gaz'd at ?   Where's the Maid
Whose lip mature is ever new ?
Where's the eye, however blue,
Doth not weary ?   Where's the face
One would meet in every place ?
Where's the voice however soft
One would hear too oft and oft ?
At a touch sweet pleasure melteth
Like to bubbles when rain pelteth.
Let then winged fancy find

Thee a Mistress to thy mind.
Dulcet-eyed as Ceres' daughter
Ere the God of torment taught her
How to frown and how to chide :
With a waist and with a side
White as Hebe's when her Zone
Slipp'd its golden clasp, and down
Fell her Kirtle to her feet
While she held the goblet sweet,
And Jove grew languid—Mistress fair !
Thou shalt have that tressed hair
Adonis tangled all for spite ;
And the mouth he would not kiss,
And the treasure he would miss ;
And the hand he would not press
And the warmth he would distress.
  O the Ravishment—the Bliss !
Fancy has her there she is—
Never fulsome, ever new,
There she steps ! and tell me who
Has a Mistress so divine ?
Be the palate ne'er so fine
She cannot sicken.   Break the Mesh
Of the Fancy's silken leash ;
Where she's tether'd to the heart.
Quickly break her prison string
And such joys as these she'll bring,
Let the winged fancy roam,
Pleasure never is at home.

I did not think this had been so long a Poem. I have
another not so long—but as it will more conveniently be
copied on the other side I will just put down here some
observations on Caleb Williams by Hazlitt—I meant to
say St. Leon, for although he has mentioned all the
Novels of Godwin very freely I do not quote them, but
this only on account of its being a specimen of his usual
abrupt manner, and fiery laconicism. He says of St.
Leon—

" He is a limb torn off society. In possession of eternal youth
and beauty he can feel no love ; surrounded, tantalised, and tormented with riches, he can do no good. The faces of Men pass
before him as in a speculum ; but he is attached to them by no
common tie of sympathy or suffering. He is thrown back into
himself and his own thoughts. He lives in the solitude of his own

breast—without wife or child or friend or Enemy in the world. *This is the solitude of the soul, not of woods or trees or mountains* —but the desert of society—the waste and oblivion of the heart. He is himself alone. His existence is purely intellectual, and is therefore intolerable to one who has felt the rapture of affection, or the anguish of woe."

As I am about it I might as well give you his character of Godwin as a Romancer :—

"Whoever else is, it is pretty clear that the author of Caleb Williams is not the author of Waverley. Nothing can be more distinct or excellent in their several ways than these two writers. If the one owes almost everything to external observations and traditional character, the other owes everything to internal conception and contemplation of the possible workings of the human Mind. There is little knowledge of the world, little variety, neither an eye for the picturesque nor a talent for the humorous in Caleb Williams, for instance, but you cannot doubt for a moment of the originality of the work and the force of the conception. The impression made upon the reader is the exact measure of the strength of the author's genius. For the effect both in Caleb Williams and St. Leon is entirely made out, not by facts nor dates, by blackletter, or magazine learning, by transcript nor record, but by intense and patient study of the human heart, and by an imagination projecting itself into certain situations, and capable of working up its imaginary feelings to the height of reality."

This appears to me quite correct—Now I will copy the other Poem—it is on the double immortality of Poets—

> Bards of Passion and of Mirth
> Ye have left your souls on earth—
> Have ye souls in heaven too,
> Double liv'd in regions new ?
> Yes—and those of heaven commune
> With the spheres of Sun and Moon ;
> With the noise of fountains wondrous
> And the parle of voices thund'rous ;
> With the Whisper of heaven's trees,
> And one another, in soft ease
> Seated on elysian Lawns
> Browsed by none but Dian's fawns ;
> Underneath large bluebells tented,
> Where the daisies are rose scented,
> And the rose herself has got
> Perfume that on Earth is not.

Where the nightingale doth sing
Not a senseless, tranced thing ;
But melodious truth divine,
Philosophic numbers fine ;
Tales and golden histories
Of Heaven and its Mysteries.
Thus ye live on Earth, and then
On the Earth ye live again ;
And the souls ye left behind you
Teach us here the way to find you,
Where your other souls are joying
Never slumber'd, never cloying.
Here your earth born souls still speak
To mortals of the little week
They must sojourn with their cares ;
Of their sorrows and delights
Of their Passions and their spites ;
Of their glory and their shame—
What doth strengthen and what maim.
Thus ye teach us every-day
Wisdom though fled far away.
　Bards of Passion and of Mirth,
Ye have left your Souls on Earth !
Ye have souls in heaven too,
Double liv'd in Regions new !

These are specimens of a sort of rondeau which I think I shall become partial to—because you have one idea amplified with greater ease and more delight and freedom than in the sonnet.   It is my intention to wait a few years before I publish any minor poems—and then I hope to have a volume of some worth—and which those people will relish who cannot bear the burthen of a long poem.   In my journal I intend to copy the poems I write the days they are written—There is just room, I see, in this page to copy a little thing I wrote off to some Music as it was playing—

I had a dove and the sweet dove died,
And I have thought it died of grieving :
O what could it mourn for ? it was tied
With a silken thread of my own hand's weaving.
Sweet little red-feet why did you die ?
Why would you leave me—sweet dove why ?
You lived alone on the forest tree.

Why pretty thing could you not live with me ?
I kissed you oft and I gave you white peas.
Why not live sweetly as in the green trees ?

Sunday [January 3].

I have been dining with Dilke to-day—He is up
to his Ears in Walpole's letters. Mr. Manker is there,
and I have come round to see if I can conjure up
anything for you. Kirkman came down to see me this
morning—his family has been very badly off lately. He
told me of a villainous trick of his Uncle William in
Newgate Street, who became sole Creditor to his father
under pretence of serving him, and put an execution on
his own Sister's goods. He went in to the family at
Portsmouth ; conversed with them, went out and sent in
the Sherriff's officer. He tells me too of abominable behaviour of Archer to Caroline Mathew—Archer has lived
nearly at the Mathews these two years ; he has been
amusing Caroline—and now he has written a Letter to
Mrs. M. declining, on pretence of inability to support
a wife as he would wish, all thoughts of marriage.
What is the worst is Caroline is 27 years old. It is
an abominable matter. He has called upon me twice
lately—I was out both times. What can it be for?—
There is a letter to-day in the Examiner to the Electors
of Westminster on Mr. Hobhouse's account. In it there
is a good character of Cobbett—I have not the paper by
me or I would copy it. I do not think I have mentioned
the discovery of an African Kingdom—the account is
much the same as the first accounts of Mexico—all
magnificence—There is a Book being written about it. I
will read it and give you the cream in my next. The
romance we have heard upon it runs thus : They have
window frames of gold—100,000 infantry—human sacri-
fices. The Gentleman who is the Adventurer has his
wife with him—she, I am told, is a beautiful little sylphid
woman—her husband was to have been sacrificed to their
Gods and was led through a Chamber filled with different
instruments of torture with privilege to choose what

death he would die, without their having a thought of
his aversion to such a death, they considering it a
supreme distinction.   However he was let off, and
became a favourite with the King, who at last openly
patronised him, though at first on account of the Jealousy
of his Ministers he was wont to hold conversations with
his Majesty in the dark middle of the night.   All this
sounds a little Bluebeardish—but I hope it is true.
There is another thing I must mention of the momentous
kind ;—but I must mind my periods in it—Mrs. Dilke
has two Cats—a Mother and a Daughter—now the
Mother is a tabby and the daughter a black and white
like the spotted child.   Now it appears to me, for the
doors of both houses are opened frequently, so that there
is a complete thoroughfare for both Cats (there being no
board up to the contrary), they may one and several of
them come into my room ad libitum.   But no—the
Tabby only comes—whether from sympathy for Ann the
Maid or me I cannot tell—or whether Brown has left
behind him any atmospheric spirit of Maidenhood I cannot
tell.   The Cat is not an old Maid herself—her daughter
is a proof of it—I have questioned her—I have look'd at
the lines of her paw—I have felt her pulse—to no purpose.
Why should the *old* Cat come to me ? I ask myself—and
myself has not a word to answer.   It may come to light
some day ; if it does you shall hear of it.

Kirkman this morning promised to write a few lines
to you and send them to Haslam.   I do not think I have
anything to say in the Business way.   You will let me
know what you would wish done with your property in
England—what things you would wish sent out—But I
am quite in the dark about what you are doing—If I do
not hear soon I shall put on my wings and be after you.
I will in my next, and after I have seen your next letter,
tell you my own particular idea of America.   Your next
letter will be the key by which I shall open your hearts
and see what spaces want filling with any particular
information—Whether the affairs of Europe are more or

P

less interesting to you—whether you would like to hear of the Theatres—of the bear Garden—of the Boxers— the Painters, the Lectures—the Dress—The progress of Dandyism—The Progress of Courtship—or the fate of Mary Millar—being a full, true, and très particular account of Miss M.'s ten Suitors—How the first tried the effect of swearing ; the second of stammering ; the third of whispering ;—the fourth of sonnets—the fifth of Spanish leather boots ;—the sixth of flattering her body—the seventh of flattering her mind—the eighth of flattering himself—the ninth stuck to the Mother—the tenth kissed the Chambermaid and told her to tell her Mistress—But he was soon discharged, his reading led him into an error ; he could not sport the Sir Lucius to any advantage. And now for this time I bid you good-bye—I have been thinking of these sheets so long that I appear in closing them to take my leave of you—but that is not it—I shall immediately as I send this off begin my journal— when some days I shall write no more than 10 lines and others 10 times as much.   Mrs. Dilke is knocking at the wall for Tea is ready—I will tell you what sort of a tea it is and then bid you Good-bye.

[January 4.]

This is Monday morning—nothing particular happened yesterday evening, except that when the tray came up Mrs. Dilke and I had a battle with celery stalks—she sends her love to you.   I shall close this and send it immediately to Haslam—remaining ever, My dearest brother and sister,

Your most affectionate Brother   JOHN.

LXXXI.—TO RICHARD WOODHOUSE.

Wentworth Place, Friday Morn [December 18, 1818].

My dear Woodhouse—I am greatly obliged to you. I must needs feel flattered by making an impression on a set of ladies.   I should be content to do so by mere-tricious romance verse, if they alone, and not men, were

to judge. I should like very much to know those ladies
—though look here, Woodhouse—I have a new leaf to
turn over : I must work ; I must read ; I must write.
I am unable to afford time for new acquaintances. I am
scarcely able to do my duty to those I have. Leave the
matter to chance. But do not forget to give my remembrances to your cousin.

Yours most sincerely   JOHN KEATS.

LXXXII.—TO MRS. REYNOLDS.

Wentworth Place, Tuesd. [December 22, 1818].

My dear Mrs. Reynolds—When I left you yesterday,
'twas with the conviction that you thought I had
received no previous invitation for Christmas day : the
truth is I had, and had accepted it under the conviction
that I should be in Hampshire at the time : else believe
me I should not have done so, but kept in Mind my old
friends. I will not speak of the proportion of pleasure
I may receive at different Houses—that never enters my
head—you may take for a truth that I would have given
up even what I did see to be a greater pleasure, for the
sake of old acquaintanceship—time is nothing—two years
are as long as twenty.

Yours faithfully   JOHN KEATS.

LXXXIII.—TO BENJAMIN ROBERT HAYDON.

Wentworth Place, Tuesday [December 22, 1818].

My dear Haydon—Upon my Soul I never felt your
going out of the room at all—and believe me I never
rhodomontade anywhere but in your Company—my
general Life in Society is silence. I feel in myself all
the vices of a Poet, irritability, love of effect and admiration—and influenced by such devils I may at times say
more ridiculous things than I am aware of—but I will
put a stop to that in a manner I have long resolved
upon—I will buy a gold ring and put it on my finger—

and from that time a Man of superior head shall never have occasion to pity me, or one of inferior Nunskull to chuckle at me.   I am certainly more for greatness in a shade than in the open day—I am speaking as a mortal —I should say I value more the privilege of seeing great things in loneliness than the fame of a Prophet.   Yet here I am sinning—so I will turn to a thing I have thought on more—I mean your means till your picture be finished : not only now but for this year and half have I thought of it.   Believe me Haydon I have that sort of fire in my heart that would sacrifice everything I have to your service—I speak without any reserve—I know you would do so for me—I open my heart to you in a few words.   I will do this sooner than you shall be distressed : but let me be the last stay—Ask the rich lovers of Art first—I'll tell you why—I have a little money which may enable me to study, and to travel for three or four years.   I never expect to get anything by my Books : and moreover I wish to avoid publishing—I admire Human Nature but I do not like *Men*.   I should like to compose things honourable to Man—but not fingerable over by *Men*.   So I am anxious to exist without troubling the printer's devil or drawing upon Men's or Women's admiration—in which great solitude I hope God will give me strength to rejoice.   Try the long purses—but do not sell your drawings or I shall consider it a breach of friendship.   I am sorry I was not at home when Salmon called.   Do write and let me know all your present whys and wherefores.

Yours most faithfully   JOHN KEATS.

LXXXIV.—TO JOHN TAYLOR.

Wentworth Place, [December 24, 1818].

My dear Taylor—Can you lend me £30 for a short time ?   Ten I want for myself—and twenty for a friend —which will be repaid me by the middle of next month. I shall go to Chichester on Wednesday and perhaps stay

a fortnight—I am afraid I shall not be able to dine with
you before I return.   Remember me to Woodhouse.

    Yours sincerely   JOHN KEATS.

LXXXV.—TO BENJAMIN ROBERT HAYDON.

Wentworth Place, [December 27, 1818].

My dear Haydon—I had an engagement to-day—and
it is so fine a morning that I cannot put it off—I will
be with you to-morrow—when we will thank the Gods,
though you have bad eyes and I am idle.

I regret more than anything the not being able to
dine with you to-day.   I have had several movements
that way—but then I should disappoint one who has
been my true friend.   I will be with you to-morrow
morning and stop all day—we will hate the profane
vulgar and make us Wings.

    God bless you.   J. KEATS.

LXXXVI.—TO FANNY KEATS.

Wentworth Place, Wednesday [December 30, 1818].

My dear Fanny—I am confined at Hampstead with
a sore throat ; but I do not expect it will keep me above
two or three days.   I intended to have been in Town
yesterday but feel obliged to be careful a little while.   I
am in general so careless of these trifles, that they tease
me for Months, when a few days' care is all that is
necessary.   I shall not neglect any chance of an endeavour to let you return to School—nor to procure you a
Visit to Mrs. Dilke's which I have great fears about.
Write me if you can find time—and also get a few lines
ready for George as the Post sails next Wednesday.

    Your affectionate Brother   JOHN ———.

LXXXVII.—TO BENJAMIN ROBERT HAYDON.

Wentworth Place, Monday Aft. [January 4, 1819].

My dear Haydon—I have been out this morning, and did not therefore see your note till this minute, or I would have gone to town directly—it is now too late for to-day. I will be in town early to-morrow, and trust I shall be able to lend you assistance noon or night. I was struck with the improvement in the architectural part of your Picture—and, now I think on it, I cannot help wondering you should have had it so poor, especially after the Solomon. Excuse this dry bones of a note : for though my pen may grow cold, I should be sorry my Life should freeze—

Your affectionate friend   JOHN KEATS.

LXXXVIII.—TO BENJAMIN ROBERT HAYDON.

Wentworth Place, [between January 7 and 14, 1819].

My dear Haydon—We are very unlucky—I should have stopped to dine with you, but I knew I should not have been able to leave you in time for my plaguy sore throat; which is getting well.

I shall have a little trouble in procuring the Money and a great ordeal to go through—no trouble indeed to any one else—or ordeal either. I mean I shall have to go to town some thrice, and stand in the Bank an hour or two—to me worse than anything in Dante —I should have less chance with the people around me than Orpheus had with the Stones. I have been writing a little now and then lately : but nothing to speak of—being discontented and as it were moulting. Yet I do not think I shall ever come to the rope or the Pistol, for after a day or two's melancholy, although I smoke more and more my own insufficiency—I see by little and little more of what is to be done, and how it is to be done, should I ever be able to do it. On my soul, there should be some reward for that continual *agonie ennuyeuse.* I was thinking of going into Hampshire for a few days. I have been delaying it longer than I intended. You shall see me soon ; and do not be at all anxious, for *this* time I really will do, what I never did before in my life, business in good time, and properly.—With respect to the Bond—it may be a satisfaction to you to let me have it : but as you love me do not let there be any mention of interest, although we are mortal men—and bind ourselves for fear of death.

Yours for ever JOHN KEATS.

LXXXIX.—TO BENJAMIN ROBERT HAYDON.

Wentworth Place, [January 1819].

My dear Haydon—My throat has not suffered me yet to expose myself to the night air : however I have been to town in the day time—have had several interviews with my guardian—have written him rather a plain-spoken Letter—which has had its effect ; and he now seems inclined to put no stumbling-block in my way : so that I see a good prospect of performing my promise. What I should have lent you ere this if I could have got it, was belonging to poor Tom—and the difficulty is whether I am to inherit it before my Sister is of age ; a period of six years. Should it be so I must incontinently take to Corduroy Trousers. But I am nearly confident 'tis all a Bam. I shall see you soon—but do let me have a line to-day or to-morrow concerning your health and spirits.

Your sincere friend JOHN KEATS.

XC.—TO FANNY KEATS.

Wentworth Place, [January 1819].

My dear Fanny—I send this to Walthamstow for fear you should not be at Pancras Lane when I call to-morrow—before going into Hampshire for a few days

—I will not be more I assure you—You may think how
disappointed I am in not being able to see you more and
spend more time with you than I do—but how can it be
helped ? The thought is a continual vexation to me—
and often hinders me from reading and composing—
Write to me as often as you can—and believe me,

Your affectionate Brother   .   JOHN ——.

XCI.—TO FANNY KEATS.

Wentworth Place, Feb^{y.} [11, 1819].   Thursday.

My dear Fanny—Your Letter to me at Bedhampton
hurt me very much,—What objection can there be to
your receiving a Letter from me ? At Bedhampton I
was unwell and did not go out of the Garden Gate but
twice or thrice during the fortnight I was there—Since
I came back I have been taking care of myself—I have
been obliged to do so, and am now in hopes that by this
care I shall get rid of a sore throat which has haunted me
at intervals nearly a twelvemonth. I had always a pre-
sentiment of not being able to succeed in persuading Mr.
Abbey to let you remain longer at School—I am very
sorry that he will not consent. I recommend you to
keep up all that you know and to learn more by yourself
however little. The time will come when you will be
more pleased with Life—look forward to that time and,
though it may appear a trifle be careful not to let the
idle and retired Life you lead fix any awkward habit or
behaviour on you—whether you sit or walk endeavour
to let it be in a seemly and if possible a graceful manner.
We have been very little together : but you have not the
less been with me in thought. You have no one in the
world besides me who would sacrifice anything for you
—I feel myself the only Protector you have. In all
your little troubles think of me with the thought that
there is at least one person in England who if he could
would help you out of them—I live in hopes of being
able to make you happy.—I should not perhaps write in

this manner, if it were not for the fear of not being able to see you often or long together. I am in hopes Mr. Abbey will not object any more to your receiving a letter now and then from me. How unreasonable! I want a few more lines from you for George—there are some young Men, acquaintances of a Schoolfellow of mine, going out to Birkbeck's at the latter end of this Month —I am in expectation every day of hearing from George —I begin to fear his last letters miscarried. I shall be in town to-morrow—if you should not be in town, I shall send this little parcel by the Walthamstow Coach—I think you will like Goldsmith—Write me soon—

Your affectionate Brother   JOHN ——.

Mrs. Dilke has not been very well—she is gone a walk to town to-day for exercise.

XCII.—TO GEORGE AND GEORGIANA KEATS.

Sunday Morn⁵· February 14, [1819].

My dear Brother and Sister—How is it that we have not heard from you from the Settlement yet? The letters must surely have miscarried. I am in expectation every day. Peachey wrote me a few days ago, saying some more acquaintances of his were preparing to set out for Birkbeck; therefore, I shall take the opportunity of sending you what I can muster in a sheet or two. I am still at Wentworth Place—indeed, I have kept indoors lately, resolved if possible to rid myself of my sore throat; consequently I have not been to see your Mother since my return from Chichester; but my absence from her has been a great weight upon me. I say since my return from Chichester—I believe I told you I was going thither. I was nearly a fortnight at Mr. John Snook's and a few days at old Mr. Dilke's. Nothing worth speaking of happened at either place. I took down some thin paper and wrote on it a little poem called St. Agnes's Eve, which you shall have as it is when I have

finished the blank part of the rest for you. I went out
twice at Chichester to dowager Card parties. I see very
little now, and very few persons, being almost tired of
men and things. Brown and Dilke are very kind and
considerate towards me. The Miss R.'s have been
stopping next door lately, but are very dull. Miss
Brawne and I have every now and then a chat and a
tiff. Brown and Dilke are walking round their garden,
hands in pockets, making observations. The literary
world I know nothing about. There is a poem from
Rogers dead born; and another satire is expected from
Byron, called "Don Giovanni." Yesterday I went to
town for the first time for these three weeks. I met
people from all parts and of all sets—Mr. Towers, one
of the Holts, Mr. Dominie Williams, Mr. Woodhouse,
Mrs. Hazlitt and son, Mrs. Webb, and Mrs. Septimus
Brown. Mr. Woodhouse was looking up at a book
window in Newgate Street, and, being short-sighted,
twisted his muscles into so queer a stage that I stood by
in doubt whether it was him or his brother, if he has
one, and turning round, saw Mrs. Hazlitt, with that
little Nero, her son. Woodhouse, on his features sub-
siding, proved to be Woodhouse, and not his brother. I
have had a little business with Mr. Abbey from time to
time; he has behaved to me with a little Brusquerie:
this hurt me a little, especially when I knew him to be
the only man in England who dared to say a thing to
me I did not approve of without its being resented, or at
least noticed—so I wrote him about it, and have made
an alteration in my favour—I expect from this to see
more of Fanny, who has been quite shut out from me.
I see Cobbett has been attacking the Settlement, but I
cannot tell what to believe, and shall be all out at
elbows till I hear from you. I am invited to Miss
Miller's birthday dance on the 19th—I am nearly sure
I shall not be able to go. A dance would injure my
throat very much. I see very little of Reynolds. Hunt,
I hear, is going on very badly—I mean in money

matters. I shall not be surprised to hear of the worst.
Haydon too, in consequence of his eyes, is out at elbows.
I live as prudently as it is possible for me to do. I have
not seen Haslam lately. I have not seen Richards for
this half year, Rice for three months, or Charles Cowden
Clarke for God knows when.

When I last called in Henrietta Street[1] Miss Millar
was very unwell, and Miss Waldegrave as staid and self-
possessed as usual. Henry was well. There are two
new tragedies—one by the apostate Maw, and one by
Miss Jane Porter. Next week I am going to stop at
Taylor's for a few days, when I will see them both and
tell you what they are. Mr. and Mrs. Bentley are well,
and all the young carrots. I said nothing of consequence
passed at Snooks's—no more than this—that I like the
family very much. Mr. and Mrs. Snooks were very kind.
We used to have a little religion and politics together
almost every evening,—and sometimes about you. He
proposed writing out for me his experience in farming,
for me to send to you. If I should have an opportunity
of talking to him about it, I will get all I can at all
events; but you may say in your answer to this what
value you place upon such information. I have not seen
Mr. Lewis lately, for I have shrunk from going up the
hill. Mr. Lewis went a few mornings ago to town with
Mrs. Brawne. They talked about me, and I heard that
Mr. L. said a thing I am not at all contented with.
Says he, "O, he is quite the little poet." Now this is
abominable—You might as well say Buonaparte is quite
the little soldier. You see what it is to be under six
foot and not a lord. There is a long fuzz to-day in the
Examiner about a young man who delighted a young
woman with a valentine—I think it must be Ollier's.
Brown and I are thinking of passing the summer at
Brussels—If we do, we shall go about the first of May.
We—*i.e.* Brown and I—sit opposite one another all day
authorizing (*N.B.*, an "s" instead of a "z" would

¹ *I.e.* on George Keats's mother-in-law, Mrs. Wylie.

give a different meaning). He is at present writing a
story of an old woman who lived in a forest, and to
whom the Devil or one of his aides-de-feu came one night
very late and in disguise. The old dame sets before him
pudding after pudding—mess after mess—which he de-
vours, and moreover casts his eyes up at a side of Bacon
hanging over his head, and at the same time asks if
her Cat is a Rabbit. On going he leaves her three pips
of Eve's Apple, and somehow she, having lived a virgin
all her life, begins to repent of it, and wished herself
beautiful enough to make all the world and even the
other world fall in love with her. So it happens, she
sets out from her smoky cottage in magnificent apparel.—
The first City she enters, every one falls in love with
her, from the Prince to the Blacksmith. A young gentleman on his way to the Church to be married leaves his
unfortunate Bride and follows this nonsuch—A whole
regiment of soldiers are smitten at once and follow her—
A whole convent of Monks in Corpus Christi procession
join the soldiers.—The mayor and corporation follow the
same road—Old and young, deaf and dumb,—all but
the blind,—are smitten, and form an immense concourse
of people, who—— what Brown will do with them I know
not. The devil himself falls in love with her, flies away
with her to a desert place, in consequence of which she
lays an infinite number of eggs—the eggs being hatched
from time to time, fill the world with many nuisances,
such as John Knox, George Fox, Johanna Southcote,
and Gifford.

There have been within a fortnight eight failures of
the highest consequence in London. Brown went a few
evenings since to Davenport's, and on his coming in he
talked about bad news in the city with such a face I
began to think of a national bankruptcy. I did not feel
much surprised and was rather disappointed. Carlisle,
a bookseller on the Hone principle, has been issuing
pamphlets from his shop in Fleet Street called the
Deist. He was conveyed to Newgate last Thursday;

he intends making his own defence. I was surprised to
hear from Taylor the amount of money of the bookseller's
last sale. What think you of £25,000 ? He sold 4000
copies of Lord Byron. I am sitting opposite the Shakspeare I brought from the Isle of Wight—and I never
look at him but the silk tassels on it give me as much
pleasure as the face of the poet itself.[1]

In my next packet, as this is one by the way, I shall
send you the Pot of Basil, St. Agnes Eve, and if
I should have finished it, a little thing called the Eve
of St. Mark. You see what fine Mother Radcliff names
I have—it is not my fault—I do not search for them.
I have not gone on with Hyperion—for to tell the
truth I have not been in great cue for writing lately—I
must wait for the spring to rouse me up a little. The
only time I went out from Bedhampton was to see a
chapel consecrated—Brown, I, and John Snook the
boy, went in a chaise behind a leaden horse. Brown
drove, but the horse did not mind him. This chapel is
built by a Mr. Way, a great Jew converter, who in that
line has spent one hundred thousand pounds. He main-
tains a great number of poor Jews—*Of course his com-
munion plate was stolen.* He spoke to the clerk about
it—The clerk said he was very sorry, adding, "*I dare
shay, your honour, it's among ush.*"

The chapel is built in Mr. Way's park. The conse-
cration was not amusing. There were numbers of car-
riages—and his house crammed with clergy—They
sanctified the Chapel, and it being a wet day, consecrated
the burial-ground through the vestry window. I begin
to hate parsons ; they did not make me love them that
day when I saw them in their proper colours. A parson
is a Lamb in a drawing-room, and a Lion in a vestry.
The notions of Society will not permit a parson to give
way to his temper in any shape—So he festers in himself
—his features get a peculiar, diabolical, self-sufficient,
iron stupid expression. He is continually acting—his

[1] The tassels were a gift from his sister-in-law.

mind is against every man, and every man's mind is
against him—He is a hypocrite to the Believer and a
coward to the unbeliever—He must be either a knave
or an idiot—and there is no man so much to be pitied
as an idiot parson.   The soldier who is cheated into an
Esprit du Corps by a red coat, a band, and colours, for
the purpose of nothing, is not half so pitiable as the
parson who is led by the nose by the Bench of Bishops
and is smothered in absurdities—a poor necessary subaltern of the Church.

Friday, Feby. 18.

The day before yesterday I went to Romney Street
—your Mother was not at home—but I have just
written her that I shall see her on Wednesday.   I
call'd on Mr. Lewis this morning—he is very well
—and tells me not to be uneasy about Letters, the
chances being so arbitrary.   He is going on as usual
among his favourite democrat papers.   We had a chat
as usual about Cobbett and the Westminster electors.
Dilke has lately been very much harrassed about the
manner of educating his son—he at length decided for a
public school—and then he did not know what school—
he at last has decided for Westminster; and as Charley
is to be a day boy, Dilke will remove to Westminster.
We lead very quiet lives here—Dilke is at present in
Greek histories and antiquities, and talks of nothing but
the electors of Westminster and the retreat of the ten-
thousand. I never drink now above three glasses of
wine—and never any spirits and water.   Though by the
bye, the other day Woodhouse took me to his coffee
house and ordered a Bottle of Claret—now I like Claret,
whenever I can have Claret I must drink it,—'tis the
only palate affair that I am at all sensual in.   Would
it not be a good speck to send you some vine roots—
could it be done?   I'll enquire—If you could make some
wine like Claret to drink on summer evenings in an
arbour!   For really 'tis so fine—it fills one's mouth with
a gushing freshness—then goes down cool and feverless

—then you do not feel it quarrelling with your liver—
no, it is rather a Peacemaker, and lies as quiet as it did
in the grape; then it is as fragrant as the Queen Bee,
and the more ethereal Part of it mounts into the brain,
not assaulting the cerebral apartments like a bully in a
bad-house looking for his trull and hurrying from door
to door bouncing against the wainstcoat, but rather
walks like Aladdin about his own enchanted palace so
gently that you do not feel his step.   Other wines of a
heavy and spirituous nature transform a Man to a Silenus:
this makes him a Hermes—and gives a Woman the soul
and immortality of Ariadne, for whom Bacchus always`
kept a good cellar of claret—and even of that he could
never persuade her to take above two cups.   I said this
same claret is the only palate-passion I have—I forgot
game—I must plead guilty to the breast of a Partridge,
the back of a hare, the backbone of a grouse, the wing
and side of a Pheasant and a Woodcock *passim*.   Talking of game (I wish I could make it), the Lady whom I
met at Hastings and of whom I said something in my
last I think has lately made me many presents of game,
and enabled me to make as many.   She made me take
home a Pheasant the other day, which I gave to Mrs.
Dilke; on which to-morrow Rice, Reynolds and the
Wentworthians will dine next door.   The next I intend
for your Mother.   These moderate sheets of paper are
much more pleasant to write upon than those large
thin sheets which I hope you by this time have received
—though that can't be, now I think of it.   I have not
said in any Letter yet a word about my affairs—in a
word I am in no despair about them—my poem has
not at all succeeded; in the course of a year or so I
think I shall try the public again—in a selfish point of
view I should suffer my pride and my contempt of public
opinion to hold me silent—but for yours and Fanny's
sake I will pluck up a spirit and try again.   I have no
doubt of success in a course of years if I persevere—but
it must be patience, for the Reviews have enervated and

made indolent men's minds—few think for themselves.
These Reviews too are getting more and more powerful,
especially the Quarterly—they are like a superstition
which the more it prostrates the Crowd and the longer
it continues the more powerful it becomes just in proportion to their increasing weakness. I was in hopes that
when people saw, as they must do now, all the trickery
and iniquity of these Plagues they would scout them,
but no, they are like the spectators at the Westminster
cock-pit—they like the battle and do not care who wins
or who loses. Brown is going on this morning with the
story of his old woman and the Devil—He makes but
slow progress—The fact is it is a Libel on the Devil,
and as that person is Brown's Muse, look ye, if he libels
his own Muse how can he expect to write? Either
Brown or his Muse must turn tail. Yesterday was
Charley Dilke's birthday. Brown and I were invited to
tea. During the evening nothing passed worth notice
but a little conversation between Mrs. Dilke and Mrs.
Brawne. The subject was the Watchman. It was ten
o'clock, and Mrs. Brawne, who lived during the summer
in Brown's house and now lives in the Road, recognised
her old Watchman's voice, and said that he came as far
as her now. "Indeed," said Mrs. D., "does he turn
the Corner?" There have been some Letters passed
between me and Haslam but I have not seen him lately.
The day before yesterday—which I made a day of Business—I called upon him—he was out as usual. Brown
has been walking up and down the room a-breeding—
now at this moment he is being delivered of a couplet,
and I daresay will be as well as can be expected.
Gracious—he has twins!

I have a long story to tell you about Bailey—I
will say first the circumstances as plainly and as well
as I can remember, and then I will make my comment. You know that Bailey was very much cut up
about a little Jilt in the country somewhere. I thought
he was in a dying state about it when at Oxford

with him : little supposing, as I have since heard,
that he was at that very time making impatient Love
to Marian Reynolds—and guess my astonishment at
hearing after this that he had been trying at Miss
Martin.   So Matters have been—So Matters stood
—when he got ordained and went to a Curacy near
Carlisle, where the family of the Gleigs reside.   There
his susceptible heart was conquered by Miss Gleig—and
thereby all his connections in town have been annulled—
both male and female.   I do not now remember clearly
the facts—These however I know—He showed his correspondence with Marian to Gleig, returned all her Letters
and asked for his own—he also wrote very abrupt Letters
to Mrs. Reynolds.   I do not know any more of the
Martin affair than I have written above.   No doubt his
conduct has been very bad.   The great thing to be considered is—whether it is want of delicacy and principle
or want of knowledge and polite experience.   And again
. weakness—yes, that is it ; and the want of a Wife—yes,
that is it ; and then Marian made great Bones of him
although her Mother and sister have teased her very
much about it.   Her conduct has been very upright
throughout the whole affair—She liked Bailey as a
Brother but not as a Husband—especially as he used to
woo her with the Bible and Jeremy Taylor under his
arm—they walked in no grove but Jeremy Taylor's.
Marian's obstinacy is some excuse, but his so quickly
taking to Miss Gleig can have no excuse—except that
of a Ploughman who wants a wife.   The thing which
sways me more against him than anything else is Rice's
conduct on the occasion ; Rice would not make an im-
mature resolve : he was ardent in his friendship for
Bailey, he examined the whole for and against minutely ;
and he has abandoned Bailey entirely.   All this I am
not supposed by the Reynoldses to have any hint of.
It will be a good lesson to the Mother and Daughters
—nothing would serve but Bailey.   If you mentioned
the word Tea-pot some one of them came out with an

Q

à propros about Bailey—noble fellow—fine fellow! was
always in their mouths—This may teach them that the
man who ridicules romance is the most romantic of Men
—that he who abuses women and slights them loves
them the most—that he who talks of roasting a Man
alive would not do it when it came to the push—and
above all, that they are very shallow people who take
everything literally. A Man's life of any worth is a continual allegory, and very few eyes can see the Mystery
of his life—a life like the scriptures, figurative—which
such people can no more make out than they can the
Hebrew Bible. Lord Byron cuts a figure but he is not
figurative—Shakspeare led a life of Allegory : his works
are the comments on it—

March 12, Friday.

I went to town yesterday chiefly for the purpose of
seeing some young Men who were to take some Letters
for us to you—through the medium of Peachey. I was
surprised and disappointed at hearing they had changed
their minds, and did not purpose going so far as Birkbeck's. I was much disappointed, for I had counted
upon seeing some persons who were to see you—and
upon your seeing some who had seen me. I have not
only lost this opportunity, but the sail of the Post-
Packet to New York or Philadelphia, by which last
your Brothers have sent some Letters. The weather in
town yesterday was so stifling that I could not remain
there though I wanted much to see Kean in Hotspur. I
have by me at present Hazlitt's Letter to Gifford—perhaps you would like an extract or two from the high-
seasoned parts. It begins thus :

"Sir, you have an ugly trick of saying what is not true of any
one you do not like ; and it will be the object of this Letter to cure
you of it. You say what you please of others ; it is time you were
told what you are. In doing this give me leave to borrow the
familiarity of your style :—for the fidelity of the picture I shall be
answerable. You are a little person but a considerable cat's paw ;
and so far worthy of notice. Your clandestine connection with
persons high in office constantly influences your opinions and

alone gives importance to them. You are the government critic, a character nicely differing from that of a government spy—the invisible link which connects literature with the Police."

Again :

"Your employers, Mr. Gifford, do not pay their hirelings for nothing—for condescending to notice weak and wicked sophistry ; for pointing out to contempt what excites no admiration ; for cautiously selecting a few specimens of bad taste and bad grammar where nothing else is to be found. They want your invisible pert- ness, your mercenary malice, your impenetrable dulness, your bare- faced impudence, your pragmatical self-sufficiency, your hypo- critical zeal, your pious frauds to stand in the gap of their Pre- judices and pretensions to fly-blow and taint public opinion, to defeat independent efforts, to apply not the touch of the scorpion but the touch of the Torpedo to youthful hopes, to crawl and leave the slimy track of sophistry and lies over every work that does not dedicate its sweet leaves to some Luminary of the treasury bench, or is not fostered in the hotbed of corruption. This is your office ; 'this is what is look'd for at your hands, and this you do not baulk'—to sacrifice what little honesty and prostitute what little intellect you possess to any dirty job you are commission'd to execute. 'They keep you as an ape does an apple in the corner of his jaw, first mouth'd to be at last swallow'd.' You are by appointment literary toadeater to greatness and taster to the court. You have a natural aversion to whatever differs from your own pretensions, and an acquired one for what gives offence to your superiors. Your vanity panders to your interest, and your malice truckles only to your love of Power. If your instructive or pre- meditated abuse of your enviable trust were found wanting in a single instance ; if you were to make a single slip in getting up your select committee of enquiry and green bag report of the state of Letters, your occupation would be gone. You would never after obtain a squeeze of the hand from acquaintance, or a smile from a Punk of Quality. The great and powerful whom you call wise and good do not like to have the privacy of their self-love startled by the obtrusive and unmanageable claims of Literature and Philosophy, except through the intervention of people like you, whom, if they have common penetration, they soon find out to be without any superiority of intellect ; or if they do not, whom they can despise for their meanness of soul. You 'have the office opposite to Saint Peter.' You keep a corner in the public mind for foul prejudice and corrupt power to knot and gender in ; you volunteer your services to people of quality to ease scruples of mind and qualms of conscience ; you lay the flattering unction of venal prose and laurell'd verse to their souls. You persuade them that there is neither purity of morals, nor depth of understanding except in themselves and their hangers-on ; and would prevent the unhallow'd names of Liberty and humanity from ever being whispered in ears polite !   You, sir, do you not all this ?   I cry you mercy then : I took you for the Editor of the Quarterly Review."

This is the sort of feu de joie he keeps up.   There is another extract or two—one especially which I will copy to-morrow—for the candles are burnt down and I am using the wax taper—which has a long snuff on it—the fire is at its last click—I am sitting with my back to it with one foot rather askew upon the rug and the other with the heel a little elevated from the carpet—I am writing this on the Maid's Tragedy, which I have read since tea with great pleasure—Besides this volume of Beaumont and Fletcher, there are on the table two volumes of Chaucer and a new work of Tom Moore's, called Tom Cribb's Memorial to Congress—nothing in it.   These are trifles—but I require nothing so much of you but that you will give one a like description of yourselves, however it may be when you are writing to me.   Could I see the same thing done of any great Man long since dead it would be a great delight : as to know in what position Shakspeare sat when he began " To be or not to be "—such things become interesting from distance of time or place.   I hope you are both now in that sweet sleep which no two beings deserve more than you do—I must fancy so—and please myself in the fancy of speaking a prayer and a blessing over you and your lives—God bless you—I whisper good-night in your ears, and you will dream of me.

March 13, Saturday.

I have written to Fanny this morning and received a note from Haslam.   I was to have dined with him to-morrow : he gives me a bad account of his Father, who has not been in Town for five weeks, and is not well enough for company.   Haslam is well—and from the prosperous state of some love affair he does not mind the double tides he has to work.   I have been a Walk past west end—and was going to call at Mr. Monk-

house's—but I did not, not being in the humour. I
know not why Poetry and I have been so distant
lately; I must make some advances soon or she will
cut me entirely. Hazlitt has this fine Passage in his
Letter: Gifford in his Review of Hazlitt's characters
of Shakspeare's plays attacks the Coriolanus critique.
He says that Hazlitt has slandered Shakspeare in saying
that he had a leaning to the arbitrary side of the question.
Hazlitt thus defends himself,

"My words are, 'Coriolanus is a storehouse of political commonplaces. The Arguments for and against aristocracy and democracy
on the Privileges of the few and the claims of the many, on Liberty
and slavery, power and the abuse of it, peace and war, are here
very ably handled, with the spirit of a Poet and the acuteness of
a Philosopher. Shakspeare himself seems to have had a leaning
to the arbitrary side of the question, perhaps from some feeling of
contempt for his own origin, and to have spared no occasion of
bating the rabble. What he says of them is very true; what he
says of their betters is also very true, though he dwells less upon
it.' I then proceed to account for this by showing how it is that
'the cause of the people is but little calculated for a subject for
poetry; or that the language of Poetry naturally falls in with the
language of power.' I affirm, Sir, that Poetry, that the imagination generally speaking, delights in power, in strong excitement,
as well as in truth, in good, in right, whereas pure reason and the
moral sense approve only of the true and good. I proceed to show
that this general love or tendency to immediate excitement or
theatrical effect, no matter how produced, gives a Bias to the
imagination often consistent with the greatest good, that in Poetry
it triumphs over principle, and bribes the passions to make a
sacrifice of common humanity. You say that it does not, that
there is no such original Sin in Poetry, that it makes no such
sacrifice or unworthy compromise between poetical effect and the
still small voice of reason. And how do you prove that there is
no such principle giving a bias to the imagination and a false
colouring to poetry? Why, by asking in reply to the instances
where this principle operates, and where no other can with much
modesty and simplicity—'But are these the only topics that afford
delight in Poetry, etc. !' No; but these objects do afford delight
in poetry, and they afford it in proportion to their strong and
often tragical effect, and not in proportion to the good produced,
or their desireableness in a moral point of view. Do we read
with more pleasure of the ravages of a beast of prey than of
the Shepherd's pipe upon the Mountain? No; but we do read

with pleasure of the ravages of a beast of prey, and we do so on the principle I have stated, namely, from the sense of power abstracted from the sense of good; and it is the same principle that makes us read with admiration and reconciles us in fact to the triumphant progress of the conquerors and mighty Hunters of mankind, who come to stop the Shepherd's Pipe upon the Mountains and sweep away his listening flock. Do you mean to deny that there is anything imposing to the imagination in power, in grandeur, in outward show, in the accumulation of individual wealth and luxury, at the expense of equal justice and the common weal? Do you deny that there is anything in the 'Pride, Pomp, and Circumstance of glorious war, that makes ambition virtue' in the eyes of admiring multitudes? Is this a new theory of the pleasures of the imagination, which says that the pleasures of the imagination do not take rise solely in the calculation of the understanding? Is it a paradox of my creating that 'one murder makes a villain, millions a Hero'? or is it not true that here, as in other cases, the enormity of the evil overpowers and makes a convert of the imagination by its very magnitude? You contradict my reasoning because you know nothing of the question, and you think that no one has a right to understand what you do not. My offence against purity in the passage alluded to, 'which contains the concentrated venom of my malignity,' is that I have admitted that there are tyrants and slaves abroad in the world; and you would hush the matter up and pretend that there is no such thing in order that there may be nothing else. Further, I have explained the cause, the subtle sophistry of the human mind, that tolerates and pampers the evil in order to guard against its approaches; you would conceal the cause in order to prevent the cure, and to leave the proud flesh about the heart to harden and ossify into one impenetrable mass of selfishness and hypocrisy, that we may not 'sympathise in the distresses of suffering virtue' in any case in which they come in competition with the fictitious wants and 'imputed weaknessess of the great.' You ask, 'Are we gratified by the cruelties of Domitian or Nero?' No, not we—they were too petty and cowardly to strike the imagination at a distance; but the Roman senate tolerated them, addressed their perpetrators, exalted them into gods, the fathers of the people, they had pimps and scribblers of all sorts in their pay, their Senecas, etc., till a turbulent rabble, thinking there were no injuries to Society greater than the endurance of unlimited and wanton oppression, put an end to the farce and abated the sin as well as they could. Had you and I lived in those times we should have been what we are now, I 'a sour malcontent,' and you 'a sweet courtier.'"

The manner in which this is managed: the force and innate power with which it yeasts and works up itself—the feeling for the costume of society; is in a style of genius. He hath a demon, as he himself says of Lord Byron. We are to have a party this evening. The Davenports from Church Row—I don't think you know anything of them—they have paid me a good deal of attention. I like Davenport himself. The names of the rest are Miss Barnes, Miss Winter with the Children.

[Later, March 17 or 18.]

On Monday we had to dinner Severn and Cawthorn, the Bookseller and print-virtuoso; in the evening Severn went home to paint, and we other three went to the play, to see Sheil's new tragedy ycleped Evadné. In the morning Severn and I took a turn round the Museum— There is a Sphinx there of a giant size, and most voluptuous Egyptian expression, I had not seen it before. The play was bad even in comparison with 1818, the Augustan age of the Drama, "comme on sait," as Voltaire says—the whole was made up of a virtuous young woman, an indignant brother, a suspecting lover, a libertine prince, a gratuitous villain, a street in Naples, a Cypress grove, lilies and roses, virtue and vice, a bloody sword, a spangled jacket, one Lady Olivia, one Miss O'Neil alias Evadné, alias Bellamira, alias—Alias —Yea, and I say unto you a greater than Elias—There was Abbot, and talking of Abbot his name puts me in mind of a spelling-book lesson, descriptive of the whole Dramatis personæ — Abbot — Abbess — Actor — Actress— The play is a fine amusement, as a friend of mine once said to me—" Do what you will," says he, " a poor gentleman who wants a guinea, cannot spend his two shillings better than at the playhouse." The pantomime was excellent, I had seen it before and I enjoyed it again. Your Mother and I had some talk about Miss H.—— Says I, will Henry have that Miss ——, a lath with a boddice, she who has been fine drawn—fit for nothing but to cut up into Cribbage pins, to the tune of B. 2; one who is all muslin; all feathers and bone; once in travelling she was made use of as a lynch pin; I hope he will not have her, though it is no uncommon thing to be *smitten with a staff;* though she might be very useful as his walking-stick, his fishing-rod, his tooth-pik, his hat-stick (she runs so much in his head)—let him turn farmer, she would cut into hurdles; let him write poetry, she would be his turn-style. Her gown is like a flag on a pole; she would do for him if he turn freemason; I hope she will prove a flag of truce; when she sits languishing with her one foot on a stool, and one elbow on the table, and her head inclined, she looks like the sign of the crooked billet—or the frontispiece to Cinderella, or a tea-paper wood-cut of Mother Shipton at her studies; she is a make-believe—She is bona side a thin young 'oman— But this is mere talk of a fellow-creature; yet pardie I would not that Henry have her—Non volo ut eam possideat, nam, for, it would be a bam, for it would be a sham—

Don't think I am writing a petition to the Governors of St. Luke—no, that would be in another style. May it please your Worships; forasmuch as the undersigned has committed, transferred, given up, made over, consigned, and aberrated himself, to the art and mystery of poetry; forasmuch as he hath cut, rebuffed, affronted, huffed, and shirked, and taken stint at, all other employments, arts, mysteries, and occupations, honest, middling, and dishonest; forasmuch as he hath at sundry times and in divers places, told truth unto the men of this generation, and eke to the women; moreover, forasmuch as he hath kept a pair of boots that did not fit, and doth not admire Sheil's play, Leigh Hunt, Tom Moore, Bob Southey, and Mr. Rogers; and does admire Wm. Hazlitt; moreoverer for as more as he liketh half of Wordsworth, and none of Crabbe; moreover-est for as most as he hath written this page of penmanship—he prayeth your Worships to give him a lodging—Witnessed by Rd. Abbey and Co., cum familiaribus et consanguineis (signed) Count de Cockaigne.

The nothing of the day is a machine called the veloci

pede. It is a wheel carriage to ride cock-horse upon, sitting astride and pushing it along with the toes, a rudder wheel in hand—they will go seven miles an hour—A handsome gelding will come to eight guineas; however they will soon be cheaper, unless the army takes to them. I look back upon the last month, I find nothing to write about; indeed I do not recollect anything particular in it. It's all alike; we keep on breathing. The only amusement is a little scandal, of however fine a shape, a laugh at a pun—and then after all we wonder how we could enjoy the scandal, or laugh at the pun.

I have been at different times turning it in my head whether I should go to Edinburgh and study for a physician; I am afraid I should not take kindly to it; I am sure I could not take fees—and yet I should like to do so; it's not worse than writing poems, and hanging them up to be fly-blown on the Review shambles. Everybody is in his own mess. Here is the parson at Hampstead quarrelling with all the world, he is in the wrong by this same token; when the black cloth was put up in the Church for the Queen's mourning, he asked the workmen to hang it the wrong side outwards, that it might be better when taken down, it being his perquisite—Parsons will always keep up their character, but as it is said there are some animals the ancients knew which we do not, let us hope our posterity will miss the black badger with tri-cornered hat; Who knows but some Reviewer of Buffon or Pliny may put an account of the parson in the Appendix; No one will then believe it any more than we believe in the Phœnix. I think we may class the lawyer in the same natural history of Monsters; a green bag will hold as much as a lawn sleeve. The only difference is that one is fustian and the other flimsy; I am not unwilling to read Church history at present and have Milner's in my eye; his is reckoned a very good one.

[18th September 1819.

[In looking over some of my papers I found the above specimen of my carelessness. It is a sheet you ought to have had long ago—my letter must have appeared very unconnected, but as I number the sheets you must have discovered how the mistake happened. How many things have happened since I wrote it—How have I acted contrary to my resolves. The interval between writing this sheet and the day I put this supplement to it, has been completely filled with generous and most friendly actions of Brown towards me. How frequently I forget to speak of things which I think of and feel most. 'Tis very singular, the idea about Buffon above has been taken up by Hunt in the Examiner, in some papers which he calls " A Preter-natural History."] [1]

Friday 19th March.

This morning I have been reading " the False One." Shameful to say, I was in bed at ten—I mean this morning. The Blackwood Reviewers have committed themselves in a scandalous heresy—they have been putting up Hogg, the Ettrick Shepherd, against Burns : the senseless villains ! The Scotch cannot manage themselves at all, they want imagination, and that is why they are so fond of Hogg, who has a little of it. This morning I am in a sort of temper, indolent and supremely careless—I long after a Stanza or two of Thomson's Castle of Indolence—my passions are all asleep, from my having slumbered till nearly eleven, and weakened the animal fibre all over me, to a delightful sensation, about three degrees on this side of faintness. If I had teeth of pearl and the breath of lilies I should call it

[1] The sheet which Keats accidentally left out in making up his packet in the spring, and which he forwarded with this supplement from Winchester the following September, seems to have begun with the words, " On Monday we had to dinner," etc. (p. 231), and to have ended with the words, " but as I am " (p. 235, line 1): at least this portion of the letter is missing in the autograph now before me. I supply it from Jeffrey's transcript.

languor, but as I am *I must call it laziness. In this
state of effeminacy the fibres of the brain are relaxed in
common with the rest of the body, and to such a happy
degree that pleasure has no show of enticement and pain
no unbearable power. Neither Poetry, nor Ambition,
nor Love have any alertness of countenance as they pass
by me; they seem rather like figures on a Greek vase—
a Man and two women whom no one but myself could
distinguish in their disguisement.[1] This is the only
happiness, and is a rare instance of the advantage of the
body overpowering the Mind. I have this moment
received a note from Haslam, in which he expects the
death of his Father, who has been for some time in a
state of insensibility; his mother bears up he says very
well—I shall go to town to-morrow to see him. This
is the world—thus we cannot expect to give way many
hours to pleasure. Circumstances are like Clouds continually gathering and bursting—While we are laughing,
the seed of some trouble is put into the wide arable land
of events—while we are laughing it sprouts it grows and
suddenly bears a poison fruit which we must pluck.
Even so we have leisure to reason on the misfortunes of
our friends; our own touch us too nearly for words.
Very few men have ever arrived at a complete disinterestedness of Mind: very few have been influenced by a
pure desire of the benefit of others,—in the greater part
of the Benefactors to Humanity some meretricious motive
has sullied their greatness—some melodramatic scenery
has fascinated them. From the manner in which I feel
Haslam's misfortune I perceive how far I am from any
humble standard of disinterestedness. Yet this feeling

* Especially as I have a black eye.

[1] To about this date must belong the posthumously printed *Ode
on Indolence*, which describes the same mood with nearly the same
imagery. Possibly the "black eye" mentioned by Keats in his
footnote, together with the reflections on street-fighting later on,
may help us to fix the date of his famous fight with the butcher
boy.

ought to be carried to its highest pitch, as there is no fear
of its ever injuring society—which it would do, I fear,
pushed to an extremity. For in wild nature the Hawk
would lose his Breakfast of Robins and the Robin his of
Worms—The Lion must starve as well as the swallow.
The greater part of Men make their way with the same
instinctiveness, the same unwandering eye from their
purposes, the same animal eagerness as the Hawk. The
Hawk wants a Mate, so does the Man—look at them
both, they set about it and procure one in the same
manner. They want both a nest and they both set
about one in the same manner—they get their food in
the same manner. The noble animal Man for his
amusement smokes his pipe—the Hawk balances about
the Clouds—that is the only difference of their leisures.
This it is that makes the Amusement of Life—to a specu-
lative Mind—I go among the Fields and catch a glimpse
of a Stoat or a fieldmouse peeping out of the withered
grass—the creature hath a purpose, and its eyes are
bright with it. I go amongst the buildings of a city and
I see a Man hurrying along—to what? the Creature
has a purpose and his eyes are bright with it. But then,
as Wordsworth says, "we have all one human heart——"
There is an electric fire in human nature tending to purify
—so that among these human creatures there is continually
some birth of new heroism. The pity is that we must
wonder at it, as we should at finding a pearl in rubbish. I
have no doubt that thousands of people never heard of
have had hearts completely disinterested : I can remember
but two—Socrates and Jesus—Their histories evince it.
What I heard a little time ago, Taylor observe with respect
to Socrates, may be said of Jesus—That he was so great a
man that though he transmitted no writing of his own to
posterity, we have his Mind and his sayings and his
greatness handed to us by others. It is to be lamented
that the history of the latter was written and revised by
Men interested in the pious frauds of Religion. Yet
through all this I see his splendour. Even here, though

I myself am pursuing the same instinctive course as the
veriest human animal you can think of, I am, however
young, writing at random, straining at particles of light
in the midst of a great darkness, without knowing the
bearing of any one assertion, of any one opinion.   Yet
may I not in this be free from sin?   May there not be
superior beings amused with any graceful, though instinctive, attitude my mind may fall into as I am entertained
with the alertness of a Stoat or the anxiety of a Deer?
Though a quarrel in the Streets is a thing to be hated,
the energies displayed in it are fine; the commonest Man
shows a grace in his quarrel.   By a superior Being our
reasonings may take the same tone—though erroneous
they may be fine.   This is the very thing in which
consists Poetry, and if so it is not so fine a thing as
philosophy—For the same reason that an eagle is not so
fine a thing as a truth.   Give me this credit—Do you
not think I strive—to know myself?   Give me this
credit, and you will not think that on my own account
I repeat Milton's lines—

> " How charming is divine Philosophy,
>   Not harsh and crabbed, as dull fools suppose,
>   But musical as is Apollo's lute."

No—not for myself—feeling grateful as I do to have got
into a state of mind to relish them properly.   Nothing
ever becomes real till it is experienced—Even a Proverb
is no proverb to you till your Life has illustrated it.   I
am ever afraid that your anxiety for me will lead you to
fear for the violence of my temperament continually
smothered down: for that reason I did not intend to have
sent you the following sonnet—but look over the two
last pages and ask yourselves whether I have not that
in me which will bear the buffets of the world.   It will
be the best comment on my sonnet; it will show you
that it was written with no Agony but that of ignorance;
with no thirst of anything but Knowledge when pushed
to the point though the first steps to it were through my
human passions—they went away and I wrote with my

Mind—and perhaps I must confess a little bit of my heart—

> Why did I laugh to-night ?   No voice will tell :
> No God, no Deamon of severe response
> Deigns to reply from heaven or from Hell.—
>   Then to my human heart I turn at once—
> Heart ! thou and I are here sad and alone ;
>   Say, wherefore did I laugh ? O mortal pain !
> O Darkness ! Darkness ! ever must I moan,
>   To question Heaven and Hell and Heart in vain !
> Why did I laugh ! I know this being's lease,
>   My fancy to its utmost blisses spreads :
> Yet could I on this very midnight cease,[1]
>   And the world's gaudy ensigns see in shreds ;
> Verse, fame and Beauty are intense indeed
> But Death intenser—Death is Life's high meed.

I went to bed and enjoyed an uninterrupted sleep.   Sane I went to bed and sane I arose.

                                        [April 15.]

This is the 15th of April—you see what a time it is since I wrote ; all that time I have been day by day expecting Letters from you.   I write quite in the dark.   In the hopes of a Letter daily I have deferred that I might write in the light.   I was in town yesterday, and at Taylor's heard that young Birkbeck had been in Town and was to set forward in six or seven days—so I shall dedicate that time to making up this parcel ready for him.   I wish I could hear from you to make me " whole and general as the casing air."[2]   A few days after the 19th of April[3] I received a note from Haslam containing the news of his father's death.   The Family has all been well.   Haslam has his father's situation.   The Framptons have behaved well to him.   The day before yesterday I went to a rout at Sawrey's—it was made pleasant by Reynolds being there and our getting into conversation with one of the most beautiful Girls I ever saw—She gave

---

[1] Compare the repetition of the same thought and phrase in the ode *To a Nightingale* written two months later.

[2] Slightly misquoted from *Macbeth* in the banquet scene.

[3] By mistake for the 19th of March.

a remarkable prettiness to all those commonplaces which
most women who talk must utter—I liked Mrs. Sawrey
very well. The Sunday before last your Brothers were
to come by a long invitation—so long that for the
time I forgot it when I promised Mrs. Brawne to dine
with her on the same day. On recollecting my engagement with your Brothers I immediately excused myself
with Mrs. Brawne, but she would not hear of it, and insisted on my bringing my friends with me. So we all
dined at Mrs. Brawne's. I have been to Mrs. Bentley's
this morning, and put all the letters to and from you
and poor Tom and me.[1] I found some of the correspondence between him and that degraded Wells and Amena.
It is a wretched business; I do not know the rights of
it, but what I do know would, I am sure, affect you so
much that I am in two minds whether I will tell you
anything about it. And yet I do not see why—for anything, though it be unpleasant, that calls to mind those
we still love has a compensation in itself for the pain it
occasions—so very likely to-morrow I may set about
copying the whole of what I have about it : with no sort
of a Richardson self-satisfaction—I hate it to a sickness—
and I am afraid more from indolence of mind than anything else. I wonder how people exist with all their
worries. I have not been to Westminster but once
lately, and that was to see Dilke in his new Lodgings—
I think of living somewhere in the neighbourhood myself.
Your mother was well by your Brothers' account. I shall
see her perhaps to-morrow—yes I shall. We have had
the Boys[2] here lately—they make a bit of a racket—I shall
not be sorry when they go. I found also this morning, in
a note from George to you and my dear sister a lock of your
hair which I shall this moment put in the miniature case.
A few days ago Hunt dined here and Brown invited
Davenport to meet him, Davenport from a sense of
weakness thought it incumbent on him to show off—and

---

[1] For "put together" ?

[2] Brown's younger brothers : see below, p. 245.

pursuant to that never ceased talking and boring all day
till I was completely fagged out.   Brown grew melancholy—but Hunt perceiving what a complimentary tendency all this had bore it remarkably well — Brown
grumbled about it for two or three days.   I went with
Hunt to Sir John Leicester's gallery; there I saw North-
cote—Hilton—Bewick, and many more of great and Little
note.   Haydon's picture is of very little progress this
year — He talks about finishing it next year.   Wordsworth is going to publish a Poem called Peter Bell—
what a perverse fellow it is !   Why will he talk about
Peter Bells—I was told not to tell—but to you it will
not be telling—Reynolds hearing that said Peter Bell
was coming out, took it into his head to write a skit
upon it called Peter Bell.   He did it as soon as thought
on, it is to be published this morning, and comes out
before the real Peter Bell, with this admirable motto
from the " Bold Stroke for a Wife " " I am the real
Simon Pure."   It would be just as well to trounce Lord
Byron in the same manner.   I am still at a stand in
versifying—I cannot do it yet with any pleasure—I mean,
however, to look round on my resources and means, and
see what I can do without poetry—To that end I shall
live in Westminster—I have no doubt of making by
some means a little to help on, or I shall be left in the
Lurch—with the burden of a little Pride—However I
look in time.   The Dilkes like their Lodgings at Westminster tolerably well.   I cannot help thinking what a
shame it is that poor Dilke should give up his comfortable
house and garden for his Son, whom he will certainly ruin
with too much care.   The boy has nothing in his ears all
day but himself and the importance of his education.
Dilke has continually in his mouth " My Boy."   This is
what spoils princes : it may have the same effect with
Commoners.   Mrs. Dilke has been very well lately—But
what a shameful thing it is that for that obstinate Boy
Dilke should stifle himself in Town Lodgings and wear
out his Life by his continual apprehension of his Boy's

fate in Westminster school, with the rest of the Boys and
the Masters.   Every one has some wear and tear.   One
would think Dilke ought to be quiet and happy—but no
—this one Boy makes his face pale, his society silent and
his vigilance jealous—He would I have no doubt quarrel
with any one who snubb'd his Boy—With all this he
has no notion how to manage him.   O what a farce is
our greatest cares!   Yet one must be in the pother for
the sake of Clothes food and Lodging.   There has been
a squabble between Kean and Mr. Bucke—There are
faults on both sides—on Bucke's the faults are positive
to the Question : Kean's fault is a want of genteel knowledge and high Policy.   The former writes knavishly
foolish, and the other silly bombast.   It was about a
Tragedy written by said Mr. Bucke which, it appears, Mr.
Kean kick'd at—it was so bad—After a little struggle
of Mr. Bucke's against Kean, Drury Lane had the Policy
to bring it out and Kean the impolicy not to appear in
it.   It was damn'd.   The people in the Pit had a
favourite call on the night of "Buck, Buck, rise up" and
"Buck, Buck, how many horns do I hold up."   Kotzebue
the German Dramatist and traitor to his country was
murdered lately by a young student whose name I forget—
he stabbed himself immediately after crying out Germany !
Germany !   I was unfortunate to miss Richards the
only time I have been for many months to see him.
    Shall I treat you with a little extempore?—

> When they were come into the Faery's Court
> They rang—no one at home—all gone to sport
> And dance and kiss and love as faerys do
> For Faries be as humans lovers true.
> Amid the woods they were so lone and wild,
> Where even the Robin feels himself exil'd,
> And where the very brooks, as if afraid,
> Hurry along to some less magic shade.
> ' No one at home !' the fretful princess cry'd ;
> ' And all for nothing such a dreary ride,
> And all for nothing my new diamond cross ;
> No one to see my Persian feathers toss,
> No one to see my Ape, my Dwarf, my Fool,

R

Or how I pace my Otaheitan mule.
Ape, Dwarf, and Fool, why stand you gaping there,
Burst the door open, quick—or I declare
I'll switch you soundly and in pieces tear.'
The Dwarf began to tremble, and the Ape
Star'd at the Fool, the Fool was all agape,
The Princess grasp'd her switch, but just in time
The dwarf with piteous face began to rhyme.
' O mighty Princess, did you ne'er hear tell
What your poor servants know but too too well ?
Know you the three great crimes in faery land ?
The first, alas ! poor Dwarf, I understand,
I made a whipstock of a faery's wand ;
The next is snoring in their company ;
The next, the last, the direst of the three,
Is making free when they are not at home.
I was a Prince—a baby prince—my doom,
You see, I made a whipstock of a wand,
My top has henceforth slept in faery land.
He was a Prince, the Fool, a grown-up Prince,
But he has never been a King's son since
He fell a snoring at a faery Ball.
Your poor Ape was a Prince, and he poor thing
Picklock'd a faery's boudoir—now no king
But ape—so pray your highness stay awhile,
'Tis sooth indeed, we know it to our sorrow—
Persist and *you* may be an ape to-morrow.'
While the Dwarf spake the. Princess, all for spite,
Peel'd the brown hazel twig to lilly white,
Clench'd her small teeth, and held her lips apart,
Try'd to look unconcern'd with beating heart.
They saw her highness had made up her mind,
A-quavering like the reeds before the wind—
And they had had it, but O happy chance
The Ape for very fear began to dance
And grinn'd as all his ugliness did ache—
She staid her vixen fingers for his sake,
He was so very ugly : then she took
Her pocket-mirror and began to look
First at herself and then at him, and then
She smil'd at her own beauteous face again.
Yet for all this—for all her pretty face—
She took it in her head to see the place.
Women gain little from experience
Either in Lovers, husbands, or expense.
The more their beauty the more fortune too—
Beauty before the wide world never knew—

So each fair reasons—tho' it oft miscarries.
She thought *her* pretty face would please the fairies.
' My darling Ape.I won't whip you to-day,
Give me the Picklock sirrah and go play.'
They all three wept but counsel was as vain
As crying cup biddy to drops of rain.
Yet lingering by did the sad Ape forth draw
The Picklock from the Pocket in his Jaw.
The Princess took it, and dismounting straight
Tripp'd in blue silver'd slippers to the gate
And touch'd the wards, the Door full courteously
Opened—she enter'd with her servants three.
Again it clos'd and there was nothing seen
But the Mule grazing on the herbage green.
End of Canto XII.

Canto the XIII.

The Mule no sooner saw himself alone
Than he prick'd up his Ears—and said ' well done ;
At least unhappy Prince I may be free—
No more a Princess shall side-saddle me.
O King of Otaheite—tho' a Mule,
    Aye, every inch a King '—tho' ' Fortune's fool,'
Well done—for by what Mr. Dwarfy said
I would not give a sixpence for her head.'
Even as he spake he trotted in high glee
To the knotty side of an old Pollard tree,
And rubb'd his sides against the mossed bark
Till his Girths burst and left him naked stark
Except his Bridle—how get rid of that
Buckled and tied with many a twist and plait.
At last it struck him to pretend to sleep,
And then the thievish Monkies down would creep
And filch the unpleasant trammels quite away.
No sooner thought of than adown he lay,
Shamm'd a good snore—the Monkey-men descended,
And whom they thought to injure they befriended.
They hung his Bridle on a topmost bough
And off he went run, trot, or anyhow—

Brown is gone to bed—and I am tired of rhyming—there
is a north wind blowing playing young gooseberry with
the trees—I don't care so it helps even with a side wind
a Letter to me—for I cannot put faith in any reports I
hear of the Settlement ; some are good and some bad.

Last Sunday I took a Walk towards Highgate and in
the lane that winds by the side of Lord Mansfield's park
I met Mr. Green our Demonstrator at Guy's in conversation with Coleridge—I joined them, after enquiring by a
look whether it would be agreeable—I walked with him
at his alderman-after-dinner pace for near two miles I
suppose.   In those two Miles he broached a thousand
things—let me see if I can give you a list—Nightingales—
Poetry—on Poetical Sensation—Metaphysics—Different
genera and species of Dreams—Nightmare—a dream
accompanied by a sense of touch—single and double
touch—a dream related—First and second consciousness
—the difference explained between will and Volition—so
say metaphysicians from a want of smoking the second
consciousness — Monsters — the Kraken — Mermaids —
Southey believes in them—Southey's belief too much
diluted—a Ghost story—Good morning—I heard his
voice as he came towards me—I heard it as he moved
away—I had heard it all the interval—if it may be
called so.   He was civil enough to ask me to call on
him at Highgate.   Good-night!

[Later, April 16 or 17.]

It looks so much like rain I shall not go to town
to-day : but put it off till to-morrow.   Brown this morning is writing some Spenserian stanzas against Mrs., Miss
Brawne and me ; so I shall amuse myself with him a
little : in the manner of Spenser—

> He is to weet a melancholy Carle
> Thin in the waist, with bushy head of hair
> As hath the seeded thistle when in parle
> It holds the Zephyr, ere it sendeth fair
> Its light balloons into the summer air
> Thereto his beard had not begun to bloom
> No brush had touch'd his chin or razor sheer
> No care had touch'd his cheek with mortal doom,
>   But new he was and bright as scarf from Persian loom.
>
> Ne cared he for wine, or half-and-half
> Ne cared he for fish or flesh or fowl,

And sauces held he worthless as the chaff
He 'sdeign'd the swineherd at the wassail bowl
Ne with lewd ribbalds sat he cheek by jowl
Ne with sly Lemans in the scorner's chair
But after water-brooks this Pilgrim's soul
Panted, and all his food was woodland air
   Though he would ofttimes feast on gilliflowers rare—

The slang of cities in no wise he knew
Tipping the wink to him was heathen Greek ;
He sipp'd no olden Tom or ruin blue
Or nantz or cheery brandy drunk full meek
By many a Damsel hoarse and rouge of cheek
Nor did he know each aged Watchman's beat—
Nor in obscured purlieus would he seek
For curled Jewesses, with ankles neat
   Who as they walk abroad make tinkling with their feet.

This character would ensure him a situation in the
establishment of patient Griselda.   The servant has come
for the little Browns this morning—they have been a
toothache to me which I shall enjoy the riddance of—
Their little voices are like wasps' stings—Sometimes am
I all wound with Browns.[1]   We had a claret feast some
little while ago.   There were Dilke, Reynolds, Skinner,
Mancur, John Brown, Martin, Brown and I.   We all got a
little tipsy—but pleasantly so—I enjoy Claret to a degree.

[Later, April 18 or 19.]

   I have been looking over the correspondence of the
pretended Amena and Wells this evening—I now see
the whole cruel deception.   I think Wells must have
had an accomplice in it—Amena's letters are in a Man's
language and in a Man's hand imitating a woman's.   The
instigations to this diabolical scheme were vanity, and the
love of intrigue.   It was no thoughtless hoax—but a cruel
deception on a sanguine Temperament, with every show
of friendship.   I do not think death too bad for the
villain.   The world would look upon it in a different

---

[1] "Sometime am I
All wound with adders, who with cloven tongues
Do hiss me into madness."
     Caliban in *Tempest*, II. ii.

light should I expose it—they would call it a frolic—so
I must be wary—but I consider it my duty to be
prudently revengeful. I will hang over his head like a
sword by a hair. I will be opium to his vanity—if I
cannot injure his interests—He is a rat and he shall
have ratsbane to his vanity—I will harm him all I possibly can—I have no doubt I shall be able to do so—
Let us leave him to his misery alone, except when we
can throw in a little more. The fifth canto of Dante
pleases me more and more—it is that one in which he
meets with Paolo and Francesca. I had passed many
days in rather a low state of mind, and in the midst of
them I dreamt of being in that region of Hell. The
dream was one of the most delightful enjoyments I ever
had in my life. I floated about the whirling atmosphere,
as it is described, with a beautiful figure, to whose lips
mine were joined as it seemed for an age—and in the
midst of all this cold and darkness I was warm—even
flowery tree-tops sprung up, and we rested on them, sometimes with the lightness of a cloud, till the wind blew us
away again. I tried a sonnet upon it—there are fourteen
lines, but nothing of what I felt in it—O that I could
dream it every night—

> As Hermes once took to his feathers light
> When lulled Argus, baffled, swoon'd and slept,
> So on a delphic reed my idle spright
> So play'd, so charm'd, so conquer'd, so bereft
> The Dragon world of all its hundred eyes ;
> And seeing it asleep, so fled away ;—
> Not to pure Ida with its snow-cold skies,
> Nor unto Tempe where Jove grieved that day ;
> But to that second circle of sad Hell
> Where in the gust, the whirlwind, and the flaw
> Of Rain and hailstones, lovers need not tell
> Their sorrows. Pale were the sweet lips I saw,
> Pale were the lips I kiss'd, and fair the form
> I floated with about that melancholy storm.

I want very very much a little of your wit, my dear
Sister—a Letter or two of yours just to bandy back a
pun or two across the Atlantic, and send a quibble over

the Floridas.   Now you have by this time crumpled up
your large Bonnet, what do you wear—a cap? do you
put your hair in papers of a night? do you pay the Miss
Birkbecks a morning visit—have you any tea? or do you
milk-and-water with them—What place of Worship do
you go to—the Quakers, the Moravians, the Unitarians,
or the Methodists?   Are there any flowers in bloom you
like—any beautiful heaths—any streets full of Corset
Makers?   What sort of shoes have you to fit those pretty
feet of yours?   Do you desire Compliments ·to one
another?   Do you ride on Horseback?   What do you
have for breakfast, dinner, and supper? without mentioning lunch and bever,[1] and wet and snack—and a bit to
stay one's stomach?   Do you get any Spirits—now you
might easily distill some whiskey—and going into the
woods, set up a whiskey shop for the Monkeys—Do you
and the Miss Birkbecks get groggy on anything—a
little so-soish so as to be obliged to be seen home with a
Lantern? You may perhaps have a game at puss in the
corner—Ladies are warranted to play at this game though
they have not whiskers.   Have you a fiddle in the Settlement—or at any rate a Jew's harp—which will play in
spite of one's teeth—When you have nothing else to do
for a whole day I tell you how you may employ it—
First get up and when you are dressed, as it would be
pretty early with a high wind in the woods, give George
a cold Pig with my Compliments.   Then you may
saunter into the nearest coffee-house, and after taking a
dram and a look at the Chronicle—go and frighten the
wild boars upon the strength—you may as well bring
one home for breakfast, serving up the hoofs garnished
with bristles and a grunt or two to accompany the singing of the kettle—then if George is not up give him a
colder Pig always with my Compliments—When you
are both set down to breakfast I advise you to eat your

---

[1] This old word for a snack between meals is used by Marlowe
and Ben Jonson, and I believe still survives at some of the public
schools.

full share, but leave off immediately on feeling yourself inclined to anything on the other side of the puffy—avoid· that, for it does not become young women—After you have eaten your breakfast keep your eye upon dinner— it is the safest way—You should keep a Hawk's eye over your dinner and keep hovering over it till due time then pounce taking care not to break any plates. While you are hovering with your dinner in prospect you may do a thousand things—put a hedgehog into George's hat —pour a little water into his rifle—soak his boots in a pail of water—cut his jacket round into shreds like a Roman kilt or the back of my grandmother's stays—Sew *off* his buttons—

[Later, April 21 or 22.]

Yesterday I could not write a line I was so fatigued, for the day before I went to town in the morning, called on your Mother, and returned in time for a few friends we had to dinner. These were Taylor, Woodhouse, Reynolds : we began cards at about 9 o'clock, and the night coming on, and continuing dark and rainy, they could not think of returning to town—So we played at Cards till very daylight—and yesterday I was not worth a sixpence. Your Mother was very well but anxious for a Letter. We had half an hour's talk and no more, for I was obliged to be home. Mrs. and Miss Millar were well, and so was Miss Waldegrave. I have asked your Brothers here for next Sunday. When Reynolds was here on Monday he asked me to give Hunt a hint to take notice of his Peter Bell in the Examiner—the best thing I can do is to write a little notice of it myself, which I will do here, and copy out if it should suit my Purpose—

Peter Bell. There have been lately advertised two Books both Peter Bell by name ; what stuff the one was made of might be seen by the motto—" I am the real Simon Pure." This false Florimel has hurried from the press and obtruded herself into public notice, while for aught we know the real one may be still wandering about the woods and mountains. Let us hope she may soon

appear and make good her right to the magic girdle.
The Pamphleteering Archimage, we can perceive, has
rather a splenetic love than a downright hatred to real
Florimels—if indeed they had been so christened—or
had even a pretention to play at bob cherry with
Barbara Lewthwaite : but he has a fixed aversion to
those three rhyming Graces Alice Fell, Susan Gale and
Betty Foy; and now at length especially to Peter Bell
—fit Apollo.   It may be seen from one or two Passages
in this little skit, that the writer of it has felt the finer
parts of Mr. Wordsworth, and perhaps expatiated with
his more remote and sublimer muse.   This as far as it
relates to Peter Bell is unlucky.   The more he may love
the sad embroidery of the Excursion, the more he will
hate the coarse Samplers of Betty Foy and Alice Fell;
and as they come from the same hand, the better will
he be able to imitate that which can be imitated, to
wit Peter Bell—as far as can be imagined from the
obstinate Name.   We repeat, it is very unlucky—this real
Simon Pure is in parts the very Man—there is a pernicious likeness in the scenery, a 'pestilent humour' in the
rhymes, and an inveterate cadence in some of the Stanzas,
that must be lamented.   If we are one part amused with
this we are three parts sorry that an appreciator of
Wordsworth should show so much temper at this really
provoking name of Peter Bell—![1]

This will do well enough—I have copied it and
enclosed it to Hunt.   You will call it a little politic—
seeing I keep clear of all parties.   I say something for
and against both parties—and suit it to the tune of the
Examiner—I meant to say I do not unsuit it—and I
believe I think what I say, nay I am sure I do—I and
my conscience are in luck to-day—which is an excellent
thing.   The other night I went to the Play with Rice,
Reynolds, and Martin—we saw a new dull and half-
damn'd opera call'd the 'Heart of Midlothian,' that was

---

[1] This notice of Reynolds's parody was printed, with some
revision, in the *Examiner* for April 26, 1819.

on Saturday—I stopt at Taylor's on Sunday with Woodhouse—and passed a quiet sort of pleasant day.   I have
been very much pleased with the Panorama of the Ship
at the North Pole—with the icebergs, the Mountains,
the Bears, the Wolves—the seals, the Penguins—and a
large whale floating back above water—it is impossible
to describe the place—

Wednesday Evening [April 28].

LA BELLE DAME SANS MERCI

O what can ail thee Knight at arms
  Alone and palely loitering ?
The sedge has withered from the Lake
  And no birds sing !

O what can ail thee Knight at arms
  So haggard, and so woe-begone ?
The squirrel's granary is full
  And the harvest's done.

I see a lily on thy brow,
  With anguish moist and fever dew,
And on thy cheek a fading rose
  Fast Withereth too—

I met a Lady in the Meads
  Full beautiful, a faery's child—
Her hair was long, her foot was light
  And her eyes were wild—

I made a Garland for her head,
  And bracelets too, and fragrant Zone
She look'd at me as she did love
  And made sweet moan—

I set her on my pacing steed
  And nothing else saw all day long,
For sidelong would she bend and sing
  A faery's song—

She found me roots of relish sweet
  And honey wild and manna dew
And sure in language strange she said
  I love thee true—

She took me to her elfin grot
  And there she wept and sigh'd full sore,
And there I shut her wild, wild eyes
  With kisses four—

And there she lulled me asleep,
  And there I dream'd Ah Woe betide !
The latest dream I ever dreamt
  On the cold hill side.

I saw pale Kings and Princes too
  Pale warriors death-pale were they all
They cried—La belle dame sans merci
  Thee hath in thrall.

I saw their starv'd lips in the gloam
  With horrid warning gaped wide,
And I awoke, and found me here
  On the cold hill's side.

And this is why I sojourn here
  Alone and palely loitering ;
Though the sedge is withered from the Lake ·
  And no birds sing.[1] . . .

Why four kisses—you will say—why four, because I
wish to restrain the headlong impetuosity of my Muse—she
would have fain said "score" without hurting the rhyme
—but we must temper the Imagination, as the Critics say,
with Judgment. I was obliged to choose an even number,
that both eyes might have fair play, and to speak truly I
think two a piece quite sufficient. Suppose I had said
seven there would have been three and a half a piece—a
very awkward affair, and well got out of on my side—

[Later.]

CHORUS OF FAIRIES. 4—FIRE, AIR, EARTH, AND WATER—
SALAMANDER, ZEPHYR, DUSKETHA, BREAMA.

Sal.   Happy happy glowing fire !
Zep.   Fragrant air, delicious light !
Dusk.   Let me to my glooms retire.
Bream. I to greenweed rivers bright.

---

[1] There is no other autograph copy of this famous poem except
the draft here given. It contains several erasures and corrections.
In verse 3 Keats had written first, for "a lily" and "a fading
rose," "death's lily" and "death's fading rose": in verse 4, for
"Meads," "Wilds": in verse 7, for "manna dew," "honey dew":
in verse 8, for "and sigh'd full sore," "and there she sigh'd"; in
verse 11, for "gaped wide," "wide agape": and in verse 12, for
"sojourn," "wither."

Salam.

Happy, happy glowing fire !
Dazzling bowers of soft retire,
Ever let my nourish'd wing,
Like a bat's still wandering,
Faintly fan your fiery spaces
Spirit sole in deadly places,
In unhaunted roar and blaze
Open eyes that never daze
Let me see the myriad shapes
Of Men and Beasts and Fish and apes,
Portray'd in many a fiery den,
And wrought by spumy bitumen
On the deep intenser roof,
Arched every way aloof.
Let me breathe upon my skies,
And anger their live tapestries ;
Free from cold and every care,
Of chilly rain and shivering air.

Zephyr.

Spright of fire—away away !
Or your very roundelay
Will sear my plumage newly budded
From its quilled sheath and studded
With the self-same dews that fell
On the May-grown Asphodel.
Spright of fire away away !

Breama.

Spright of fire away away !
Zephyr blue-eyed faery turn,
And see my cool sedge-shaded urn,
Where it rests its mossy brim
Mid water-mint and cresses dim ;
And the flowers, in sweet troubles,
Lift their eyes above the bubbles,
Like our Queen when she would please
To sleep, and Oberon will tease—
Love me blue-eyed Faery true
Soothly I am sick for you.

Zephyr.

Gentle Breama ! by the first
Violet young nature nurst,
I will bathe myself with thee,
So you sometime follow me

To my home far far in west,
Far beyond the search and quest
Of the golden-browed sun.
Come with me, o'er tops of trees,
To my fragrant Palaces,
Where they ever-floating are
Beneath the cherish of a star
Call'd Vesper—who with silver veil
Ever Hides his brilliance pale,
Ever gently drows'd doth keep
Twilight of the Fays to sleep.
Fear not that your watery hair
Will thirst in drouthy ringlets there—
Clouds of stored summer rains
Thou shalt taste before the stains
Of the mountain soil they take,
And too unlucent for thee make.
I love thee, Crystal faery true
Sooth I am as sick for you—

Salam.

Out ye agueish Faeries out !
Chilly Lovers, what a rout
Keep ye with your frozen breath
Colder than the mortal death—
Adder-eyed Dusketha speak,
Shall we leave them and go seek
In the Earth's wide Entrails old
Couches warm as their's is cold ?
O for a fiery gloom and thee,
Dusketha, so enchantingly
Freckle-wing'd and lizard-sided !

Dusketha.

By thee Spright will I be guided
I care not for cold or heat
Frost and Flame or sparks or sleet
To my essence are the same—
But I honour more the flame—
Spright of fire I follow thee
Wheresoever it may be ;
To the torrid spouts and fountains,
Underneath earth-quaked mountains
Or at thy supreme desire,
Touch the very pulse of fire
With my bare unlidded eyes.

Salam.

Sweet Dusketha ! Paradise !
Off ye icy Spirits fly !
Frosty creatures of the Sky !

Dusketha.

Breathe upon them fiery Spright !

Zephyr, Breama (to each other).

Away Away to our delight !

Salam.

Go feed on icicles while we
Bedded in tongued-flames will be.

Dusketha.

Lead me to those fev'rous glooms,
Spright of fire—

Breama.

Me to the blooms
Blue-eyed Zephyr of those flowers
Far in the west where the May cloud lours ;
And the beams of still Vesper, where winds are all whist,
Are shed through the rain and the milder mist,
And twilight your floating bowers—

I have been reading lately two very different books,
Robertson's America and Voltaire's Siècle de Louis XIV.
It is like walking arm and arm between Pizarro and the
great-little Monarch.   In how lamentable a case do we
see the great body of the people in both instances ; in
the first, where Men might seem to inherit quiet of Mind
from unsophisticated senses ; from uncontamination of
civilisation, and especially from their-being, as it were,
estranged from the mutual helps of Society and its
mutual injuries—and thereby more immediately under
the Protection of Providence—even there they had
mortal pains to bear as bad, or even worse than Bailiffs,
Debts, and Poverties of civilised Life.   The whole appears
to resolve into this—that Man is originally a poor forked
creature subject to the same mischances as the beasts of
the forest, destined to hardships and disquietude of some

kind or other.   If he improves by degrees his bodily
accommodations and comforts—at each stage, at each
ascent there are waiting for him a fresh set of annoyances—
he is mortal, and there is still a heaven with its Stars
above his head.   The most interesting question that can
come before us is, How far by the persevering endeavours
of a seldom appearing Socrates Mankind may be made
happy — I can imagine such happiness carried to an
extreme, but what must it end in ?—Death—and who
could in such a case bear with death?   The whole troubles
of life, which are now frittered away in a series of years,
would then be accumulated for the last days of a being
who instead of hailing its approach would leave this
world as Eve left Paradise.   But in truth I do not at all
believe in this sort of perfectibility—the nature of the
world will not admit of it—the inhabitants of the world
will correspond to itself.   Let the fish Philosophise the
ice away from the Rivers in winter time, and they shall
be at continual play in the tepid delight of summer.
Look at the Poles and at the Sands of Africa, whirlpools
and volcanoes—Let men exterminate them and I will
say that they may arrive at earthly Happiness.   The
point at which Man may arrive is as far as the parallel
state in inanimate nature, and no further.   For instance
suppose a rose to have sensation, it blooms on a beautiful
morning, it enjoys itself, but then comes a cold wind, a
hot sun—it cannot escape it, it cannot destroy its annoyances—they are as native to the world as itself : no more
can man be happy in spite, the worldly elements will
prey upon his nature.   The common cognomen of this
world among the misguided and superstitious is "a vale
of tears," from which we are to be redeemed by a certain
arbitrary interposition of God and taken to Heaven—
What a little circumscribed straightened notion !   Call
the world if you please "The vale of Soul-making."
Then you will find out the use of the world (I am speaking
now in the highest terms for human nature admitting it
to be immortal which I will here take for granted for the

purpose of showing a thought which has struck me concerning it) I say '*Soul-making*'—Soul as distinguished from an Intelligence.   There may be intelligences or sparks of the divinity in millions—but they are not Souls till they acquire identities, till each' one is personally itself.   Intelligences are atoms of perception—they know and they see and they are pure, in short they are God—how then are Souls to be made?   How then are these sparks which are God to have identity given them —so as ever to possess a bliss peculiar to each one's individual existence?   How, but by the medium of a world like this?   This point I sincerely wish to consider because I think it a grander system of salvation than the Christian religion—or rather it is a system of Spirit-creation—This is effected by three grand materials acting the one upon the other for a series of years—These three Materials are the *Intelligence*—the *human heart* (as distinguished from intelligence or Mind), and the *World* or *Elemental space* suited for the proper action of *Mind and Heart* on each other for the purpose of forming the *Soul* or *Intelligence destined to possess the sense of Identity*. I can scarcely express what I but dimly perceive—and yet I think I perceive it—that you may judge the more clearly I will put it in the most homely form possible.   I will call the *world* a School instituted for the purpose of teaching little children to read—I will call the *human heart* the *horn Book* used in that School—and I will call the *Child able to read, the Soul* made from that *School* and its *horn book*.   Do you not see how necessary a World of Pains and troubles is to school an Intelligence and make it a soul?   A Place where the heart must feel and suffer in a thousand diverse ways.   Not merely is the Heart a Hornbook, It is the Mind's Bible, it is the Mind's experience, it is the text from which the Mind or Intelligence sucks its identity.   As various as the Lives of Men are—so various become their souls, and thus does God make individual beings, Souls, Identical Souls of the sparks of his own essence.   This appears to me a faint sketch of a system of Salvation which does not offend our reason and humanity—I am convinced that many difficulties which Christians labour under would vanish before it—there is one which even now strikes me—the salvation of Children.   In them the spark or intelligence returns to God without any identity—it having had no time to learn of and be altered by the heart—or seat of the human Passions.   It is pretty generally suspected that the Christian scheme has been copied from the ancient Persian and Greek Philosophers.   Why may they not have made this simple thing even more simple for common apprehension by introducing Mediators and Personages, in the same manner as in the heathen mythology abstractions are personified?   Seriously I think it probable that this system of Soul-making may have been the Parent of all the more palpable and personal schemes ot Redemption among the Zoroastrians the Christians and the Hindoos.   For as one part of the human species must have their carved Jupiter; so another part must have the palpable and named Mediator and Saviour, their Christ, their Oromanes, and their Vishnu.   If what I have said should not be plain enough, as I fear it may not be, I will put you in the place where I began in this series of thoughts—I mean I began by seeing how man was formed by circumstances—and what are circumstances but touchstones of his heart? and what are touchstones but provings of his heart, but fortifiers or alterers of his nature? and what is his altered nature but his Soul?—and what was his Soul before it came into the world and had these provings and alterations and perfectionings?—An intelligence without Identity—and how is this Identity to be made? Through the medium of the Heart? and how is the heart to become this Medium but in a world of Circumstances?

There now I think what with Poetry and Theology, you may thank your stars that my pen is not very long-winded. Yesterday I received two Letters from your Mother and Henry, which I shall send by young Birkbeck with this.

s

Friday, April 30.

Brown has been here rummaging up some of my old sins—that is to say sonnets. I do not think you remember them, so I will copy them out, as well as two or three lately written. I have just written one on Fame—which Brown is transcribing and he has his book and mine. I must employ myself perhaps in a sonnet on the same subject—

ON FAME

You cannot eat your cake and have it too.—Proverb.

How fever'd is that Man who cannot look
   Upon his mortal days with temperate blood
Who vexes all the leaves of his Life's book
   And robs his fair name of its maidenhood.
It is as if the rose should pluck herself
   Or the ripe plum finger its misty bloom,
As if a clear Lake meddling with itself
   Should cloud its clearness with a muddy gloom.
But the rose leaves herself upon the Briar
For winds to kiss and grateful Bees to feed,
And the ripe plum still wears its dim attire,
The undisturbed Lake has crystal space—
Why then should man, teasing the world for grace,
Spoil his salvation by a fierce miscreed ?

ANOTHER ON FAME

Fame like a wayward girl will still be coy
   To those who woo her with too slavish knees
But makes surrender to some thoughtless boy
   And dotes the more upon a heart at ease—
She is a Gipsy will not speak to those
   Who have not learnt to be content without her,
A Jilt whose ear was never whisper'd close,
   Who think they scandal her who talk about her—
A very Gipsy is she Nilus born,
Sister-in-law to jealous Potiphar—
Ye lovesick Bards, repay her scorn for scorn,
Ye lovelorn Artists, madmen that ye are,
Make your best bow to her and bid adieu,
Then if she likes it she will follow you.

TO SLEEP

O soft embalmer of the still midnight
  Shutting with careful fingers and benign
Our gloom-pleased eyes embowered from the light
  Enshaded in forgetfulness divine—
O soothest sleep, if so it please thee close
  In midst of this thine hymn my willing eyes,
Or wait the amen, ere thy poppy throws
  Around my bed its dewy Charities.
Then save me or the passed day will shine
Upon my pillow breeding many woes.
Save me from curious conscience that still lords
Its strength for darkness, burrowing like a Mole—
Turn the key deftly in the oiled wards,
And seal the hushed Casket of my soul.

The following Poem—the last I have written—is the first and the only one with which I have taken even moderate pains. I have for the most part dash'd off my lines in a hurry. This I have done leisurely—I think it reads the more richly for it, and will I hope encourage me to write other things in even a more peaceable and healthy spirit. You must recollect that Psyche was not embodied as a goddess before the time of Apuleius the Platonist who lived after the Augustan age, and consequently the Goddess was never worshipped or sacrificed to with any of the ancient fervour—and perhaps never thought of in the old religion—I am more orthodox than to let a heathen Goddess be so neglected—

ODE TO PSYCHE

O Goddess hear these tuneless numbers, wrung
  By sweet enforcement and remembrance dear,
And pardon that thy secrets should be sung
  Even into thine own soft-conched ear !
Surely I dreamt to-day ; or did I see
  The winged Psyche, with awaked eyes ?
I wandered in a forest thoughtlessly,
  And on the sudden, fainting with surprise,
Saw two fair Creatures couched side by side
  In deepest grass, beneath the whisp'ring fan

Of leaves and trembled blossoms, where there ran
  A Brooklet scarce espied
'Mid hush'd, cool-rooted flowers, fragrant-eyed,
  Blue, freckle pink, and budded Syrian
They lay, calm-breathing on the bedded grass ;
  Their arms embraced and their pinions too ;
Their lips touch'd not, but had not bid adieu,
As if disjoined by soft-handed slumber,
And ready still past kisses to outnumber
At tender dawn of aurorian love.
  The winged boy I knew :
But who wast thou O happy happy dove !
  His Psyche true ?
O latest born, and loveliest vision far
  Of all Olympus' faded Hierarchy !
Fairer than Phœbe's sapphire-region'd star,
  Or Vesper amorous glow-worm of the sky ;
Fairer than these though Temple thou hadst none,
  Nor Altar heap'd with flowers ;
Nor virgin-choir to make delicious moan
  Upon the midnight hours ;
No voice, no lute, no pipe no incense sweet
  From chain-swung Censer teeming—
No shrine, no grove, no Oracle, no heat
  Of pale mouth'd Prophet dreaming !

O Bloomiest ! though too late for antique vows ;
  Too, too late for the fond believing Lyre,
When holy were the haunted forest boughs,
  Holy the Air, the water and the fire ;
Yet even in these days so far retir'd
  From happy Pieties, thy lucent fans,
Fluttering among the faint Olympians,
  I see, and sing by my own eyes inspired.
O let me be thy Choir and make a moan
  Upon the midnight hours ;
Thy voice, thy lute, thy pipe, thy incense sweet
  From swinged Censer teeming ;
Thy Shrine, thy Grove, thy Oracle, thy heat
  Of pale-mouth'd Prophet dreaming !
Yes, I will be thy Priest and build a fane
  In some untrodden region of my Mind,
Where branched thoughts, new grown with pleasant pain,
  Instead of pines shall murmur in the wind.
Far, far around shall those dark cluster'd trees
  Fledge the wild-ridged mountains steep by steep ;

And there by Zephyrs streams and birds and bees
  The moss-lain Dryads shall be lulled to sleep.
And in the midst of this wide-quietness
  A rosy Sanctuary will I dress
With the wreath'd trellis of a working brain;
  With buds and bells and stars without a name;
With all the gardener-fancy e'er could feign,
  Who breeding flowers will never breed the same—
And there shall be for thee all soft delight
  That shadowy thought can win;
A bright torch and a casement ope at night
  To let the warm Love in.

Here endethe ye Ode to Psyche.

———

Incipit altera Sonneta

———

I have been endeavouring to discover a better Sonnet
Stanza than we have. The legitimate does not suit the
language over well from the pouncing rhymes—the other
kind appears too elegiac—and the couplet at the end of it
has seldom a pleasing effect—I do not pretend to have
succeeded—it will explain itself.

If by dull rhymes our English must be chained,
And, like Andromeda, the sonnet sweet
Fetter'd, in spite of pained Loveliness;
Let us find out, if we must be constrain'd,
Sandals more interwoven and complete
To fit the naked foot of poesy;
Let us inspect the lyre, and weigh the stress
Of every chord, and see what may be gain'd
By ear industrious, and attention meet;
Misers of sound and syllable, no less
Than Midas of his coinage, let us be
Jealous of dead leaves in the bay wreath crown,
So, if we may not let the muse be free,
She will be bound with Garlands of her own.

[May 3.]

This is the third of May, and everything is in delightful forwardness; the violets are not withered before the
peeping of the first rose. You must let me know every·

thing—how parcels go and come, what papers you have,
and what newspapers you want, and other things.   God
bless you, my dear brother and sister.

Your ever affectionate Brother   JOHN KEATS.

XCIII.—TO FANNY KEATS.

Wentworth Place. Saturday Morn.
[*Postmark*, February 27, 1819.]

My dear Fanny—I intended to have not failed to do
as you requested, and write you as you say once a fortnight.   On looking to your letter I find there is no date ;
and not knowing how long it is since I received it I do
not precisely know how great a sinner I am.   I am getting quite well, and Mrs. Dilke is getting on pretty well.
You must pay no attention to Mrs. Abbey's unfeeling
and ignorant gabble.   You can't stop an old woman's
crying more than you can a Child's.   The old woman is
the greatest nuisance because she is too old for the rod.
Many people live opposite a Blacksmith's till they cannot hear the hammer.   I have been in Town for two or
three days and came back last night.   I have been a
little concerned at not hearing from George—I continue
in daily expectation.   Keep on reading and play as much
on the music and the grassplot as you can.   I should
like to take possession of those Grassplots for a Month
or so ; and send Mrs. A. to Town to count coffee berries
instead of currant Bunches, for I want you to teach me a
few common dancing steps—and I would buy a Watch
box to practise them in by myself.   I think I had better
always pay the postage of these Letters.   I shall send
you another book the first time I am in Town early
enough to book it with one of the morning Walthamstow
Coaches.   You did not say a word about your Chillblains.
Write me directly and let me know about them—Your
Letter shall be answered like an echo.

Your affectionate Brother   JOHN ——.

XCIV.—TO FANNY KEATS.

Wentworth Place, March 18 [1819].

My dear Fanny—I have been employed lately in
writing to George—I do not send him very short letters,
but keep on day after day.   There were some young Men
I think I told you of who were going to the Settlement :
they have changed their minds, and I am disappointed in
my expectation of sending Letters by them.—I went
lately to the only dance I have been to these twelve
months or shall go to for twelve months again—it was
to our Brother in law's cousin's—She gave a dance for
her Birthday and I went for the sake of Mrs. Wylie.   I
am waiting every day to hear from George—I trust there
is no harm in the silence : other people are in the same
expectation as we are.   On looking at your seal I cannot
tell whether it is done or not with a Tassie—it seems
to me to be paste.   As I went through Leicester Square
lately I was going to call and buy you some, but not
knowing but you might have some I would not run the
chance of buying duplicates.   Tell me if you have any or
if you would like any—and whether you would rather
have motto ones like that with which I seal this letter ;
or heads of great Men such as Shakspeare, Milton, etc.—
or fancy pieces of Art; such as Fame, Adonis, etc.—those
gentry you read of at the end of the English Dictionary.
Tell me also if you want any particular Book ; or Pencils,
or drawing paper—anything but live stock.   Though I
will not now be very severe on it, remembering how fond
I used to be of Goldfinches, Tomtits, Minnows, Mice,
Ticklebacks, Dace, Cock salmons and all the whole tribe
of the Bushes and the Brooks : but verily they are better
in the Trees and the water—though I must confess even
now a partiality for a handsome Globe of gold-fish—then
I would have it hold 10 pails of water and be fed continually fresh through a cool pipe with another pipe to
let through the floor—well ventilated they would preserve
all their beautiful silver and Crimson.   Then I would

put it before a handsome painted window and shade it all round with myrtles and Japonicas.   I should like the window to open onto the Lake of Geneva—and there I'd sit and read all day like the picture ·of somebody reading.   The weather now and then begins to feel like spring ; and therefore I have begun my walks on the heath again.   Mrs. Dilke is getting better than she has been as she has at length taken a Physician's advice. She ever and anon asks after you and always bids me remember her in my Letters to you.   She is going to leave Hampstead for the sake of educating their son Charles at the Westminster School.   We (Mr. Brown and I) shall leave in the beginning of May ; I do not know what I shall do or where be all the next summer.   Mrs. Reynolds has had a sick house ; but they are all well now.   You see what news I can send you I do—we all live one day like the other as well as you do—the only difference is being sick and well—with the variations of single and double knocks, and the story of a dreadful fire in the Newspapers.   I mentioned Mr. Brown's name —yet I do not think I ever said a word about him to you.   He is a friend of mine of two years' standing, with whom I walked through Scotland : who has been very kind to me in many things when I most wanted his assistance and with whom I keep house till the first of May—you will know him some day.   The name of the young Man who came with me is William Haslam.

Ever your affectionate Brother   JOHN.

XCV.—TO FANNY KEATS.

[*Postmark*, Hampstead, March 24, 1819.]

My dear Fanny—It is impossible for me to call on you to-day—for I have particular Business at the other end of the Town this morning, and must be back to Hampstead with all speed to keep a long agreed on appointment.   To-morrow I shall see you.

Your affectionate Brother   JOHN ——.

Wentworth Place, Monday Aft. [March 29 ? 1819].

My dear Severn—Your note gave me some pain, not
on my own account, but on yours. Of course I should
never suffer any petty vanity of mine to hinder you in
any wise; and therefore I should say "put the miniature
in the exhibition" if only myself was to be hurt. But,
will it not hurt you? What good can it do to any future
picture. Even a large picture is lost in that canting
place—what a drop of water in the ocean is a Miniature.
Those who might chance to see it for the most part if
they had ever heard of either of us and know what we
were and of what years would laugh at the puff of the
one and the vanity of the other. I am however in these
matters a very bad judge—and would advise you to act
in a way that appears to yourself the best for your interest. As your "Hermia and Helena" is finished send
that without the prologue of a Miniature. I shall see
you soon, if you do not pay me a visit sooner—there's a
Bull for you.

Yours ever sincerely   JOHN KEATS.

XCVII.—TO FANNY KEATS.

Wentworth Place [April 13, 1819].

My dear Fanny—I have been expecting a Letter from
you about what the Parson said to your answers. I have
thought also of writing to you often, and I am sorry to
confess that my neglect of it has been but a small instance of my idleness of late—which has been growing
upon me, so that it will require a great shake to get rid
of it. I have written nothing and almost read nothing
—but I must turn over a new leaf. One most discourag-
ing thing hinders me—we have no news yet from George
—so that I cannot with any confidence continue the
Letter I have been preparing for him. Many are in the

same state with us and many have heard from the Settlement. They must be well however: and we must consider this silence as good news. I ordered some bulbous roots for you at the Gardener's, and they sent me some, but they were all in bud—and could not be sent—so I put them in our Garden. There are some beautiful heaths now in bloom in Pots—either heaths or some seasonable plants I will send you instead—perhaps some that are not yet in bloom that you may see them come out. To-morrow night I am going to a rout, a thing I am not at all in love with. Mr. Dilke and his Family have left Hampstead—I shall dine with them to-day in Westminster where I think I told you they were going to reside for the sake of sending their son Charles to the Westminster School. I think I mentioned the Death of Mr. Haslam's Father. Yesterday week the two Mr. Wylies dined with me. I hope you have good store of double violets—I think they are the Princesses of flowers, and in a shower of rain, almost as fine as barley sugar drops are to a schoolboy's tongue. I suppose this fine weather the lambs' tails give a frisk or two extraordinary —when a boy would cry huzza and a Girl O my! a little Lamb frisks its tail. I have not been lately through Leicester Square—the first time I do I will remember your Seals. I have thought it best to live in Town this Summer, chiefly for the sake of books, which cannot be had with any comfort in the Country—besides my Scotch journey gave me a dose of the Picturesque with which I ought to be contented for some time. Westminster is the place I have pitched upon—the City or any place very confined would soon turn me pale and thin—which is to be avoided. You must make up your mind to get stout this summer—indeed I have an idea we shall both be corpulent old folks with triple chins and stumpy thumbs.

Your affectionate Brother   JOHN.

XCVIII.—TO BENJAMIN ROBERT HAYDON.

Tuesday [April 13, 1819].

My dear Haydon—When I offered you assistance I thought I had it in my hand; I thought I had nothing to do but to do. The difficulties I met with arose from the alertness and suspicion of Abbey : and especially from the affairs being still in a Lawyer's hand—who has been draining our Property for the last six years of every charge he could make. I cannot do two things at once, and thus this affair has stopped my pursuits in every way— from the first prospect I had of difficulty. I assure you I have harassed myself ten times more than if I alone had been concerned in so much gain or loss. I have also ever told you the exact particulars as well as and as literally as any hopes or fear could translate them : for it was only by parcels that I found all those petty obstacles which for my own sake should not exist a moment—and yet why not—for from my own imprudence and neglect all my accounts are entirely in my Guardian's Power. This has taught me a Lesson. Hereafter I will be more correct. I find myself possessed of much less than I thought for and now if I had all on the table all I could do would be to take from it a moderate two years' subsistence and lend you the rest; but I cannot say how soon I could become possessed of it. This would be no sacrifice nor any matter worth thinking of —much less than parting as I have more than once done with little sums which might have gradually formed a library to my taste. These sums amount together to nearly £200, which I have but a chance of ever being repaid or paid at a very distant period. I am humble enough to put this in writing from the sense I have of your struggling situation and the great desire that you should do me the justice to credit me the unostentatious and willing state of my nerves on all such occasions. It has not been my fault. I am doubly hurt at the slightly reproachful tone of your note and at the occasion of it,—for it must be some other disappointment; you seem'd so sure of some important help when I last saw you—now you have maimed me again ; I was whole, I had began reading again—when your note came I was engaged in a Book.　I dread as much as a Plague the idle fever of two months more without any fruit.　I will walk over the first fine day : then see what aspect your affairs have taken, and if they should continue gloomy walk into the City to Abbey and get his consent for I am persuaded that to me alone he will not concede a jot.

XCIX.—TO FANNY KEATS.

Wentworth Place, Saturday.
[April 17, 1819 ?]

My dear Fanny—If it were but six o'Clock in the morning I would set off to see you to-day : if I should do so now I could not stop long enough for a how d'ye do—it is so long a walk through Hornsey and Tottenham—and as for Stage Coaching it besides that it is very expensive it is like going into the Boxes by way of the pit.　I cannot go out on Sunday—but if on Monday it should promise as fair as to-day I will put on a pair of loose easy palatable boots and me rendre chez vous.　I continue increasing my letter to George to send it by one of Birkbeck's sons who is going out soon—so if you will let me have a few more lines, they will be in time.　I am glad you got on so well with Monsr. le Curé.　Is he a nice clergyman ?—a great deal depends upon a cock'd hat and powder—not gunpowder, lord love us, but lady-meal, violet-smooth, dainty-scented, lilly-white, feather-soft, wigsby-dressing, coat-collar-spoiling, whisker-reaching, pig-tail-loving, swans-down-puffing, parson-sweetening powder.　I shall call in passing at the Tottenham nursery and see if I can find some seasonable plants for you. That is the nearest place—or by our la'kin or lady kin, that is by the virgin Mary's kindred, is there not a twig-manufacturer in Walthamstow? Mr. and Mrs. Dilke are coming to dine with us to-day. They will enjoy the country after Westminster. O there is nothing like fine weather, and health, and Books, and a fine country, and a contented Mind, and diligent habit of reading and thinking, and an amulet against the ennui—and, please heaven, a little claret wine cool out of a cellar a mile deep—with a few or a good many ratafia cakes—a rocky basin to bathe in, a strawberry bed to say your prayers to Flora in, a pad nag to go you ten miles or so; two or three sensible people to chat with; two or three spiteful folks to spar with; two or three odd fishes to laugh at and two or three numskulls to argue with—instead of using dumb bells on a rainy day—

Two or three Posies
With two or three simples—
Two or three Noses
With two or three pimples—
Two or three wise men
And two or three ninny's—
Two or three purses
And two or three guineas—
Two or three raps
At two or three doors—
Two or three naps
Of two or three hours—
Two or three Cats
And two or three mice—
Two or three sprats
At a very great price—
Two or three sandies
And two or three tabbies—
Two or three dandies
And two Mrs. ——   mum!
Two or three Smiles
And two or three frowns—
Two or three Miles
To two or three towns—
Two or three pegs
For two or three bonnets—
Two or three dove eggs
To hatch into sonnets—

Good-bye I've an appointment—can't
stop pon word—good-bye—now
don't get up—open the door myself—good-bye—see ye Monday.

J. K.

C.—TO FANNY KEATS.

[Hampstead, May 13, 1819.]

My dear Fanny—I have a Letter from George at
last—and it contains, considering all things, good news—
I have been with it to-day to Mrs. Wylie's, with whom
I have left it.   I shall have it again as soon as possible
and then I will walk over and read it to you.   They are
quite well and settled tolerably in comfort after a great
deal of fatigue and harass.   They had the good chance
to meet at Louisville with a Schoolfellow of ours.   You
may expect me within three days.   I am writing to-night
several notes concerning this to many of my friends.
Good-night ! God bless you.

JOHN KEATS.

CI.—TO FANNY KEATS.

[Hampstead, May 26, 1819.]

My dear Fanny—I have been looking for a fine day
to pass at Walthamstow : there has not been one Morning (except Sunday and then I was obliged to stay at
home) that I could depend upon.   I have I am sorry to
say had an accident with the Letter—I sent it to Haslam
and he returned it torn into a thousand pieces.   So I
shall be obliged to tell you all I can remember from
Memory.   You would have heard from me before this
but that I was in continual expectation of a fine Morning—I want also to speak to you concerning myself.
Mind I do not purpose to quit England, as George has
done ; but I am afraid I shall be forced to take a voyage
or two.   However we will not think of that for some

Months.   Should it be a fine morning to-morrow you will see me.

Your affectionate Brother   JOHN ——.

CII.—TO FANNY KEATS.

Wentworth Place [June 9, 1819].

My dear Fanny—I shall be with you next Monday at the farthest.   I could not keep my promise of seeing you again in a week because I am in so unsettled a state of mind about what I am to do—I have given up the Idea of the Indiaman; I cannot resolve to give up my favorite studies : so I purpose to retire into the Country and set my Mind at work once more.   A Friend of Mine who has an ill state of health called on me yesterday and proposed to spend a little time with him at the back of the Isle of Wight where he said we might live very cheaply.   I agreed to his proposal.   I have taken a great dislike to Town—I never go there—some one is always calling on me and as we have spare beds they often stop a couple of days.   I have written lately to some acquaintances in Devonshire concerning a cheap Lodging and they have been very kind in letting me know all I wanted. They have described a pleasant place which I think I shall eventually retire to.   How came you on with my young Master Yorkshire Man?   Did not Mrs. A. sport her Carriage and one?   They really surprised me with super civility—how did Mrs. A. manage it?   How is the old tadpole gardener and little Master next door? it is to be hop'd they will both die some of these days. Not having been to Town I have not heard whether Mr. A. purposes to retire from business.   Do let me know if you have heard anything more about it.   If he should not I shall be very disappointed.   If any one deserves to be put to his shifts it is that Hodgkinson—as for the other he would live a long time upon his fat and be none the worse for a good long lent.   How came miledi to give one Lisbon wine—had she drained the Gooseberry?

Truly I cannot delay making another visit—asked to take Lunch, whether I will have ale, wine, take sugar,—objection to green—like cream—thin bread and butter—another cup—agreeable—enough sugar—little more cream—too weak—12 shillin etc. etc. etc.—Lord I must come again. We are just going to Dinner I must must[1] with this to the Post——

Your affectionate Brother   JOHN —.

CIII.—TO JAMES ELMES.

Wentworth Place, Hampstead [June 12, 1819].

Sir—I did not see your Note till this Saturday evening, or I should have answered it sooner—However as it happens I have but just received the Book which contains the only copy of the verses in question.[2] I have asked for it repeatedly ever since I promised Mr. Haydon and could not help the delay; which I regret. The verses can be struck out in no time, and will I hope be quite in time. If you think it at all necessary a proof may be forwarded; but as I shall transcribe it fairly perhaps there may be no need.

I am, Sir, your obed[t] Serv[t]   JOHN KEATS.

CIV.—TO FANNY KEATS.

Wentworth Place, [June 14, 1819].

My dear Fanny—I cannot be with you to-day for two reasons—1[ly] I have my sore-throat coming again to prevent my walking. 2[ly] I do not happen just at present to be flush of silver so that I might ride. To-morrow I am engaged—but the day after you shall see me. Mr. Brown is waiting for me as we are going to Town together, so good-bye.

Your affectionate Brother   JOHN.

---

[1] *Sic:* obviously for "run" or "go."

[2] In all probability the *Ode to a Nightingale*, published in the July number of the *Annals of the Fine Arts*, of which James Elmes was editor.

CV.—TO FANNY KEATS,

Wentworth Place [June 16, 1819].

My dear Fanny—Still I cannot afford to spend money by Coachhire and still my throat is not well enough to warrant my walking. I went yesterday to ask Mr. Abbey for some money; but I could not on account of a Letter he showed me from my Aunt's solicitor. You do not understand the business. I trust it will not in the end be detrimental to you. I am going to try the Press once more, and to that end shall retire to live cheaply in the country and compose myself and verses as well as I can. I have very good friends ready to help me—and I am the more bound to be careful of the money they lend me. It will all be well in the course of a year I hope. I am confident of it, so do not let it trouble you at all. Mr. Abbey showed me a Letter he had received from George containing the news of the birth of a Niece for us—and all doing well—he said he would take it to you—so I suppose to-day you will see it. I was preparing to en-quire for a situation with an apothecary, but Mr. Brown persuades me to try the press once more; so I will with all my industry and ability. Mr. Rice a friend of mine in ill health has proposed retiring to the back of the Isle of Wight—which I hope will be cheap in the summer—I am sure it will in the winter. Thence you shall frequently hear from me and in the Letters I will copy those lines I may write which will be most pleasing to you in the confidence you will show them to no one. I have not run quite aground yet I hope, having written this morning to several people to whom I have lent money requesting repayment. I shall henceforth shake off my indolent fits, and among other reformation be more diligent in writing to you, and mind you always answer me. I shall be obliged to go out of town on Saturday and shall have no money till to-morrow, so I am very sorry to think I shall not be able to come to Wal-

T

thamstow.   The Head Mr. Severn did of me is now
too dear, but here inclosed is a very capital Profile done
by Mr. Brown.   I will write again on Monday or Tuesday—Mr. and Mrs. Dilke are well.

Your affectionate Brother   JOHN ——.

CVI.—TO BENJAMIN ROBERT HAYDON.

Wentworth Place.
Thursday Morning [June 17, 1819].

My dear Haydon—I know you will not be prepared
for this, because your Pocket must needs be very low
having been at ebb tide so long: but what can I do?
mine is lower.   I was the day before yesterday much in
want of Money: but some news I had yesterday has
driven me into necessity.   I went to Abbey's for some
Cash, and he put into my hand a letter from my Aunt's
Solicitor containing the pleasant information that she was
about to file a Bill in Chancery against us.   Now in case
of a defeat Abbey will be very undeservedly in the wrong
box; so I could not ask him for any more money, nor
can I till the affair is decided; and if it goes against him
I must in conscience make over to him what little he
may have remaining.   My purpose is now to make one
more attempt in the Press—if that fail, "ye hear no
more of me" as Chaucer says.   Brown has lent me some
money for the present.   Do borrow or beg somehow
what you can for me.   Do not suppose I am at all uncomfortable about the matter in any other way than as
it forces me to apply to the needy.   I could not send
you those lines, for I could not get the only copy of them
before last Saturday evening.   I sent them Mr. Elmes
on Monday.   I saw Monkhouse on Sunday—he told me
you were getting on with the Picture.   I would have
come over to you to-day, but I am fully employed.

Yours ever sincerely   JOHN KEATS.

CVII.—TO FANNY KEATS.

Shanklin, Isle of Wight, Tuesday, July 6.

My dear Fanny—I have just received another Letter from George—full of as good news as we can expect. I cannot inclose it to you as I could wish because it contains matters of Business to which I must for a Week to come have an immediate reference. I think I told you the purpose for which I retired to this place—to try the fortune of my Pen once more, and indeed I have some confidence in my success: but in every event, believe me my dear sister, I shall be sufficiently comfortable, as, if I cannot lead that life of competence and society I should wish, I have enough knowledge of my gallipots to ensure me an employment and maintenance. The Place I am in now I visited once before and a very pretty place it is were it not for the bad weather. Our window looks over house-tops and Cliffs onto the Sea, so that when the Ships sail past the Cottage chimneys you may take them for weathercocks. We have Hill and Dale, forest and Mead, and plenty of Lobsters. I was on the Portsmouth Coach the Sunday before last in that heavy shower— and I may say I went to Portsmouth by water—I got a little cold, and as it always flies to my throat I am a little out of sorts that way. There were on the Coach with me some common French people but very well behaved—there was a woman amongst them to whom the poor Men in ragged coats were more gallant than ever I saw gentleman to Lady at a Ball. When we got down to walk up hill—one of them pick'd a rose, and on remounting gave it to the woman with "Ma'mselle voila une belle rose!" I am so hard at work that perhaps I should not have written to you for a day or two if George's Letter had not diverted my attention to the interests and pleasure of those I love—and ever believe that when I do not behave punctually it is from a very necessary occupation, and that my silence is no proof of my not thinking of you, or that I want more than a gentle fillip to bring your image with every claim before me. You have never seen mountains, or I might tell you that the hill at Steephill is I think almost of as much consequence as Mount Rydal on Lake Winander. Bonchurch too is a very delightful Place— as I can see by the Cottages, all romantic—covered with creepers and honeysuckles, with roses and eglantines peeping in at the windows. Fit abodes for the People I guess live in them, romantic old maids fond of novels, or soldiers' widows with a pretty jointure—or any body's widows or aunts or anythings given to Poetry and a Piano-forte—as far as in 'em lies—as people say. If I could play upon the Guitar I might make my fortune with an old song—and get two blessings at once—a Lady's heart and the Rheumatism. But I am almost afraid to peep at those little windows—for a pretty window should show a pretty face, and as the world goes chances are against me. I am living with a very good fellow indeed, a Mr. Rice.—He is unfortunately labouring under a complaint which has for some years been a burthen to him. This is a pain to me. He has a greater tact in speaking to people of the village than I have, and in those matters is a great amusement as well as good friend to me. He bought a ham the other day for says he "Keats, I don't think a Ham is a wrong thing to have in a house." Write to me, Shanklin, Isle of Wight, as soon as you can; for a Letter is a great treat to me here—believing me ever,

Your affectionate Brother   JOHN ——.

CVIII.—TO JOHN HAMILTON REYNOLDS.

Extract from a letter dated Shanklin, nʳ Ryde, Isle of Wight,
Sunday, 12th [for 11th] July, 1819.

You will be glad to hear, under my own hand (though Rice says we are like Sauntering Jack and Idle Joe),

how diligent I have been, and am being. I have finished
the Act, and in the interval of beginning the 2^d have
proceeded pretty well with Lamia, finishing the 1st
part which consists of about 400 lines. I have great
hopes of success, because I make use of my Judgment more deliberately than I have yet done; but in
case of failure with the world, I shall find my content.
And here (as I know you have my good at heart as
much as a Brother), I can only repeat to you what I
have said to George—that however I should like to
enjoy what the competencies of life procure, I am in no
wise dashed at a different prospect. I have spent too
many thoughtful days and moralised through too many
nights for that, and fruitless would they be indeed, if
they did not by degrees make me look upon the affairs
of the world with a healthy deliberation. I have of late
been moulting: not for fresh feathers and wings: they
are gone, and in their stead I hope to have a pair of
patient sublunary legs. I have altered, not from a Chry-
salis into a butterfly, but the contrary; having two little
loopholes, whence I may look out into the stage of the
world: and that world on our coming here I almost
forgot. The first time I sat down to write, I could
scarcely believe in the necessity for so doing. It struck
me as a great oddity—Yet the very corn which is now
so beautiful, as if it had only took to ripening yesterday,
is for the market; so, why should I be delicate?

.   .   .   .

CIX.—TO CHARLES WENTWORTH DILKE.

Shanklin, Saturday Evening [July 31, 1819].

My dear Dilke—I will not make my diligence an
excuse for not writing to you sooner—because I consider
idleness a much better plea.   A Man in the hurry of
business of any sort is expected and ought to be expected
to look to everything—his mind is in a whirl, and what
matters it what whirl?   But to require a Letter of a

Man lost in idleness is the utmost cruelty; you cut the thread of his existence, you beat, you pummel him, you sell his goods and chattels, you put him in prison; you impale him; you crucify him. If I had not put pen to paper since I saw you this would be to me a vi et armis taking up before the Judge; but having got over my darling lounging habits a little, it is with scarcely any pain I come to this dating from Shanklin and Dear Dilke. The Isle of Wight is but so so, etc. Rice and I passed rather a dull time of it. I hope he will not repent coming with me. He was unwell, and I was not in very good health: and I am afraid we made each other worse by acting upon each other's spirits. We would grow as melancholy as need be. I confess I cannot bear a sick person in a House, especially alone—it weighs upon me day and night—and more so when perhaps the Case is irretrievable. Indeed I think Rice is in a dangerous state. I have had a Letter from him which speaks favourably of his health at present. Brown and I are pretty well harnessed again to our dog-cart. I mean the Tragedy, which goes on sinkingly. We are thinking of introducing an Elephant, but have not historical reference within reach to determine us as to Otho's Menagerie. When Brown first mentioned this I took it for a joke; however he brings such plausible reasons, and discourses so eloquently on the dramatic effect that I am giving it a serious consideration. The Art of Poetry is not sufficient for us, and if we get on in that as well as we do in painting, we shall by next winter crush the Reviews and the Royal Academy. Indeed, if Brown would take a little of my advice, he could not fail to be first palette of his day. But odd as it may appear, he says plainly that he cannot see any force in my plea of putting skies in the background, and leaving Indian ink out of an ash tree. The other day he was sketching Shanklin Church, and as I saw how the business was going on, I challenged him to a trial of skill—he lent me Pencil and Paper— we keep the Sketches to contend for the Prize at the

Gallery. I will not say whose I think best—but really
I do not think Brown's done to the top of the Art.

A word or two on the Isle of Wight. I have been no
further than Steephill. If I may guess, I should say
that there is no finer part in the Island than from this
Place to Steephill. I do not hesitate to say it is fine.
Bonchurch is the best. But I have been so many finer
walks, with a background of lake and mountain instead
of the sea, that I am not much touch'd with it, though
I credit it for all the Surprise I should have felt if it had
taken my cockney maidenhead. But I may call myself
an old Stager in the picturesque, and unless it be something very large and overpowering, I cannot receive any
extraordinary relish.

I am sorry to hear that Charles is so much oppress'd
at Westminster, though I am sure it will be the finest
touchstone for his Metal in the world. His troubles will
grow day by day less, as his age and strength increase.
The very first Battle he wins will lift him from the Tribe
of Manasseh. I do not know how I should feel were I
a Father—but I hope I should strive with all my Power
not to let the present trouble me. When your Boy shall
be twenty, ask him about his childish troubles and he will
have no more memory of them than you have of yours.
Brown tells me Mrs. Dilke sets off to-day for Chichester.
I am glad—I was going to say she had a fine day—but
there has been a great Thunder cloud muttering over
Hampshire all day—I hope she is now at supper with a
good appetite.

So Reynolds's Piece succeeded—that is all well.
Papers have with thanks been duly received. We leave
this place on the 13th, and will let you know where we
may be a few days after—Brown says he will write when
the fit comes on him. If you will stand law expenses I'll
beat him into one before his time. When I come to
town I shall have a little talk with you about Brown and
one Jenny Jacobs. Open daylight! he don't care. I
am afraid there will be some more feet for little stock-

ings—[*of Keats's making. (I mean the feet.*)[1]] Brown here tried at a piece of Wit but it failed him, as you see, though long a brewing.—[*this is a 2*d *lie.*] Men should never despair—you see he has tried again and succeeded to a miracle.—He wants to try again, but as I have a right to an inside place in my own Letter—I take possession.

Your sincere friend   JOHN KEATS.

CX.—TO BENJAMIN BAILEY.

[*Fragment (outside sheet) of a letter addressed to Bailey at St. Andrews.*   Winchester, August 15, 1819.]

We removed to Winchester for the convenience of a library, and find it an exceeding pleasant town, enriched with a beautiful Cathedral, and surrounded by a fresh-looking country. We are in tolerably good and cheap lodgings—Within these two months I have written 1500 lines, most of which, besides many more of prior composition, you will probably see by next winter. I have written 2 tales, one from Boccaccio, called the Pot of Basil, and another called St. Agnes's Eve, on a popular Superstition, and a 3rd called Lamia (half finished). I have also been writing parts of my "Hyperion," and completed 4 Acts of a tragedy. It was the opinion of most of my friends that I should never be able to write a scene. I will endeavour to wipe away the prejudice—I sincerely hope you will be pleased when my labours, since we last saw each other, shall reach you. One of my Ambitions is to make as great a revolution in modern dramatic writing as Kean has done in acting. Another to upset the drawling of the blue-stocking literary world—if in the Course of a few years I do these two things, I ought to die content, and my friends should drink a dozen of claret on my tomb. I am convinced more and more every day that (excepting

---

[1] This and the next interpolation are Brown's.

the human friend philosopher), a fine writer is the most
genuine being in the world. Shakspeare and the Paradise lost every day become greater wonders to me. I
look upon fine phrases like a lover. I was glad to see
by a passage of one of Brown's letters, some time ago,
from the North that you were in such good spirits.
Since that you have been married, and in congratulating
you I wish you every continuance of them. Present my
respects to Mrs. Bailey. This sounds oddly to me, and
I daresay I do it awkwardly enough : but I suppose by
this time it is nothing new to you. Brown's remembrances to you. As far as I know, we shall remain at
Winchester for a goodish while.

Ever your sincere friend   JOHN KEATS.

CXI.—TO JOHN TAYLOR.

Winchester, Monday morn [August 23, 1819].

My dear Taylor—. . . Brown and I have together
been engaged (this I should wish to remain secret) on a
Tragedy which I have just finished and from which we
hope to share moderate profits. . . . I feel every confidence
that, if I choose, I may be a popular writer. That I will
never be; but for all that I will get a livelihood. I equally
dislike the favour of the public with the love of a woman.
They are both a cloying treacle to the wings of Independ-
ence. I shall ever consider them (People) as debtors to me
for verses, not myself to them for admiration—which I can
do without. I have of late been indulging my spleen by
composing a preface AT them : after all resolving never
to write a preface at all. "There are so many verses,"
would I have said to them, "give so much means for
me to buy pleasure with, as a relief to my hours of
labour"—You will observe at the end of this if you put
down the letter, "How a solitary life engenders pride
and egotism !" True—I know it does : but this pride
and egotism will enable me to write finer things than
anything else could—so I will indulge it. Just so much

as I am humbled by the genius above my grasp am I exalted and look with hate and contempt upon the literary world.—A drummer-boy who holds out his hand familiarly to a field Marshal,—that drummer-boy with me is the good word and favour of the public. Who could wish to be among the common-place crowd of the little famous—who are each individually lost in a throng made up of themselves? Is this worth louting or playing the hypocrite for? To beg suffrages for a seat on the benches of a myriad-aristocracy in letters? This is not wise.—I am not a wise man—'Tis pride—I will give you a definition of a proud man—He is a man who has neither Vanity nor Wisdom—One filled with hatreds cannot be vain, neither can he be wise. Pardon me for hammering instead of writing. Remember me to Woodhouse Hessey and all in Percy Street.

Ever yours sincerely   JOHN KEATS.

CXII.—TO JOHN HAMILTON REYNOLDS.

Winchester, August 25 [1819].

My dear Reynolds—By this post I write to Rice, who will tell you why we have left Shanklin; and how we like this place. I have indeed scarcely anything else to say, leading so monotonous a life, except I was to give you a history of sensations, and day-nightmares. You would not find me at all unhappy in it, as all my thoughts and feelings which are of the selfish nature, home speculations, every day continue to make me more iron—I am convinced more and more, every day, that fine writing is, next to fine doing, the top thing in the world; the Paradise Lost becomes a greater wonder. The more I know what my diligence may in time probably effect, the more does my heart distend with Pride and Obstinacy— I feel it in my power to become a popular writer— I feel it in my power to refuse the poisonous suffrage of a public. My own being which I know to be becomes of more consequence to me than the crowds of Shadows

in the shape of men and women that inhabit a kingdom.
The soul is a world of itself, and has enough to do in its
own home. Those whom I know already, and who have
grown as it were a part of myself, I could not do without:
but for the rest of mankind, they are as much a dream
to me as Milton's Hierarchies. I think if I had a free
and healthy and lasting organisation of heart, and lungs
as strong as an ox's so as to be able to bear unhurt the
shock of extreme thought and sensation without weariness, I could pass my life very nearly alone though it
should last eighty years. But I feel my body too weak
to support me to the height, I am obliged continually
to check myself, and be nothing. It would be vain for
me to endeavour after a more reasonable manner of writing to you. I have nothing to speak of but myself, and
what can I say but what I feel? If you should have any
reason to regret this state of excitement in me, I will
turn the tide of your feelings in the right Channel, by
mentioning that it is the only state for the best sort of
Poetry—that is all I care for, all I live for. Forgive me
for not filling up the whole sheet; Letters become so
irksome to me, that the next time I leave London I
shall petition them all to be spared me. To give me
credit for constancy, and at the same time waive letter
writing will be the highest indulgence I can think of.

Ever your affectionate friend   JOHN KEATS.

CXIII.—TO FANNY KEATS.

Winchester, August 28 [1819].

My dear Fanny—You must forgive me for suffering
so long a space to elapse between the dates of my letters.
It is more than a fortnight since I left Shanklin chiefly
for the purpose of being near a tolerable Library, which
after all is not to be found in this place. However we
like it very much: it is the pleasantest Town I ever was
in, and has the most recommendations of any. There is
a fine Cathedral which to me is always a source of

amusement, part of it built 1400 years ago; and the
more modern by a magnificent Man, you may have read
of in our History, called William of Wickham. The
whole town is beautifully wooded. From the Hill at
the eastern extremity you see a prospect of Streets, and
old Buildings mixed up with Trees. Then there are the
most beautiful streams about I ever saw—full of Trout.
There is the Foundation of St. Croix about half a mile
in the fields—a charity greatly abused. We have a
Collegiate School, a Roman catholic School; a chapel
ditto and a Nunnery! And what improves it all is, the
fashionable inhabitants are all gone to Southampton.
We are quiet—except a fiddle that now and then goes
like a gimlet through my Ears—our Landlady's son not
being quite a Proficient. I have still been hard at work,
having completed a Tragedy I think I spoke of to you.
But there I fear all my labour will be thrown away for
the present, as I hear Mr. Kean is going to America.
For all I can guess I shall remain here till the middle of
October—when Mr. Brown will return to his house at
Hampstead; whither I shall return with him. I some
time since sent the Letter I told you I had received
from George to Haslam with a request to let you and
Mrs. Wylie see it: he sent it back to me for very in-
sufficient reasons without doing so; and I was so irritated
by it that I would not send it travelling about by the
post any more: besides the postage is very expensive.
I know Mrs. Wylie will think this a great neglect. I
am sorry to say my temper gets the better of me—I will
not send it again. Some correspondence I have had
with Mr. Abbey about George's affairs—and I must
confess he has behaved very kindly to me as far as the
wording of his Letter went. Have you heard any
further mention of his retiring from Business? I am
anxious to hear whether Hodgkinson, whose name I
cannot bear to write, will in any likelihood be thrown
upon himself. The delightful Weather we have had for
two Months is the highest gratification I could receive—

no chill'd red noses—no shivering—but fair atmosphere
to think in—a clean towel mark'd with the mangle and
a basin of clear Water to drench one's face with ten
times a day: no need of much exercise—a Mile a day
being quite sufficient.   My greatest regret is that I have
not been well enough to bathe though I have been two
Months by the seaside and live now close to delicious
bathing—Still I enjoy the Weather—I adore fine
Weather as the greatest blessing I can have.   Give me
Books, fruit, French wine and fine weather and a little
music out of doors, played by somebody I do not know—
not pay the price of one's time for a jig—but a little
chance music: and I can pass a summer very quietly
without caring much about Fat Louis, fat Regent or the
Duke of Wellington.   Why have you not written to me ?
Because you were in expectation of George's Letter and
so waited ? Mr. Brown is copying out our Tragedy of
Otho the Great in a superb style—better than it deserves
—there as I said is labour in vain for the present.   I
had hoped to give Kean another opportunity to shine.
What can we do now ? There is not another actor of
Tragedy in all London or Europe.   The Covent Garden
Company is execrable.   Young is the best among them
and he is a ranting coxcombical tasteless Actor—a Disgust, a Nausea—and yet the very best after Kean.
What a set of barren asses are actors ! I should like
now to promenade round your Gardens—apple tasting
—pear-tasting—plum-judging—apricot-nibbling—peach-
scrunching—nectarine-sucking and Melon-carving.   I
have also a great feeling for antiquated cherries full of
sugar cracks—and a white currant tree kept for company.
I admire lolling on a lawn by a water lilied pond to eat
white currants and see gold-fish: and go to the Fair in
the Evening if I'm good.   There is not hope for that—
one is sure to get into some mess before evening.   Have
these hot days I brag of so much been well or ill for
your health ? Let me hear soon.

Your affectionate Brother   JOHN ——.

CXIV.—TO JOHN TAYLOR.

Winchester, September 1, 1819.

My dear Taylor—Brown and I have been employed for these 3 weeks past from time to time in writing to our different friends—a dead silence is our only answer —we wait morning after morning.   Tuesday is the day for the Examiner to arrive, this is the 2d Tuesday which has been barren even of a newspaper—Men should be in imitation of spirits "responsive to each other's note."   Instead of that I pipe and no one hath danced. We have been cursing like Mandeville and Lisle—With this I shall send by the same post a 3d letter to a friend of mine, who though it is of consequence has neither answered right or left.   We have been much in want of news from the Theatres, having heard that Kean is going to America—but no—not a word.   Why I should come on you with all these complaints I cannot explain to myself, especially as I suspect you must be in the country. Do answer me soon for I really must know something. I must steer myself by the rudder of Information. . . .

Ever yours sincerely   JOHN KEATS.

CXV.—TO JOHN TAYLOR.

Winchester, September 5 [1819].

My dear Taylor—This morning I received yours of the 2d, and with it a letter from Hessey enclosing a Bank post Bill of £30, an ample sum I assure you—more I had no thought of.—You should not have delayed so long in Fleet St.—leading an inactive life as you did was breathing poison : you will find the country air do more for you than you expect.   But it must be proper country air. You must choose a spot.   What sort of a place is Retford ? You should have a dry, gravelly, barren, elevated country, open to the currents of air, and such a place is generally furnished with the finest springs—The neighbourhood of a rich enclosed fulsome manured arable land, especially in a valley and almost as bad on a flat, would be almost as bad as the smoke of Fleet St. — Such a place as this was Shanklin, only open to the south-east, and surrounded by hills in every other direction. From this south-east came the damps of the sea; which, having no egress, the air would for days together take on an unhealthy idiosyncrasy altogether enervating and weakening as a city smoke—I felt it very much. Since I have been here at Winchester I have been improving in health—it is not so confined—and there is on one side of the City a dry chalky down, where the air is worth Sixpence a pint. So if you do not get better at Retford, do not impute it to your own weakness before you have well considered the Nature of the air and soil—especially as Autumn is encroaching—for the Autumn fog over a rich land is like the steam from cabbage water. What makes the great difference between valesmen, flatlandmen and mountaineers? The cultivation of the earth in a great measure—Our health temperament and disposition are taken more (notwithstanding the contradiction of the history of Cain and Abel) from the air we breathe, than is generally imagined. See the difference between a Peasant and a Butcher.—I am convinced a great cause of it is the difference of the air they breathe: the one takes *his* mingled with the fume of slaughter, the other from the dank exhalement from the glebe; the teeming damp that comes up from the plough-furrow is of great effect in taming the fierceness of a strong man—more than his labour—Let him be mowing furze upon a mountain, and at the day's end his thoughts will run upon a .. axe[1] if he ever had handled one; let him leave the plough, and he will think quietly of his supper. Agriculture is the tamer of men—the steam from the earth is like drinking their Mother's milk—it enervates their nature—this appears a great cause of the imbecility of the Chinese: and if this sort of atmosphere is a mitigation to the energy

---

[1] So copied by Woodhouse: query "battle-axe"?

of a strong man, how much more must it injure a weak one unoccupied unexercised—For what is the cause of so many men maintaining a good state in Cities, but occupation—An idle man, a man who is not sensitively alive to self-interest in a city cannot continue long in good health.   This is easily explained—If you were to walk leisurely through an unwholesome path in the fens, with a little horror of them, you would be sure to have your ague.   But let Macbeth cross the same path, with the dagger in the air leading him on, and he would never have an ague or anything like it—You should give these things a serious consideration.   Notts, I believe, is a flat county—You should be on the slope of one of the dry barren hills in Somersetshire.   I am convinced there is as harmful air to be beathed in the country as in town. I am greatly obliged to you for your letter.   Perhaps, if you had had strength and spirits enough, you would have felt offended by my offering a note of hand, or rather expressed it.   However, I am sure you will give me credit for not in anywise mistrusting you: or imagining that you would take advantage of any power I might give you over me.   No—It proceeded from my serious resolve not to be a gratuitous borrower, from a great desire to be correct in money matters, to have in my desk the Chronicles of them to refer to, and know my worldly non-estate : besides in case of my death such documents would be but just, if merely as memorials of the friendly turns I had done to me—Had I known of your illness I should not have written in such fiery phrase in my first letter.   I hope that shortly you will be able to bear six times as much.   Brown likes the tragedy very much : But he is not a fit judge of it, as I have only acted as midwife to his plot ; and of course he will be fond of his child.   I do not think I can make you any extracts without spoiling the effect of the whole when you come to read it—I hope you will then not think my labour misspent.   Since I finished it, I have finished Lamia, and am now occupied in revising St. Agnes's Eve, and study-

ing Italian.   Ariosto I find as diffuse, in parts, as Spenser
—I understand completely the difference between them.
I will cross the letter with some lines from Lamia.
Brown's kindest remembrances to you—and I am ever
your most sincere friend   JOHN KEATS.

> A haunting Music sole perhaps and lone
> Supportress of the fairy roof made moan
> Throughout as fearful the whole charm might fade.
> Fresh Carved Cedar mimicking a glade
> Of Palm and Plantain met from either side
> In the high midst in honour of the Bride—
> Two Palms, and then two plantains and so on
> From either side their stems branch'd one to one
> All down the aisled place—and beneath all
> There ran a stream of lamps straight on from wall to wall.
> So canopied lay an untasted feast
> Teeming a perfume.   Lamia regal drest
> Silverly paced about and as she went
> Mission'd her viewless servants to enrich
> The splendid finish of each nook and niche—
> Between the tree stems wainscoated at first
> Came jasper panels—then anon there burst
> Forth creeping imagery of slighter trees
> And with the larger wove in small intricacies—
> And so till she was sated—then came down
> Soft lighting on her head a brilliant crown
> Wreath'd turban-wise of tender wannish fire
> And sprinkled o'er with stars like Ariadne's tiar,
> Approving all—she faded at self will
> And shut the Chamber up close hush'd and still ;
> Complete, and ready, for the revels rude
> When dreadful Guests would come to spoil her solitude.
> The day came soon and all the gossip-rout—
> O senseless Lycius[1] . . .

This is a good sample of the story.   Brown is gone to
Chichester a-visiting—I shall be alone here for 3 weeks,
expecting accounts of your health.

[1] Keats's quotation from his first draft of Lamia continued, says
Woodhouse, for thirty lines more : but as the text varied much
from that subsequently printed, and as Woodhouse's notes of these
variations are lost, I can only give thus much, from an autograph
first draft of the passage in the possession of Lord Houghton.

CXVI.—TO GEORGE AND GEORGIANA KEATS.

Winchester, September [17, 1819], Friday.

My dear George—I was closely employed in reading and composition in this place, whither I had come from Shanklin for the convenience of a library, when I received your last dated 24th July. You will have seen by the short letter I wrote from Shanklin how matters stand between us and Mr. Jennings. They had not at all moved, and I knew no way of overcoming the inveterate obstinacy of our affairs. On receiving your last, I immediately took a place in the same night's coach for London. Mr. Abbey behaved extremely well to me, appointed Monday evening at seven to meet me, and observed that he should drink tea at that hour. I gave him the enclosed note and showed him the last leaf of yours to me. He really appeared anxious about it, and promised he would forward your money as quickly as possible. I think I mentioned that Walton was dead. . . . He will apply to Mr. Gliddon the partner, endeavour to get rid of Mr. Jenning's claim, and be expeditious. He has received an answer from my letter to Fry. That is something. We are certainly in a very low estate—I say we, for I am in such a situation, that were it not for the assistance of Brown and Taylor, I must be as badly off as a man can be. I could not raise any sum by the promise of any poem, no, not by the mortgage of my intellect. We must wait a little while. I really have hopes of success. I have finished a tragedy, which if it succeeds will enable me to sell what I may have in manuscript to a good advantage. I have passed my time in reading, writing, and fretting— the last I intend to give up, and stick to the other two. They are the only chances of benefit to us. Your wants will be a fresh spur to me. I assure you you shall more than share what I can get whilst I am still young. The time may come when age will make me more selfish. I have not been well treated by the world, and yet I have,

capitally well. I do not know a person to whom so many
purse-strings would fly open as to me, if I could possibly
take advantage of them, which I cannot do, for none of
the owners of these purses are rich.   Your present situation I will not suffer myself to dwell upon.   When misfortunes are so real, we are glad enough to escape them
and the thought of them.   I cannot help thinking Mr.
Audubon a dishonest man.   Why did he make you believe that he was a man of property?   How is it that his
circumstances have altered so suddenly?   In truth, I do
not believe you fit to deal with the world, or at least the
American world.   But, good God! who can avoid these
chances?   You have done your best.   Take matters as
coolly as you can; and confidently expecting help from
England, act as if no help were nigh.   Mine, I am sure,
is a tolerable tragedy; it would have been a bank to me,
if just as I had finished it, I had not heard of Kean's
resolution to go to America.   That was the worst news I
could have had.   There is no actor can do the principal
character besides Kean.   At Covent Garden there is a
great chance of its being damm'd.   Were it to succeed
even there it would lift me out of the mire; I mean the
mire of a bad reputation which is continually rising against
me.   My name with the literary fashionables is vulgar.
I am a weaver-boy to them.   A tragedy would lift me
out of this mess, and mess it' is as far as regards our
pockets.   But be not cast down any more than I am; I
feel that I can bear real ills better than imaginary ones.
Whenever I find myself growing vapourish, I rouse myself,
wash, and put on a clean shirt, brush my hair and clothes,
tie my shoestrings neatly, and in fact adonise as I were
going out.   Then, all clean and comfortable, I sit down
to write.   This I find the greatest relief.   Besides I am
becoming accustomed to the privations of the pleasures of
sense.   In the midst of the world I live like a hermit.
I have forgot how to lay plans for the enjoyment of any
pleasure.   I feel I can bear anything,—any misery, even
imprisonment, so long as I have neither wife nor child.

Perhaps you will say yours are your only comfort; they
must be. I returned to Winchester the day before yesterday, and am now here alone, for Brown, some days before
I left, went to Bedhampton, and there he will be for the
next fortnight. The term of his house will be up in the
middle of next month when we shall return to Hampstead.
On Sunday, I dined with your mother and Hen and
Charles in Henrietta Street. Mrs. and Miss Millar were
in the country. Charles had been but a few days returned from Paris. I daresay you will have letters
expressing the motives of his journey. Mrs. Wylie and
Miss Waldegrave seem as quiet as two mice there alone.
I did not show your last. I thought it better not, for
better times will certainly come, and why should they
be unhappy in the meantime? On Monday morning I
went to Walthamstow. Fanny looked better than I had
seen her for some time. She complains of not hearing
from you, appealing to me as if it were half my fault. I
had been so long in retirement that London appeared a
very odd place. I could not make out I had so many
acquaintances, and it was a whole day before I could feel
among men. I had another strange sensation. There
was not one house I felt any pleasure to call at. Reynolds was in the country, and, saving himself, I am
prejudiced against all that family. Dilke and his wife
and child were in the country. Taylor was at Notting-
ham. I was out, and everybody was out. I walked
about the streets as in a strange land. Rice was the only
one at home. I passed some time with him. I know him
better since we have lived a month together in the Isle
of Wight. He is the most sensible and even wise man I
know. He has a few John Bull prejudices, but they
improve him. His illness is at times alarming. We are
great friends, and there is no one I like to pass a day
with better. Martin called in to bid him good-bye before
he set out for Dublin. If you would like to hear one of
his jokes, here is one which, at the time, we laughed at
a good deal: A Miss ——, with three young ladies, one

of them Martin's sister, had come a-gadding in the Isle of
Wight and took for a few days a cottage opposite ours. We
dined with them one day, and as I was saying they had
fish. Miss —— said she thought *they tasted of the boat.*
"No" says Martin, very seriously, "they haven't been
kept long enough." I saw Haslam. He is very much
occupied with love and business, being one of Mr.
Saunders' executors and lover to a young woman. He
showed me her picture by Severn. I think she is, though
not very cunning, too cunning for him. Nothing strikes
me so forcibly with a sense of the ridiculous as love. A
man in love I do think cuts the sorriest figure in the
world; queer, when I know a poor fool to be really in
pain about it, I could burst out laughing in his face.
His pathetic visage becomes irresistible. Not that I take
Haslam as a pattern for lovers; he is a very worthy man
and a good friend. His love is very amusing. Somewhere in the Spectator is related an account of a man
inviting a party of stutterers and squinters to his table.
It would please me more to scrape together a party of
lovers—not to dinner, but to tea. There would be no
fighting as among knights of old.

> Pensive they sit, and roll their languid eyes,
> Nibble their toast and cool their tea with sighs;
> Or else forget the purpose of the night,
> Forget their tea, forget their appetite.
> See, with cross'd arms they sit—Ah! hapless crew,
> The fire is going out and no one rings
> For coals, and therefore no coals Betty brings.
> A fly is in the milk-pot. Must he die
> Circled by a humane society?
> No, no; there, Mr. Werter takes his spoon,
> Inserts it, dips the handle, and lo! soon
> The little straggler, sav'd from perils dark,
> Across the tea-board draws a long wet mark.
> Romeo! Arise take snuffers by the handle,
> There's a large cauliflower in each candle.
> A winding sheet—ah, me! I must away
> To No. 7, just beyond the circus gay.
> Alas, my friend, your coat sits very well;
> Where may your Taylor live? I may not tell.

O pardon me.   I'm absent now and then.
Where *might* my Taylor live ?   I say again
I cannot tell.   Let me no more be teased ;
He lives in Wapping, might live where he pleased.

You see, I cannot get on without writing, as boys do at
school, a few nonsense verses.   I begin them, and before
I have written six the whim has passed—if there is anything deserving so respectable a name in them.   I shall
put in a bit of information anywhere, just as it strikes
me.   Mr. Abbey is to write to me as soon as he can bring
matters to bear, and then I am to go to town and tell
him the means of forwarding to you through Capper and
Hazlewood.   I wonder I did not put this before.   I shall
go on to-morrow; it is so fine now I must take a bit of a
walk.

Saturday [September 18].

With my inconstant disposition it is no wonder that
this morning, amid all our bad times and misfortunes,
I should feel so alert and well-spirited.   At this moment
you are perhaps in a very different state of mind.   It is
because my hopes are ever paramount to my despair.
I have been reading over a part of a short poem I have
composed lately, called Lamia, and I am certain there
is that sort of fire in it that must take hold of people
some way.   Give them either pleasant or unpleasant sensation—what they want is a sensation of some sort.   I
wish I could pitch the key of your spirits as high as mine
is ; but your organ-loft is beyond the reach of my voice.

I admire the exact admeasurement of my niece in your
mother's letter—O ! the little span-long elf.   I am not
in the least a judge of the proper weight and size of an
infant.   Never trouble yourselves about that.   She is
sure to be a fine woman.   Let her have only delicate nails
both on hands and feet, and both as small as a May-fly's,
who will live you his life on a 3 square inch of oak-leaf;
and nails she must have, quite different from the market-
women here, who plough into butter and make a quarter
pound taste of it.   I intend to write a letter to your wife,

and there I may say more on this little plump subject—
I hope she's plump. Still harping on my daughter. This
Winchester is a place tolerably well suited to me. There
is a fine cathedral, a college, a Roman Catholic chapel, a
Methodist do., and Independent do. ; and there is not one
loom, or anything like manufacturing beyond bread and
butter, in the whole city. There are a number of rich
Catholics in the place. It is a respectable, ancient,
aristocratic place, and moreover it contains a nunnery.
Our set are by no means so hail fellow well met on literary
subjects as we were wont to be. Reynolds has turn'd to the
law. By the bye, he brought out a little piece at the
Lyceum call'd One, Two, Three, Four : by Advertisement.
It met with complete success. The meaning of this odd
title is explained when I tell you the principal actor is a
mimic, who takes off four of our best performers in the
course of the farce. Our stage is loaded with mimics.
I did not see the piece, being out of town the whole time
it was in progress. Dilke is entirely swallowed up in his
boy. It is really lamentable to what a pitch he carries
a sort of parental mania. I had a letter from him at
Shanklin. He went on, a word or two about the Isle of
Wight, which is a bit of hobby horse of his, but he soon
deviated to his boy. "I am sitting," says he, "at the
window expecting my boy from ——." I suppose I told
you somewhere that he lives in Westminster, and his boy
goes to school there, where he gets beaten, and every
bruise he has, and I daresay deserves, is very bitter to
Dilke. The place I am speaking of puts me in mind of
a circumstance which occurred lately at Dilke's. I think
it very rich and dramatic and quite illustrative of the
little quiet fun that he will enjoy sometimes. First I
must tell you that their house is at the corner of Great
Smith Street, so that some of the windows look into one
street, and the back windows into another round the
corner. Dilke had some old people to dinner—I know
not who, but there were two old ladies among them.
Brown was there—they had known him from a child.

Brown is very pleasant with old women, and on that day
it seems behaved himself so winningly that they became
hand and glove together, and a little complimentary.
Brown was obliged to depart early.   He bid them good-
bye and passed into the passage.   No sooner was his back
turned than the old women began lauding him.   When
Brown had reached the street door, and was just going,
Dilke threw up the window and called : " Brown ! Brown !
They say you look younger than ever you did !"   Brown
went on, and had just turned the corner into the other
street when Dilke appeared at the back window, crying :
" Brown ! Brown ! By God, they say you're handsome !"
You see what a many words it requires to give any identity
to a thing I could have told you in half a minute.

I have been reading lately Burton's Anatomy of
Melancholy, and I think you will be very much amused
with a page I here copy for you.   I call it a Feu de Joie
round the batteries of Fort St. Hyphen-de-Phrase on the
birthday of the Digamma.   The whole alphabet was
drawn up in a phalanx on the corner of an old dictionary,
band playing, " Amo, amas," etc.

" Every lover admires his mistriss, though she be very deformed
of herself, ill-favoured, wrinkled, pimpled, pale, red, yellow, tan'd,
tallow-faced, have a swoln juglers platter face, or a thin, lean,
chitty face, have clouds in her face, be crooked, dry, bald, goggle-
ey'd, blear-ey'd or with staring eys, she looks like a squis'd cat,
hold her head still awry, heavy, dull, hollow-mouthed, Persean
hook-nosed, have a sharp Jose nose, a red nose, China flat, great
nose, *nare simo patuloque*, a nose like a promontory, gubber-tushed,
rotten teeth, black, uneven, brown teeth, beetle browed, a witches
beard, her breath stink all over the room, her nose drop winter
and summer with a Bavarian poke under her chin, a sharp chin,
lave eared, with a long cranes neck, which stands awry too, *pen-
dulis mammis, her dugs like two double jugs,* or else no dugs in the
other extream, bloody faln fingers, she have filthy long unpaired
nails, scabbed hands or wrists, a tan'd skin, a rotten carkass,
crooked back, she stoops, is lame, splea-footed, *as slender in the
middle as a cow in the waste,* gowty legs, her ankles hang over her
shooes, her feet stink, she breed lice, a mere changeling, a very
monster, an aufe imperfect, her whole complexion savours, an
harsh voyce, incondite gesture, vile gait, a vast virago, or an ugly

tit, a slug, a fat fustilugs, a truss, a long lean rawbone, a skeleton,
a sneaker (*si qua latent meliora puta*), and to thy judgment looks
like a Mard in a lanthorn, whom thou couldst not fancy for a
world, but hatest, lothest, and wouldst have spit in her face, or
blow thy nose in her bosome, *remedium amoris* to another man,
a dowdy, a slut, a scold, a nasty, rank, rammy, filthy, beastly
quean, dishonest peradventure, obscene, base, beggerly, rude,
foolish, untaught, peevish, Irus' daughter, Thersite's sister,
Grobian's schollar; if he love her once, he admires her for all
this, he takes no notice of any such errors, or imperfections of
body or minde."

There's a dose for you. Fire!! I would give my
favourite leg to have written this as a speech in a play.
With what effect could Matthews pop-gun it at the pit!
This I think will amuse you more than so much poetry.
Of that I do not like to copy any, as I am afraid it is too
mal à propos for you at present ; and yet I will send you
some, for by the time you receive it, things in England
may have taken a different turn.   When I left Mr. Abbey
on Monday evening, I walked up Cheapside, but returned
to put some letters in the post, and met him again in
Bucklesbury.   We walked together through the Poultry
as far as the baker's shop he has some concern in—He
spoke of it in such a way to me, I thought he wanted me
to make an offer to assist him in it.   I do believe if I
could be a hatter I might be one.   He seems anxious
about me.   He began blowing up Lord Byron while I
was sitting with him : "However, may be the fellow says
true now and then," at which he took up a magazine, and
read me some extracts from Don Juan (Lord Byron's
last flash poem), and particularly one against literary
ambition.   I do think I must be well spoken of among
sets, for Hodgkinson is more than polite, and the coffee
German endeavoured to be very close to me the other
night at Covent Garden, where I went at half price before
I tumbled into bed.   Every one, however distant an
acquaintance, behaves in the most conciliating manner to
me.   You will see I speak of this as a matter of interest.
On the next sheet I will give you a little politics.

In every age there has been in England, for two or
three centuries, subjects of great popular interest on the
carpet, so that however great the uproar, one can scarcely
prophecy any material change in the Government, for as
loud disturbances have agitated the country many times.
All civilised countries become gradually more enlightened,
and there should be a continual change for the better.
Look at this country at present, and remember it when
it was even thought impious to doubt the justice of a
trial by combat.   From that time there has been a
gradual change.   Three great changes have been in progress : first for the better, next for the worse, and a third
for the better once more.   The first was the gradual
annihilation of the tyranny of the nobles, when kings
found it their interest to conciliate the common people,
elevate them, and be just to them.   Just when baronial
power ceased, and before standing armies were so dangerous, taxes were few, kings were lifted by the people over
the heads of their nobles, and those people held a rod over
kings.   The change for the worse in Europe was again
this : the obligation of kings to the multitude began to
be forgotten.   Custom had made noblemen the humble
servants of kings.   Then kings turned to the nobles as
the adorners of their power, the slaves of it, and from the
people as creatures continually endeavouring to check
them.   Then in every kingdom there was a long struggle
of kings to destroy all popular privileges.   The English
were the only people in Europe who made a grand kick
at this.   They were slaves to Henry VIII, but were
freemen under William III at the time the French were
abject slaves under Louis XIV.   The example of England,
and the liberal writers of France and England, sowed the
seed of opposition to this tyranny, and it was swelling in
the ground till it burst out in the French Revolution.
That has had an unlucky termination.   It put a stop to
the rapid progress of free sentiments in England, and
gave our Court hopes of turning back to the despotism
of the eighteenth century.   They have made a handle of

this event in every way to undermine our freedom. They spread a horrid superstition against all innovation and improvement. The present struggle in England of the people is to destroy this superstition. What has roused them to do it is their distresses. Perhaps, on this account, the present distresses of this nation are a fortunate thing though so horrid in their experience. You will see I mean that the French Revolution put a temporary stop to this third change—the change for the better—Now it is in progress again, and I think it is an effectual one. This is no contest between Whig and Tory, but between right and wrong. There is scarcely a grain of party spirit now in England. Right and wrong considered by each man abstractedly, is the fashion. I know very little of these things. I am convinced, however, that apparently small causes make great alterations. There are little signs whereby we may know how matters are going on. This makes the business of Carlisle the bookseller of great amount in my mind. He has been selling deistical pamphlets, republished Tom Paine, and many other works held in superstitious horror. He even has been selling, for some time, immense numbers of a work called The Deist, which comes out in weekly numbers. For this conduct he, I think, has had about a dozen indictments issued against him, for which he has found bail to the amount of many thousand pounds. After all, they are afraid to prosecute. They are afraid of his defence; it would be published in all the papers all over the empire. They shudder at this. The trials would light a flame they could not extinguish. Do you not think this of great import? You will hear by the papers of the proceedings at Manchester, and Hunt's triumphal entry into London. It would take me a whole day and a quire of paper to give you anything like detail. I will merely mention that it is calculated that 30,000 people were in the streets waiting for him. The whole distance from the Angel at Islington to the Crown and Anchor was lined with multitudes.

As I passed Colnaghi's window I saw a profile portrait of Sandt, the destroyer of Kotzebue. His very look must interest every one in his favour. I suppose they have represented him in his college dress. He seems to me like a young Abelard—a fine mouth, cheek bones (and this is no joke) full of sentiment, a fine, unvulgar nose, and plump temples.

On looking over some letters I found the one I wrote, intended for you, from the foot of Helvellyn to Liverpool; but you had sailed, and therefore it was returned to me. It contained, among other nonsense, an acrostic of my sister's name—and a pretty long name it is. I wrote it in a great hurry which you will see. Indeed I would not copy it if I thought it would ever be seen by any but yourselves.

> Give me your patience, sister, while I frame
> Exact in capitals your golden name,
> Or sue the fair Apollo, and he will
> Rouse from his heavy slumber and instil
> Great love in me for thee and Poesy.
> Imagine not that greatest mastery
> And kingdom over all the realms of verse
> Nears more to Heaven in aught than when we nurse
> And surety give to love and brotherhood.
>
> Anthropopagi in Othello's mood ;
> Ulysses storm'd, and his enchanted belt
> Glowed with the Muse : but they are never felt
> Unbosom'd so, and so eternal made,
> Such tender incense in their laurel shade
> To all the recent sisters of the Nine,
> As this poor offering to you, sister mine.
>
> Kind sister ! aye, this third name says you are ;
> Enchanted has it been the Lord knows where ;
> And may its taste to you, like good old wine,
> Take you to real happiness, and give
> Sons, daughters, and a home like honied hive.

Foot of Helvellyn, June 27.

I sent you in my first packet some of my Scotch letters. I find I have one kept back, which was written in the most interesting part of our tour, and will copy

part of it in the hope you will not find it unamusing. I
would give now anything for Richardson's power of
making mountains of molehills.

Incipit epistola caledoniensa—

"Dunancullen."

(I did not know the day of the month, for I find
I have not added it. Brown must have been asleep).
"Just after my last had gone to the post" (before I
go any further, I must premise that I would send the
identical letter, instead of taking the trouble to copy it;
I do not do so, for it would spoil my notion of the neat
manner in which I intend to fold these three genteel
sheets. The original is written on coarse paper, and the
soft one would ride in the post bag very uneasy. Perhaps
there might be a quarrel)[1]   .   .   .   .

.   .   .   .   .   .

I ought to make a large "?" here, but I had better
take the opportunity of telling you I have got rid of my
haunting sore throat, and conduct myself in a manner
not to catch another.

You speak of Lord Byron and me. There is this
great difference between us : he describes what he sees—
I describe what I imagine. Mine is the hardest task;
now see the immense difference. The Edinburgh Reviewers are afraid to touch upon my poem. They do not
know what to make of it; they do not like to condemn
it, and they will not praise it for fear. They are as shy
of it as I should be of wearing a Quaker's hat. The fact
is, they have no real taste. They dare not compromise
their judgments on so puzzling a question. If on my

---

[1] Keats here copies, with slight changes and abridgments, his
letter to Tom of July 23, 1818 (see above, p. 147), ending with
the lines written after visiting Staffa : as to which he adds, "I find
I must keep memorandums of the verses I send you, for I do not
remember whether I have sent the following lines upon Staffa. I
hope not ; 'twould be a horrid bore to you, especially after reading
this dull specimen of description. For myself I hate descriptions.
I would not send it if it were not mine."

next publication they should praise me, and so lug in Endymion, I will address them in a manner they will not at all relish. The cowardliness of the Edinburgh is more than the abuse of the Quarterly.

Monday [September 20].

This day is a grand day for Winchester. They elect the mayor. It was indeed high time the place should have some sort of excitement. There was nothing going on—all asleep. Not an old maid's sedan returning from a card party; and if any old women have got tipsy at christenings, they have not ~~exposed~~ themselves in the street. The first night, though, of our arrival here there was a slight uproar took place at about ten of the clock. We heard distinctly a noise patting down the street, as of a walking-cane of the good old dowager breed; and a little minute after we heard a less voice observe, "What a noise the ferril made—it must be loose." Brown wanted to call the constables, but I observed it was only a little breeze, and would soon pass over. The side streets here are excessively maiden-lady-like; the door-steps always fresh from the flannel. The knockers have a very staid, serious, nay almost awful quietness about them. I never saw so quiet a collection of lions' and rams' heads. The doors most part black, with a little brass handle just above the keyhole, so that you may easily shut yourself out of your own house. He! He! There is none of your Lady Bellaston ringing and rapping here; no thundering Jupiter-footmen, no opera-treble tattoos, but a modest lifting up of the knocker by a set of little wee old fingers that peep through the gray mittens, and a dying fall thereof. The great beauty of poetry is that it makes everything in every place interesting. The palatine Venice and the abbotine Winchester are equally interesting. Some time since I began a poem called "The Eve of St. Mark," quite in the spirit of town quietude. I think I will give you the sensation of walking about an old country

town in a coolish evening.   I know not whether I shall
ever finish it; I will give it as far as I have gone.   Ut
tibi placeat—

THE EVE OF ST. MARK.

Upon a Sabbath-day it fell ;
Twice holy was the Sabbath-bell,
That call'd the folk to evening prayer ;
The city streets were clean and fair
From wholesome drench of April rains ;
And, when on western window panes,
The chilly sunset faintly told
Of unmatured green vallies cold,
Of the green thorny bloomless hedge,
Of rivers new with spring-tide sedge,
Of primroses by shelter'd rills,
And daisies on the aguish hills.
Twice holy was the Sabbath-bell :
The silent streets were crowded well
With staid and pious companies,
Warm from their fireside orat'ries ;
And moving, with demurest air,
To even-song, and vesper prayer.
Each arched porch, and entry low,
Was fill'd with patient folk and slow,
With whispers hush, and shuffling feet,
While play'd the organ loud and sweet.

The bells had ceas'd, the prayers begun,
And Bertha had not yet half done
A curious volume, patch'd and torn,
That all day long, from earliest morn,
Had taken captive her two eyes,
Among its golden broideries ;
Perplex'd her with a thousand things,--
The stars of Heaven, and angels' wings,
Martyrs in a fiery blaze,
Azure saints and silver rays,
Moses' breastplate, and the seven
Candlesticks John saw in Heaven,
The winged Lion of St. Mark,
And the Covenantal Ark,
With its many mysteries,
Cherubim and golden mice.
Bertha was a maiden fair,
Dwelling in the old Minster-square ;

From her fireside she could see,
Sidelong, its rich antiquity,
Far as the Bishop's garden-wall,
Where sycamores and elm-trees tall,
Full-leav'd the forest had outstript,
By no sharp north-wind ever nipt,
So shelter'd by the mighty pile.
Bertha arose, and read awhile,
With forehead 'gainst the window-pane.
Again she try'd, and then again,
Until the dusk eve left her dark
Upon the legend of St. Mark.
From plaited lawn-frill, fine and thin,
She lifted up her soft warm chin,
With aching neck and swimming eyes,
And dazed with saintly imageries.

All was gloom, and silent all,
Save now and then the still footfall
Of one returning homewards late,
Past the echoing minster-gate.
The clamorous daws, that all the day
Above tree-tops and towers play,
Pair by pair had gone to rest,
Each in ancient belfry-nest,
Where asleep they fall betimes,
To music and the drowsy chimes.

All was silent, all was gloom,
Abroad and in the homely room:
Down she sat, poor cheated soul!
And struck a lamp from the dismal coal;
Lean'd forward, with bright drooping hair
And slant book, full against the glare.
Her shadow, in uneasy guise,
Hover'd about, a giant size,
On ceiling-beam and old oak chair,
The parrot's cage, and panel square;
And the warm angled winter-screen,
On which were many monsters seen,
Call'd doves of Siam, Lima mice,
And legless birds of Paradise,
Macaw and tender Avadavat,
And silken-furr'd Angora cat.
Untir'd she read, her shadow still
Glower'd about, as it would fill
The room with wildest forms and shades,
As though some ghostly queen of spades

Had come to mock behind her back,
And dance, and ruffle her garments black.
Untir'd she read the legend page,
Of holy Mark, from youth to age,
On land, on sea, in pagan chains,
Rejoicing for his many pains.
Sometimes the learned eremite,
With golden star, or dagger bright,
Referr'd to pious poesies
Written in smallest crow-quill size
Beneath the text ; and thus the rhyme
Was parcelled out from time to time :
". . . Als writith he of swevenis,
Man han beforne they wake in bliss,
Whanne that hir friendes thinke him bound
In crimped shroude farre under grounde ;
And how a litling child mote be
A saint er its nativitie,
Gif that the modre (God her blesse !)
Kepen in solitarinesse,
And kissen devoute the holy croce.
Of Goddes love, and Sathan's force,—
He writith ; and thinges many mo
Of swiche thinges I may not show.
Bot I must tellen verilie
Somdel of Saintè Cicilie,
And chieflie what he auctorethe
Of Saintè Markis life and dethe : "

At length her constant eyelids come
Upon the fervent martyrdom ;
Then lastly to his holy shrine,
Exalt amid the tapers' shine .
At Venice,—

I hope you will like this for all its carelessness.   I
must take an opportunity here to observe that though I
am writing *to* you, I am all the while writing *at* your
wife.   This explanation will account for my speaking
sometimes hoity-toity-ishly, whereas if you were alone, I
should sport a little more sober sadness.   I am like a
squinty gentleman, who, saying soft things to one lady
ogles another, or what is as bad, in arguing with a person
on his left hand, appeals with his eyes to one on the
right.   His vision is elastic ; he bends it to a certain

object, but having a patent spring it flies off. Writing
has this disadvantage of speaking—one cannot write a
wink, or a nod, or a grin, or a purse of the lips, or a
smile—O law! One cannot put one's finger to one's
nose, or yerk ye in the ribs, or lay hold of your button in
writing; but in all the most lively and titterly parts of
my letter you must not fail to imagine me, as the epic
poets say, now here, now there; now with one foot
pointed at the ceiling, now with another; now with my
pen on my ear, now with my elbow in my mouth.   O,
my friends, you lose the action, and attitude is everything,
as Fuseli said when he took up his leg like a musket to
shoot a swallow just darting behind his shoulder.   And
yet does not the word "mum" go for one's finger beside
the nose? I hope it does. I have to make use of the
word "mum" before I tell you that Severn has got a
little baby—all his own, let us hope.   He told Brown he
had given up painting, and had turned modeller.   I hope
sincerely 'tis not a party concern—that no Mr. —— or
——is the real Pinxit and Severn the poor Sculpsit to
this work of art.   You know he has long studied in the
life Academy.   "Haydon—yes," your wife will say, "Here
is a sum total account of Haydon again.   I wonder your
brother don't put a monthly bulletin in the Philadelphia
papers about him.   I won't hear—no.   Skip down to
the bottom, and there are some more of his verses—skip
(lullaby-by) them too."—"No, let's go regularly through."
—"I won't hear a word about Haydon—bless the child,
how rioty she is—there, go on there."

Now, pray go on here, for I have a few words to say
about Haydon.   Before this chancery threat had cut off
every legitimate supply of cash from me, I had a little at
my disposal.   Haydon being very much in want, I lent
him £30 of it.   Now in this see-saw game of life, I got
nearest to the ground, and this chancery business rivetted
me there, so that I was sitting in that uneasy position
where the seat slants so abominably.   I applied to him
for payment.   He could not.   That was no wonder;

but Goodman Delver, where was the wonder then?
Why marry in this: he did not seem to care much about
it, and let me go without my money with almost non-
chalance, when he ought to have sold his drawings to
supply me. I shall perhaps still be acquainted with
him, but for friendship, that is at an end. Brown has
been my friend in this. He got him to sign a bond,
payable at three months. Haslam has assisted me with
the return of part of the money you lent him.

Hunt—"there," says your wife, "there's another of
those dull folk! Not a syllable about my friends? Well,
Hunt—What about Hunt? You little thing, see how she
bites my finger! My! is not this a tooth?" Well when
you have done with the tooth, read on. Not a syllable
about your friends! Here are some syllables. As far as
I could smoke things on the Sunday before last, thus
matters stood in Henrietta Street. Henry was a greater
blade then ever I remember to have seen him. He had
on a very nice coat, a becoming waistcoat, and buff
trousers. I think his face has lost a little of the
Spanish-brown, but no flesh. He carved some beef
exactly to suit my appetite, as if I had been measured
for it. As I stood looking out of the window with
Charles, after dinner, quizzing the passengers,—at which
I am sorry to say he is too apt,—I observed that this
young son of a gun's whiskers had begun to curl and
curl, little twists and twists, all down the sides of his
face, getting properly thickest on the angles of the
visage. He certainly will have a notable pair of whiskers.
"How shiny your gown is in front," says Charles. "Why
don't you see? 'tis an apron," says Henry; whereat I
scrutinised, and behold your mother had a purple stuff
gown on, and over it an apron of the same colour, being
the same cloth that was used for the lining. And
furthermore to account for the shining, it was the first
day of wearing. I guessed as much of the gown—but
that is entre nous. Charles likes England better than
France. They've got a fat, smiling, fair cook as ever

you saw; she is a little lame, but that improves her; it
makes her go more swimmingly.   When I asked "Is
Mrs. Wylie within?" she gave me such a large five-and-
thirty-year-old smile, it made me look round upon the
fourth stair—it might have been the fifth; but that's a
puzzle.   I shall never be able, if I were to set myself a
recollecting for a year, to recollect.   I think I remember
two or three specks in her teeth, but I really can't say
exactly.   Your mother said something about Miss Keasle
—what that was is quite a riddle to me now, whether she
had got fatter or thinner, or broader or longer, straiter,
or had taken to the zigzags—whether she had taken to or
had left off asses' milk.   That, by the bye, she ought never
to touch.   How much better it would be to put her out
to nurse with the wise woman of Brentford.   I can say
no more on so spare a subject.   Miss Millar now is a
different morsel, if one knew how to divide and sub-
divide, theme her out into sections and subsections, lay a
little on every part of her body as it is divided, in
common with all her fellow-creatures, in Moor's Almanack.
But, alas, I have not heard a word about her, no cue to
begin upon: there was indeed a buzz about her and her
mother's being at old Mrs. So and So's, *who was like to
die,* as the Jews say.   But I dare say, keeping up their
dialect, *she was not like to die.*   I must tell you a good
thing Reynolds *did.*   'Twas the best thing he ever *said.*
You know at taking leave of a party at a doorway,
sometimes a man dallies and foolishes and gets awkward,
and does not know how to make off to advantage.
Good-bye—well, good-bye—and yet he does not go;
good-bye, and so on,—well, good bless you—you know
what I mean.   Now Reynolds was in this predicament,
and got out of it in a very witty way.   He was leaving
us at Hampstead.   He delayed, and we were pressing at
him, and even said "be off," at which he put the tails of
his coat between his legs and sneak'd off as nigh like a
spaniel as could be.   He went with flying colours.   This
is very clever.   I must, being upon the subject, tell you

another good thing of him. He began, for the service it might be of to him in the law, to learn French ; he had lessons at the cheap rate of 2s. 6d. per fag, and observed to Brown, " Gad," says he, " the man sells his lessons so cheap he must have stolen 'em." You have heard of Hook, the farce writer. Horace Smith said to one who asked him if he knew Hook, " Oh yes, Hook and I are very intimate." There's a page of wit for you, to put John Bunyan's emblems out of countenance.

Tuesday [September 21].

You see I keep adding a sheet daily till I send the packet off, which I shall not do for a few days, as I am inclined to write a good deal ; for there can be nothing so remembrancing and enchaining as a good long letter, be it composed of what it may. From the time you left me our friends say I have altered completely—am not the same person. Perhaps in this letter I am, for in a letter one takes up one's existence from the time we last met. I daresay you have altered also—every man does —our bodies every seven years are completely material'd. Seven years ago it was not this hand that clinched itself against Hammond. We are like the relict garments of a saint—the same and not the same, for the careful monks patch it and patch it till there's not a thread of the original garment left, and still they show it for St. Anthony's shirt. This is the reason why men who have been bosom friends, on being separated for any number of years meet coldly, neither of them knowing why. The fact is they are both altered.

Men who live together have a silent moulding and influencing power over each other. They interassimilate. 'Tis an uneasy thought, that in seven years the same hands cannot greet each other again. All this may be obviated by a wilful and dramatic exercise of our minds towards each other. Some think I have lost that poetic ardour and fire 'tis said I once had—the fact is, perhaps I have ; but, instead of that, I hope I shall substitute a more thoughtful and quiet power. I am more frequently now contented to read and think, but now and then haunted with ambitious thoughts. Quieter in my pulse, improved in my digestion, exerting myself against vexing speculations, scarcely content to write the best verses for the fever they leave behind. I want to compose without this fever. I hope I one day shall. You would scarcely imagine I could live alone so comfortably. "Kepen in solitarinesse." I told Anne, the servant here, the other day, to say I was not at home if any one should call. I am not certain how I should endure loneliness and bad weather together. Now the time is beautiful. I take a walk every day for an hour before dinner, and this is generally my walk : I go out the back gate, across one street into the cathedral yard, which is always interesting; there I pass under the trees along a paved path, pass the beautiful front of the cathedral, turn to the left under a stone doorway,—then I am on the other side of the building,—which leaving behind me, I pass on through two college-like squares, seemingly built for the dwelling-place of deans and prebendaries, garnished with grass and shaded with trees; then I pass through one of the old city gates, and then you are in one college street, through which I pass, and at the end thereof crossing some meadows, and at last a country alley of gardens, I arrive, that is my worship arrives, at the foundation of St. Cross, which is a very interesting old place, both for its gothic tower and alms square and for the appropriation of its rich rents to a relation of the Bishop of Winchester. Then I pass across St. Cross meadows till you come to the most beautifully clear river—now this is only one mile of my walk. I will spare you the other two till after supper, when they would do you more good. You must avoid going the first mile best after dinner—

[Wednesday, September 22.]

I could almost advise you to put by this nonsense until you are lifted out of your difficulties; but when

you come to this part, feel with confidence what I now
feel, that though there can be no stop put to troubles we
are inheritors of, there can be, and must be, an end to
immediate difficulties. Rest in the confidence that I will
not omit any exertion to benefit you by some means or
other—If I cannot remit you hundreds, I will tens, and
if not that, ones. Let the next year be managèd by you
as well as possible—the next month, I mean, for I trust
you will soon receive Abbey's remittance. What he can
send you will not be a sufficient capital to ensure you
any command in America. What he has of mine I have
nearly anticipated by debts, so I would advise you not to
sink it, but to live upon it, in hopes of my being able to
increase it. To this end I will devote whatever I may
gain for a few years to come, at which period I must
begin to think of a security of my own comforts, when
quiet will become more pleasant to me than the world.
Still, I would have you doubt my success. 'Tis at present
the cast of a die with me. You say, "These things will
be a great torment to me." I shall not suffer them to be
so. I shall only exert myself the more, while the serious-
ness of their nature will prevent me from nursing up
imaginary griefs. I have not had the blue devils once
since I received your last. I am advised not to publish
till it is seen whether the tragedy will or not succeed.
Should it, a few months may see me in the way of
acquiring property. Should it not, it will be a drawback, and I shall have to perform a longer literary
pilgrimage. You will perceive that it is quite out of
my interest to come to America. What could I do
there? How could I employ myself out of reach of
libraries? You do not mention the name of the gentleman who assists you. 'Tis an extraordinary thing. How
could you do without that assistance? I will not trust
myself with brooding over this. The following is an
extract from a letter of Reynolds to me :—

"I am glad to hear you are getting on so well with
your writings. I hope you are not neglecting the revision

of your poems for the press, from which I expect more than you do."

The first thought that struck me on reading your last was to mortgage a poem to Murray, but on more consideration, I made up my mind not to do so; my reputation is very low; he would not have negotiated my bill of intellect, or given me a very small sum. I should have bound myself down for some time. 'Tis best to meet present misfortunes; not for a momentary good to sacrifice great benefits which one's own untrammell'd and free industry may bring one in the end. In all this do never think of me as in any way unhappy: I shall not be so. I have a great pleasure in thinking of my responsibility to you, and shall do myself the greatest luxury if I can succeed in any way so as to be of assistance to you. We shall look back upon these times, even before our eyes are at all dim—I am convinced of it. But be careful of those Americans. I could almost advise you to come, whenever you have the sum of £500, to England. Those Americans will, I am afraid, still fleece you. If ever you think of such a thing, you must bear in mind the very different state of society here,—the immense difficulties of the times, the great sum required per annum to maintain yourself in any decency. In fact the whole is with Providence. I know not how to advise you but by advising you to advise with yourself. In your next tell me at large your thoughts about America —what chance there is of succeeding there, for it appears to me you have as yet been somehow deceived. I cannot help thinking Mr. Audubon has deceived you. I shall not like the sight of him. I shall endeavour to avoid seeing him. You see how puzzled I am. I have no meridian to fix you to, being the slave of what is to happen. I think I may bid you finally remain in good hopes, and not tease yourself with my changes and variations of mind. If I say nothing decisive in any one particular part of my letter, you may glean the truth from the whole pretty correctly. You may wonder why I had not put your affairs with Abbey in train on receiving your letter before last, to which there will reach you a short answer dated from Shanklin. I did write and speak to Abbey, but to no purpose. Your last, with the enclosed note, has appealed home to him. He will not see the necessity of a thing till he is hit in the mouth. 'Twill be effectual.

I am sorry to mix up foolish and serious things together, but in writing so much I am obliged to do so, and I hope sincerely the tenor of your mind will maintain itself better. In the course of a few months I shall be as good an Italian scholar as I am a French one. I am reading Ariosto at present, not managing more than six or eight stanzas at a time. When I have done this language, so as to be able to read it tolerably well, I shall set myself to get complete in Latin, and there my learning must stop. I do not think of returning upon Greek. I would not go even so far if I were not persuaded of the power the knowledge of any language gives one. The fact is I like to be acquainted with foreign languages. It is, besides, a nice way of filling up intervals, etc. Also the reading of Dante is well worth the while; and in Latin there is a fund of curious literature of the Middle Ages, the works of many great men—Aretino and Sannazaro and Machiavelli. I shall never become attached to a foreign idiom, so as to put it into my writings. The Paradise Lost, though so fine in itself, is a corruption of our language. It should be kept as it is—unique, a curiosity, a beautiful and grand curiosity, the most remarkable production of the world; a northern dialect accommodating itself to Greek and Latin inversions and intonations. The purest English, I think—or what ought to be purest—is Chatterton's. The language had existed long enough to be entirely uncorrupted of Chaucer's Gallicisms, and still the old words are used. Chatterton's language is entirely northern. I prefer the native music of it to Milton's, cut by feet. I have but lately stood on my guard against Milton. Life to him would be death to me. Miltonic verse cannot be written, but is the verse of art. I wish to devote myself to another verse alone.

Friday [September 24].

I have been obliged to intermit your letter for two days (this being Friday morning), from having had to attend to other correspondence. Brown, who was at Bedhampton, went thence to Chichester, and I am still directing my letters Bedhampton. There arose a misunderstanding about them. I began to suspect my letters had been stopped from curiosity. However, yesterday Brown had four letters from me all in a lump, and the matter is cleared up. Brown complained very much in his letter to me of yesterday of the great alteration the disposition of Dilke has undergone. He thinks of nothing but political justice and his boy. Now, the first political duty a man ought to have a mind to is the happiness of his friends. I wrote Brown a comment on the subject, wherein I explained what I thought of Dilke's character, which resolved itself into this conclusion, that Dilke was a man who cannot feel he has a personal identity unless he has made up his mind about everything. The only means of strengthening one's intellect is to make up one's mind about nothing—to let the mind be a thoroughfare for all thoughts, not a select party. The genus is not scarce in population; all the stubborn arguers you meet with are of the same brood. They never begin upon a subject they have not preresolved on. They want to hammer their nail into you, and if you have the point, still they think you wrong. Dilke will never come at a truth as long as he lives, because he is always trying at it. He is a Godwin Methodist.

I must not forget to mention that your mother show'd me the lock of hair—'tis of a very dark colour for so young a creature. Then it is two feet in length. I shall not stand a barley corn higher. That's not fair;

one ought to go on growing as well as others. At the
end of this sheet I shall stop for the present and send it
off. You may expect another letter immediately after it.
As I never know the day of the month but by chance, I
put here that this is the 24th September.

I would wish you here to stop your ears, for I have
a word or two to say to your wife.

My dear Sister—In the first place I must quarrel
with you for sending me such a shabby piece of paper,
though that is in some degree made up for by the beautiful impression of the seal. You should like to know
what I was doing the first of May. Let me see—I
cannot recollect. I have all the Examiners ready to
send—they will be a great treat to you when they reach
you. I shall pack them up when my business with
Abbey has come to a good conclusion, and the remittance
is on the road to you. I have dealt round your best
wishes like a pack of cards, but being always given to
cheat myself, I have turned up acc. You see I am
making game of you. I see you are not all happy in
that America. England, however, would not be over
happy for you if you were here. Perhaps 'twould be
better to be teased here than there. I must preach
patience to you both. No step hasty or injurious to you
must be taken. You say let one large sheet be all to
me. You will find more than that in different parts of
this packet for you. Certainly, I have been caught in
rains. A catch in the rain occasioned my last sore
throat; but as for red-haired girls, upon my word, I do
not recollect ever having seen one. Are you quizzing
me or Miss Waldegrave when you talk of promenading ?
As for pun-making, I wish it was as good a trade as
pin-making. There is very little business of that sort
going on now. We struck for wages, like the Manchester
weavers, but to no purpose. So we are all out of employ. I am more lucky than some, you see, by having
an opportunity of exporting a few—getting into a little

foreign trade, which is a comfortable thing. I wish one
could get change for a pun in silver currency. I would
give three and a half any night to get into Drury pit,
but they won't ring at all. No more will notes you will
say; but notes are different things, though they make
together a pun-note as the term goes. If I were your
son, I shouldn't mind you, though you rapt me with
the scissors. But, Lord! I should be out of favour when
the little un be comm'd. You have made an uncle of
me, you have, and I don't know what to make of myself.
I suppose next there will be a nevey. You say in my
last, write directly. I have not received your letter
above ten days. The thought of your little girl puts me
in mind of a thing I heard a Mr. Lamb say. A child in
arms was passing by towards its mother, in the nurse's
arms. Lamb took hold of the long clothes, saying:
" Where, God bless me, where does it leave off ?"

Saturday [September 25].

If you would prefer a joke or two to anything
else, I have two for you, fresh hatched, just ris, as
the bakers' wives say by the rolls. The first I played
off on Brown; the second I played on myself. Brown,
when he left me, "Keats," says he, "my good fellow"
(staggering upon his left heel and fetching an irregular
pirouette with his right); "Keats," says he (depressing his
left eyebrow and elevating his right one), though by the
way at the moment I did not know which was the right
one; "Keats," says he (still in the same posture, but
furthermore both his hands in his waistcoat pockets and
putting out his stomach), "Keats—my—go-o-ood fell-
o-o-ooh," says he (interlarding his exclamation with
certain ventriloquial parentheses),—no, this is all a lie—
He was as sober as a judge, when a judge happens to be
sober, and said: " Keats, if any letters come for me, do
not forward them, but open them and give me the marrow
of them in a few words." At the time I wrote my first
to him no letter had arrived. I thought I would invent

one, and as I had not time to manufacture a long one, I dabbed off a short one, and that was the reason of the joke succeeding beyond my expectations. Brown let his house to a Mr. Benjamin—a Jew. Now, the water which furnishes the house is in a tank, sided with a composition of lime, and the lime impregnates the water unpleasantly. Taking advantage of this circumstance, I pretended that Mr. Benjamin had written the following short note—

Sir—By drinking your damn'd tank water I have got the gravel. What reparation can you make to me and my family ?   NATHAN BENJAMIN.

By a fortunate hit, I hit upon his right—heathen name—his right pronomen. Brown in consequence, it appears, wrote to the surprised Mr. Benjamin the following—

Sir—I cannot offer you any remuneration until your gravel shall have formed itself into a stone—when I will cut you with pleasure.   C. BROWN.

This of Brown's Mr. Benjamin has answered, insisting on an explanation of this singular circumstance. B. says : "When I read your letter and his following, I roared ; and in came Mr. Snook, who on reading them seem'd likely to burst the hoops of his fat sides." So the joke has told well.

Now for the one I played on myself. I must first give you the scene and the dramatis personæ. There are an old major and his youngish wife here in the next apartments to me. His bedroom door opens at an angle with my sitting-room door. Yesterday I was reading as demurely as a parish clerk, when I heard a rap at the door. I got up and opened it ; no one was to be seen. I listened, and heard some one in the major's room. Not content with this, I went upstairs and down, looked in the cupboards and watch'd. At last I set myself to read again, not quite so demurely, when there came a louder rap. I was determined to find out who it was. I looked out; the staircases were all silent. "This must be the major's wife," said I. "At all events I will see the truth." So I rapt me at the major's door and went in, to the utter surprise and confusion of the lady, who was in reality there. After a little explanation, which I can no more describe than fly, I made my retreat from her, convinced of my mistake. She is to all appearance a silly body, and is really surprised about it. She must have been, for I have discovered that a little girl in the house was the rapper. I assure you she has nearly made me sneeze. If the lady tells tits, I shall put a very grave and moral face on the matter with the old gentleman, and make his little boy a present of a humming top.

[Monday, September 27.]

My dear George—This Monday morning, the 27th, I have received your last, dated 12th July. You say you have not heard from England for three months. Then my letter from Shanklin, written, I think, at the end of June, has not reach'd you. You shall not have cause to think I neglect you. I have kept this back a little time in expectation of hearing from Mr. Abbey. You will say I might have remained in town to be Abbey's messenger in these affairs. That I offered him, but he in his answer convinced me that he was anxious to bring the business to an issue. He observed, that by being himself the agent in the whole, people might be more expeditious. You say you have not heard for three months, and yet your letters have the tone of knowing how our affairs are situated, by which I conjecture I acquainted you with them in a letter previous to the Shanklin one. That I may not have done. To be certain, I will here state that it is in consequence of Mrs. Jennings threatening a chancery suit that you have been kept from the receipt of monies, and myself deprived of any help from Abbey. I am glad you say you keep up your spirits. I hope you make a true statement on that score. Still keep them up, for we are all young. I can only repeat here that you shall hear from me again immediately. Notwithstanding this bad intelligence, I have experienced some pleasure in receiving so correctly two letters from you, as it gives me, if I may so say, a distant idea of proximity. This last improves upon my little niece—kiss her for me. Do not fret yourself about the delay of money on account of my immediate opportunity being lost, for in a new country whoever has money must have an opportunity of employing it in many ways. The report runs now more in favour of Kean stopping in England. If he should, I have confident hopes of our tragedy. If he invokes the hot-blooded character of Ludolph,—and he is the only actor that can do it,—he will add to his own fame and improve my fortune. I will give you a half-dozen lines of it before I part as a specimen—

> Not as a swordsman would I pardon crave,
> But as a son : the bronz'd Centurion,
> Long-toil'd in foreign wars, and whose high deeds
> Are shaded in a forest of tall spears,
> Known only to his troop, hath greater plea
> Of favour with my sire than I can have.

Believe me, my dear brother and sister, your affectionate and anxious Brother   JOHN KEATS.

CXVII.—TO JOHN HAMILTON REYNOLDS.

Winchester, September 22, 1819.

My dear Reynolds—I was very glad to hear from Woodhouse that you would meet in the country. I hope you will pass some pleasant time together. Which I wish to make pleasanter by a brace of letters, very highly to be estimated, as really I have had very bad luck with this sort of game this season. I "kepen in solitarinesse," for Brown has gone a-visiting. I am surprised myself at

the pleasure I live alone in.   I can give you no news of
the place here, or any other idea of it but what I have
to this effect written to George.   Yesterday I say to
him was a grand day for Winchester.   They elected a
Mayor.   It was indeed high time the place should receive
some sort of excitement.   There was nothing going on :
all asleep : not an old maid's sedan returning from a card
party : and if any old woman got tipsy at Christenings
they did not expose it in the streets.   The first night
though of our arrival here, there was a slight uproar took
place at about 10 o' the Clock.   We heard distinctly a
noise pattering down the High Street as of a walking cane
of the good old Dowager breed; and a little minute after
we heard a less voice observe " What a noise the ferril
made—it must be loose."   Brown wanted to call the
constables, but I observed 'twas only a little breeze and
would soon pass over.—The side streets here are excessively maiden-lady-like : the door-steps always fresh from
the flannel.   The knockers have a staid serious, nay
almost awful quietness about them.   I never saw so quiet
a collection of Lions' and Rams' heads.   The doors are
most part black, with a little brass handle just above
the keyhole, so that in Winchester a man may very
quietly shut himself out of his own house.   How beautiful the season is now—How fine the air.   A temperate
sharpness about it.   Really, without joking, chaste
weather—Dian skies—I never liked stubble-fields so
much as now—Aye better than the chilly green of the
Spring.   Somehow, a stubble-field looks warm—in the
same way that some pictures look warm.   This struck
me so much in my Sunday's walk that I composed upon
it.[1]

I hope you are better employed than in gaping after
weather.   I have been at different times so happy as
not to know what weather it was—No I will not copy a

---

[1] The beautiful *Ode to Autumn*, the draft of which Keats had
copied in a letter (unluckily not preserved) written earlier in the
same day to Woodhouse.

parcel of verses. I always somehow associate Chatterton
with autumn. He is the purest writer in the English
Language. He has no French idiom or particles, like
Chaucer—'tis genuine English Idiom in English words.
I have given up Hyperion — there were too many
Miltonic inversions in it — Miltonic verse cannot be
written but in an artful, or, rather, artist's humour. I
wish to give myself up to other sensations. English
ought to be kept up. It may be interesting to you to
pick out some lines from Hyperion, and put a mark
× to the false beauty proceeding from art, and one ‖ to
the true voice of feeling. Upon my soul 'twas imagination—I cannot make the distinction—Every now and then
there is a Miltonic intonation—But I cannot make the
division properly. The fact is, I must take a walk: for
I am writing a long letter to George: and have been employed at it all the morning. You will ask, have I heard
from George. I am sorry to say not the best news—I
hope for better. This is the reason, among others, that
if I write to you it must be in such a scrap-like way. I
have no meridian to date interests from, or measure
circumstances—To-night I am all in a mist; I scarcely
know what's what—But you knowing my unsteady and
vagarish disposition, will guess that all this turmoil will
be settled by to-morrow morning. It strikes me to-night
that I have led a very odd sort of life for the two or
three last years—Here and there—no anchor—I am glad
of it.—If you can get a peep at Babbicombe before you
leave the country, do.—I think it the finest place I have
seen, or is to be seen, in the South. There is a Cottage
there I took warm water at, that made up for the tea.
I have lately shirk'd some friends of ours, and I advise
you to do the same, I mean the blue-devils—I am
never at home to them. You need not fear them while
you remain in Devonshire—there will be some of the
family waiting for you at the Coach office—but go by
another Coach.

I shall beg leave to have a third opinion in the first

discussion you have with Woodhouse—just half-way, between both. You know I will not give up my argument—In my walk to-day I stoop'd under a railing that lay across my path, and asked myself "Why I did not get over." "Because," answered I, "no one wanted to force you under." I would give a guinea to be a reasonable man—good sound sense—a says what he thinks and does what he says man—and did not take snuff. They say men near death, however mad they may have been, come to their senses—I hope I shall here in this letter—there is a decent space to be very sensible in—many a good proverb has been in less—nay, I have heard of the statutes at large being changed into the Statutes. at Small and printed for a watch paper.

Your sisters, by this time, must have got the Devonshire "ees"—short ees—you know 'em—they are the prettiest ees in the language. O how I admire the middle-sized delicate Devonshire girls of about fifteen. There was one at an Inn door holding a quartern of . brandy—the very thought of her kept me warm a whole stage—and a 16 miler too—"You'll pardon me for being jocular."

Ever your affectionate friend   JOHN KEATS.

CXVIII.—TO CHARLES WENTWORTH DILKE.

Winchester, Wednesday Eve.
[September 22, 1819.]

My dear Dilke—Whatever I take to for the time I cannot leave off in a hurry; letter writing is the go now; I have consumed a quire at least. You must give me credit, now, for a free Letter when it is in reality an interested one, on two points, the one requestive, the other verging to the pros and cons. As I expect they will lead me to seeing and conferring with you in a short time, I shall not enter at all upon a letter I have lately received from George, of not the most comfortable intelligence : but proceed to these two points, which if you can theme

out into sections and subsections, for my edification, you
will oblige me. The first I shall begin upon, the other
will follow like a tail to a Comet. I have written to
Brown on the subject, and can but go over the same
ground with you in a very short time, it not being more
in length than the ordinary paces between the Wickets.
It concerns a resolution I have taken to endeavour to
acquire something by temporary writing in periodical
works. You must agree with me how unwise it is to
keep feeding upon hopes, which depending so much on
the state of temper and imagination, appear gloomy or
bright, near or afar off, just as it happens. Now an act
has three parts—to act, to do, and to perform—I mean I
should *do* something for my immediate welfare. Even if I
am swept away like a spider from a drawing-room, I am
determined to spin—homespun anything for sale. Yea,
I will traffic. Anything but Mortgage my Brain to
Blackwood. I am determined not to lie like a dead
lump. If Reynolds had not taken to the law, would he
not be earning something? Why cannot I. You may
say I want tact—that is easily acquired. You may be
up to the slang of a cock pit in three battles. It is
fortunate I have not before this been tempted to venture
on the common. I should a year or two ago have spoken
my mind on every subject with the utmost simplicity.
I hope I have learned a little better and am confident I
shall be able to cheat as well as any literary Jew of the
Market and shine up an article on anything without
much knowledge of the subject, aye like an orange. I
would willingly have recourse to other means. I cannot;
I am fit for nothing but literature. Wait for the issue
of this Tragedy? No—there cannot be greater uncertainties east, west, north, and south than concerning
dramatic composition. How many months must I wait!
Had I not better begin to look about me now? If better
events supersede this necessity what harm will be done?
I have no trust whatever on Poetry. I don't wonder at
it—the marvel is to me how people read so much of it.

I think you will see the reasonableness of my plan.   To
forward it I purpose living in cheap Lodging in Town,
that I may be in the reach of books and information, of
which there is here a plentiful lack.   If I can find any
place tolerably comfortable I will settle myself and fag
till I can afford to buy Pleasure—which if I never can
afford I must go without.   Talking of Pleasure, this
moment I was writing with one hand, and with the other
holding to my Mouth a Nectarine—good God how fine.
It went down soft, pulpy, slushy, oozy—all its delicious
embonpoint melted down my throat like a large beatified
Strawberry.   I shall certainly breed.   Now I come to
my request.   Should you like me for a neighbour again?
Come, plump it out, I won't blush.   I should also be in
the neighbourhood of Mrs. Wylie, which I should be glad
of, though that of course does not influence me.   Therefore will you look about Marsham, or Rodney Street for
a couple of rooms for me.   Rooms like the gallant's legs
in Massinger's time, "as good as the times allow, Sir."
I have written to-day to Reynolds, and to Woodhouse.
Do you know him?   He is a Friend of Taylor's at whom
Brown has taken one of his funny odd dislikes.   I'm
sure he's wrong, because Woodhouse likes my Poetry—
conclusive.   I ask your opinion and yet I must say to
you as to him, Brown, that if you have anything to say
against it I shall be as obstinate and heady as a Radical.
By the Examiner coming in your handwriting you must
be in Town.   They have put me into spirits.   Notwithstanding my aristocratic temper I cannot help being
very much pleased with the present public proceedings.
I hope sincerely I shall be able to put a Mite of help to
the Liberal side of the Question before I die.   If you
should have left Town again (for your Holidays cannot
be up yet) let me know when this is forwarded to you.
A most extraordinary mischance has befallen two letters
I wrote Brown—one from London whither I was obliged
to go on business for George; the other from this place
since my return.   I can't make it out.   I am excess-

ively sorry for it. I shall hear from Brown and from you almost together, for I have sent him a Letter to-day : you must positively agree with me or by the delicate toe nails of the virgin I will not open your Letters. If they are as David says "suspicious looking letters" I won't open them. If St. John had been half as cunning he might have seen the revelations comfortably in his own room, without giving angels the trouble of breaking open seals. Remember me to Mrs. D. and the West-monasteranian and believe me

Ever your sincere friend   JOHN KEATS.

CXIX.—TO CHARLES BROWN.

Winchester, September 23, 1819.

. . . . . .

Now I am going to enter on the subject of. self. It is quite time I should set myself doing something, and live no longer upon hopes. I have never yet exerted myself. I am getting into an idle-minded, vicious way of life, almost content to live upon others. In no period of my life have I acted with any self-will but in throwing up the apothecary profession. That I do not repent of. Look at Reynolds, if he was not in the law, he would be acquiring, by his abilities, something towards his support. My occupation is entirely literary : I will do so, too. I will write, on the liberal side of the question, for whoever will pay me. I have not known yet what it is to be diligent. I purpose living in town in a cheap lodging, and endeavouring, for a beginning, to get the theatricals of some paper. When I can afford to compose deliberate poems, I will. I shall be in expectation of an answer to this. Look on my side of the question. I am convinced I am right. Suppose the tragedy should succeed,—there will be no harm done. And here I will take an opportunity of making a remark or two on our friendship, and on all your good offices to me. I have a natural timidity

of mind in these matters ; liking better to take the feeling between us for granted, than to speak of it.   But,
good God ! what a short while you have known me !   I
feel it a sort of duty thus to recapitulate, however unpleasant it may be to you.   You have been living for
others more than any man I know.   This is a vexation
to me, because it has been depriving you, in the very
prime of your life, of pleasures which it was your duty to
procure.   As I am speaking in general terms, this may
appear nonsense ; you perhaps will not understand it ;
but if you can go over, day by day, any month of the
last year, you will know what I mean.   On the whole however this is a subject that I cannot express myself upon—
I speculate upon it frequently ; and believe me the end
of my speculations is always an anxiety for your happiness.   This anxiety will not be one of the least incite-
ments to the plan I purpose pursuing.   I had got into a
habit of mind of looking towards you as a help in all
difficulties — This very habit would be the parent of
idleness and difficulties.   You will see it is a duty I owe
myself to break the neck of it.   I do nothing for my
subsistence—make no exertion—At the end of another
year you shall applaud me, not for verses, but for conduct.   While I have some immediate cash, I had better
settle myself quietly, and fag on as others do.   I shall
apply to Hazlitt, who knows the market as well as any
one, for something to bring me in a few pounds as soon
as possible.   I shall not suffer my pride to hinder me.
·The whisper may go round ; I shall not hear it.   If I can
get an article in the Edinburgh, I will.   One must not
be delicate — Nor let this disturb you longer than·a
moment.   I look forward with a good hope that we
shall one day be passing free, untrammelled, unanxious
time together.   That can never be if I continue a dead
lump.   I shall be expecting anxiously an answer from
you.   If it does not arrive in a few days this will have
miscarried, and I shall come straight to —— before I
go to town, which you I am sure will agree had better

be done while I still have some ready cash. By the middle of October I shall expect you in London. We will then set at the theatres. If you have anything to gainsay, I shall be even as the deaf adder which stoppeth her ears.

.   .   .   .   .   .

CXX.—TO CHARLES BROWN.

Winchester, September 23, 1819.

.   .   .   .   .

Do not suffer me to disturb you unpleasantly: I do not mean that you should not suffer me to occupy your thoughts, but to occupy them pleasantly; for I assure you I am as far from being unhappy as possible. Imaginary grievances have always been more my torment than real ones—You know this well—Real ones will never have any other effect upon me than to stimulate me to get out of or avoid them. This is easily accounted for—Our imaginary woes are conjured up by our passions, and are fostered by passionate feeling: our real ones come of themselves, and are opposed by an abstract exertion of mind. Real grievances are displacers of passion. The imaginary nail a man down for a sufferer, as on a cross; the real spur him up into an agent. I wish, at one view, you would see my heart towards you. 'Tis only from a high tone of feeling that I can put that word upon paper—out of poetry. I ought to have waited for your answer to my last before I wrote this. I felt however compelled to make a rejoinder to yours. I had written to Dilke on the subject of my last, I scarcely know whether I shall send my letter now. I think he would approve of my plan; it is so evident. Nay, I am convinced, out and out, that by prosing for a while in periodical works I may maintain myself decently.

.   .   .   .   .   .

CXXI.—TO CHARLES WENTWORTH DILKE.

Winchester, Friday, October 1 [1819].

My dear Dilke—For sundry reasons, which I will explain to you when I come to Town, I have to request you will do me a great favour as I must call it knowing how great a Bore it is. That your imagination may not have time to take too great an alarm I state immediately that I want you to hire me a couple of rooms (a Sitting Room and bed room for myself alone) in Westminster. Quietness and cheapness are the essentials: but as I shall with Brown be returned by next Friday you cannot in that space have sufficient time to make any choice selection, and need not be very particular as I can when on the spot suit myself at leisure. Brown bids me remind you not to send the Examiners after the third. Tell Mrs. D. I am obliged to her for the late ones which I see are directed in her hand. Excuse this mere business letter for I assure you I have not a syllable at hand on any subject in the world.

Your sincere friend   JOHN KEATS.

CXXII.—TO BENJAMIN ROBERT HAYDON.

Winchester, Sunday Morn [October 3, 1819].

My dear Haydon—Certainly I might: but a few Months pass away before we are aware. I have a great aversion to letter writing, which grows more and more upon me; and a greater to summon up circumstances before me of an unpleasant nature. I was not willing to trouble you with them. Could I have dated from my Palace of Milan you would have heard from me. Not even now will I mention a word of my affairs—only that "I Rab am here" but shall not be here more than a Week more, as I purpose to settle in Town and work my way with the rest. I hope I shall never be so silly as to injure my health and industry for the future by speaking,

writing or fretting about my non-estate. I have no
quarrel, I assure you, of so weighty a nature, with the
world, on my own account as I have on yours. I have
done nothing—except for the amusement of a few people
who refine upon their feelings till anything in the un-
understandable way will go down with them—people
predisposed for sentiment. I have no cause to complain
because I am certain anything really fine will in these
days be felt. I have no doubt that if I had written
Othello I should have been cheered by as good a mob as
Hunt. So would you be now if the operation of painting
was as universal as that of Writing. It is not: and
therefore it did behove men I could mention among whom
I must place Sir George Beaumont to have lifted you up
above sordid cares. That this has not been done is a
disgrace to the country. I know very little of Painting,
yet your pictures follow me into the Country. When I
am tired of reading I often think them over and as often
condemn the spirit of modern Connoisseurs. Upon the
whole, indeed, you have no complaint to make, being able
to say what so few Men can, "I have succeeded." On
sitting down to write a few lines to you these are the
uppermost in my mind, and, however I may be beating
about the arctic while your spirit has passed the line, you
may lay to a minute and consider I am earnest as far
as I can see. Though at this present "I have great dispositions to write" I feel every day more and more content to read. Books are becoming more interesting and
valuable to me. I may say I could not live without
them. If in the course of a fortnight you can procure
me a ticket to the British Museum I will make a better
use of it than I did in the first instance. I shall go on
with patience in the confidence that if I ever do anything
worth remembering the Reviewers will no more be able
to stumble-block me than the Royal Academy could you.
They have the same quarrel with you that the Scotch
nobles had with Wallace. The fame they have lost
through you is no joke to them. Had it not been for

you Fuseli would have been not as he is major but
maximus domo.   What Reviewers can put a hindrance
to must be—a nothing—or mediocre which is worse.   I
am sorry to say that since I saw you I have been guilty
of a practical joke upon Brown which has had all the
success of an innocent Wildfire among people.   Some
day in the next week you shall hear it from me by word
of Mouth.   I have not seen the portentous Book which
was skummer'd at you just as I left town.   It may be
light enough to serve you as a Cork Jacket and save you
for a while the trouble of swimming.   I heard the Man
went raking and rummaging about like any Richardson.
That and the Memoirs of Menage are the first I shall be
at.   From Sr. G. B.'s, Lord Ms[1] and particularly Sr. John
Leicesters good lord deliver us.   I shall expect to see
your Picture plumped out like a ripe Peach—you would
not be very willing to give me a slice of it.   I came to
this place in the hopes of meeting with a Library but was
disappointed.   The High Street is as quiet as a Lamb.
The knockers are dieted to three raps per diem.   The
walks about are interesting from the many old Buildings
and archways.   The view of the High Street through the
Gate of the City in the beautiful September evening light
has amused me frequently.   The bad singing of the
Cathedral I do not care to smoke—being by myself I am
not very coy in my taste.   At St. Cross there is an interesting picture of Albert Dürer's—who living in such war-
like times perhaps was forced to paint in his Gauntlets—
so we must make all allowances.

I am, my dear Haydon, Yours ever

JOHN KEATS.

Brown has a few words to say to you and will cross
this.

[1] Sir George Beaumonts and Lord Mulgraves : compare Haydon's *Life* and *Correspondence.*

CXXIII.—TO FANNY KEATS.

Wentworth Place [1] [October 16, 1819].

My dear Fanny—My Conscience is always reproaching me for neglecting you for so long a time. I have been returned from Winchester this fortnight, and as yet I have not seen you. I have no excuse to offer—I should have no excuse. I shall expect to see you the next time I call on Mr. A. about George's affairs which perplex me a great deal—I should have to-day gone to see if you were in town—but as I am in an industrious humour (which is so necessary to my livelihood for the future) I am loath to break through it though it be merely for one day, for when I am inclined I can do a great deal in a day—I am more fond of pleasure than study (many men have prefer'd the latter) but I have become resolved to know something which you will credit when I tell you I have left off animal food that my brains may never henceforth be in a greater mist than is theirs by nature—I took lodgings in Westminster for the purpose of being in the reach of Books, but am now returned to Hampstead being induced to it by the habit I have acquired in this room I am now in and also from the pleasure of being free from paying any petty attentions to a diminutive house-keeping. Mr. Brown has been my great friend for some time—with-

---

[1] In the interval between the last letter and this, Keats had tried the experiment of living alone in Westminster lodgings, and failed. After a visit to his beloved at Hampstead, he could keep none of his wise resolutions, but wrote to her, "I can think of nothing else . . . I cannot exist without you . . . you have absorb'd me . . . I shall be able to do nothing—I should like to cast the die for Love or Death—I have no patience with anything else " . . . and at the end of a week he had gone back to live next door to her with Brown at Wentworth Place. Here he quickly fell into that state of feverish despondency and recklessness to which his friends, especially Brown, have borne witness, and the signs of which are perceptible in his letters of the time, and still more in his verse, viz. the remodelled *Hyperion* and the *Cap and Bells :* see *Keats* (Men of Letters Series), pp. 180-190.

out him I should have been in, perhaps, personal distress
—as I know you love me though I do not deserve it, I
am sure you will take pleasure in being a friend to Mr.
Brown even before you know him.—My lodgings for two
or three days were close in the neighbourhood of Mrs.
Dilke who never sees me but she enquires after you—I
have had letters from George lately which do not contain,
as I think I told you in my last, the best news—I have
hopes for the best—I trust in a good termination to his
affairs which you please God will soon hear of — It is
better you should not be teased with the particulars. The
whole amount of the ill news is that his mercantile speculations have not had success in consequence of the general
depression of trade in the whole province of Kentucky
and indeed all America.—I have a couple of shells for
you you will call pretty.

Your affectionate Brother   JOHN ——.

CXXIV.—TO JOSEPH SEVERN.

Wentworth Place, Wednesday
[October 27 ? 1819].

Dear Severn—Either your joke about staying at home
is a very old one or I really call'd. I don't remember
doing so. I am glad to hear you have finish'd the Picture
and am more anxious to see it than I have time to spare :
for I have been so very lax, unemployed, unmeridian'd,
and objectless these two months that I even grudge indulging (and that is no great indulgence considering the
Lecture is not over till 9 and the lecture room seven
miles from Wentworth Place) myself by going to Hazlitt's
Lecture. If you have hours to the amount of a brace of
dozens to throw away you may sleep nine of them here
in your little Crib and chat the rest. When your Picture
is up and in a good light I shall make a point of meeting
you at the Academy if you will let me know when. If
you should be at the Lecture to-morrow evening I shall

see you—and congratulate you heartily—Haslam I know
" is very Beadle to an amorous sigh."

Your sincere friend   JOHN KEATS.

CXXV.—TO JOHN TAYLOR.

Wentworth Place, Hampstead,
November 17 [1819].

My dear Taylor—I have come to a determination not
to publish anything I have now ready written : but, for
all that, to publish a poem before long, and that I hope
to make a fine one. As the marvellous is the most enticing, and the surest guarantee of harmonious numbers,
I have been endeavouring to persuade myself to untether
Fancy, and to let her manage for herself.[1] I and myself
cannot agree about this at all. Wonders are no wonders
to me. I am more at home amongst men and women.
I would rather read Chaucer than Ariosto. The little
dramatic skill I may as yet have, however badly it might
show in a drama, would, I think, be sufficient for a poem.
I wish to diffuse the colouring of St. Agnes's Eve throughout a poem in which character and sentiment would be
the figures to such drapery. Two or three such poems,
if God should spare me, written in the course of the next
six years, would be a famous Gradus ad Parnassum
altissimum—I mean they would nerve me up to the
writing of a few fine plays—my greatest ambition, when
I do feel ambitious. I am sorry to say that is very
seldom. The subject we have once or twice talked of
appears a promising one—The Earl of Leicester's history.
I am this morning reading Holinshed's "Elizabeth."
You had some books a while ago, you promised to send
me, illustrative of my subject. If you can lay hold of
them, or any others which may be serviceable to me, I
know you will encourage my low-spirited muse by send-

---

[1] Referring to the fairy poem of *The Cap and Bells*, the writing
of which, says Brown, was Keats's morning occupation during
these weeks.

ing them, or rather by letting me know where our errand-cart man shall call with my little box.   I will endeavour to set myself selfishly at work on this poem that is to be.

Your sincere friend   JOHN KEATS.

CXXVI.—TO FANNY KEATS.

Wednesday Morn—[November 17, 1819].

My dear Fanny—I received your letter yesterday Evening and will obey it to-morrow.   I would come to-day—but I have been to Town so frequently on George's Business it makes me wish to employ to-day at Hampstead.   So I say Thursday without fail.   I have no news at all entertaining—and if I had I should not have time to tell them as I wish to send this by the morning Post.

Your affectionate Brother   JOHN.

CXXVII.—TO JOSEPH SEVERN.

Wentworth Place, Monday Morn—
[December 6 ? 1819].

My dear Severn—I am very sorry that on Tuesday I have an appointment in the City of an undeferable nature; and Brown on the same day has some business at Guildhall.   I have not been able to figure your manner of executing the Cave of despair,[1] therefore it will be at any rate a novelty and surprise to me—I trust on the right side.   I shall call upon you some morning shortly, early enough to catch you before you can get out—when we will proceed to the Academy.   I think you must be suited with a good painting light in your Bay window. I wish you to return the Compliment by going with me to see a Poem I have hung up for the Prize in the Lecture Room of the Surry Institution.   I have many Rivals,

---

[1] Spenser's Cave of Despair was the subject of the picture (already referred to in Letter CXXIV.) with which Severn won the Royal Academy premium, awarded December 10 of this year.

the most threatening are An Ode to Lord Castlereagh,
and a new series of Hymns for the New, new Jerusalem
Chapel. (You had best put me into your Cave of despair.)
Ever yours sincerely   JOHN KEATS.

CXXVIII.—TO JAMES RICE.

Wentworth Place [December 1819].

My dear Rice—As I want the coat on my back mended,
I would be obliged if you would send me the one Brown
left at your house by the Bearer—During your late contest I had regular reports of you, how that your time was
completely taken up and your health improving—I shall
call in the course of a few days, and see whether your
promotion has made any difference in your Behaviour to
us. I suppose Reynolds has given you an account of
Brown and Elliston. As he has not rejected our Tragedy,
I shall not venture to call him directly a fool; but as he
wishes to put it off till next season, I cannot help thinking him little better than a knave.—That it will not be
acted this season is yet uncertain. Perhaps we may
give it another furbish and try it at Covent Garden.
'Twould do one's heart good to see Macready in Ludolph.
If you do not see me soon it will be from the humour of
writing, which I have had for three days continuing. I
must say to the Muses what the maid says to the Man—
"Take me while the fit is on me." . . .
Ever yours sincerely   JOHN KEATS.

CXXIX.—TO FANNY KEATS.

Wentworth Place, Monday Morn—
[December 20, 1819.]

My dear Fanny—When I saw you last, you ask'd me
whether you should see me again before Christmas. You
would have seen me if I had been quite well. I have not,

though not unwell enough to have prevented me—not indeed at all—but fearful lest the weather should affect my throat which on exertion or cold continually threatens me.—By the advice of my Doctor I have had a warm great Coat made and have ordered some thick shoes—so furnish'd I shall be with you if it holds a little fine before Christmas day.—I have been very busy since I saw you, especially the last Week, and shall be for some time, in preparing some Poems to come out in the Spring, and also in brightening the interest of our Tragedy.—Of the Tragedy I can give you but news semigood. It is accepted at Drury Lane with a promise of coming out next season : as that will be too long a delay we have determined to get Elliston to bring it out this Season or to transfer it to Covent Garden. This Elliston will not like, as we have every motive to believe that Kean has perceived how suitable the principal Character will be for him. My hopes of success in the literary world are now better than ever. Mr. Abbey, on my calling on him lately, appeared anxious that I should apply myself to something else— He mentioned Tea Brokerage. I supposed he might per- haps mean to give me the Brokerage of his concern which might be executed with little trouble and a good profit ; and therefore said I should have no objection to it, especially as at the same time it occurred to me that I might make over the business to George—I questioned him about it a few days after. His mind takes odd turns. When I became a Suitor he became coy. He did not seem so much inclined to serve me. He described what I should have to do in the progress of business. It will not suit me. I have given it up. I have not heard again from George, which rather disappoints me, as I wish to hear before I make any fresh remittance of his property. I received a note from Mrs. Dilke a few days ago inviting me to dine with her on Xmas day which I shall do. Mr. Brown and I go on in our old dog trot of Breakfast, dinner (not tea, for we have left that off), supper, Sleep, Confab, stirring the fire and reading. Whilst I was in

the Country last Summer, Mrs. Bentley tells me, a woman
in mourning call'd on me,—and talk'd something of an
aunt of ours—I am so careless a fellow I did not enquire,
but will particularly :   On Tuesday I am going to hear
some Schoolboys Speechify on breaking up day—I'll lay
you a pocket piece we shall have " My name is Norval."
I have not yet look'd for the Letter you mention'd as it
is mix'd up in a box full of papers—you must tell me, if
you can recollect, the subject of it.   This moment Bentley
brought a Letter from George for me to deliver to Mrs.
Wylie—I shall see her and it before I see you.   The
Direction was in his best hand written with a good Pen
and sealed with a Tassie's Shakspeare such as I gave
you—We judge of people's hearts by their Countenances;
may we not judge of Letters in the same way ?—if so,
the Letter does not contain unpleasant news—Good or
bad spirits have an effect on the handwriting.   This
direction is at least unnervous and healthy.   Our Sister
is also well, or George would have made strange work
with Ks and Ws.   The little Baby is well or he would
have formed precious vowels and Consonants—He sent
off the Letter in a hurry, or the mail bag was rather a
warm berth, or he has worn out his Seal, for the Shakspeare's head is flattened a little.   This is close muggy
weather as they say at the Ale houses.

I am ever, my dear Sister, yours affectionately

JOHN KEATS.

CXXX.—TO FANNY KEATS.

Wentworth Place, Wednesday.
[December 22, 1819.]

My dear Fanny—I wrote to you a Letter directed
Walthamstow the day before yesterday wherein I promised to see you before Christmas day.   I am sorry to
say I have been and continue rather unwell, and therefore shall not be able to promise certainly.   I have not

z

seen Mrs. Wylie's Letter.   Excuse my dear Fanny this very shabby note.

Your affectionate Brother   JOHN.

CXXXI.—TO GEORGIANA KEATS.

Thursday, January 13, 1820.

My dear Sister—By the time you receive this your trouble will be over. I wish you knew they were half over. I mean that George is safe in England and in good health.[1] To write to you by him is almost like following one's own letter in the mail. That it may not be quite so, I will leave common intelligence out of the question, and write wide of him as I can. I fear I must be dull, having had no good-natured flip from Fortune's finger since I saw you, and no sideway comfort in the success of my friends. I could almost promise that if I had the means I would accompany George back to America, and pay you a visit of a few months. I should not think much of the time, or my absence from my books ; or I have no right to think, for I am very idle. But then I ought to be diligent, and at least keep myself within the reach of materials for diligence. Diligence, that I do not mean to say ; I should say dreaming over my books, or rather other people's books. George has promised to bring you to England when the five years have elapsed. I regret very much that I shall not be able to see you before that time, and even then I must hope that your affairs will be in so prosperous a way as to induce you to stop longer. Yours is a hardish fate, to be so divided among your friends and settled among a people you hate. You will find it improve. You have a heart that will take hold of your children ; even George's absence will make things better. His return will banish what must be your greatest sorrow, and at the same time minor ones with it. Robinson Crusoe, when he

[1] George Keats had come over for a hurried visit to England on business.

saw himself in danger of perishing on the waters, looked back to his island as to the haven of his happiness, and on gaining it once more was more content with his solitude. We smoke George about his little girl. He runs the common-beaten road of every father, as I dare say you do of every mother: there is no child like his child, so original,—original forsooth! However, I take you at your words. I have a lively faith that yours is the very gem of all children. Ain't I its uncle?

On Henry's marriage there was a piece of bride cake sent me. It missed its way. I suppose the carrier or coachman was a conjuror, and wanted it for his own private use. Last Sunday George and I dined at Millar's. There were your mother and Charles with Fool Lacon, Esq., who sent the sly, disinterested shawl to Miss Millar, with his own heathen name engraved in the middle. Charles had a silk handkerchief belonging to a Miss Grover, with whom he pretended to be smitten, and for her sake kept exhibiting and adoring the handkerchief all the evening. Fool Lacon, Esq., treated it with a little venturesome, trembling contumely, whereupon Charles set him quietly down on the floor, from where he as quietly got up. This process was repeated at supper time, when your mother said, "If I were you Mr. Lacon I would not let him do so." Fool Lacon, Esq., did not offer any remark. He will undoubtedly die in his bed. Your mother did not look quite so well on Sunday. Mrs. Henry Wylie is excessively quiet before people. I hope she is always so. Yesterday we dined at Taylor's, in Fleet Street. George left early after dinner to go to Deptford; he will make all square there for me. I could not go with him—I did not like the amusement. Haslam is a very good fellow indeed; he has been excessively anxious and kind to us. But is this fair? He has an innamorata at Deptford, and he has been wanting me for some time past to see her. This is a thing which it is impossible not to shirk. A man is like a magnet—he must have a repelling end. So how am I to see

Haslam's lady and family, if I even went? for by the time I got to Greenwich I should have repell'd them to Blackheath, and by the time I got to Deptford they would be on Shooter's Hill; when I came to Shooter Hill they would alight at Chatham, and so on till I drove them into the sea, which I think might be indictable. The evening before yesterday we had a pianoforte hop at Dilke's. There was very little amusement in the room, but a Scotchman to hate. Some people, you must have observed, have a most unpleasant effect upon you when you see them speaking in profile. This Scotchman is the most accomplished fellow in this way I ever met with. The effect was complete. It went down like a dose of bitters, and I hope will improve my digestion. At Taylor's too, there was a Scotchman,—not quite so bad, for he was as clean as he could get himself. Not having succeeded in Drury Lane with our tragedy, we have been making some alterations, and are about to try Covent Garden. Brown has just done patching up the copy—as it is altered. The reliance I had on it was in Kean's acting. I am not afraid it will be damn'd in the Garden. You said in one of your letters that there was nothing but Haydon and Co. in mine. There can be nothing of him in this, for I never see him or Co. George has introduced to us an American of the name of Hart. I like him in a moderate way. He was at Mrs. Dilke's party—and sitting by me; we began talking about English and American ladies. The Miss —— and some of their friends made not a very enticing row opposite us. I bade him mark them and form his judgment of them. I told him I hated Englishmen because they were the only men I knew. He does not understand this. Who would be Braggadochio to Johnny Bull? Johnny's house is his castle—and a precious dull castle it is; what a many Bull castles there are in so-and-so crescent! I never wish myself an unversed writer and newsmonger but when I write to you. I should like for a day or two to have somebody's knowledge—Mr.

Lacon's for instance—of all the different folks of a wide acquaintance, to tell you about. Only let me have his knowledge of family minutiæ and I would set them in a proper light; but, bless me, I never go anywhere. My pen is no more garrulous than my tongue. Any third person would think I was addressing myself to a lover of scandal. But we know we do not love scandal, but fun; and if scandal happens to be fun, that is no fault of ours. There were very good pickings for me in George's letters about the prairie settlement, if I had any taste to turn them to account in England. I knew a friend of Miss Andrews, yet I never mentioned her to him; for after I had read the letter I really did not recollect her story. Now I have been sitting here half an hour with my invention at work, to say something about your mother or Charles or Henry, but it is in vain. I know not what to say. Three nights since, George went with your mother to the play. I hope she will soon see mine acted. I do not remember ever to have thanked you for your tassels to my Shakspeare—there he hangs so ably supported opposite me. I thank you now. It is a continual memento of you. If you should have a boy, do not christen him John, and persuade George not to let his partiality for me come across. 'Tis a bad name, and goes against a man. If my name had been Edmund I should have been more fortunate.

I was surprised to hear of the state of society at Louisville; it seems to me you are just as ridiculous there as we are here—threepenny parties, halfpenny dances. The best thing I have heard of is your shooting; for it seems you follow the gun. Give my compliments to Mrs. Audubon, and tell her I cannot think her either good-looking or honest. Tell Mr. Audubon he's a fool, and Briggs that 'tis well I was not Mr. A.

Saturday, January 15.

It is strange that George having to stop so short a time in England, I should not have seen him for nearly two days. He has been to Haslam's and does not encourage me to follow his example. He had given promise to dine with the same party to-morrow, but has sent an excuse which I am glad of, as we shall have a pleasant party with us to-morrow. We expect Charles here to-day. This is a beautiful day. I hope you will not quarrel with it if I call it an American one. The sun comes upon the snow and makes a prettier candy than we have on twelfth-night cakes. George is busy this morning in making copies of my verses. He is making one now of an "Ode to the Nightingale," which is like reading an account of the Black Hole at Calcutta on an iceberg.

You will say this is a matter of course. I am glad it is—I mean that I should like your brothers more the more I know them. I should spend much more time with them if our lives were more run in parallel; but we can talk but on one subject—that is you.

The more I know of men the more I know how to value entire liberality in any of them. Thank God, there are a great many who will sacrifice their worldly interest for a friend. I wish there were more who would sacrifice their passions. The worst of men are those whose self-interests are their passion; the next, those whose passions are their self-interest. Upon the whole I dislike mankind. Whatever people on the other side of the question may advance, they cannot deny that they are always surprised at hearing of a good action, and never of a bad one. I am glad you have something to like in America—doves. Gertrude of Wyoming and Birkbeck's book should be bound up together like a brace of decoy ducks—one is almost as poetical as the other. Precious miserable people at the prairie. I have been sitting in the sun whilst I wrote this till it's become quite oppressive—this is very odd for January. The vulcan fire is the true natural heat for winter. The sun has nothing to do in winter but to give a little glooming light much like a shade. Our Irish servant has piqued me this morning by saying that her father in Ireland was very much like my Shakspeare, only he had more colour than the engraving. You will find on George's return that I have not been neglecting your affairs. The delay was unfortunate, not faulty. Perhaps by this time you have received my three last letters, not one of which had reached before George sailed. I would give two-pence to have been over the world as much as he has. I wish I had money enough to do nothing but travel about for years. Were you now in England I dare say you would be able (setting aside the pleasure you would have in seeing your mother) to suck out more amusement for society than I am able to do. To me it is all as dull here as Louisville could be. I am tired of the theatres. Almost all the parties I may chance to fall into I know by heart. I know the different styles of talk in different places,—what subjects will be started, how it will proceed like an acted play, from the first to the last act. If I go to Hunt's I run my head into many tunes heard before, old puns, and old music; to Haydon's worn-out discourses of poetry and painting. The Miss —— I am afraid to speak to, for fear of some sickly reiteration of phrase or sentiment. When they were at the dance the other night I tried manfully to sit near and talk to them, but to no purpose; and if I had it would have been to no purpose still. My question or observation must have been an old one, and the rejoinder very antique indeed. At Dilke's I fall foul of politics. 'Tis best to remain aloof from people and like their good parts without being eternally troubled with the dull process of their every-day lives. When once a person has smoked the vapid-ness of the routine of society he must either have self-interest or the love of some sort of distinction to keep him in good humour with it. All I can say is that, standing at Charing Cross and looking east, west, north, and south, I can see nothing but dulness. I hope while I am young to live retired in the country. When I grow in years and have a right to be idle, I shall enjoy

cities more. If the American ladies are worse than the
English they must be very bad. You say you should
like your Emily brought up here. You had better bring
her up yourself. You know a good number of English
ladies; what encomium could you give of half a dozen of
them? The greater part seem to me downright American.
I have known more than one Mrs. Audubon. Her
affectation of fashion and politeness cannot transcend
ours. Look at our Cheapside tradesmen's sons and
daughters—only fit to be taken off by a plague. I hope
now soon to come to the time when I shall never be
forced to walk through the city and hate as I walk.

Monday, January 17.

George had a quick rejoinder to his letter of excuse
to Haslam, so we had not his company yesterday,
which I was sorry for as there was our old set. I know
three witty people all distinct in their excellence—Rice,
Reynolds, and Richards. Rice is the wisest, Reynolds
the playfullest, Richards the out-o'-the-wayest. The
first makes you laugh and think, the second makes you
laugh and not think, the third puzzles your head. I admire
the first, I enjoy the second, I stare at the third. The
first is claret, the second ginger-beer, the third crême de
Byrapymdrag. The first is inspired by Minerva, the
second by Mercury, the third by Harlequin Epigram,
Esq. The first is neat in his dress, the second slovenly,
the third uncomfortable. The first speaks adagio, the
second allegretto, the third both together. The first is
Swiftean, the second Tom-Crib-ean, the third Shandean.
And yet these three eans are not three eans but one ean.

Charles came on Saturday but went early; he seems
to have schemes and plans and wants to get off. He is
quite right; I am glad to see him employed at business.
You remember I wrote you a story about a woman named
Alice being made young again, or some such stuff. In
your next letter tell me whether I gave it as my own, or
whether I gave it as a matter Brown was employed upon

at the time. He read it over to George the other day, and George said he had heard it all before. So Brown suspects I have been giving you his story as my own. I should like to set him right in it by your evidence. George has not returned from town; when he does I shall tax his memory. We had a young, long, raw, lean Scotchman with us yesterday, called Thornton. Rice, for fun or for mistake, would persist in calling him Stevenson. I know three people of no wit at all, each distinct in his excellence—A, B, and C. A is the foolishest, B the sulkiest, C is a negative. A makes you yawn, B makes you hate, as for C you never see him at all though he were six feet high—I bear the first, I forbear the second, I am not certain that the third is. The first is gruel, the second ditch-water, the third is spilt—he ought to be wip'd up. A is inspired by Jack-o'-the-clock, B has been drilled by a Russian serjeant, C, they say, is not his mother's true child, but she bought him of the man who cries, Young lambs to sell.

Twang-dillo-dee—This you must know is the amen to nonsense. I know a good many places where Amen should be scratched out, rubbed over with ponce made of Momus's little finger bones, and in its place Twang-dillo-dee written. This is the word I shall be tempted to write at the end of most modern poems. Every American book ought to have it. It would be a good distinction in society. My Lords Wellington and Castlereagh, and Canning, and many more, would do well to wear Twang-dillo-dee on their backs instead of Ribbons at their button-holes; how many people would go sideways along walls and quickset hedges to keep their "Twang-dillo-dee" out of sight, or wear large pig-tails to hide it. However there would be so many that the Twang-dillo-dees would keep one another in countenance—which Brown cannot do for me—I have fallen away lately. Thieves and murderers would gain rank in the world, for would any of them have the poorness of spirit to condescend to be a Twang-dillo-dee? "I have robbed

many a dwelling house; I have killed many a fowl,
many a goose, and many a Man (would such a gentleman
say) but, thank Heaven, I was never yet a Twang-dillo-
dee." Some philosophers in the moon, who spy at our
globe as we do at theirs, say that Twang-dillo-dee is
written in large letters on our globe of earth; they say
the beginning of the "T" is just on the spot where
London stands, London being built within the flourish;
"wan" reaches downward and slants as far as Timbuctoo
in Africa; the tail of the "g" goes slap across the
Atlantic into the Rio della Plata; the remainder of the
letters wrap around New Holland, and the last "e"
terminates in land we have not yet discovered. However, I must be silent; these are dangerous times to libel
a man in—much more a world.

Friday 27 [for 28th January 1820].

I wish you would call me names: I deserve them so
much. I have only written two sheets for you, to carry
by George, and those I forgot to bring to town and
have therefore to forward them to Liverpool. George
went this morning at 6 o'clock by the Liverpool coach.
His being on his journey to you prevents my regretting
his short stay. I have no news of any sort to tell you.
Henry is wife bound in Camden Town; there is no
getting him out. I am sorry he has not a prettier wife:
indeed 'tis a shame: she is not half a wife. I think I
could find some of her relations in Buffon, or Captn Cook's
voyages or the hierogueglyphics in Moor's Almanack, or
upon a Chinese clock door, the shepherdesses on her own
mantelpiece, or in a *cruel* sampler in which she may find
herself worsted, or in a Dutch toyshop window, or one of
the daughters in the ark, or any picture shop window.
As I intend to retire into the country where there will
be no sort of news, I shall not be able to write you very
long letters. Besides I am afraid the postage comes to
too much; which till now I have not been aware of.

People in military bands are generally seriously occu-

pied. None may or can laugh at their work but the
Kettle Drum, Long Drum, Do. Triangle and Cymbals.
Thinking you might want a rat-catcher I put your
mother's old quaker-colour'd cat into the top of your
bonnet. She's wi' kitten, so you may expect to find a
whole family. I hope the family will not grow too
large for its lodging. I shall send you a close written
sheet on the first of next month, but for fear of missing
the Liverpool Post I must finish here. God bless you
and your little girl.

Your affectionate Brother　　　JOHN KEATS.

CXXXII.—TO FANNY KEATS.

Wentworth Place, Sunday Morning.
[February 6, 1820.]

My dear Sister—I should not have sent those Letters
without some notice if Mr. Brown had not persuaded me
against it on account of an illness with which I was
attack'd on Thursday.[1] After that I was resolved not to
write till I should be on the mending hand; thank God,
I am now so. From imprudently leaving off my great
coat in the thaw I caught cold which flew to my Lungs.
Every remedy that has been applied has taken the desired
effect, and I have nothing now to do but stay within
doors for some time. If I should be confined long I shall
write to Mr. Abbey to ask permission for you to visit me.
George has been running great chance of a similar attack,
but I hope the sea air will be his Physician in case of
illness—the air out at sea is always more temperate than
on land—George mentioned, in his Letters to us, something of Mr. Abbey's regret concerning the silence kept
up in his house. It is entirely the fault of his Manner.

[1] Hemorrhage from the lungs; in which Keats recognised his
death-warrant, and after which the remainder of his life was but
that of a doomed invalid. The particulars of the attack, as related
by Charles Brown, are given by Lord Houghton, and in *Keats*
(Men of Letters Series), p. 193.

You must be careful always to wear warm clothing not only in frost but in a Thaw.—I have no news to tell you. The half-built houses opposite us stand just as they were and seem dying of old age before they are brought up. The grass looks very dingy, the Celery is all gone, and there is nothing to enliven one but a few Cabbage Stalks that seem fix'd on the superannuated List. Mrs. Dilke has been ill but is better. Several of my friends have been to see me. Mrs. Reynolds was here this morning and the two Mr. Wylie's. Brown has been very alert about me, though a little wheezy himself this weather. Everybody is ill. Yesterday evening Mr. Davenport, a gentleman of Hampstead, sent me an invitation to supper, instead of his coming to see us, having so bad a cold he could not stir out—so you see 'tis the weather and I am among a thousand. Whenever you have an inflammatory fever never mind about eating. The day on which I was getting ill I felt this fever to a great height, and therefore almost entirely abstained from food the whole day. I have no doubt experienced a benefit from so doing—The Papers I see are full of anecdotes of the late King: how he nodded to a Coal-heaver and laugh'd with a Quaker and lik'd boiled Leg of Mutton. Old Peter Pindar is just dead: what will the old King and he say to each other? Perhaps the King may confess that Peter was in the right, and Peter maintain himself to have been wrong. You shall hear from me again on Tuesday.

Your affectionate Brother   JOHN.

CXXXIII.—TO FANNY KEATS.

Wentworth Place, Tuesday Morn.
[February 8, 1820.]

My dear Fanny—I had a slight return of fever last night, which terminated favourably, and I am now tolerably well, though weak from the small quantity of food to which I am obliged to confine myself: I am sure a

mouse would starve upon it. Mrs. Wylie came yesterday.
I have a very pleasant room for a sick person. A Sofa
bed is made up for me in the front Parlour which looks
on to the grass plot as you remember Mrs. Dilke's does.
How much more comfortable than a dull room up stairs,
where one gets tired of the pattern of the bed curtains.
Besides I see all that passes—for instance now, this
morning—if I had been in my own room I should not
have seen the coals brought in. On Sunday between
the hours of twelve and one I descried a Pot boy. I
conjectured it might be the one o'Clock beer—Old
women with bobbins and red cloaks and unpresuming
bonnets I see creeping about the heath. Gipsies after
hare skins and silver spoons. Then goes by a fellow
with a wooden clock under his arm that strikes a hundred and more. Then comes the old French emigrant
(who has been very well to do in France) with his hands
joined behind on his hips, and his face full of political
schemes. Then passes Mr. David Lewis, a very good-
natured, good-looking old gentleman who has been very
kind to Tom and George and me. As for those fellows
the Brickmakers they are always passing to and fro. I
mus'n't forget the two old maiden Ladies in Well Walk
who have a Lap dog between them that they are very
anxious about. It is a corpulent Little beast whom it is
necessary to coax along with an ivory-tipp'd cane. Carlo
our Neighbour Mrs. Brawne's dog and it meet sometimes.
Lappy thinks Carlo a devil of a fellow and so do his
Mistresses. Well they may—he would sweep 'em all
down at a run ; all for the Joke of it. I shall desire him
to peruse the fable of the Boys and the frogs : though he
prefers the tongues and the Bones. You shall hear from
me again the day after to-morrow.

Your affectionate Brother   JOHN KEATS.

CXXXIV.—TO FANNY KEATS.

Wentworth Place [February 11, 1820].

My dear Fanny—I am much the same as when I last wrote. I hope a little more verging towards improvement. Yesterday morning being very fine, I took a walk for a quarter of an hour in the garden and was very much refresh'd by it. You must consider no news, good news —if you do not hear from me the day after to-morrow.

Your affectionate Brother   JOHN.

CXXXV.—TO FANNY KEATS.

Wentworth Place, Monday Morn.
[February 14, 1820.]

My dear Fanny—I am improving but very gradually and suspect it will be a long while before I shall be able to walk six miles—The Sun appears half inclined to shine ; if he obliges us I shall take a turn in the garden this morning. No one from Town has visited me since my last. I have had so many presents of jam and jellies that they would reach side by side the length of the sideboard. I hope I shall be well before it is all consumed. I am vexed that Mr. Abbey will not allow you pocket money sufficient. He has not behaved well—By detaining money from me and George when we most wanted it he has increased our expenses. In consequence of such delay George was obliged to take his voyage to England which will be £150 out of his pocket. I enclose you a note—You shall hear from me again the day after to-morrow.

Your affectionate Brother   JOHN.

CXXXVI.—TO JAMES RICE.

Wentworth Place, February 16, 1820.

My dear Rice—I have not been well enough to make any tolerable rejoinder to your kind letter. I will, as you advise, be very chary of my health and spirits. I am sorry to hear of your relapse and hypochondriac symptoms attending it. Let us hope for the best, as you say. I shall follow your example in looking to the future good rather than brooding upon the present ill. I have not been so worn with lengthened illnesses as you have, therefore cannot answer you on your own ground with respect to those haunting and deformed thoughts and feelings you speak of. When I have been, or supposed myself in health, I have had my share of them, especially within the last year. I may say, that for six months before I was taken ill I had not passed a tranquil day. Either that gloom overspread me, or I was suffering under some passionate feeling, or if I turned to versify, that acerbated the poison of either sensation. The beauties of nature had lost their power over me. How astonishingly (here I must premise that illness, as far as I can judge in so short a time, has relieved my mind of a load of deceptive thoughts and images, and makes me perceive things in a truer light),—how astonishingly does the chance of leaving the world impress a sense of its natural beauties upon us! Like poor Falstaff, though I do not "babble," I think of green fields; I muse with the greatest affection on every flower I have known from my infancy—their shapes and colours are as new to me as if I had just created them with a superhuman fancy. It is because they are connected with the most thoughtless and the happiest moments of our lives. I have seen foreign flowers in hothouses, of the most beautiful nature, but I do not care a straw for them. The simple flowers of our Spring are what I want to see again.

Brown has left the inventive and taken to the imitative art. He is doing his forte, which is copying Hogarth's heads. He has just made a purchase of the Methodist Meeting picture, which gave me a horrid dream a few nights ago. I hope I shall sit under the trees with you again in some such place as the Isle of Wight. I do not mind a game of cards in a saw-pit or waggon, but if ever you catch me on a stage-coach in the winter full against the wind, bring me down with a brace of bullets, and I promise not to 'peach.   Remember me to Reynolds, and say how much I should like to hear from him ; that Brown returned immediately after he went on Sunday, and that I was vexed at forgetting to ask him to lunch ; for as he went towards the gate, I saw he was fatigued and hungry.

I am, my dear Rice, ever most sincerely yours

JOHN KEATS.

I have broken this open to let you know I was surprised at seeing it on the table this morning, thinking it had gone long ago.

CXXXVII.—TO FANNY KEATS.

[February 19, 1820.]

My dear Fanny—Being confined almost entirely to vegetable food and the weather being at the same time so much against me, I cannot say I have much improved since I wrote last.   The Doctor tells me there are no dangerous Symptoms about me, and quietness of mind and fine weather will restore me.   Mind my advice to be very careful to wear warm cloathing in a thaw.   I will write again on Tuesday when I hope to send you good news.

Your affectionate Brother   JOHN ——.

CXXXVIII.—TO JOHN HAMILTON REYNOLDS.

[February 23 or 25, 1820.]

My dear Reynolds—I have been improving since you saw me : my nights are better which I think is a very encouraging thing.   You mention your cold in rather too slighting a manner—if you travel outside have some flannel against the wind—which I hope will not keep on

at this rate when you are in the Packet boat. Should
it rain do not stop upon deck though the Passengers
should vomit themselves inside out. Keep under Hatches
from all sort of wet.

I am pretty well provided with Books at present,
when you return I may give you a commission or two.
Mr. B. C. has sent me not only his Sicilian Story but
yesterday his Dramatic Scenes—this is very polite, and
I shall do what I can to make him sensible I think so.
I confess they teaze me—they are composed of amiability,
the Seasons, the Leaves, the Moons, etc., upon which he
rings (according to Hunt's expression), triple bob majors.
However that is nothing—I think he likes poetry for its
own sake, not his. I hope I shall soon be well enough
to proceed with my faeries and set you about the notes
on Sundays and Stray-days. If I had been well enough
I should have liked to cross the water with you. Brown
wishes you a pleasant vóyage—Have fish for dinner at
the sea ports, and don't forget a bottle of Claret. You
will not meet with so much to hate at Brussels as at
Paris. Remember me to all my friends. If I were well
enough I would paraphrase an ode of Horace's for you,
on your embarking in the seventy years ago style. The
Packet will bear a comparison with a Roman galley at
any rate.

· Ever yours affectionately   J. KEATS.

CXXXIX.—TO FANNY KEATS.

Wentworth Place, Thursday.
[February 24, 1820.]

My dear Fanny—I am sorry to hear you have been
so unwell : now you are better, keep so. Remember to
be very careful of your clothing—this climate requires
the utmost care. There has been very little alteration
in me lately. I am much the same as when I wrote
last. When I am well enough to return to my old diet
I shall get stronger. If my recovery should be delay'd

2 A

long I will ask Mr. Abbey to let you visit me—keep
up your Spirits as well as you can. You shall hear soon
again from me.

    Your affectionate Brother   JOHN ——.

CXL.—TO CHARLES WENTWORTH DILKE.

                    [Hampstead, March 4, 1820.]

    My dear Dilke—Since I saw you I have been gradu-
ally, too gradually perhaps, improving; and though
under an interdict with respect to animal food, living
upon pseudo victuals, Brown says I have pick'd up a
little flesh lately. If I can keep off inflammation for the
next six weeks I trust I shall do very well. You certainly should have been at Martin's dinner, for making
an index is surely as dull work as engraving. Have you
heard that the Bookseller is going to tie himself to the
manger eat or not as he pleases. He says Rice shall
have his foot on the fender notwithstanding. Reynolds
is going to sail on the salt seas. Brown has been
mightily progressing with his Hogarth. A damn'd
melancholy picture it is, and during the first week of
my illness it gave me a psalm-singing nightmare, that
made me almost faint away in my sleep. I know I am
better, for I can bear the Picture. I have experienced
a specimen of great politeness from Mr. Barry Cornwall.
He has sent me his books. Some time ago he had given
his first publish'd book to Hunt for me; Hunt forgot to
give it and Barry Cornwall thinking I had received it
must have thought me a very neglectful fellow. Notwithstanding he sent me his second book and on my
explaining that I had not received his first he sent me
that also. I am sorry to see by Mrs. D.'s note that she
has been so unwell with the spasms. Does she continue
the Medicines that benefited her so much? I am afraid
not. Remember me to her, and say I shall not expect
her at Hampstead next week unless the Weather changes
for the warmer. It is better to run no chance of a

supernumerary cold in March. As for you, you must come. You must improve in your penmanship; your writing is like the speaking of a child of three years old, very understandable to its father but to no one else. The worst is it looks well—no, that is not the worst—the worst is, it is worse than Bailey's. Bailey's looks illegible and may perchance be read ; yours looks very legible and may perchance not be read. I would endeavour to give you a fac-simile of your word Thistlewood if I were not minded on the instant that Lord Chesterfield has done some such thing to his son. Now I would not bathe in the same River with Lord C. though I had the upper hand of the stream. I am grieved that in writing and speaking it is necessary to make use of the same particles as he did. Cobbett is expected to come in. O that I had two double plumpers for him. The ministry are not so inimical to him but it would like to put him out of Coventry. Casting my eye on the other side I see a long word written in a most vile manner, unbecoming a Critic. You must recollect I have served no apprenticeship to old plays. If the only copies of the Greek and Latin authors had been made by you, Bailey and Haydon they were as good as lost. It has been said that the Character of a Man may be known by his handwriting—if the Character of the age may be known by the average goodness of said, what a slovenly age we live in. Look at Queen Elizabeth's Latin exercises and blush. Look at Milton's hand. I can't say a word for Shakspeare's.

Your sincere friend　　　　JOHN KEATS.

CXLI.—TO FANNY KEATS.

[March 20, 1820.]

My dear Fanny—According to your desire I write to-day. It must be but a few lines, for I have been attack'd several times with a palpitation at the heart and the Doctor says I must not make the slightest exertion. I am much the same to-day as I have been for a week past. They say 'tis nothing but debility and will entirely cease on my recovery of my strength which is the object of my present diet. As the Doctor will not suffer me to write I shall ask Mr. Brown to let you hear news of me for the future if I should not get stronger soon. I hope I shall be well enough to come and see your flowers in bloom.

Ever your most affectionate Brother

JOHN ——.

CXLII.—TO FANNY KEATS.

Wentworth Place, April 1 [1820].

My dear Fanny—I am getting better every day and should think myself quite well were I not reminded every now and then by faintness and a tightness in the Chest. Send your Spaniel over to Hampstead, for I think I know where to find a Master or Mistress for him. You may depend upon it if you were even to turn it loose in the common road it would soon find an owner. If I keep improving as I have done I shall be able to come over to you in the course of a few weeks. I should take the advantage of your being in Town but I cannot bear the City though I have already ventured as far as the west end for the purpose of seeing Mr. Haydon's Picture, which is just finished and has made its appearance. I have not heard from George yet since he left Liverpool. Mr. Brown wrote to him as from me the other day— Mr. B. wrote two Letters to Mr. Abbey concerning me— Mr. A. took no notice and of course Mr. B. must give up such a correspondence when as the man said all the Letters are on one side. I write with greater ease than I had thought, therefore you shall soon hear from me again.

Your affectionate Brother   JOHN ——.

CXLIII.—TO FANNY KEATS.

[April 1820.]

My dear Fanny—Mr. Brown is waiting for me to take a walk. Mrs. Dilke is on a visit next door and desires her love to you. The Dog shall be taken care of and for his name I shall go and look in the parish register where he was born—I still continue on the mending hand.

Your affectionate Brother   JOHN ——.

CXLIV.—TO FANNY KEATS.

Wentworth Place, April 12 [1820].

My dear Fanny—Excuse these shabby scraps of paper I send you—and also from endeavouring to give you any consolation just at present, for though my health is tolerably well I am too nervous to enter into any discussion in which my heart is concerned. Wait patiently and take care of your health, being especially careful to keep yourself from low spirits which are great enemies to health. You are young and have only need of a little patience. I am not yet able to bear the fatigue of coming to Walthamstow, though I have been to Town once or twice. I have thought of taking a change of air. You shall hear from me immediately on my moving anywhere. I will ask Mrs. Dilke to pay you a visit if the weather holds fine, the first time I see her. The Dog is being attended to like a Prince.

Your affectionate Brother   JOHN.

CXLV.—TO FANNY KEATS.

[Hampstead, April 21, 1820.]

My dear Fanny—I have been slowly improving since I wrote last. The Doctor assures me that there is nothing the matter with me except nervous irritability and a general weakness of the whole system, which has proceeded from my anxiety of mind of late years and the too great excitement of poetry.   Mr. Brown is going to Scotland by the Smack, and I am advised for change of exercise and air to accompany him and give myself the chance of benefit from a Voyage.   Mr. H. Wylie call'd on me yesterday with a letter from George to his mother : George is safe at the other side of the water, perhaps by this time arrived at his home.   I wish you were coming to town that I might see you ; if you should be coming write to me, as it is quite a trouble to get by the coaches to Walthamstow.   Should you not come to Town I must see you before I sail, at Walthamstow.   They tell me I must study lines and tangents and squares and angles to put a little Ballast into my mind.   We shall be going in a fortnight and therefore you will see me within that space.   I expected sooner, but I have not been able to venture to walk across the country.   Now the fine Weather is come you will not find your time so irksome.   You must be sensible how much I regret not being able to alleviate the unpleasantness of your situation, but trust my dear Fanny that better times are in wait for you.

Your affectionate Brother   JOHN ——.

CXLVI.—TO FANNY KEATS.

Wentworth Place, Thursday [May 4, 1820].

My dear Fanny—I went for the first time into the City the day before yesterday, for before I was very disinclined to encounter the scuffle, more from nervousness than real illness ; which notwithstanding I should not have suffered to conquer me if I had not made up my mind not to go to Scotland, but to remove to Kentish Town till Mr. Brown returns.   Kentish Town is a mile nearer to you than Hampstead—I have been getting gradually better, but am not so well as to trust myself to the casualties of rain and sleeping out which I am liable to in visiting you. Mr. Brown goes on Saturday, and by that time I shall have settled in my new lodging, when I will certainly venture to you. You will forgive me I hope when I confess that I endeavour to think of you as little as possible and to let George dwell upon my mind but slightly. The reason being that I am afraid to ruminate on anything which has the shade of difficulty or melancholy in it, as that sort of cogitation is so pernicious to health, and it is only by health that I can be enabled to alleviate your situation in future. For some time you must do what you can of yourself for relief; and bear your mind up with the consciousness that your situation cannot last for ever, and that for the present you may console yourself against the reproaches of Mrs. Abbey. Whatever obligations you may have had to her you have none now, as she has reproached you. I do not know what property you have, but I will enquire into it: be sure however that beyond the obligation that a lodger may have to a landlord you have none to Mrs. Abbey. Let the surety of this make you laugh at Mrs. A.'s foolish tattle. Mrs. Dilke's Brother has got your Dog. She is now very well—still liable to Illness. I will get her to come and see you if I can make up my mind on the propriety of introducing a stranger into Abbey's house. Be careful to let. no fretting injure your health as I have suffered it—health is the greatest of blessings—with *health* and *hope* we should be content·to live, and so you will find as you grow older.

I am, my dear Fanny, your affectionate Brother
JOHN ——.

CXLVII.—TO CHARLES WENTWORTH DILKE.

[Hampstead, May 1820].

My dear Dilke—As Brown is not to be a fixture at Hampstead, I have at last made up my mind to send home all lent books. I should have seen you before this, but my mind has been at work all over the world to find

out what to do. I have my choice of three things, or at
least two,—South America, or Surgeon to an Indiaman ;
which last, I think, will be my fate. I shall resolve in
a few days. Remember me to Mrs. D. and Charles,
and your father and mother.

Ever truly yours   JOHN KEATS.

CXLVIII.—TO JOHN TAYLOR.

[Wesleyan Place, Kentish Town][1]
June 11 [1820].

My dear Taylor—In reading over the proof of St.
Agnes's Eve since I left Fleet Street, I was struck with
what appears to me an alteration in the seventh stanza very
much for the worse. The passage I mean stands thus—

> her maiden eyes incline
> Still on the floor, while many a sweeping train
> Pass by.

'Twas originally written—

> her maiden eyes divine
> Fix'd on the floor, saw many a sweeping train
> Pass by.

My meaning is quite destroyed in the alteration. I do
not use *train* for *concourse of passers by*, but for *skirts*
sweeping along the floor.

In the first stanza my copy reads, second line—

> bitter *chill* it was,

to avoid the echo *cold* in the second line.

Ever yours sincerely   JOHN KEATS.

CXLIX.—TO CHARLES BROWN.

[Wesleyan Place, Kentish Town, June 1820.]

My dear Brown—I have only been to ——'s once since
you left, when —— could not find your letters. Now

---

[1] Brown having let his house (Wentworth Place) when he
started for a fresh Scotch tour on May 7, Keats moved to lodgings
at the above address in order to be near Leigh Hunt, who was then
living in Mortimer Terrace, Kentish Town.

this is bad of me. I should, in this instance, conquer the great aversion to breaking up my regular habits, which grows upon me more and more. True, I have an excuse in the weather, which drives one from shelter to shelter in any little excursion. I have not heard from George. My book is coming out with very low hopes, though not spirits, on my part. This shall be my last trial; not succeeding, I shall try what I can do in the apothecary line. When you hear from or see —— it is probable you will hear some complaints against me, which this notice is not intended to forestall. The fact is, I did behave badly; but it is to be attributed to my health, spirits, and the disadvantageous ground I stand on in society. I could go and accommodate matters if I were not too weary of the world. I know that they are more happy and comfortable than I am; therefore why should I trouble myself about it? I foresee I shall know very few people in the course of a year or two. Men get such different habits that they become as oil and vinegar to one another. Thus far I have a consciousness of having been pretty dull and heavy, both in subject and phrase; I might add, enigmatical. I am in the wrong, and the world is in the right, I have no doubt. Fact is, I have had so many kindnesses done me by so many people, that I am cheveaux-de-frised with benefits, which I must jump over or break down. I met —— in town, a few days ago, who invited me to supper to meet Wordsworth, Southey, Lamb, Haydon, and some more; I was too careful of my health to risk being out at night. Talking of that, I continue to improve slowly, but I think surely. There is a famous exhibition in Pall-Mall of the old English portraits by Vandyck and Holbein, Sir Peter Lely, and the great Sir Godfrey. Pleasant countenances predominate; so I will mention two or three unpleasant ones. There is James the First, whose appearance would disgrace a "Society for the Suppression of Women;" so very squalid and subdued to nothing he looks. Then, there is old Lord Burleigh, the high-priest of economy, the political save-all, who has the appearance of a Pharisee just rebuffed by a Gospel bon-mot. Then, there is George the Second, very like an unintellectual Voltaire, troubled with the gout and a bad temper. Then, there is young Devereux, the favourite, with every appearance of as slang a boxer as any in the Court ; his face is cast in the mould of blackguardism with jockey-plaster. I shall soon begin upon "Lucy Vaughan Lloyd." [1]   I do not begin composition yet, being willing, in case of a relapse, to have nothing to reproach myself with. I hope the weather will give you the slip; let it show itself and steal out of your company. When I have sent off this, I shall write another to some place about fifty miles in advance of you.

Good morning to you. Yours ever sincerely
JOHN KEATS.

CL.—TO FANNY KEATS.

Friday Morn [Wesleyan Place, Kentish Town,
June 26, 1820.]

My dear Fanny—I had intended to delay seeing you till a Book which I am now publishing was out,[2] expecting that to be the end of this week when I would have brought it to Walthamstow : on receiving your Letter of course I set myself to come to town, but was not able, for just as I was setting out yesterday morning a slight spitting of blood came on which returned rather more copiously at night. I have slept well and they tell me there is nothing material to fear. I will send my Book soon with a Letter which I have had from George who is with his family quite well.

Your affectionate Brother   JOHN ——.

[1] The *Cap and Bells* was to have appeared under this pseudonym. By "begin" Keats means begin again (compare above, CXXXVIII.): he did not, however, do so, and the eighty-eight stanzas of the poem which are left all belong to the previous year (end of October—beginning of December 1819).

[2] The volume containing *Lamia, Isabella, The Eve of St. Agnes, Hyperion*, and the *Odes*.

CLI.—TO FANNY KEATS.

Mortimer Terrace,[1] Wednesday [July 5, 1820].

My dear Fanny—I have had no return of the spitting of blood, and for two or three days have been getting a little stronger. I have no hopes of an entire re-establishment of my health under some months of patience. My Physician tells me I must contrive to pass the Winter in Italy. This is all very unfortunate for us—we have no recourse but patience, which I am now practising better than ever I thought it possible for me. I have this moment received a Letter from Mr. Brown, dated Dunvegan Castle, Island of Skye. He is very well in health and spirits. My new publication has been out for some days and I have directed a Copy to be bound for you, which you will receive shortly. No one can regret Mr. Hodgkinson's ill fortune : I must own illness has not made such a Saint of me as to prevent my rejoicing at his reverse. Keep yourself in as good hopes as possible ; in case my illness should continue an unreasonable time many of my friends would I trust for my sake do all in their power to console and amuse you, at the least word from me—You may depend upon it that in case my strength returns I will do all in my power to extricate you from the Abbeys. Be above all things careful of your health which is the corner stone of all pleasure.

Your affectionate Brother   JOHN ——.

CLII.—TO BENJAMIN ROBERT HAYDON.

[Mortimer Terrace, July 1820.]

My dear Haydon—I am sorry to be obliged to try your patience a few more days when you will have the Book[2] sent from Town. I am glad to hear you are in

---

[1] After the attack last mentioned, Keats went to be taken care of in Hunt's house, and stayed there till August 12.

[2] Chapman's *Homer*.

progress with another Picture.   Go on.   I am afraid I
shall pop off just when my mind is able to run alone.
     Your sincere friend   JOHN KEATS.

CLIII.—TO FANNY KEATS.

Mortimer Terrace [July 22, 1820].

My dear Fanny—I have been gaining strength for
some days : it would be well if I could at the same time
say I am gaining hopes of a speedy recovery.   My constitution has suffered very much for two or three years past,
so as to be scarcely able to make head against illness,
which the natural activity and impatience of my Mind
renders more dangerous.   It will at all events be a very
tedious affair, and you must expect to hear very little
alteration of any sort in me for some time.   You ought
to have received a copy of my Book ten days ago.   I shall
send another message to the Booksellers.   One of the
Mr. Wylie's will be here to-day or to-morrow when I will
ask him to send you George's Letter.   Writing the
smallest note is so annoying to me that I have waited
till I shall see him.   Mr. Hunt does everything in his
power to make the time pass as agreeably with me as
possible.   I read the greatest part of the day, and generally take two half-hour walks a-day up and down the
terrace which is very much pester'd with cries, ballad
singers, and street music.   We have been so unfortunate
for so long a time, every event has been of so depressing
a nature that I must persuade myself to think some
change will take place in the aspect of our affairs.   I shall
be upon the look out for a trump card.
     Your affectionate Brother   JOHN ——.

CLIV.—TO FANNY KEATS.

Wentworth Place [August 14, 1820].

My dear Fanny—'Tis a long time since I received
your last.   An accident of an unpleasant nature occurred

at Mr. Hunt's and prevented me from answering you,
that is to say made me nervous. That you may not
suppose it worse I will mention that some one of Mr.
Hunt's household opened a Letter of mine—upon which
I immediately left Mortimer Terrace, with the intention
of taking to Mrs. Bentley's again ; fortunately I am not
in so lone a situation, but am staying a short time with
Mrs. Brawne who lives in the house which was Mrs.
Dilke's. I am excessively nervous : a person I am not
quite used to entering the room half chokes me. 'Tis
not yet Consumption I believe, but it would be were I to
remain in this climate all the Winter : so I am thinking
of either voyaging or travelling to Italy. Yesterday I
received an invitation from Mr. Shelley, a Gentleman re-
siding at Pisa, to spend the Winter with him : if I go I
must be away in a month or even less. I am glad you
like the Poems, you must hope with me that time and
health will produce you some more. This is the first
morning I have been able to sit to the paper and have
many Letters to write if I can manage them. God bless
you my dear Sister.

Your affectionate Brother   JOHN ——.

CLV.—TO PERCY BYSSHE SHELLEY.

[Wentworth Place, Hampstead, August 1820.]

My dear Shelley—I am very much gratified that you,
in a foreign country, and with a mind almost over-occu-
pied, should write to me in the strain of the letter beside
me. If I do not take advantage of your invitation, it
will be prevented by a circumstance I have very much at
heart to prophesy. There is no doubt that an English
winter would put an end to me, and do so in a lingering,
hateful manner. Therefore, I must either voyage or
journey to Italy, as a soldier marches up to a battery.
My nerves at present are the worst part of me, yet they
feel soothed that, come what extreme may, I shall not be
destined to remain in one spot long enough to take a

hatred of any four particular bedposts. I am glad you take any pleasure in my poor poem, which I would willingly take the trouble to unwrite, if possible, did I care so much as I have done about reputation. I received a copy of the Cenci, as from yourself, from Hunt. There is only one part of it I am judge of—the poetry and dramatic effect, which by many spirits nowadays is considered the Mammon. A modern work, it is said, must have a purpose, which may be the God. An artist must serve Mammon; he must have "self-concentration"—selfishness, perhaps. You, I am sure, will forgive me for sincerely remarking that you might curb your magnanimity, and be more of an artist, and load every rift of your subject with ore. The thought of such discipline must fall like cold chains upon you, who perhaps never sat with your wings furled for six months together. And is not this extraordinary talk for the writer of Endymion, whose mind was like a pack of scattered cards? I am picked up and sorted to a pip. My imagination is a monastery, and I am its monk. I am in expectation of Prometheus every day. Could I have my own wish effected, you would have it still in manuscript, or be but now putting an end to the second act. I remember you advising me not to publish my first blights, on Hampstead Heath. I am returning advice upon your hands. Most of the poems in the volume I send you have been written above two years, and would never have been published but for hope of gain, so you see I am inclined enough to take your advice now. I must express once more my deep sense of your kindness, adding my sincere thanks and respects for Mrs. Shelley.

In the hope of soon seeing you, I remain most sincerely yours   JOHN KEATS.

CLVI.—TO JOHN TAYLOR.

Wentworth Place [August 14, 1820].

My dear Taylor—My chest is in such a nervous state, that anything extra, such as speaking to an unaccustomed person, or writing a note, half suffocates me.   This journey to Italy wakes me at daylight every morning, and haunts me horribly.   I shall endeavour to go, though it be with the sensation of marching up against a battery. The first step towards it is to know the expense of a journey and a year's residence, which if you will ascertain for me, and let me know early, you will greatly serve me. I have more to say, but must desist, for every line I write increases the tightness of my chest, and I have many more to do.   I am convinced that this sort of thing does not continue for nothing.   If you can come, with any of our friends, do.

Your sincere friend   JOHN KEATS.

CLVII.—TO BENJAMIN ROBERT HAYDON.

Mrs. Brawne's Next door to Brown's,
Wentworth Place, Hampstead,
[August] 1820.

My dear Haydon—I am much better this morning than I was when I wrote the note: that is my hopes and spirits are better which are generally at a very low ebb from such a protracted illness.   I shall be here for a little time and at home all and every day.   A journey to Italy is recommended me, which I have resolved upon and am beginning to prepare for.   Hoping to see you shortly

I remain your affectionate friend

JOHN KEATS.

CLVIII.—TO CHARLES BROWN.

[Wentworth Place, August 1820.]

My dear Brown—You may not have heard from ——,
or ——, or in any way, that an attack of spitting of
blood, and all its weakening consequences, has prevented
me from writing for so long a time. I have matter now
for a very long letter, but not news : so I must cut everything short. I shall make some confession, which you
will be the only person, for many reasons, I shall trust
with. A winter in England would, I have not a doubt,
kill me ; so I have resolved to go to Italy, either by sea
or land. Not that I have any great hopes of that, for, I
think, there is a core of disease in me not easy to pull out.
I shall be obliged to set off in less than a month. Do
not, my dear Brown, teaze yourself about me. You must
fill up your time as well as you can, and as happily. You
must think of my faults as lightly as you can. When I
have health I will bring up the long arrear of letters I
owe you. My book has had good success among the literary people, and I believe has a moderate sale. I have
seen very few people we know. —— has visited me more
than any one. I would go to —— and make some inquiries after you, if I could with any bearable sensation ;
but a person I am not quite used to causes an oppression
on my chest. Last week I received a letter from Shelley,
at Pisa, of a very kind nature, asking me to pass the
winter with him. Hunt has behaved very kindly to me.
You shall hear from me again shortly.

Your affectionate friend   JOHN KEATS.

CLIX.—TO FANNY KEATS.

Wentworth Place, Wednesday Morning.
[August 23, 1820.]

My dear Fanny—It will give me great Pleasure to see
you here, if you can contrive it ; though I confess I should

have written instead of calling upon you before I set out on my journey, from the wish of avoiding unpleasant partings. Meantime I will just notice some parts of your Letter. The seal-breaking business is over blown. I think no more of it. A few days ago I wrote to Mr. Brown, asking him to befriend me with his company to Rome. His answer is not yet come, and I do not know when it will, not being certain how far he may be from the Post Office to which my communication is addressed. Let us hope he will go with me. George certainly ought to have written to you: his troubles, anxieties and fatigues are not quite a sufficient excuse. In the course of time you will be sure to find that this neglect, is not forgetfulness. I am sorry to hear you have been so ill and in such low spirits. Now you are better, keep so. Do not suffer your Mind to dwell on unpleasant reflections—that sort of thing has been the destruction of my health. Nothing is so bad as want of health—it makes one envy scavengers and cinder-sifters. There are enough real distresses and evils in wait for every one to try the most vigorous health. Not that I would say yours are not real—but they are such as to tempt you to employ your imagination on them, rather than endeavour to dismiss them entirely. Do not diet your mind with grief, it destroys the constitution ; but let your chief care be of your health, and with that you will meet your share of Pleasure in the world—do not doubt it. If I return well from Italy I will turn over a new leaf for you. I have been improving lately, and have very good hopes of "turning a Neuk" and cheating the consumption. I am not well enough to write to George myself—Mr Haslam will do it for me, to whom I shall write to-day, desiring him to mention as gently as possible your complaint. I am, my dear Fanny,

Your affectionate Brother JOHN.

CLX.—TO CHARLES BROWN.

[Wentworth Place, August 1820.]

My dear Brown—I ought to be off at the end of this week, as the cold winds begin to blow towards evening;—but I will wait till I have your answer to this.   I am to be introduced, before I set out, to a Dr. Clark, a physician settled at Rome, who promises to befriend me in every way there.   The sale of my book is very slow, though it has been very highly rated.   One of the causes, I understand from different quarters, of the unpopularity of this new book, is the offence the ladies take at me.   On thinking that matter over, I am certain that I have said nothing in a spirit to displease any woman I would care to please ; but still there is a tendency to class women in my books with roses and sweetmeats,—they never see themselves dominant.   I will say no more, but, waiting in anxiety for your answer, doff my hat, and make a purse as long as I can.

Your affectionate friend   JOHN KEATS.

CLXI.—TO CHARLES BROWN.

Saturday, September 28 [1820], *Maria Crowther*,
Off Yarmouth, Isle of Wight.

My dear Brown—The time has not yet come for a pleasant letter from me.   I have delayed writing to you from time to time, because I felt how impossible it was to enliven you with one heartening hope of my recovery ; this morning in bed the matter struck me in a different manner ; I thought I would write "while I was in some liking," or I might become too ill to write at all ; and then if the desire to have written should become strong it would be a great affliction to me.   I have many more letters to write, and I bless my stars that I have begun, for time seems to press,—this may be my best opportunity.   We are in a calm, and I am easy enough this

morning. If my spirits seem too low you may in some
degree impute it to our having been at sea a fortnight
without making any way.[1] I was very disappointed at
not meeting you at Bedhampton, and am very provoked
at the thought of you being at Chichester to-day. I
should have delighted in setting off for London for the
sensation merely,—for what should I do there? I could
not leave my lungs or stomach or other worse things
behind me. I wish to write on subjects that will not
agitate me much—there is one I must mention and have
done with it. Even if my body would recover of itself,
this would prevent it. The very thing which I want to
live most for will be a great occasion of my death. I
cannot help it. Who can help it? Were I in health it
would make me ill, and how can I bear it in my state!
I daresay you will be able to guess on what subject I am
harping—you know what was my greatest pain during
the first part of my illness at your house. I wish for
death every day and night to deliver me from these pains,
and then I wish death away, for death would destroy
even those pains which are better than nothing. Land
and sea, weakness and decline, are great separators, but
death is the great divorcer for ever. When the pang of
this thought has passed through my mind, I may say the
bitterness of death is passed. I often wish for you that
you might flatter me with the best. I think without my
mentioning it for my sake you would be a friend to Miss
Brawne when I am dead. You think she has many
faults—but for my sake think she has not one. If there
is anything you can do for her by word or deed I know
you will do it. I am in a state at present in which
woman merely as woman can have no more power over
me than stocks and stones, and yet the difference of my
sensations with respect to Miss Brawne and my sister is

---

[1] The *Maria Crowther* had in fact sailed from London September 18 : contrary winds holding her in the Channel, Keats had
landed at Portsmouth for a night's visit to the Snooks of Bedhampton.

amazing. The one seems to absorb the other to a degree incredible. I seldom think of my brother and sister in America. The thought of leaving Miss Brawne is beyond everything horrible—the sense of darkness coming over me—I eternally see her figure eternally vanishing. Some of the phrases she was in the habit of using during my last nursing at Wentworth Place ring in my ears. Is there another life? Shall I awake and find all this a dream? There must be, we cannot be created for this sort of suffering. The receiving this letter is to be one of yours. I will say nothing about our friendship, or rather yours to me, more than that, as you deserve to escape, you will never be so unhappy as I am. I should think of—you in my last moments. I shall endeavour to write to Miss Brawne if possible to-day. A sudden stop to my life in the middle of one of these letters would be no bad thing, for it keeps one in a sort of fever awhile. Though fatigued with a letter longer than any I have written for a long while, it would be better to go on for ever than awake to a sense of contrary winds. We expect to put into Portland Roads to-night. The captain, the crew, and the passengers, are all ill-tempered and weary. I shall write to Dilke. I feel as if I was closing my last letter to you.

My dear Brown, your affectionate friend

JOHN KEATS.

CLXII.—TO MRS. BRAWNE.

October 24 [1820], Naples Harbour.

My dear Mrs. Brawne—A few words will tell you what sort of a Passage we had, and what situation we are in, and few they must be on account of the Quarantine, our Letters being liable to be opened for the purpose of fumigation at the Health Office. We have to remain in the vessel ten days and are at present shut in a tier of ships. The sea air has been beneficial to me about to as great an extent as squally weather and bad accommodations

and provisions has done harm.   So I am about as I was.
Give my Love to Fanny and tell her, if I were well there
is enough in this Port of Naples to fill a quire of Paper
—but it looks like a dream—every man who can row his
boat and walk and talk seems a different being from myself.   I do not feel in the world.   It has been unfortunate for me that one of the Passengers is a young Lady in
a Consumption—her imprudence has vexed me very much
—the knowledge of her complaints—the flushings in her
face, all her bad symptoms have preyed upon me—they
would have done so had I been in good health.   Severn
now is a very good fellow but his nerves are too strong
to be hurt by other people's illnesses—I remember poor
Rice wore me in the same way in the Isle of Wight—I
shall feel a load off me when the Lady vanishes out of
my sight.   It is impossible to describe exactly in what
state of health I am—at this moment I am suffering from
indigestion very much, which makes such stuff of this
Letter.   I would always wish you to think me a little
worse than I really am ; not being of a sanguine disposition I am likely to succeed.   If I do not recover your
regret will be softened—if I do your pleasure will be
doubled.   I dare not fix my Mind upon Fanny, I have
not dared to think of her.   The only comfort I have had
that way has been in thinking for hours together of having the knife she gave me put in a silver-case—the hair
in a Locket—and the Pocket Book in a gold net.   Show
her this.   I dare say no more.   Yet you must not believe
I am so ill as this Letter may look, for if ever there was
a person born without the faculty of hoping I am he.
Severn is writing to Haslam, and I have just asked him
to request Haslam to send you his account of my health.
O what an account I could give you of the Bay of Naples
if I could once more feel myself a Citizen of this world—
I feel a spirit in my Brain would lay it forth pleasantly
—O what a misery it is to have an intellect in splints !
My Love again to Fanny—tell Tootts I wish I could pitch
her a basket of grapes—and tell Sam the fellows catch

here with a line a little fish much like an anchovy, pull them up fast. Remember me to Mr. and Mrs. Dilke— mention to Brown that I wrote him a letter at Portsmouth which I did not send and am in doubt if he ever will see it.

My dear Mrs. Brawne, yours sincerely and affectionate
JOHN KEATS.

Good bye Fanny! God bless you.

CLXIII.—TO CHARLES BROWN.

Naples, November 1 [1820].

My dear Brown—Yesterday we were let out of quarantine, during which my health suffered more from bad air and the stifled cabin than it had done the whole voyage. The fresh air revived me a little, and I hope I am well enough this morning to write to you a short calm letter; —if that can be called one, in which I am afraid to speak of what I would fainest dwell upon. As I have gone thus far into it, I must go on a little;—perhaps it may relieve the load of WRETCHEDNESS which presses upon me. The persuasion that I shall see her no more will kill me. My dear Brown, I should have had her when I was in health, and I should have remained well. I can bear to die—I cannot bear to leave her. Oh, God! God! God! Every thing I have in my trunks that reminds me of her goes through me like a spear. The silk lining she put in my travelling cap scalds my head. My imagination is horribly vivid about her—I see her—I hear her. There is nothing in the world of sufficient interest to divert me from her a moment. This was the case when I was in England; I cannot recollect, without shuddering, the time that I was a prisoner at Hunt's, and used to keep my eyes fixed on Hampstead all day. Then there was a good hope of seeing her again—Now!—O that I could be buried near where she lives! I am afraid to write to her—to receive a letter from her—to see her handwriting

would break my heart—even to hear of her anyhow, to
see her name written, would be more than I can bear.
My dear Brown, what am I to do? Where can I look
for consolation or ease? If I had any chance of recovery,
this passion would kill me. Indeed, through the whole
of my illness, both at your house and at Kentish Town,
this fever has never ceased wearing me out. When you
write to me, which you will do immediately, write to
Rome (poste restante)—if she is well and happy, put a
mark thus + ; if——

Remember me to all. I will endeavour to bear my
miseries patiently. A person in my state of health
should not have such miseries to bear. Write a short
note to my sister, saying you have heard from me.
Severn is very well. If I were in better health I would
urge your coming to Rome. I fear there is no one can
give me any comfort. Is there any news of George? O
that something fortunate had ever happened to me or my
brothers !—then I might hope, — but despair is forced
upon me as a habit. My dear Brown, for my sake be
her advocate for ever. I cannot say a word about Naples ;
I do not feel at all concerned in the thousand novelties
around me. I am afraid to write to her—I should like
her to know that I do not forget her. Oh, Brown I have
coals of fire in my breast—It surprises me that the
human heart is capable of containing and bearing so
much misery. Was I born for this end ? God bless her,
and her mother, and my sister, and George, and his wife,
and you, and all !

Your ever affectionate friend   JOHN KEATS.

[Thursday, November 2.]

I was a day too early for the Courier. He sets out
now. I have been more calm to-day, though in a half
dread of not continuing so. I said nothing of my health ;
I know nothing of it ; you will hear Severn's account from
Haslam. I must leave off. You bring my thoughts too
near to Fanny. God bless you !

CLXIV.—TO CHARLES BROWN.

Rome, November 30, 1820.

My dear Brown—'Tis the most difficult thing in the world to me to write a letter. My stomach continues so bad, that I feel it worse on opening any book,—yet I am much better than I was in quarantine. Then I am afraid to encounter the pro-ing and con-ing of anything interesting to me in England. I have an habitual feeling of my real life having passed, and that I am leading a posthumous existence. God knows how it would have been—but it appears to me—however, I will not speak of that subject. I must have been at Bedhampton nearly at the time you were writing to me from Chichester—how unfortunate—and to pass on the river too! There was my star predominant! I cannot answer anything in your letter, which followed me from Naples to Rome, because I am afraid to look it over again. I am so weak (in mind) that I cannot bear the sight of any handwriting of a friend I love so much as I do you. Yet I ride the little horse, and at my worst even in quarantine, summoned up more puns, in a sort of desperation, in one week than in any year of my life. There is one thought enough to kill me; I have been well, healthy, alert, etc., walking with her, and now—the knowledge of contrast, feeling for light and shade, all that information (primitive sense) necessary for a poem, are great enemies to the recovery of the stomach. There, you rogue, I put you to the torture; but you must bring your philosophy to bear, as I do mine, really, or how should I be able to live? Dr. Clark is very attentive to me; he says, there is very little the matter with my lungs, but my stomach, he says, is very bad. I am well disappointed in hearing good news from George, for it runs in my head we shall all die young. I have not written to Reynolds yet, which he must think very neglectful; being anxious to send him a good account of my health, I have delayed it

from week to week.   If I recover, I will do all in my
power to correct the mistakes made during sickness; and
if I should not, all my faults will be forgiven.   Severn
is very well, though he leads so dull a life with me.
Remember me to all friends, and tell Haslam I should
not have left London without taking leave of him, but
from being so low in body and mind.   Write to George
as soon as you receive this, and tell him how I am, as
far as you can guess; and also a note to my sister—who
walks about my imagination like a ghost—she is so like
Tom.   I can scarcely bid you good-bye, even in a letter.
I always made an awkward bow.

    God bless you !   JOHN KEATS.[1]

   [1] On the 10th of December following came a renewal of fever
and hemorrhage, extinguishing the last hope of recovery: and
after eleven more weeks of suffering, only alleviated by the devoted
care of Severn, the poet died in his friend's arms on the 23d of
February 1821.

THE END.

Printed by R. & R. CLARK, *Edinburgh*.

Lightning Source UK Ltd.
Milton Keynes UK
UKHW022233251022
411098UK00003B/50